MAKING MICHAEL

Mike Smallcombe

Clink Street

London | New York

Published by Clink Street Publishing 2015

First edition.

Cover photo courtesy of © Sam Emerson/Polaris

Photo credits:
© Matt Forger: 7, 97
© Bernie Ilson Public Relations: 16 (Creative Commons)
© Bruce Swedien: 36
© Michael Salisbury: 43
© Nick Truger: 72
© Antony Payne: 76
© Zoran Veselinovic: 127 (Creative Commons)
© John Wiley: 131 (Creative Commons)
© Brad Sundberg: 152, 227
© Jennifer Fasano Wolf: 196
© Sjors Provoost: 242 (Creative Commons)
© Georges Biard: 260 (Creative Commons)
© Youssefza: 338 (Creative Commons)
© Amin Eshaiker: 361 (Creative Commons)

Every effort has been made to trace copyright holders and to obtain their permission for the use of copyright material. The author apologises for any errors or omissions in the above list and would be grateful if notified of any corrections that should be incorporated in future reprints or editions of this book.

ISBN: PB: 978-1-910782-51-4
EB: 978-1-910782-52-1

For Mum. *Gone Too Soon.*

CONTENTS

AUTHOR'S NOTE

Having risen from humble beginnings to become a child star with The Jackson 5, and then the most successful entertainer of all time, Michael Joseph Jackson was the epitome of the American Dream.

But he didn't do it quietly. His personal life enhanced the feeling that he really was bigger than life; from another planet. The Pepsi burn incident, Bubbles the chimp, Neverland Ranch, the skin colour change, the plastic surgery, the Peter Pan image, the child abuse allegations, the drug abuse, his children, his reclusiveness, his finances and a marriage to Elvis Presley's daughter, among many other things, kept the world guessing for decades. Just when a life couldn't get any more mysterious, he died in shocking, unique circumstances, right before the start of a monumental comeback. Even in death, the life of Michael Jackson has been far from straightforward.

Amid the chaos, it's easy to forget what all the fuss was about in the first place. Ultimately, it was the music, stage performances and videos that made Michael Jackson arguably the biggest superstar that has ever walked the planet. He is the most-awarded recording artist in the history of popular music, and his *Thriller* album is the biggest-selling of all time. On stage he danced and performed like no other, with the moonwalk and single white glove becoming instantly recognisable symbols. Michael's undying love for film also saw him transform music videos into an art form and promotional tool in the early eighties, with 'Thriller' breaking racial barriers and having a huge impact on popular culture.

Like millions across the globe, I was shocked when Michael died on that unforgettable day in June 2009. He kept a low profile after the image-shattering second child abuse allegations culminated in an acquittal in court four years earlier. But three months before his untimely death, he announced

50 shows at London's O2 Arena as part of a comeback tour called This Is It. All 50 dates sold out in record time, and I somehow obtained tickets for the opening night on July 8, which was later pushed back five days.

After Michael's death, which placed him in the spotlight more than ever before, I read the few credible Michael Jackson biographies that were available. Although they provide plenty of insight, the primary focus is the personal life; in terms of his career, there are several gaps. There is almost zero information about Michael's final three studio albums, *Dangerous*, *HIStory* and *Invincible*, or the remix album *Blood on the Dance Floor*. Other gaps include parts of Michael's career outside the studio, such as the world tours, his fall out with Sony Music, his movie dreams, his work in the secretive last five years of his life and the preparations for This Is It.

I couldn't fathom how there wasn't a book based solely on the 45-year career of a man many believe to be the greatest entertainer of all time. Then, one night early in 2010, something just clicked. I felt confident I could take on the challenge. I wanted to know a different Michael Jackson; to discover the untold stories and secrets behind an enthralling, albeit turbulent career. The aim was to write a biography about a whole other life; the Michael Jackson who made making music his life's work rather than the one portrayed on the front pages of the tabloids. I wanted to delve deeper into his career than ever before, and I didn't want to leave any stones unturned. But it was also important to remain objective and not take a fan's point of view.

I decided to base the book on Michael's career using a unique 'behind the scenes' structure, like the reader is there for the ride; like a fly on the wall. Initially, I envisioned it as a 25-year timeline from the early recordings sessions in 1978 for Michael's first major solo album, *Off the Wall*, up to his last release of original music in 2003, the 'One More Chance' single. I then realised I had to go further – after all, Michael's career didn't end until the day he died; less than 12 hours earlier he was in rehearsals for This Is It at the Staples Center in Downtown Los Angeles. So I went all the way up until his death.

I also figured I had to explain to readers how Michael reached the point of recording *Off the Wall*, as his work with his brothers in The Jackson 5 set the tone for his adult solo career. But I wanted to keep this brief, to simply set the scene, as much of the information about the Jackson 5 days is already out there.

The starting point was to gather all the relevant information that was already in the public domain but hidden in online forums, court transcripts, web interviews and old magazine and newspaper articles, and bring it under one umbrella. But I knew the only way I could really go behind the scenes and deliver an accurate and fresh account of Michael's career was to contact as many people who had worked with him as possible. Over 60 of his collaborators agreed to be interviewed; I was both shocked and pleasantly surprised at how open and generous these individuals were with their time and insights.

I twice travelled to Los Angeles, 'The Entertainment Capital of the World', to conduct some of these interviews face to face, and to get a feel for the city where Michael made most of his music. That was important for me. As well as interviewing, I visited several of the recording studios where Michael worked, including Westlake Studio on Beverly Boulevard, where *Thriller* was recorded, and Record Plant in Hollywood, where *Blood on the Dance Floor* and *Invincible* were made. I also took a trip to 100 North Carolwood Drive in Holmby Hills, where Michael was living when he passed.

Although I tried to avoid using secondary sources as much as possible, I used them in instances where the person is either deceased, such as Michael himself or his former manager Frank DiLeo, or where the person in question did not wish to be interviewed. There were also instances where I interviewed an individual about a certain subject, but they had already covered the matter in an online forum, in their own book or with a magazine, so they referred me to that.

To achieve my aim of making this book a fly on the wall experience, I was very strict with myself with regard to how the timeline is presented. This became an incredibly difficult challenge, as the estate of Michael Jackson does not grant access to the archives as a research tool for third parties. Some of Michael's albums took two or three years to record, and it was difficult to determine the points during this period that he began writing or recording certain songs. But the structure of the book is one of the aspects that makes it a very unique product, so it was never going to be a simple task.

It has taken me more than five years to research and write this book, much longer than I anticipated. I was always seeking to discover new information and to take different paths in an attempt to make the most complete anthology possible. Although costly, I chose to self-publish this work rather than seek a traditional publisher, for one simple reason: control. I wanted to fully realise my creative vision and not that of somebody else; to have the final say on everything from the title to the content, the length of the book, the layout, the front cover design and the photos inside.

My hope is that I have created an account of Michael Jackson's career that has been missing for far too long. Now Michael has passed, more and more people are fascinated by the man who changed the course of music history rather than the eccentric side show, and appreciate that there will never be another performer like him.

Mike Smallcombe
January 2015

FOREWORD

Michael Jackson was an extraordinary talent, and an exceptional person to work with.

Michael's career was longer than that of most other entertainers, and starting at such an early age allowed him to learn so much along the way. Working with so many of the world's great musical talents, he was always studying and learning.

When Michael began his solo career, he wanted it to be set apart. Not only did he want to better what he had already accomplished with The Jackson 5, but he also had a desire to make the biggest-selling album of all time, and to create songs that would live on and be part of history. He was always searching for something that nobody had ever heard, seen or experienced before.

It was this drive within that was most striking, because he was so quiet and seemingly shy. But under a very polite and respectful exterior, he was a confident creator of music, dance and visual ideas that would transform the music business. When he let loose with a musical idea or performance, he could stun you with his talent and ability. He became the measure of success that others were measured against. His desire for perfection and emotional quality set him apart as a dancer, a singer and an entertainer.

Michael would demand perfection, and those who also were perfectionists understood this. In return, he also understood if something would take time to complete, or if it involved a difficult process. It was this trust that his professional relationships were built on. If you couldn't stand the heat, then you didn't want to stand too close to the fire, because 'almost' wasn't good enough. The respect he had in the world of entertainment was hard earned, but justified.

But for all these attributes, he was still a polite and considerate person who I loved to spend time with. He had a wonderful sense of humour, and when he laughed it was both deep and hearty.

As time went on, Michael matured. While his writing started with songs that were fun to create and sing, he later developed material that had a much deeper meaning. His need to have a voice that reflected humanity became more pronounced. The emotions in his songs reached a greater depth, and touched more people around the world.

Michael was always thankful for the entertainer and person he was allowed to become, and he never took for granted the appreciation his fans had for both him and his music. He knew that without them, he had nothing. His energy and commitment never wavered, but he also enjoyed watching his children grow up. Once again, he appreciated the joy of youth.

To work alongside Michael was such a privilege and honour. To see the creative process come to life and to learn from a master what is possible, to be encouraged by him and to see him encourage others to follow their dreams, meant so very much. As Mike Smallcombe demonstrates in this captivating book, Michael was such a unique individual, both in spirit and in the beauty he created. There is no doubt that his songs will live on for as long as music is appreciated.

MATT FORGER *was one of Michael Jackson's most trusted collaborators. Few, if any, have more knowledge of Michael's adult recording career and creative process than Forger. Over a period of 15 years, he worked closely with Michael on several projects as a sound engineer. Forger was working with Quincy Jones when he first met Michael during the* Thriller *sessions in the summer of 1982. The pair then developed a close friendship as Forger went on to work with Michael on The Jacksons'* Victory *album in 1984, before transitioning into the* Captain EO *project in early 1985. He then spent two years working at Michael's home studio in Encino, California, as they created and sculpted the songs that formed the* Bad *album. After Michael's professional split with Quincy Jones, Forger went on to play a central role as they recorded the* Dangerous,

HIStory *and* Blood on the Dance Floor *albums in studios in Los Angeles, New York and Europe.*

Michael Jackson and Matt Forger during the *Thriller* recording sessions in 1982

PROLOGUE

It was a Friday evening in January 1984, a little over a year since Michael Jackson released his blockbuster *Thriller* album. Michael was at the Shrine Auditorium in Los Angeles filming a commercial for drinks company Pepsi with his brothers, in front of three thousand people who were seated in the venue to simulate a live concert.

At the start of the fateful sixth take Michael began dancing at the top of the stage, but the pyrotechnic devices either side of him went off too early, showering him in sparks and catching his hair – lagged in cosmetic spray – on fire.

Unaware that his head was engulfed in flames, Michael continued to perform for around six seconds as he descended down the staircase. Once at the bottom he felt the searing heat on his scalp and performed two quick spins, with the force putting the fire out almost immediately. He then disappeared below a frantic crowd of assistants and stage crews. As Michael rose from the floor, a glow was visible on his crown where the fire had caused nasty second and third degree burns.

It is a popular opinion that Michael's career went downhill after that infamous incident. In terms of sales figures none of his subsequent albums would reach the heights of *Thriller*, and due to painful surgery to reduce scarring on his scalp he also began taking prescription drugs, which ultimately led to his death.

But in reality, his staggering success continued. By early 1993, with the successful release of the *Bad* album and then his latest smash *Dangerous*, Michael had become the most international music star ever; more than three-quarters of sales of *Dangerous* were made outside the United States.

A record-breaking performance at the Super Bowl XXVII halftime show in January 1993 encapsulated Michael at the very peak of his powers, because his world would come crashing down only seven months later.

On August 23, 1993, a day before Michael was to start the third leg of the Dangerous Tour with a concert in Bangkok, news broke around the globe that he had been accused of sexually abusing a thirteen-year-old boy.

It was a major turning point that split the adult solo career of Michael Jackson in two. The period before August 1993 saw him crowned as the King of Pop, but after that his musical achievements were largely ignored in favour of coverage of his personal life.

It could be said that this post-August 1993 part – which was just as fascinating as the more successful periods of Michael's career – began in a Moscow hotel room only three weeks after the allegations became public knowledge.

Despite having been accused of such a heinous crime, Michael continued to tour. He performed in the Russian capital on Wednesday, September 15, 1993, becoming the first international pop star to put on a concert in post-Soviet-era Russia. Having arrived in Moscow on the Sunday, Michael was in good spirits as he took in a variety of tourist sites over the next two days to sample the way of life behind the former Iron Curtain.

But by the morning of the show, his mood had changed. Heavy rain clouds descended on the city, and Michael spent the day holed up in his $1,500-a-night Presidential Suite at the luxury Hotel Metropol near Red Square. As usual, hundreds of fans were gathered in the streets below, eager to catch a glimpse of their idol. But as Michael looked out of his window at the faces outside, he felt like the loneliest man in the world.

Sitting on the closet floor in his hotel suite listening to the rain, his eyes were filled with tears, and his mind with fear and loneliness. The night before, he had received the news that his accuser's father had officially filed a $30 million civil lawsuit against him. Michael described it as a 'strange' and 'eerie' time. "Outside my hotel was just a sea of faces, of fans chanting and screaming," he recalled. "But I was inside my room and I felt so all alone, like I was the last person on the planet."

Even in one of his darkest hours, Michael's creativity did not desert him; instead he poured his emotions into lyrics about how he was feeling. If any moment summed up the creative mind of Michael Jackson, this was it.

Once Michael worked out the accompanying music with his collaborator Brad Buxer, the song became arguably one of his finest musical creations – the haunting 'Stranger in Moscow'. Michael explained the emotion which sparked the idea: "In the song I say 'How does it feel when you're alone and you're cold inside'. I say it's 'like a stranger in Moscow', and that's pretty much how I felt."

Hours later, Michael was due on stage at the city's Luzhniki Stadium. Ticket sales for the show were slow by his standards, with factors including the admission prices; an average ticket cost about $30, a little less than an average monthly salary in Moscow. With the Cold War having only just ended, there was also scepticism among locals that such a huge American star would even show up.

The show at the roofless Luzhniki was scheduled to begin at 7pm, but the rain continued to lash down all day, soaking the stage and making it impossible for a performer like Michael to dance. By 9pm, when the rain began to relent, he finally exploded onto the stage.

For the next two months Michael continued to hit the road as the tour moved on to South America and Mexico, but eventually the stress of the allegations caught up with him. In mid-November he cancelled the remaining tour dates to seek help for a prescription drug dependency, which was first triggered by pain from scar revision surgery performed on his scalp earlier in the year, a whole nine years after the original Pepsi burn incident. Michael said the stress of the allegations worsened this dependency.

Michael settled the civil lawsuit out of court in January 1994. Even though the authorities failed to find enough evidence to pursue a criminal trial, many saw the settling of the suit as an admission of guilt. His image may have taken a severe hit as a result, but this didn't deter him.

If anything, the allegations increased his musical creativity, because as well as 'Stranger in Moscow', several songs from his next album, *HIStory*, were written in response to this turbulent time in his life. It is a testament to Michael's superstardom that this album, released in 1995, is the best-selling multiple-disc release ever, because a child abuse allegation would likely have finished the career of any other entertainer. "I've been through hell and back and still I'm able to do what I do and nothing can stop me," Michael said when explaining the significance of his 2001 song 'Unbreakable'.

But when a second set of damaging allegations culminated in an acquittal in court in the summer of 2005, Michael seemed truly broken. Slowly he began to recover from his ordeal, enough to feel there was still time for one epic final curtain call to seal his legacy.

"I stop when I'm ready to stop," he said.

CHAPTER 1: HUMBLE BEGINNINGS

1958 – 1975

Friday, August 29, 1958, 7.33pm
Gary, IN

It was just another ordinary late summer's evening in the gritty industrial city located on Lake Michigan roughly 30 miles south of downtown Chicago. At that very moment an African-American woman by the name of Katherine Jackson gave birth to her seventh child, Michael Joseph, at the city's Mary Mercy Hospital.

When Katherine returned with her newborn son to the Jackson family's tiny two-bedroom house on Jackson Street, of all places, she had little reason to believe her baby boy would later amaze the world with his mesmerising ability to entertain. It was the beginning of the ultimate American Dream.

Katherine was a devout Jehovah's Witness and housewife who also worked part-time as a store clerk to make ends meet, while husband Joseph worked in a steel mill in nearby East Chicago. Eventually Michael had three sisters – Rebbie (born 1950), La Toya (1956), and Janet (1966), and five brothers – Jackie (1951), Tito (1953), Jermaine (1954), Marlon (1957) and Randy (1961). Brandon, a twin of older brother Marlon, died shortly after birth.

Through the fifties Joseph was a musician in a small-time rhythm and blues band, The Falcons, but they eventually disbanded after failing to secure a recording deal. Joseph stashed his guitar in the bedroom closet, and by the early sixties his three eldest sons would secretly borrow it while he was at work; Tito would play the instrument while Jackie and Jermaine made harmonies.

One night, Joseph discovered one of his children had been playing his guitar after finding a string had been broken. Tito owned up, and initially upset with his sons for using it behind his back, Joseph saw their potential after the three performed in front of him. Keen to exorcise his frustrations over his own failed musical career by nurturing the talents of his children, Joseph soon began rehearsing his sons at home, and formed a little group.

Michael joined his brothers in rehearsal by the time he was five, after showing an ability to sing and play the bongos. Jermaine said Marlon also joined at the same time, as their mother didn't want him to feel left out. Soon after, Michael also became the first brother to sing before a live audience, with a kindergarten rendition of 'Climb Ev'ry Mountain' from *The Sound of Music*.

The group continued to rehearse before performing at their first talent show in 1965, when 'The Jackson 5' name was also formed. By now Michael was the lead singer, as he could reach high notes that original frontman Jermaine couldn't. "He [Michael] found octaves that I didn't know existed and our father was blown away," Jermaine recalls.

That year The Jackson 5 also played their first paying performance at Mr Lucky's nightclub in Gary. Although little Michael was only seven years old, he was performing late nights in strip joints and clubs, sometimes not returning home until four or five in the morning on school nights. "When we sang, people would throw all this money on the floor, tons of dollars, 10s, 20s, lots of change," Michael recalled. "I remember my pockets being so full of money that I couldn't keep my pants up. I'd wear a real tight belt. And I'd buy candy like crazy."

Many neighbourhood boys would accompany the brothers as musicians from time to time, including Johnny Jackson (no relation). Between 1966 and 1968 The Jackson 5 spent most weekends on the road, with Michael on lead vocals, Jermaine on bass guitar, Tito on guitar, Jackie on shakers, Johnny on drums, Marlon singing harmony and another boy, Ronnie Rancifer, on keyboard.

Michael always emphasised the heavy price he paid for such an unusual childhood. He would often hear other children playing in the street and desperately want to join them, rather than sit in a recording studio or rehearse.

It is also no secret that young Michael was terribly frightened of his own father. He said Joseph used force to keep his sons in check during rehearsals, with Marlon suffering the most. "We were nervous rehearsing," Michael admitted, "because he sat in the chair and he had this belt in his hand, and if you didn't do it the right way, he would tear you up, really get you. He was tough." Michael said Joseph would use 'whatever's around' to hit his children, and also threw them up against walls as hard as he could.

Although Marlon was punished the most during practice, Michael said he would get beaten more than all his brothers combined outside rehearsal time, because he always tried to fight back. "[I was] scared, so scared that I would regurgitate just seeing him," he admitted. Michael also said his father often verbally abused him, with the term 'fat nose' hurting him the most. It is these experiences that are believed to have triggered a deep dissatisfaction with his appearance, and the desire to remain childlike throughout his adult life.

However controversial they may have been, Joseph's disciplinarian ways seemed to have a positive effect on his sons on stage. The group went on to win several talent competitions throughout 1967, including one at the legendary Apollo Theater in Harlem, New York. Later that year the brothers signed a short-term deal with Gordon Keith's Gary-based record label Steeltown Records, where they recorded their first major song, 'Big Boy', released in January 1968.

The group's big break came six months later, when they were asked to audition for Motown Records, the famous Detroit-based label founded in 1959 by African-American producer Berry Gordy. Top artists signed with Motown at the time included Diana Ross, Stevie Wonder and Marvin Gaye. Gordy said he knew as early as the very first audition that Michael possessed an unknown quality he didn't completely understand. He was sufficiently impressed by what he saw, and officially signed the group in March 1969 following a delay due to a dispute with Steeltown.

The Jackson 5 in December 1969. Top row: Tito, Jermaine and Jackie. Bottom row: Marlon and Michael, aged eleven.

In the summer of 1969 Gordy moved the entire Jackson family to Los Angeles, leasing a house on Queen's Road in the Hollywood Hills after they initially stayed in motels in the city. For Michael, the change was enormous. "To come from our part of Indiana, which is so urban and often bleak, and to land in Southern California was like having the world transformed into a wonderful dream," he said. Mentoring the boys in Los Angeles was Gordy's creative assistant Suzanne de Passe, who became a big influence on Michael as she was given responsibility for live shows, choreography, schooling, clothing, public relations and personal aspects like doctor appointments.

The brothers attended a public school in Los Angeles, lasting an entire seven days. "It didn't work, because a bunch of fans would break into the classroom, or we'd come out of school and there'd be a bunch of kids waiting to take pictures and stuff like that," Michael recalled. "We stayed at that school a week. The rest was private school with other entertainment kids or stars' kids, where you wouldn't have to be hassled."

Success for the Jacksons at Motown came instantly through hits written by 'The Corporation', a record production team created specifically for the band consisting of Gordy, Alphonso Mizell, Freddie Perren and Deke Richards. Gordy labelled the music 'soul bubble-gum', a style aimed at younger teens. When The Corporation disbanded in 1972, Motown producer Hal Davis took over songwriting and production duties.

Between 1969 and 1970, the group's first four singles with Motown, 'I Want You Back', 'ABC', 'The Love You Save' and 'I'll Be There', all went to number one on the American singles chart, the *Billboard* Hot 100. Further hits included 'Mama's Pearl' and 'Never Can Say Goodbye', which both peaked at number two on the *Billboard* 100 in 1971.

While the brothers were topping the charts, Michael was also releasing solo albums with Motown under the suggestion of Berry Gordy. In January 1972, at the age of 13, he became the first Jackson brother to release a solo album, although like the group, he had no say in songwriting or production. *Got to Be There* peaked at 14 on the American album chart (*Billboard* 200), and featured two top-five singles in 'Rockin' Robin' and the title track. "In our early years at Motown, he [Gordy] thought that I should spin out and do different kinds of music and not be obligated to one sound," Michael said. "And so when I recorded the song 'Got to Be There', it was a different type of music that I loved. Of course it had its soul flavourings as well as a pop feel, [but] it was music and it was beautiful." Seven months later Michael released his second solo album, *Ben*, which charted at number five in America. The album spawned Michael's first number one hit, 'Ben', which tells the story of a young boy and his pet rat.

The brothers had landed on their feet, but growing up in the adult world of show business would leave a mark for life on an adolescent Michael Jackson. From the age of 11 and through his early teenage years he was surrounded mostly by bodyguards, tutors, record producers, executives and fellow celebrities. Years later, he admitted he felt 'strange' around everyday people. "See, my whole life has been onstage," Michael explained. "And the impression I get of people is applause, standing ovations and running after you. In a crowd I'm afraid. Onstage I feel safe. If I could, I would sleep on the stage. I'm serious."

The Jackson 5 may have become the fastest-selling act in Motown's history, but after 1972, the brothers' records began plummeting down the charts at an alarming rate. Joseph and four of his sons, including Michael, pointed the finger firmly at the record label.

CHAPTER 2: THE ROAD TO *OFF THE WALL*

1975 – 1978

In January 1975, Motown released Michael's fourth solo album, *Forever, Michael*. The album performed poorly, peaking at 101 on the *Billboard* 200 chart. This was eight places lower than Michael's previous album of two years earlier, *Music and Me*, which includes songs such as the title track and 'With a Child's Heart'. Neither album reached the top 50 in the United Kingdom, selling poorly at a time when The Jackson 5's record sales as a whole were declining.

The group felt Motown was holding them back, not allowing them to write or produce their own music or play their own instruments. They were unhappy with the sound of their music, and there was a real concern that more contemporary groups would overtake them if something didn't change. "We want to try different things; we want to grow," Michael explained. "It's like the caterpillar must come out of the cocoon and be a butterfly. We have to try different things and grow and become all those different colours and elements and things like that. We've always wanted to write on Motown but it was never in our contract. And we could have changed our contract at Motown. But I don't think people had confidence in us; they didn't believe in us. They say, 'Oh, you guys [are] just kids. Just go behind the mike'."

Neither Michael's father Joseph nor his brothers spoke out about the issue, so Michael felt it was up to him to confront Berry Gordy about their feelings. But after meeting Gordy at his Bel Air mansion, Michael was told in no uncertain terms that the group's songs would still be controlled by Motown's writers and producers. If the brothers wanted to progress there was only one choice left, and that was to leave the label altogether.

Joseph and his attorney, Richard Arons, began began looking for a new record deal and chose to sign with CBS Records, headed by the volatile New Yorker Walter Yetnikoff, in the summer of 1975. CBS offered a royalty rate of 27% of the wholesale price for each record sold in the United States, compared with Motown's standard 2.7%; and although Yetnikoff was sceptical about allowing the brothers to write and produce all of their own music, there would be more creative opportunities there than at Motown.

Life at CBS didn't get off to the smoothest of starts; first the group were forced to change their name to The Jacksons, as Motown laid claim to the 'Jackson 5' name. Jermaine also felt compelled to leave the group and stay with Motown and release solo albums, having married Berry Gordy's daughter Hazel in 1973. He was replaced by the youngest Jackson brother, fourteen-year-old Randy, who had been an unofficial member of the group since 1972, playing congas onstage as part of their live act.

At CBS, The Jacksons' albums were produced by Philadelphia production duo Kenny Gamble and Leon Huff, who had success with artists like The O'Jays and Harold Melvin & The Blue Notes. Michael learnt a great deal watching Gamble and Huff in the studio, which helped to develop his own songwriting skills. "When you really can see the science, the anatomy and the structure of how it all works, it's just so wonderful," Michael said. "I used to say to myself, 'I want to write more'."

Even from a young age, Michael never stopped studying in his quest for perfection. There were no doubts that he was the most naturally talented Jackson, but he was also much more dedicated to his craft than his brothers were. Michael studied not only producers and singers, but also entertainers, and had his favourites. "Everybody has to start out looking up to someone," he said. "For me it was James Brown, Sammy Davis Jr., Jackie Wilson, Fred Astaire and Gene Kelly."

Michael would get the chance to write more, as the Jackson brothers' CBS deal, signed in May 1975, included an arrangement that the record company would handle any future Michael Jackson solo project. Michael believed CBS may have signed him as an insurance policy in case The Jacksons' next few albums continued to be unsuccessful.

The brothers' first album with their new label, simply titled *The Jacksons*, was released in 1976 under CBS subsidiary Epic Records. Despite peaking at a disappointing number 36 on the *Billboard* 100, eighteen-year-old Michael was able to write his first major song, 'Blues Away', one of two he wrote for the album. The other, 'Style of Life', was written with his brother Tito. One of the highlights of the record, Gamble and Huff's 'Show You the Way to Go', became the group's only number one hit in the United Kingdom. The brothers also wrote two songs for their next album, *Goin' Places*, which was released in October 1977 but also performed poorly, charting at 52. By now they hadn't had a number one single since 1971, and so far the relationship with CBS wasn't working out.

Michael found the transition between Motown and CBS particularly tough, and struggled with the enormous change. "At Motown it's a much smaller company, you know every face that's there," he said. "You even know the secretaries by name. And when you have a problem about anything you can call Berry Gordy right up he'll come down and he'll discuss it. Now CBS, it has millions of employees all over the world, and God, it was hard to adjust to such a big family of people. And when you do want to call somebody you call long distance to New York, long distance to Brazil or England. You get to know the person by business but not like a personal friend. And Berry, as well as our manager, he was fatherly too. We could relate to him much better."

CBS was ready to drop The Jacksons altogether, but after a meeting with Michael and Joseph the label decided to give them one more chance. This time they would finally be allowed to write and produce their own material. "I had a meeting with Walter Yetnikoff, I told him to give us that chance," Michael said. "I said, 'I know my potential and I know what we can do.' I think what really convinced people was when we wrote a song on the *Goin' Places* album, 'Different Kind of Lady', which was a big hit in the clubs. Even Kenny Gamble came and told us, 'You are all good enough to do your own stuff'." Michael was relieved. "That was the most tense situation ever," he admitted. "I was in a whole nother world, I didn't know what was happening and there was so much going on, so much tension."

It was a small victory for Michael, but in the year 1977 he was at a stage where he was unsure of what he wanted to do with his life now he was an adult. He was anxiously preparing to make decisions that would have repercussions for his entire career. A major turning point came in late 1977, when Michael was in New York filming *The Wiz*, a musical film adaptation of the 1975 Broadway musical of the same name, with an entirely African-American cast. The film production arm of Motown Records had acquired the rights for the movie, and Michael landed a role as the Scarecrow despite the supposed bad blood between the Jacksons and Berry Gordy.

On set Michael met producer Quincy Jones, who was the musical supervisor and music producer for the film and had previously worked with the likes of Frank Sinatra, Sammy Davis Jr. and Aretha Franklin. Quincy produced the soundtrack album, which features performances by the stars of the film. Michael's contributions include 'You Can't Win', a solo effort, and 'Ease on Down the Road', a collaboration with co-star Diana Ross. During filming, Michael and Quincy developed a rapport that Michael compared to a father-and-son relationship. The acquaintance would not only solve Michael's concerns about his future, but would also become one of the most significant moments in the history of the music industry.

Living in Manhattan, with older sister La Toya for company, the role also presented Michael with his first opportunity of escapism from his father and brothers. He spent numerous nights in the hottest nightclub in town, the iconic Studio 54, which opened only a few months before Michael's arrival in the city. During an interview on the premises, Michael admitted that he didn't usually enjoy discos or going out at night. But Studio 54 possessed a different kind of atmosphere. "It's just exciting," he said, "I'm ready to have a good time, it's where you come when you want to escape. It's really escapism, it's getting away from reality."

After filming of *The Wiz* was completed in January 1978, Michael returned to Los Angeles. He was now 19 years old and ready to resume a stalling solo career. CBS president Walter Yetnikoff sensed *The Wiz* had 'renewed' Michael's confidence, as it was done without his father or brothers. Although he had already released four solo albums with Motown, the next project was set to become Michael's first major release, and his first as an adult. It would mark the beginning of a journey which would lead to Michael Jackson becoming the most successful entertainer of all time, and one of the most famous people to ever live. Such an astronomical level of fame usually has a price, and for Michael, that price was huge.

CHAPTER 3:
LIVE IT *OFF THE WALL*

EARLY 1978 – LATE 1981

Back in 1978, nobody could imagine just how famous Michael Jackson would eventually become. Seen as nothing more than an innocent and gifted child star, he was desperate to shed that image and be taken seriously as a solo artist in his own right.

After returning from his film work in New York, Michael called his new mentor Quincy Jones, asking him if he could recommend any suitable producers for his upcoming solo project. He had already considered American film composer Walter Scharf, who had written his first number one hit 'Ben' six years earlier. Quincy mulled over the options, and eventually suggested himself for the role.

Michael was surprised that Quincy was even interested in his music, and didn't think twice about accepting the offer. "I said [to Quincy], 'I'm ready to do an album. Do you think…could you recommend anybody who would be interested in producing it with me or working with me?' He paused and said, 'Why don't you let me do it?' I said to myself, 'I don't know why I didn't think of that.' Probably because I was thinking that he was more [like] my father, kind of jazzy. I said, 'Wow, that would be great'."

When Michael told CBS that he wanted Quincy to produce his album, the label executives had certain reservations. They said Quincy was too 'jazzy' and would be unable to handle what they considered to be Michael's genre of disco and bubble-gum pop. Quincy claims CBS preferred Kenny Gamble and Leon Huff, who were producing The Jacksons' albums at the time. "Epic [Records] felt that Quincy was too old for Michael, who, in their minds, was a bubble-gum kid who needed a bubble-gum producer, they believed Quincy was out of touch with what young people were listening to," explained one of Michael's managers, Ron Weisner. Joseph hired Weisner to manage his sons in 1978, alongside Weisner's management partner Freddy DeMann. The pair replaced Joseph's original partner and attorney, Richard Arons, because Joseph claimed he needed 'white help' in dealing with the corporate structure at CBS.

Despite the label's reservations over Quincy, Michael held firm and demanded he produce the record. "Eventually, after a lot of kicking and screaming, Epic reluctantly acquiesced," Weisner added. "I think part of the reason Epic gave Quincy the thumbs up was the fact that he didn't take much money up front."

In the summer of 1978, Michael was ready to enter the studio with Quincy. But his brothers wanted him to prioritise The Jacksons' next album, *Destiny*, the first the group were to write and produce as a whole. After years of disappointing sales it was a make or break album for the brothers, and Michael reluctantly agreed to put family ahead of his own solo ambitions.

Destiny was released in December 1978 and had hit singles in 'Blame It on the Boogie' and 'Shake Your Body (Down to the Ground)', which was one of three songs Michael and his little brother Randy wrote for the album. Music critic Nelson George said it's 'appropriate' to see 'Shake Your Body' as 'the true start' of the adult Michael Jackson's solo career. The single was a top ten hit in both the United States and the United Kingdom, and the album also re-established The Jacksons as a top-selling group after the disappointments of the previous two records.

After attending the premiere of *The Wiz* in Los Angeles in late October 1978, Michael was able to put both the film and the *Destiny* album to the back of his mind. In November Quincy's contract to produce his new record became active, and the pair began planning the album.

When they spoke about the kind of sound they wanted, Michael told Quincy he wanted one that was different from that of The Jacksons. "Hard words to spit out," Michael said, but that was the primary reason why he hired an outside producer not affiliated with the group in any form. After all, if Michael wanted an album that sounded like The Jacksons, he would have just made another record with his brothers after *Destiny*. This album needed a new sound, especially as his last solo record – the Motown produced *Forever, Michael* – could only hit the dizzy heights of 101 on the *Billboard* 200 chart. Michael felt no guilt in working without his brothers. "They understand," he said. "Why hide something? Share it!"

During preproduction, Michael and Quincy began listening to dozens of songs from outside writers. Michael didn't have time to write a whole album's worth of songs due to album and touring commitments with his brothers, so he needed 'someone with a good ear' to help him choose material from other writers. Michael was still encouraged by Quincy to go into the studio and write a handful of songs for the project, a show of trust which he appreciated.

In late 1978, while Quincy was lining up the musicians for the main studio sessions, Michael began writing songs and creating demos (early, incomplete versions of songs) in his home studio at the Jackson family estate at 4641 Hayvenhurst Avenue in Encino, an affluent neighbourhood in the San Fernando Valley region of Los Angeles. The Jacksons moved into the ranch-style property, which became known simply as Hayvenhurst, in May 1971.

Michael was joined at the home studio by the talented young session keyboardist Greg Phillinganes, who had already worked with Michael and his brothers on *Destiny*. Significantly, Phillinganes also helped to mould the sounds of Stevie Wonder's 1976 smash album *Songs in the Key of Life*, a record which Michael loved. Songs that Michael wrote during this period include what became 'Don't Stop 'Til You Get Enough' and 'Workin' Day and Night'. Although Michael struggled with lyric writing at this time, he loved creating melodies, and his experiences of nightlife at New York's Studio 54 in 1977 no doubt shaped the sounds and rhythms of some of this new material.

For the main sessions, Quincy assembled a team of musicians and engineers which he called his 'killer Q posse'. They included drummer John 'J.R.' Robinson, bassist Louis Johnson from the funk duo The Brothers Johnson, percussionist Paulinho Da Costa, keyboardists/synthesists Michael Boddicker and Toto member Steve Porcaro, guitarist David Williams and members of the jazz fusion group Seawinds, led by trumpeter Jerry Hey.

Other members of the Seawinds hired to play on the album include saxophonists Larry Williams and Kim Hutchcroft, trombonist Bill Reichenbach and trumpeter Gary Grant. "We did the Brothers Johnson album *Blam!* with Quincy Jones in 1978 and he loved our work," Grant recalls. "He said to us, 'From now on, you are my horn section for every album I do'!"

Horn sections were extremely popular at the time and the Seawinds were in real demand. "Michael knew from our earlier work on *The Wiz* and with The Jacksons what the Seawinds represented in terms of quality," Kim Hutchcroft said. "Quincy would say how refreshing it was to have us come in and do live stuff."

Bruce Swedien, a deep voiced big bear of a man who Quincy had known and worked with since the late fifties, was appointed as the project's chief engineer. Quincy also brought in another trusted ally as associate producer, the talented composer Tom Bahler, whom he had worked with since 1973. Michael had prior experience of working with Bahler during the recording of *The Wiz* soundtrack, which Bahler co-produced with Quincy.

Musician Michael Boddicker said Quincy had a knack for choosing the right songs for each album, and effectively knew every musician and arranger in Los Angeles. "He went through hundreds of songs and would pull out the ones that leapt out," Boddicker said. "Then he would keep whittling them down. Other than Michael doing basic track cutting and vocals, Quincy was the producer. Michael wasn't very hands on during these sessions. This was Quincy's record, it was his show, he was the one who was hands on, hiring the musicians and arrangers and bringing in songs from other writers. At this stage, Michael was simply the star – the singer and the dancer – and would come in when he was needed."

Although Quincy was the chief producer and most certainly in charge, he still involved Michael in all aspects of the production, and the two shared responsibilities and constantly consulted with one another. Quincy admitted Michael was still shy and non-assertive in the studio. When the pair rehearsed for the album at Quincy's house on Stone Canyon Road in Bel Air, Michael forced the producer to hold his hands over his eyes and switch off the lights while he sang behind a couch. But Quincy was certainly impressed with Michael's work rate. "He can come to a session and put down two lead vocals and three background parts in one day," the producer said in 1979. "He does his homework, rehearses and works hard at home. Most singers want to do everything in the studio – write words and music, figure out harmonies, try different approaches to a song. That makes me crazy. All I can see is dollar signs going up. Studio time is expensive, and that's why someone like Michael is a producer's dream artist. He walks in prepared. We accomplish so much in a single session, it stuns me."

Once Michael and Quincy had chosen the first bunch of tracks to record, the main sessions began in early December of 1978 in two West Hollywood studios, Allen Zentz Recording on North Sycamore Avenue and Cherokee Studios on Fairfax Avenue. The recording process merely began that winter – nothing on the album was fully completed until the very end of production the following summer. This was the case for all of Michael's albums throughout his career.

Although the studios were only a short drive away from Michael's house in Encino, he would often get lost in his Rolls Royce. "He didn't like the freeways so he used back streets and side roads, and most of the time he would get lost," studio engineer Ed Cherney recalls. "He would pull over, knock on somebody's door and ring the studio from wherever he was. Sometimes I would go find him and pick him up. He was so sweet, he would ring and say, 'Ed, can you come and get me? I'm at so and so address.' And because we were using different studios for the production, Michael would also sometimes get confused and turn up at the wrong studio!"

On other occasions, Michael would drive to the studio with his brothers or an assistant. "One memory is of one of those Excalibur cars with a long hood and bulbous fenders pulling into the parking lot at the studio, and five or six Jacksons piling out of it," engineer Jim Fitzpatrick remembers. "It was just kind of a classic moment when I look back on it, something you'd expect to see on a Monkees TV show. They were all just so happy and seemed to be really having fun."

'SHE'S OUT OF MY LIFE'

The first song recorded for the album, 'She's Out of My Life', was a ballad written by associate producer Tom Bahler. Michael felt it was the ballads that would make this new album more his own, as his brothers were never overly enthusiastic about them. "On my own album I can do some things I can't do on The Jacksons' albums, I can do the ballads I want," Michael explained in 1979.

Bahler disclosed the full story of how 'She's Out of My Life', which he wrote in 1977, came to be considered for the album. "Everybody seemed to believe this fantasy story that it was about [singer] Karen Carpenter," Bahler said. "But the song wasn't inspired by Karen, by the time I became involved with her I had already written it. I actually wrote the song after splitting up with Rhonda Rivera, it was that break up that inspired it. I was with Rhonda for two years…all my relationships seemed to last for two years! That's why I wrote the line 'To think for two years she was here'."

One day Bahler played the song for Quincy, who immediately knew it would be a hit. "Quincy said to me, 'Tom, if you trust me, I'll make this into a hit record with somebody.' So he sat on it for two years, waiting for the right artist to come along and sing it. When I wrote it, I originally saw Frank Sinatra doing it."

Having still not found the right person to sing 'She's Out of My Life', Quincy suggested that Michael record it. "After Quincy agreed to produce Michael's record, he said to me, 'I think we should do 'She's Out of My Life' with Michael'," Bahler recalls. "I wasn't so sure because Michael was very young at the time – I felt maybe he wasn't mature enough for the song. But Quincy said, 'Hey, it'll give him adult emotions'."

Bahler revealed that Michael loved 'She's Out of My Life' and even wanted it to be the lead single. "It's so pretty that I think it could be another 'Ben'," Michael said shortly after recording the song. But Quincy made it clear they would certainly not be opening the album with a ballad.

Chief engineer Bruce Swedien recalls how Michael would refuse to curse, especially in the late seventies and eighties, which in turn meant he struggled to sing certain lyrics. Michael was rehearsing his vocals in the studio one day before the music track for 'She's Out of My Life' was to be recorded, with the musicians due to arrive later in the afternoon.

"Michael was seated at the drums, singing his heart out," Swedien recalls. "Every time we came to the third verse, and the line 'Damned indecision and cursed pride', Michael couldn't say the word 'damned'. He just couldn't bring himself to do it! He would stop singing and, with his foot, hit the bass drum foot pedal as loud as possible. He just couldn't curse. When the rehearsal ended, Quincy told Michael that he would absolutely have to sing the word 'damned' for the recording. Michael nodded and said to Q, 'I know'. He did."

The song was recorded with just Michael singing and Greg Phillinganes playing piano, which Quincy originally wanted Tom Bahler to play. "Quincy loved the way I played the piano, even though I wasn't a pianist," Bahler said. "I originally wrote the song in E-flat, but Michael sang it a step higher, in E, which kind of screwed that up for me! So I played the song and made a tape for Greg to study. Greg played the song in the end and did a beautiful job. He was only 22 at the time, but he played the song with the maturity of a man 100 years old."

The recording of the vocals for 'She's Out of My Life' became one of the more eventful studio sessions in Michael's career. He got too immersed in the emotion of the song, crying at the end of every one of the numerous takes he did. "The words suddenly had such a strong effect on me," Michael explained. "I had been letting so much passion build up inside me."

In the end, Quincy and Bahler chose the first vocal they recorded with Michael, because none of the subsequent takes hit them quite like that one. "It really took some courage for Michael to sing it the way he did," Bahler said. "He had no confidence at the time, he just showed up and sang the song, and was told every move he should make. It was just great, amazing in fact, what he did with that vocal."

When Michael broke down yet again at the end of what would be the last take, he was both apologetic and embarrassed. "Michael was too embarrassed to come into the control room, and just tippy-toed out of the back door of the Allen Zentz Studio, got in his car, and left the building," Bruce Swedien recalls. "Quincy said to me, 'Hey – that's supposed to be, leave it on there, leave it there'."

MATURE THEMES

Another song Michael and Quincy chose to record was written by Paul McCartney. Michael recalled how, when bumping into McCartney at a party at the Harold Lloyd estate in Los Angeles in June 1976, the former Beatle told him he had written a song for him, despite the pair having never met before.

McCartney began singing a song called 'Girlfriend' to Michael and the pair exchanged phone numbers, vowing to write songs together in the near future. But different commitments got in the way, and McCartney put the song on the Wings (his band) album *London Town*, released in March 1978.

What happened next was, as Michael put it, quite a coincidence. While considering songs for the album, Quincy suggested Michael record 'Girlfriend'. Quincy had no idea that McCartney wrote the song with Michael in mind in the first place, and the easy decision was made to include it on the album. At the time 'Girlfriend' was even considered as a potential album title.

Michael also had another surprise up his sleeve for Quincy. Stevie Wonder was working on his 1976 album *Songs in the Key of Life* with Susaye Greene of legendary Motown girl group The Supremes, when the two came up with 'I Can't Help It'. Greene said Wonder expressed a desire to write something for Michael, who was invited to sit in on the production sessions. "He [Wonder] had part of the hook – 'Can't help it, if I wanted to', but [for the rest] there weren't any real words there," Greene recalls. "So we just sat down and that song came together very quickly."

During one session Wonder was speaking to Michael in the studio about his plans for the future, before playing him 'I Can't Help It'. Michael was mesmerised and eager to find out when Wonder was planning to release the song, only for Wonder to reveal he had written it especially for him. Michael was delighted and gratefully accepted it for his next solo album. Wonder was equally excited. "He was just like a little boy," Greene said. "We were over the moon that this [Michael recording the song] would happen."

Observing Wonder in the studio would also prove invaluable for the development of Michael's production skills. Michael said he learnt so much by simply sitting like a fly on the wall. "Stevie Wonder, he's a musical prophet," Michael said. "I got to see *Songs in the Key of Life* get made, some of the most golden things."

Fast forward to 1978, and Quincy agreed that it was another perfect song for Michael to sing. To help the session musicians record the music track, Quincy demonstrated a certain Marvin Gaye song and told them, "This is the vibe I want to get."

"If a certain author of a piece of music inspired Quincy, he would use it as a demonstration to the musicians," Michael Boddicker said. "Don't get me wrong, he would never copy anyone's melody, it was the tempo that he would use as an example. He would say, 'This is the tempo we need, this is the feeling'."

Quincy also suggested Michael cover 'It's the Falling in Love', a ballad which American singer Carole Bayer Sager had written and included on her own 1978 album, *Too*. Quincy brought in Grammy-winning singer, producer and composer David Foster to adapt it, and the Canadian was given a writing credit for his work. The song features guest vocals by Quincy's goddaughter, Patti Austin.

Quincy chose songs such as 'She's Out of My Life', 'Girlfriend', 'I Can't Help It' and 'It's the Falling in Love' because he was eager for Michael to sing songs with more mature themes, including relationships.

"HEY MICHAEL, YOU'RE A WRITER ALL RIGHT!"

During the main sessions Michael and Greg Phillinganes also began laying down the foundations for the up-tempo songs they had worked on together at Michael's home studio – 'Don't Stop 'Til You Get Enough' and 'Workin' Day and Night'. Quincy hadn't done much dance or disco music before, so Michael brought in Phillinganes to help build a thicker wall of sound.

'Don't Stop' was an important song for Michael, as it was the very first one he had written as a whole. At the time, disco songs were the easiest songs for him to write, because he was so used to singing and dancing to them with his brothers.

The melody to 'Don't Stop' came to Michael one day in 1978 as he walked around his house in Encino. "I just started singing, 'da-da—da-da-da-da-da', and said, 'Ah, that sounds kinda nice'," he recalled. "I kept singing it and gradually it came about."

Later he went into his home studio and asked his younger brother Randy to play the melody that he was hearing in his head on the piano, as he couldn't play. Once the time had come to cut a demo, Michael was joined in the studio by Randy and their sister Janet. The three of them composed percussion sounds using glass bottles, cowbells and the cabasa, sounds that would all make it onto the final version. "It turned out real funky," Michael said. Greg Phillinganes created the bridge – a short, unique passage that comes between and connects two different sections of a song, often to build anticipation for an upcoming chorus – and received a rhythm arrangement credit.

The lyrical content of the song shocked Michael's mother Katherine, who pointed out that the title could easily be misinterpreted. But Michael told her it wasn't a reference to sex; it could mean whatever people wanted it to mean.

When Michael finally played the track for Quincy, he loved it. Michael may still have been experimenting and developing his songwriting, but Quincy and his right-hand man Tom Bahler were immediately impressed with what he brought to the table. "Michael wasn't even sure he was a writer at the time," Bahler said. "But then he came in with 'Don't Stop', and we said, 'Hey Michael, you're a writer all right'!"

Quincy wanted to add a string section (small orchestra) to the track, so he gave composer Benjamin Wright a call. When Wright picked up the phone, he thought a guitar player was playing a joke on him. "I was like, 'Quincy who'? I didn't really believe it was Quincy *Jones*. Somehow, he convinced me it was him, and gave me an address for his house in Bel Air. So I turned up at his house, and saw a familiar face at the door from TV, Peggy Lipton. It was his wife. Now I knew this really was *the* Quincy! I was scared to death."

Three days before the recording session, Wright still hadn't written any notes. "Quincy called me and said, 'Ben, you need to get some notes down on paper!' So the first song I worked on was 'Don't Stop' at Cherokee studio where all the strings were done. When I got there I saw Bruce Swedien, who I knew from days gone by. Bruce said to me, 'Don't worry Ben, this is a piece of cake.' I was thinking, 'Man, Bruce, don't put more pressure on me, I'm scared as it is!' Thankfully Quincy was really impressed with my work on 'Don't Stop', so after that session I was given two more songs to work on."

Performing drums on the track was John 'J.R.' Robinson, drummer for the funk band Rufus. Robinson's involvement on the album began when Quincy asked him to perform on 'Girlfriend' and 'It's the Falling in Love'. Robinson recalls: "That was on a Thursday, the following Monday I was called in by Quincy to come in and do the rest of the record, and the next song I did was 'Don't Stop'. The session began at noon at the Allen Zentz Studio. When that session finished, everybody in the room knew we were making history. It was electric."

The next song Michael submitted to Quincy was another of the home demos he worked on with Greg Phillinganes, 'Workin' Day and Night'.

The track, which Michael described as autobiographical due to its theme of working hard, was Brazilian percussionist Paulinho Da Costa's chance to shine. Da Costa, along with Phillinganes and Jerry Hey, was another musician who worked with The Jacksons prior to this project.

As with 'Don't Stop', Michael again contributed to the percussion sounds, as did John Robinson. "When we did the percussion for 'Workin' Day and Night', I used a really old wine bottle," the drummer recalls. "The sun was shining through the studio and it was a great session. So there we were, using this old wine bottle, but the fucking thing shattered on me. Michael was there, and when he saw what happened, he just said in his voice, 'Oh J.R.! Let me help!' There he was, picking all this glass off my arms, bit by bit. Soon after, Bruce [Swedien] came marching in, and with his deep voice, he was like, 'What the hell's going on in there?!' It was a funny moment."

Once the sessions were underway Michael wrote 'Get on the Floor' with musician Louis Johnson, who was performing bass on other tracks. Johnson had been working on a bass idea with his band The Brothers Johnson for their upcoming album *Light Up the Night*, but it had no melody. Michael heard the bass track and liked it, so Quincy suggested that the pair complete the song, with Michael adding the missing melody. Michael returned the favour by writing 'This Had to Be' with the Johnson brothers for *Light Up the Night*.

ENTER: ROD TEMPERTON

Michael was forced to leave the studio in January 1979 to begin rehearsing with his brothers for their forthcoming Destiny Tour, which was due to kick off in the German city of Bremen on January 22. The tour would keep Michael out of the studio until late March, when The Jacksons took a break and returned to Los Angeles.

That spring, associate producer Tom Bahler left the production for another project at New York's Radio City Music Hall. "Going to Radio City was a once in a lifetime opportunity and Quincy gave his blessing," Bahler said. "He said, 'Go Tom, you have to do it'."

Michael Boddicker said Quincy wanted something 'smooth, dreamy and lush' for Michael to sing. So the producer called in Rod Temperton, an English songwriter from the Lincolnshire seaside town of Cleethorpes who was also a member of the band Heatwave, famous for their 1976 hit 'Boogie Nights'.

Both Quincy and Bruce Swedien knew what Temperton had to offer and were impressed with his songwriting abilities. Quincy called him 'one of the best songwriters who ever lived', and Swedien said, "I simply loved Rod's musical feeling – everything about it – Rod's arrangements, his tunes, his songs – was exceedingly hip."

Temperton was recording an album with his band in a New York studio in the spring of 1979 when he got a call from Quincy, who wanted him to write some funky disco tunes for Michael. "In the end I wrote three songs, in order for Michael and Quincy to choose one song to go on the album," Temperton recalls. "They booked the studio in Los Angeles at the weekend when I wasn't working, and I flew in over the weekend to cut the tracks." In two six-hour sessions, Temperton and Quincy cut the three rhythm tracks (the basic foundations of a song such as bass guitar and drums).

Quincy Jones, Rod Temperton and Bruce Swedien at Allen Zentz Studio during the *Off the Wall* sessions

Bruce Swedien will never forget the moment when Temperton arrived at the studio to begin work. "The first day we met, it was a Saturday morning, I was already at Allen Zentz's studio waiting for Rod and Quincy to come from LAX [airport]," Swedien recalls. "Rod had flown all night on the red-eye from New York. When Quincy's car pulled into the parking lot at the studio, Quincy and his driver were in the front seat. In the back seat was this exhausting-looking dude in a wrinkled trench coat. His eyes were red-rimmed with fatigue, and he was staring into space. A Marlboro cigarette with a three-inch ash was dangling from his lower lip. That was my first impression of Rod Temperton."

After cutting the rhythm tracks Temperton returned to New York, where he completed the lyrics, before flying back to Los Angeles the following weekend to record vocals with Michael. Background vocals were recorded on the Saturday afternoon, and the three lead vocals were done the next day. Temperton described Michael as 'amazing', because he stayed up the whole of the Saturday night to learn the lyrics so that he wouldn't have to read them from the paper in front of him.

The three songs Temperton submitted for the album, 'Off the Wall', 'Rock With You' and 'Burn This Disco Out', are all disco themed. Michael felt he and Temperton were similar in the sense that they both felt more comfortable singing and writing about nightlife than actually experiencing it.

Temperton waited until he met Michael before completing lyrics for the three tracks, as he wanted to find out about his character first. 'Off the Wall' was the first song recorded; of the three, Temperton thought it would be Michael and Quincy's first choice.

"With all of the artists, I have to try to understand them so that they can sing the songs from the heart," Temperton explained. "When I met Michael, we talked about his love of movies and Hollywood and when I came up with that lyric ['Off the Wall'], it was a phrase that was used in New York a lot at the time. What I made of the meaning of the lyric was he was a little bit off-centre – and when you look at Michael, there was a little bit of eccentricity there that gave him an amazing energy. So I thought it was a fun idea to write a song with the lyric, 'Off the Wall'."

'Rock With You' was originally called 'I Want to Eat You Up', but the title was changed to fit in with Michael's image. Temperton knew Michael thrived when he was tasked with singing and dancing to melodic songs, and Michael acknowledged that 'Rock With You' was perfect for him.

By the time 'Rock With You' was recorded, the team began using another studio, Westlake, which was located on Wilshire Boulevard in Hollywood. Production was switched there from Allen Zentz because they needed a bigger studio, especially during the mixing stage, which was yet to come. Mixing is the technical and creative process of combining all the individual elements which are recorded separately, such as guitars, drums and vocals, and mixing them down to a single stereo track.

It was at Westlake where John Robinson performed the drum sections for 'Rock With You'. "That opening drum section of the song has become one of the most recognisable song intros in history," Robinson said. "And in my own opinion, I think 'Rock With You' is Michael's greatest ever song." Bruce Swedien, who wanted those drums to have their 'own acoustic space', had the studio carpenters build him a wooden drum platform so the unpainted plywood surface reflected Robinson's drum sounds back to the microphone. Over the years, Swedien would also record many of Michael's vocals on this platform.

'Rock With You' was the first song on the album that musician Michael Boddicker worked on. "The song was fabulous – as a musician it wasn't hard to be inspired," he said. "The objective, when we first heard Rod's demos, was to turn them into something really special. When I played my part it was just the four of us at Westlake; me, Quincy, Bruce and Greg Phillinganes. Rod and Michael weren't there. Greg played the synth solo, and I played the outro based on Greg's solo. I played that from A to Z, all the way through with no breaks. In those days nothing was done on computer, there was no cutting and pasting or flying things in. Rod really put in the hours, he was so disciplined, and he had little sleep. He was just working constantly."

Other musicians who worked on the album also remember Temperton as extremely dedicated. Trumpeter Gary Grant, a member of the Seawinds, said the Englishman would work on his songs both day and night. "He was the epitome of a songwriter and was capable of a rare art," Grant said. "He knew his songs. He knew how they flowed, how they were delivered and how they made sense." Steve Porcaro remembers Temperton as very demanding. "He knew exactly what he wanted in the studio," he said.

Temperton's arrival on the scene also motivated Michael to further his own songwriting skills. "He [Temperton] comes in the studio with this killer melody and chorus, 'Rock With You'," Michael recalled. "I go, 'Wow'! So when I heard that I said, 'Okay, I really have to work now'. So every time Rod would present something, I would present something, and we'd form a little friendly competition."

Once all three of his songs had been recorded, Temperton asked Quincy which one he wanted for the album. Much to Temperton's surprise, the producer wanted all of them.

The songs completed what would be the final tracklist: 'Don't Stop 'Til You Get Enough', 'Rock With You', 'Workin' Day and Night', 'Get on the Floor', 'Off the Wall', 'Girlfriend', 'She's Out of My Life', 'I Can't Help It', 'It's the Falling in Love' and 'Burn This Disco Out'.

It was decided the album would take the title of one of Temperton's tracks, 'Off the Wall'.

LIVING LIFE *OFF THE WALL*

Recording Michael Jackson's first adult solo album was a magical experience for everyone involved. Michael, Quincy and the musicians had complete artistic freedom; they could take chances in the studio because they didn't have any big sales to follow. But making *Off the Wall* also required hard work and dedication. Michael Boddicker described Quincy as one of the most detailed and focused men he has ever seen. "Quincy got things done in good time, but he was also a perfectionist," the musician said. "He wasn't afraid to erase things. He would say, 'This is great, but this could be better. We're 99% there, let's get to 110%'. During those sessions Quincy was very organised, and everything ran smoothly. He really trusted the musicians and gave us freedom. But nothing ever happened without his direct approval."

Michael certainly had a great rapport with the musicians, with whom he would often sing live. They spent a great deal of time together during the hours they weren't recording. "Michael was so accessible then," John Robinson remembers. "Girls would come by the studio regularly; he was so shy, but he would talk to them. He was open, and just about everybody could talk to him." Kim Hutchcroft too has fond memories of those sessions, and found Michael similarly accessible. "He once held my daughter, who was only a baby at the time," the saxophonist recalls.

The one person who did make Michael feel uncomfortable in the studio was his father, Joseph, who, alongside Ron Weisner and Freddy DeMann, was still his manager. "Quincy was criticised by Joe for being too jazzy," Bruce Swedien said. "I remember at one point Joe had to be escorted out of the studio because he was making Michael so nervous."

Having artistic freedom meant the atmosphere was always relaxed, and the team found time to have fun in the studio. "Gary Grant loved to mess around," fellow Seawind Larry Williams recalls. "We would be in the kitchen at the studio, and Gary would play practical jokes. Michael was very naïve…some of the things Gary said or did would shock Michael to the point where his eyes would widen with disbelief. But Gary would say, 'I'm only kidding, Michael.' But it got him every time!" Grant himself too remembers the fun times. "There was a lot of laughing, but the work was always serious," he said. "Michael was very serious about his work." The world would soon learn just how serious Michael was about his art.

By mid-April 1979, Michael was back on the road with his brothers to resume the Destiny Tour. His work in the studio was now complete and all of his vocals had been recorded. Bruce Swedien and the assistant engineers mixed the album while Michael was away.

Michael may not have been physically present during mixing, but he was involved in every part of the process. "When he was away, we would send him the mix tapes via courier or private messenger and then wait for his response, to see if he was happy or felt something needed changing," engineer Ed Cherney said. "While we were waiting, we would sit around and tell stories." Swedien mixed the record at Westlake. Cherney said Swedien liked one of the consoles (an electronic device used for mixing) located in a back room at the studio, which was built especially for Stevie Wonder.

The last day of mixing was on June 3, when Michael was on tour in South Carolina. But he was back in Los Angeles by the time Bernie Grundman mastered the album at A&M Recording Studios in Hollywood on July 17. Mastering is the final stage of album production and ensures the recording is balanced, equalised and enhanced.

Celebrity photographer Mike Salisbury was the man behind the album sleeve design. The final photo shoot took place in an alley behind what is now Lester Carpet, near the CBS television studio complex on Beverly Boulevard in Los Angeles. Yet before Salisbury brought his ideas to the table, the cover image saw Michael seated on a bale of straw wearing cowboy clothes.

Salisbury contacted Michael's managers, Freddy DeMann and Ron Weisner, after being impressed with Michael's work in *The Wiz*, and told them he would be anxious to work on something with their client. Salisbury was called to DeMann and Weisner's office, and shown the original album cover mock up.

"I told them that it looked like a cheap ad for the children's department of a failing discount store," Salisbury recalls. "Michael was sitting on straw bales, with his elbows on his knees and wearing striped pants. It was corny, and didn't mean much, and they didn't like it either, so I said I could come up with something. So I did some drawings, brought them back and told the managers that Michael was just a kid out from under his father, and that I thought the album cover should make a big statement about his solo debut. Pointing to the fashion drawing I said, 'I put him in a tuxedo. That says big deal'."

Salisbury said they didn't respond or react, until Michael stepped out and said he liked the design. "Michael liked everything about my concept and only requested one change, to wear white socks, which were custom made for him by famous Hollywood costume designer Bob Mackie. My wife at the time found an Yves St. Laurent woman's tux in Beverly Hills that fitted Michael's slim frame."

The first photo shoot took place at the Griffith Observatory in Los Angeles, but didn't go so well. "Michael was late when he drove up the hill to where we were waiting in the front of the observatory," Salisbury said. "The location was his idea, and it wouldn't work. There was no place for Michael to change and we were under a time constraint because we had no permit to shoot there. And the men's room was locked, but the women's restroom was open and like a real trouper he ran in there and put on the tux."

Salisbury had to dissuade Michael from a wide shot showing the landmark observatory that the photographer felt would only 'diminish' him. "I found a round deco corner of a tower at the top of a curved stairway. I would use a piece of it and we were shooting into the sunset which would give us some drama. But all Michael could do was lean against the wall; he was just not into it."

After Salisbury showed Michael the film, the pair agreed to a reshoot in a studio. "At the studio in front of a white backdrop dressed in the tux, it still wasn't working. I pushed my way out into the alley to find a better location – there was a plant covered trellis, some trashcans and boxes, a van and wrinkled blacktop. Walking down the alley I saw it, a loading dock and a brick wall behind a store. I jumped up on the dock, and said 'This is it'!"

Salisbury then positioned Michael up against the bare brick wall. "His pants were rolled up but not enough to show the socks, so I told Michael to put his thumbs in the tux pockets with his fingers out, and to pull his pants up so we could see the socks. Then I told him to smile, and we shot it. On the final print of the cover shot I had a glow airbrushed around the socks. Magic."

'Not into it': Michael leaning against a wall during the *Off the Wall* cover shoot at the Griffith Observatory

OFF THE WALL **– THE AFTERMATH**

In late June 1979, right after the mixing of *Off the Wall* was finalised and the first leg of The Jacksons' Destiny Tour was complete, Michael got straight back into the studio with his brothers to record the group's next album, *Triumph*. There's no rest for the wicked.

Off the Wall was released on August 10, peaking at number three on the *Billboard* album chart and at five in the United Kingdom. At the end of the month Michael turned 21, and made the tough decision not to renew his father's contract as one of his managers. Michael said the decision was made for both personal and creative reasons. "I just didn't like the way certain things were being handled," he said. "I was beginning to feel that I was working for him rather than he was working for me. And on the creative side we are two completely different minds." Management partners Ron Weisner and Freddy DeMann remained in place.

In early 1980, Michael took another step towards creative independence when he chose to hire his own attorney. One of those interviewed for the position was John Branca, a New Yorker who had a background in corporate tax law. Branca said Michael came to the meeting with his accountant, who did most of the talking. "In the meeting, he was trying to read and gather every piece of information he could," Branca recalls. "Behind his sunglasses, he studied the entire conversation. Michael had definite objectives. He wanted all of his business affairs reviewed, including his publishing and his record deal. And with the success of *Off the Wall*, he wanted a new contract."

Branca delivered on all fronts. He negotiated a new recording deal with CBS Records, one which gave Michael the highest royalty rate in the business at the time, at 37% of wholesale. Branca also had an agreement with CBS that Michael could leave The Jacksons at any time without it affecting his brothers' standing with the label.

The songs Michael had written with The Jacksons, as well as the three self-penned tracks from *Off the Wall*, were part of music publishing companies Michael created and owned with his brothers, Peacock and Miran Publishing. With Branca's guidance he formed his own publishing company, Mijac Music, which would include his future compositions, but not songs written by others such as Rod Temperton. The company is responsible for collecting royalties and licensing his music. A management and music production company, MJJ Productions, was also created.

In February 1980, Michael was nominated for two Grammy Awards for 'Don't Stop 'Til You Get Enough'. Although he won Best R&B Vocal Performance and became the first solo artist to have four singles from the same album reach the top ten of the *Billboard* 100, Michael felt ignored by his peers and hurt that *Off the Wall* only received a total of two nominations. His disappointment would only serve as motivation for the future. "I was disappointed and then I got excited thinking about the album to come," he said. "I said to myself, 'Wait until next time – they won't be able to ignore the next album'."

Despite Michael's Grammy frustration, *Off the Wall* would go on to sell ten million copies in three years, making it the biggest-selling album of all time by a black artist. Most importantly, the album showed the world that Michael wasn't about to go down the same road as so many child stars before him; the music created with his brothers was just the beginning of a great adventure. To date, it is estimated that more than 30 million copies of *Off the Wall* have been sold worldwide.

This success came despite a huge disco backlash in 1979, when the music industry in the United States crashed to its lowest ebb in decades. Rock music fans in particular blamed disco, which had been hugely popular throughout the seventies, and suddenly slogans such as 'disco sucks' and 'death to disco' became common.

Disco Demolition Night came only four weeks before the release of *Off the Wall*. The event was an anti-disco demonstration held during a baseball doubleheader in Chicago, and became known as 'the day disco died'. Two rock station DJs staged the promotional event, blowing up a box filled with disco records on the field between games. The backlash changed the face of radio, as American stations began to play other formats of music, but *Off the Wall* weathered the storm. It didn't prevent two of the disco orientated tracks from the album, 'Don't Stop 'Til You Get Enough' and 'Rock With You', going to number one on the *Billboard* 100.

'Don't Stop 'Til You Get Enough' was also the subject of Michael's first solo music video (called 'promos' in the pre-MTV era), followed by 'Rock With You' and 'She's Out of My Life'. The latter two were filmed on the same day at a Los Angeles stage and directed by Englishman Bruce Gowers, the man behind Queen's 1975 'Bohemian Rhapsody' video. Gowers estimates that making the 'Rock With You' video cost as little as $3,000. "In those days [videos] were done for peanuts. Absolute peanuts. I think about all we could afford [for the 'Rock With You' video] was the laser. If you look at it, there's nothing there but a laser and Michael Jackson." All three videos appear basic compared with what Michael would create only three years later.

Although the recording and release of *Off the Wall* was clearly an exciting time for Michael, he also described it as one of the most difficult periods of his life up to that date. All of his brothers, including young Randy, had moved out of the family home and Michael struggled to adapt. "Even at home I'm lonely," he admitted in 1981. "I sit in my room and sometimes cry. It is so hard to make friends and there are some things you can't talk to your parents or family about. I sometimes walk around the neighbourhood at night, just hoping to find someone to talk to. But I just end up coming home." Throughout his adult years, Michael would describe himself as one of the loneliest people on the planet.

Off the Wall may have been an instant success, but Michael was still juggling his own solo career ambitions with his work with The Jacksons. "This has been the major problem for me, trying to work with the group and do solo things as well," Michael admitted at the time. "I want to do more films and things."

The brothers finalised the recording of the *Triumph* album in June 1980, a year after recording first began. Part of the reason for the delay was the Destiny Tour, which was still ongoing and eventually finished in Los Angeles in September 1980. Michael incorporated his new solo material by singing songs including 'Don't Stop 'Til You Get Enough' on the second and third legs. On the day of the final show the *Triumph* album was released, which includes the hits 'This Place Hotel', written by Michael alone, 'Can You Feel It', written with older brother Jackie, and 'Lovely One', written with Randy.

With his confidence at an all-time high, Michael decided to call Paul McCartney about a collaboration in December 1980, as he wanted to repay McCartney for contributing 'Girlfriend' to *Off the Wall*. Initially, McCartney thought a female fan was on the other end of the phone line. "One Christmas I got a call on my private home number and I thought it was a girl fan, so I was a bit apprehensive," McCartney recalls. After realising it was Michael, the pair arranged to meet up in the New Year and write some songs. "Why not," McCartney said, "I really liked his singing, dancing and acting abilities."

Michael's former record label, Motown, released a compilation album in March 1981 which includes six tracks from his 1975 solo record *Forever, Michael*, padded out with four Jackson 5 songs. Motown later admitted it only released the album due to the commercial interest generated from the sales of *Off the Wall*. The release was significant because the album contained Michael's first solo number one hit in the United Kingdom, 'One Day in Your Life', which was recorded over six years earlier for *Forever, Michael*.

Two months later, Michael flew to London to work on music with McCartney. After meeting in the former Beatle's office, the two immediately got down to business. McCartney began playing the guitar, and soon enough they had the basis of a song that became 'Say Say Say'. Michael then returned to his hotel room and wrote most of the lyrics, before presenting them to McCartney the next day. Recording began during the remainder of Michael's stay, at famous Beatles producer George Martin's AIR Studios on Oxford Street in central London.

McCartney also played Michael a song on the piano that he had not yet completed, called 'The Man', and Michael again completed the lyrics. As most of McCartney's 1982 album *Tug of War* was already completed at this stage, he chose to keep the songs for his next record. This also gave the pair time to fine-tune the tracks later down the line.

While in London Michael was invited to spend time at McCartney's country estate in Sussex, just over an hour away from the English capital. Michael often had dinner with Paul and his wife Linda, and the three would hang out in the kitchen for conversation. "We really had some fun times," McCartney said. "I had an elder-brother attitude with him. I'd say, 'Michael, you're not eating enough,' and he'd say, 'Oh, Paul, you're so funny,' and giggle, and I'd say, 'C'mon, Michael, finish your vegetables.' So it was great, I'd take the mickey, and we made some nice music together."

After his London adventure, Michael turned his attention back to his work with The Jacksons. The brothers started a short three-month tour, supporting the *Triumph* album, in July 1981. After that, the time had come for Michael to begin work on the follow up to *Off the Wall*. As part of his contract, Quincy Jones had the option to produce Michael's next solo record, one which he exercised in October 1979. But to avoid overexposure, Michael wanted a gap of at least two years between the release of *Off the Wall* and starting work.

Hurt by his Grammy disappointment, Michael wanted every song on the next album to be a hit record. He didn't believe in albums where songs are included just to make up the numbers, and cited Russian composer Pyotr Ilyich Tchaikovsky's *The Nutcracker* as an inspiration. "It's an album where every song is like a great song," Michael explained. But he didn't just want to make great songs; he also wanted the album to be the biggest-selling of all time. Many felt this was maybe a little too ambitious.

CHAPTER 4: MAKING MUSIC HISTORY

LATE 1981 – LATE 1982

After The Jacksons' Triumph Tour finished with four concerts at the Forum in Los Angeles in September 1981, Michael got straight back into his home studio at Hayvenhurst to write songs and record demos for the next project. Excited to start work, he was constantly filling notebooks with lyrics, singing melodies into tape recorders and studying songs that outside writers had submitted to him.

The three main tracks Michael worked on in this period became 'Wanna Be Startin' Somethin'', 'Billie Jean' and 'The Girl Is Mine'. Another track that came out of these sessions, 'Behind the Mask', was released posthumously. Michael had actually written 'Wanna Be Startin' Somethin'' during his *Off the Wall* home studio sessions in 1978, but couldn't bring himself to present it to Quincy in case the producer rejected it. Michael's brothers' wives were the inspiration for the song as they were "always creating trouble", Bruce Swedien said.

Michael also knew he wanted to write a song with a great bass hook. "I just let it go," he said, not wishing to force the issue. After a distinctive bassline came to him one day, he went into the Hayvenhurst studio to work out the arrangement with musician Bill Wolfer. Michael sat with Wolfer at a Rhodes piano, and sang him the bassline, chords and harmonies. "I started playing the bassline, and then he sang the top three notes of chords that go over it," Wolfer recalls. "We then tried to figure out what the underlying harmonies were. There are a thousand different ways to do that, but

Michael had a very specific idea in his mind. He didn't play an instrument, but he really was a musician. He arranged entire songs in his head, and no matter what you played to him, he stood by the vision in his head." The next step was to create sounds on the synthesizer (an electronic instrument played with a keyboard), which Wolfer compared to human voices, before they recorded a demo. Even at this early stage Michael said he knew he had a hit on his hands, and called the song 'Billie Jean'.

About a girl who accuses him of fathering her child, there has been speculation whether there was ever a real 'Billie Jean', but Michael insisted she simply represents numerous girls that pursued the Jackson brothers over the years. "I wrote this out of experience with my brothers when I was little – there were a lot of Billie Jeans out there," he said. Michael recalled how fans would visit Hayvenhurst equipped with sleeping bags, before jumping over the wall and sleeping in the yard. Some even entered the house itself. "We found people everywhere," he said. "Even with 24-hour guards they find a way to slip in. One day my brother woke up and saw this girl standing over him in his bedroom. People hitch-hike to the house and say they want to sleep with us, stay with us, and it usually ends up that one of the neighbours takes them in."

'The Girl Is Mine', which is about two men fighting over a girl, came about after Quincy set Michael the task of writing a song he could sing with Paul McCartney. The two agreed to get together to record more music after their exploits in London earlier in the year. Michael awoke one night with a melody idea in his head and sang it straight into a tape recorder, along with the instrumental parts such as keyboards and strings.

Michael knew this latest idea would suit both his and McCartney's voice, so he recorded a demo and played it to Quincy. It was exactly what Quincy was looking for, although the producer felt it was missing a rap verse. "Quincy called me up one morning and says, 'Smelly' – he calls me Smelly – 'We have to have some rapping in this'," Michael recalled. Quincy later explained the nickname. "I called Michael 'Smelly' because when he liked a piece of music or a certain beat, instead of calling it funky, he'd call it 'smelly jelly'," the producer said. "When it was really good, he'd say, 'That's some smelly jelly'."

McCartney agreed to sing the song with Michael despite having doubts about some of the lyrics, which he described as 'shallow'. "There was even a word – 'doggone' – that I wouldn't have put in it," the former Beatle admitted. "When I checked it out with Michael, he explained that he wasn't going for depth – he was going for rhythm, he was going for feel. And he was right. It's not the lyrics that are important on this particular song – it's much more the noise, the performance, my voice, his voice." In December 1981, the pair rehearsed the song with Quincy at McCartney's ranch in Arizona.

UNREALISTIC AMBITIONS

After the rehearsal session, a date was chosen for the pair to record the song in the main studio. At noon on Wednesday, April 14, 1982, McCartney joined Michael in the new Westlake Studio on Beverly Boulevard for what became a three-day recording session. Working with Michael for the first time was an engineer called Matt Forger. "I met Michael because I was working with Quincy at the time, and Michael's project was simply the next one on Quincy's schedule," Forger said. It was the start of a professional relationship and friendship that would last more than 20 years. Forger said 'The Girl Is Mine' was recorded in April because it was a good time for all parties involved, even though the main sessions for Michael's album weren't due to start for a few months.

With two stars such as Michael Jackson and Paul McCartney collaborating, the session was particularly enjoyable for the musicians involved. Steve Porcaro described it as 'incredible'. "Michael and Paul sang live with the band, I sat down with Paul's wife Linda and had a chat…it was great," the Toto keyboardist recalls. "So many people came in. At the end of the session, a whole entourage of people left the studio, including Michael, Paul, Linda, Quincy, Michael's people, Paul's people, musicians and engineers. But somehow, Paul managed to escape from the crowd. I stayed behind in the studio with my brother Jeff, who was playing the drums on the track, and we were having a smoke of something. All of a sudden, this head pops around the corner. It was Paul. He had snuck back into the studio! When he saw us, he just said, 'Ahhhh, musicians…' So he sat down and had a smoke with us. How he managed to lose everyone without anyone noticing I'll never know."

Michael said recording 'The Girl Is Mine' was one of the most enjoyable studio moments of his entire career. McCartney arrived at Westlake with a personal movie crew in tow to film the session, and celebrities who visited the studio include Christopher Cross, Dick Clark and Lionel Richie. "Working with Paul McCartney was pretty exciting and we just literally had fun," Michael said. "It was like lots of kibitzing and playing, and throwing stuff at each other, and making jokes. We actually recorded the track and the vocals pretty much live at the same time." Although he enjoyed recording 'The Girl Is Mine', Michael later admitted the song never fully satisfied him.

The late seventies disco backlash meant Michael's next album needed a totally different sound from *Off the Wall.* Although the album was a massive success, Michael admitted he was hurt by the anti-disco movements. "Disco was just a happy medium of making people dance at the time, but it was so popular that the society was turning against it," he said. The animosity towards the genre required Michael to adopt a more electronic funk sound, which later became known as 'post-disco'.

It was not only time for Michael to move away from the disco themes of The Jacksons and *Off the Wall*, but also to grow as an artist and a producer. He was certainly ready to become more hands on with his next album than *Off the Wall*, which was mainly Quincy's show. Musician Michael Boddicker said there was a completely different approach. "Michael was certainly more present in the studio than during the *Off the Wall* sessions, and he had far more input," Boddicker said.

After recording 'The Girl Is Mine', the team took a break as Quincy and his production crew recorded an album with Donna Summer. In August 1982, Michael, Quincy, Bruce Swedien, the returning songwriter Rod Temperton and the rest of the team gathered at Westlake's Studio A to begin recording the follow up to *Off the Wall.* Quincy brought back most of the *Off the Wall* session players, with three other Toto band members joining Steve Porcaro – guitarist Steve Lukather, keyboardist David Paich and Porcaro's younger brother, drummer Jeff. Drummer Ndugu Chancler was another new face. The team would only have around three months to finish the album in time for CBS Records' strict Thanksgiving deadline, but fortunately there were no big sales expectations.

In the summer of 1982 America was in the midst of a severe recession, and the music industry was in tatters. When the team walked through the studio doors on day one, Quincy confided to Westlake studio manager Jim Fitzpatrick that he simply hoped the album would match the sales of *Off the Wall*. "Quincy said to me, 'Gosh Jim, this record business is in such a slump, I only hope this next one can sell as well as *Off the Wall*'," Fitzpatrick recalls.

Despite the industry crisis Michael had higher hopes for the album, even if other members of the production team didn't. He was in the studio with Quincy and Rod Temperton one day when the pair dared to mention that sales may not reach the heights of *Off the Wall*. "I admitted that I wanted this album to be the biggest-selling album of all time," Michael said. "They started laughing. It was a seemingly unrealistic thing to want. There were times when I would get emotional or upset because I couldn't get the people working with me to see what I saw." Proving people wrong had been Michael's goal ever since *Off the Wall* only won one Grammy Award in 1980.

POLAROIDS

Before submitting his own songs to Quincy, Michael wanted to see what had come in from other writers. After writing three hits for *Off the Wall*, Rod Temperton was asked to come up with more material for the next project. Quincy figured there was no reason to break with a successful formula. "You managed to come up with a title for the last album, see what you can do for this album," he told the Englishman.

Temperton's demos were the first the team worked on. After Temperton whittled his ideas down from 40 to five, he went to Hayvenhurst with Quincy to present them to Michael. The demos were mostly complete, with the beginnings of lyric schemes and several different titles for each track, and included 'Baby Be Mine', 'Starlight', 'The Lady in My Life' and 'Hot Street'.

Michael and Quincy saw potential in the 'Starlight' demo; Temperton said the title was 'just some rubbish word' he used to demonstrate to Michael how the melody went. After leaving Hayvenhurst Temperton went back to his hotel and wrote two or three hundred alternative titles, one of which was 'Midnight Man'. During breakfast the next morning, the word 'Thriller' suddenly shot into his head. "It was like electricity and immediately I started thinking of the lyrics," he said. "That's how 'Thriller' came to be."

The original hook lyrics were 'Starlight! Starlight sun…', but when the title was changed to 'Thriller', the line was rewritten to 'Thriller! Thriller night…' With both titles in hand, Temperton asked Michael which one he would prefer. "I thought kids would enjoy something more fun like 'Thriller', so we went with the 'Thriller' idea," Michael explained.

The team spent a great deal of time creating the spooky intro to 'Thriller', which features creaking doors, wind, footsteps, thunder and wolf howls. Bruce Swedien, who worked on the sound effects with film editor Bruce Cannon, even wanted his own Great Dane, Max, to make a cameo after seeing a similar dog in the Sherlock Holmes movie *The Hound of The Baskervilles.* "We bribed Max with hamburgers, we put him out by the barn to listen to the coyotes at night, but Max wasn't interested in being part of 'Thriller'," Swedien said.

When Temperton wrote 'Thriller' he envisioned a spooky horror rap to come in at the end of the track, and wanted a famous voice in the horror genre to perform the vocal. Much to his delight, Quincy's then wife Peggy Lipton knew Hollywood horror film actor Vincent Price, who agreed to participate. "The idea was going to be that he would just talk some horror talk from the type of lines he would deliver in some of his famous roles," Temperton said.

Temperton planned to write the rap verses on the morning of Price's studio session, but a lengthy business meeting meant he had only two hours to complete them. "I frantically started to write some stuff, and it was just one of those lucky times that it flowed out of me," Temperton said. Some of the verses were written in the back of a taxi on the way to the studio. "As I arrived at the studio I saw a car pull up, and out steps Vincent Price, and the taxi pulled me round the back of the studio and I dived out of the cab, raced in the back door and said to the secretary, 'Photocopy this quick'. They put it on the music stand and he walked in, sat down in his chair and off we went."

The session was completed in around two hours, and Price did his part in only two takes. Although he had performed on a record before, Price was still a little out of his comfort zone in the recording studio. "When the music track for 'Thriller' started, Vincent jumped up from his stall with a very startled look on his face," Bruce Swedien recalls. "He asked Rod to come out of the studio with him and help him by cueing him where to come in and speak his verses." Price was offered either $20,000 for his work, or a percentage of the album royalties. He chose to take the money upfront, a move he would later regret.

Michael revealed that another of Temperton's songs, 'The Lady in My Life', was one of the most challenging to record in the entire project. Quincy wasn't satisfied with Michael's vocals even after dozens of takes. Late one session, he took him aside and said, "Smelly, I need you to beg on this. I want a serious beg on this one, which is convincing the lady that this is the way that she should go."

"Michael knew exactly what I was talking about," Quincy said. "He got all embarrassed and started to blush." With the lights off and the curtain between the studio and control room drawn, Michael went back before the microphone and begged. His self-consciousness meant his vocals were almost always recorded with the lights off. "I like to just feel everything, I don't like people looking at me unless I'm on stage," he explained.

Much like Tom Bahler's role during the production of *Off the Wall*, Temperton would effectively act as Quincy's right-hand man in finding the right songs for the album. The pair went through between 600 and 800 songs and demos from outside writers. Quincy said the producer's main job is to 'find the right tunes', a process he called 'polaroids'. Describing the process, Matt Forger said: "He would 'snapshot' the best songs to get a feel for the key, tempo, how Michael's voice would react to the song, that type of thing." One song that impressed Quincy was 'Carousel', a ballad written by Michael Sembello and Don Freeman.

Quincy was also looking for a racy, up-tempo song about women. His wife, Peggy Lipton, had some lingerie with 'Pretty Young Things' written on it at the time, which he thought would make a great song title. The producer asked Michael, Temperton and several others to write a song around the title. Michael created a melodic mid-tempo version with musician Greg Phillinganes, while musician Michael Boddicker also took a shot at it. "Quincy said he wanted a song about women's behinds, and I took it literally and wrote a song called 'Love Them Buns'," Boddicker said. "But I think he wanted something a little subtler!" Of all the attempts, Quincy's favourite was a funky up-tempo demo written by singer James Ingram. The full title became 'P.Y.T. (Pretty Young Thing)'.

Meanwhile, Rod Temperton had again written the title track, as they chose to call the album *Thriller*.

THE MAKING OF 'BILLIE JEAN'

Once Michael had heard the material from the other writers, he finally showed Quincy what he had been working on over the previous year. 'The Girl Is Mine' was already completed, and the next demo he had was 'Wanna Be Startin' Somethin'', written around four years earlier during the *Off the Wall* home studio sessions.

Years later, Michael revealed his disappointment that he couldn't get 'Wanna Be Startin' Somethin'' to sound the way he wanted, despite its eventual popularity. "Song-writing is a very frustrating art form, you have to get on tape exactly what's playing in your head," he explained. "When I hear it up here [his head], it's wonderful. [But] I have to transcribe that onto tape."

Michael also had 'Billie Jean' up his sleeve. Before they recorded the song in the studio, Quincy told Bruce Swedien the music had to have more 'sonic personality' than anything they had ever done. Swedien believes they achieved just that. "The bottom line is that there aren't many pieces of music where you can hear the first three or four notes of the drums, and immediately tell what the piece of music is," he said. "But I think that is the case with 'Billie Jean' – and that I attribute to sonic personality."

Those now famous drum parts were played by top session musician Ndugu Chancler. "Playing that was very challenging, because I had to simultaneously mirror the drum machine for my parts," Chancler recalls. "It was originally just a drum machine track, but I replaced that with the live drums."

David Williams's guitar solo, about three quarters of the way through the song, was actually taken from Michael's original demo. Williams tried many times to replay it to the same effect at Westlake, but Swedien said it was never the same.

The distinctive bassline was performed by bassist Louis Johnson, another musician to return after working on *Off the Wall*. "Michael was very specific about how he wanted the bassline to sound," Johnson said. "He had me bring all my guitars to see how they sounded playing the part. I tried three of four basses before we settled on the Yamaha."

Michael's entire lead vocal was performed in one take; he received training from his vocal coach, Seth Riggs, every morning throughout production. "During *Thriller*, I would work with Michael for two hours a day, I thought it was too much but it's what Quincy wanted," Riggs recalls. "I had to make sure I didn't tire Michael's voice but massage it, and prepare it."

Before Michael recorded a song, he would vocalise with Riggs for at least an hour. Riggs said Michael's voice had a range of three-and-a-half octaves, mostly high tenor. "Michael could also sing bass or baritone and his speaking voice was actually four or five notes higher than his lowest singing voice," he said. "I had to make Michael's voice sound like a man's voice, not just a voice of a boy going through puberty. I was able to make him vocalise a man's voice. But as Michael got older, his voice also got deeper." In order to keep his voice clear Michael would drink scalding hot water while he sang, sometimes supplemented with Ricola cough drops.

Musician Gary Grant says he was amazed by Michael's vocal delivery in every single session. "His timing, his delivery of the vocals, it was always done perfectly," Grant said. "The pitch was wonderful; he was 'on it' every time. That maturity at his age was rare to see. The timing of the execution and the phrasing…it was outstanding."

Bruce Swedien ended up mixing 'Billie Jean' 91 times; a staggering figure considering he usually only mixed a song once. After two days of mixing, Swedien felt his second effort was 'a killer'. Michael and Quincy also loved this mix, but kept asking for minor alterations. "This went on for about a week, soon I was up to mix number 91," Swedien said. "I played mix number 91 for the boys and everybody smiled. Quincy said, 'Just for the fun of it, can we listen to one of your earlier mixes?' My heart jumped because I knew my earlier mixes were dynamite. We listened to mix number two again and it was slammin'! Everyone was grooving and dancing. Mix number two was the final decision and that is exactly what you hear on the record."

Quincy originally wanted to change the song title to 'Not My Lover', as he believed people may have thought it was about the female tennis player Billie Jean King. The chorus included the line 'not my lover' over and over again, which he also felt was significant. But Michael stood his ground, and the title was kept. With hindsight, Quincy believes it was the correct decision. "Sitting here today, I would say it is good that Michael enforced the song to be named 'Billie Jean'," he said.

Quincy also wanted to shorten the song's long 29-second introduction. "You could shave on that intro it was so long," he said. Again, Michael held firm and insisted the long intro remain, because it made him want to dance. There have been claims that Quincy didn't even feel 'Billie Jean' was strong enough to be included on the album, which the producer has flatly denied.

Either way, 'Billie Jean' would never have been completed if Michael's Rolls Royce had blown up on the journey home from the studio one day.

COURAGE UNDER FIRE

While recording *Thriller*, Michael was living temporarily in a small condominium at 5420 Lindley Avenue in Encino, a ten minute drive from Hayvenhurst, which was being remodelled. Engineer Nelson Hayes, who worked with Michael on his home demos and also acted as an assistant, was tasked with driving him to the studio as he hated to use the freeways of Los Angeles. Before heading to Westlake the two would often stop at the Golden Temple, a nearby Sikh restaurant. It was the only Los Angeles restaurant Michael would dine in, as he knew the owners. "We would have a quick bite and Yogi tea before heading to Westlake," Hayes recalls. "Mike loved their vegetarian cuisine, and he could also dine there unnoticed by other customers."

Upon arrival at Westlake Hayes would park at the back of the studio, before the two entered through the rear entrance. At the end of a session, Bruce Swedien would give Michael a demo cassette containing the work they had done that day. During the drive back to Encino, Michael would listen to the cassette on his Walkman or the custom audio system of his Rolls Royce. "One afternoon we came out of the studio ready to go home after a short session, and Mike had other appointments that day and was somewhat rushed," Hayes said. "A heatwave was over Los Angeles that week, so we were using Mike's car because the air conditioning in his Rolls sure beat the hell out of the conditioning in my Fiat 128 Sport Coupe."

Hayes noticed a small pool of clear liquid was leaking from the Rolls, so the two drove to a repair shop in Hollywood. "The mechanic there said we were leaking brake fluid and could take care of it, but all loaners were out," Hayes said. "They could get a rental for us, but it would take a while and Mike said he needed to get home, and asked if the brakes would be okay for the 20 minute ride to Encino. The mechanic said he didn't recommend it, and warned that brake fluid is highly flammable should it get on a hot manifold or muffler. All this had taken about 20 more minutes of Mike's time, so he said, 'Let's chance it and let's roll'." Hayes planned to drive Michael home before taking the vehicle to a local dealer.

Once on the road Michael was grooving to 'Billie Jean' on his headphones while sat in the passenger seat, quietly composing music in his head. Coming off the Ventura Freeway and down the White Oak Avenue exit ramp, Hayes noticed somebody on a bicycle waving and pointing at them while stopped at a red light. "I powered down my window and heard the kid holler, 'Hey, your car's on fire'," Hayes recalls. "As he said that, the light turned green and I sped out of that exit and stopped out of traffic flow at the west curb." The two immediately jumped out of the car and noticed small flames flickering from the car's undercarriage.

Hayes opened the bonnet only to be greeted by billowing flames, and ran to a petrol station to retrieve a fire extinguisher. Michael was now seated under the shade of a small tree, still absorbed by 'Billie Jean' and composing additional material in his head. "Mike couldn't care less about his Rolls, but God bless him, he stopped the Walkman to scream another stay away warning at me," Hayes said. "By now I was on a mission, I pulled out the pin and squeezed the trigger but nothing happened…the extinguisher's charge date had expired. Mike howled with laughter; put his headphones back on and got back to boppin' to the music. Courage under fire? How about care less during fire!"

By the time firefighters arrived, the flames had burnt out. Hayes called for a tow truck to take the car to the repair shop, before calling Jackie – who was living in the same condo as Michael – to pick up his little brother. Michael admitted he didn't focus on the potential consequences until later. "That's how involved I was with 'Billie Jean'," he said. "The kid probably saved our lives, if the car had exploded, we could have been killed."

THE *E.T.* STORYBOOK

It was September 1982, and the team were working hard in the studio in order to meet the record label's Thanksgiving deadline for completing *Thriller*. The task was about to get much harder.

Film director Steven Spielberg asked Quincy if he could cut a song for the *E.T. the Extra-Terrestrial* storybook album, with Michael singing. The film, directed by Spielberg, had been released a few months earlier and was already a huge box-office hit. Quincy agreed because it was only one song, and asked Rod Temperton to write it, together with Academy Award winning songwriters Marilyn and Alan Bergman.

Spielberg loved the song, which became 'Someone in the Dark', so he asked Michael and Quincy if they would record the entire soundtrack album. "This was quite a challenge given that we had to boil down a two-hour-long visual experience – one of the most successful films in history – to a forty-minute listening experience," Quincy said. "Steven had no idea of the kind of time involved in putting together this kind of record."

But for Michael, this was a chance not to be missed. "He felt like this was a window of opportunity and took up the offer," Matt Forger said. "But the project wasn't as quick and easy as they thought – it took up a few weeks right during the middle of the *Thriller* sessions, which meant we were working on both albums at the same time."

Although Quincy and his writers didn't have to write any more material, as they were using composer John Williams's *E.T.* film score, they still had to rewrite the narrative and transform it into an audio experience. "It was a nightmare," Quincy admitted.

For Michael it was far from a nightmare; he developed a sense of attachment to the alien character while narrating the story. "I felt like I was there with them, like behind a tree or something, watching everything that happened," Michael said. "That's what I loved about doing *E.T.* I was actually there. The next day, I missed him a lot. I wanted to go back to that spot I was at yesterday in the forest. I wanted to be there."

MCA Records, which distributed the *E.T.* storybook, got into a bit of bother with Walter Yetnikoff and CBS after not getting the necessary clearance for Michael to feature on the album. It was eventually agreed that MCA could release it, but only after Christmas 1982 so it wouldn't compete directly with *Thriller*. 'Someone in the Dark' was also prohibited from ever being released as a single.

STUDIO LIFE

Although recording both albums was putting the team in a tight position, there was still time to have fun in the studio. One of Greg Phillinganes's fondest memories was 'Animal Day'. "Michael brought in his pet snake, Muscles, and we all had a group shot with it," he recalls. Michael's personal assistant at the time, Shari Dub, also remembers the day well. "Michael draped Muscles around me, which normally would not be alarming, except for the fact that it was a snake of course, but I also happened to be very, very pregnant which freaked everyone out, including Quincy," Dub said. "Michael and I thought it was fine and slightly funny, but not everyone agreed with us! Michael just adored animals, even Muscles."

Young women were also frequent visitors to the studio. "Girls came by all the time," saxophonist Larry Williams said. "James Ingram brought Jodie Foster in one day, but Michael was very shy with the girls, it was sweet to watch." On other occasions, when Michael wasn't in direct contact with the women, he wasn't quite so shy. "[One day] A healthy young Los Angeles lady walked slowly by the front of the studio," Bruce Swedien recalls. "That window was made of a one-way glass facing the sidewalk and the street. All of a sudden, while we were watching, she pulled her dress high up over her head. She was wearing absolutely nothing underneath. Quincy, Rod and I got a very good look! We just stood there, gawking. We turned around and there was Michael, devoted Jehovah's Witness and all, hiding behind the big Harrison console getting an eyeful all the same!"

Although he was now one of the biggest stars in the world thanks to the huge success of *Off the Wall*, Michael was still very humble and trusting. "He was still very approachable and accessible during this time," musician Steve Porcaro remembers. Trumpeter Gary Grant recollects a particular moment that was perhaps an example of Michael's modest background. "During a break at the studio I went over to the piano with Larry Williams, who played some things," Grant said. "I had two dollars on me and put it down on the piano – Michael was listening to us fooling around and must have seen me put my money down. A few hours later he came up to me and said, 'Hey Gary, you left your money on the piano.' Michael was a wealthy man by then after *Off the Wall*, but for him to be concerned that I left two dollars lying around was a testimony to the man."

In order to get out and sample everyday normality, Michael would often dress up in disguise so he could mix with the public. "We were at Westlake on Beverly Boulevard and the Beverly Center was just across the road," Greg Phillinganes recalls. "We had some downtime in the studio and Michael said to me, 'Hey Greg, you wanna go to the mall?' I said, 'Sure.'

So Michael dressed up with an afro wig, sunglasses and bucked teeth. We walked over with no security, no nothing…I just couldn't believe I was walking across La Cienega Boulevard with Michael Jackson next to me. We went in there and eventually people started to look twice at Michael; they were a bit suspicious. At the checkout Michael whipped out his credit card, and the cashiers saw the name on the front of the card. They were in disbelief and stared at Michael, but still weren't quite sure if it was him!"

THE SEARCH FOR MICHAEL'S 'MY SHARONA'

By the fall, it was certain that Michael's three songs, 'The Girl Is Mine', 'Wanna Be Startin' Somethin'' and 'Billie Jean', were going to make the final cut, as well as Rod Temperton's 'Thriller'. At this stage these songs were considered to be the cornerstones of the album. Songs such as 'Carousel', 'Got the Hots' (written by Michael and Quincy), 'Nightline' (Glen Ballard) and 'She's Trouble' (Terry Britten, Sue Shifrin and Bill Livsey), as well as Temperton's 'Baby Be Mine', 'The Lady in My Life' and 'Hot Street', were also being strongly considered.

But a few of these songs were causing Quincy and Temperton to reconsider the direction of the album. They realised songs such as 'Hot Street', 'She's Trouble' and 'Got the Hots' were 'a little too poppy' and 'straightforward' in comparison with 'Wanna Be Startin' Somethin'', 'Billie Jean' and 'Thriller'. What the album was really missing, according to Quincy, was a big rock song. He encouraged Michael, as well as others, to try to write it. Musician Steve Porcaro said Quincy was looking for something in the vein of 'My Sharona' by The Knack, and asked Porcaro's fellow band member David Paich to try to come up with something. But instead of getting a rock song from Paich, it was by complete chance that another ballad caught Quincy's attention.

Porcaro, working on *Thriller* as a musician, was living at Paich's house at the time and assisted him in throwing down his ideas on tape while he was trying to come up with material for Michael. "There was a week long period where Quincy would send his assistant to David's studio every day to pick up a cassette of what he was working on," Porcaro recalls. "One day, David told me to take the two grooves he had worked on the previous day and make a cassette copy of them, because Quincy's assistant was on the way to pick something up. When I went in the studio to do this, I found we had run out of blank cassettes."

Porcaro had been working on a new tune, called 'Human Nature', although it was far from finished. "The demo I had of it at the time was a very rough track with no verse lyrics, just me horribly singing the same thing over and over, but the chorus was intact. I was hoping Toto would do it. I had that on a cassette and figured I would fast forward it, flip it over to the B-side, and record David's two grooves. I relabelled the cassette so that David's tunes were on the A-side, but didn't label the B-side. That was what was sent over to Quincy."

Quincy played Paich's demos, but he forgot to turn the tape off at the end and it kicked into auto reverse. "All of a sudden, at the end, there was all this silence," Quincy recalls. "There was, 'why, why, dah dah dum dum dum dum dum dum, why, why'. I get goose bumps just talking about it. I said, 'What the hell is that, this is where we wanna go,' because it's got such a wonderful flavour." The producer called Paich the next day, and told him he loved the 'why, why' song. "David told me it took him half an hour to figure out what he was talking about," Porcaro said.

After Porcaro agreed to let Michael have the song, Quincy asked him to finish the lyrics. "As much as Quincy loved the chorus, he was underwhelmed with my verses for a very good reason...they were horrible," Porcaro admitted. "He asked if I would mind letting a lyricist named John Bettis take a shot at the verses, which I agreed to, and he just knocked it out of the park. His very first draft that he presented to me is what you hear on the record. John turned my tune into a song. He did change my title, 'Human Nature', but Quincy wanted to keep it. Michael, Quincy and Bruce, my brother Jeff, Steve Lukather, David Paich and Michael Boddicker turned it into a record. Talk about a fluke."

When the time came for Michael to record his vocals, Porcaro was present to assist him. It is a session he will never forget. "I was standing next to him in the vocal booth, feeding him lines and guiding him," he recalls. "He pretty much did that in one take, apart from a couple of little things.

Michael barely knew the words or melody but he nailed it. And he improvised, the high ad-lib parts [improvised lines] he sang were all him, that wasn't written in beforehand."

'BEAT IT'

Although Quincy had just stumbled upon another wonderful melody, the rock song he so desired was still evading him. "The deadline for finishing the production was drawing ever closer, and it appeared that although Quincy had been asking him for months to try and write a rock song, Michael couldn't come up with anything," Matt Forger said. "Suddenly, he came in with a song called 'Beat It', and everything changed."

Michael actually held on to the song for a long time, even though Quincy was constantly challenging him to come up with something. He was shy about playing his songs for people right away, to avoid the potentially painful experience of rejection. When Quincy finally convinced Michael to let him hear what he had been keeping from him, the producer was amazed. "He went crazy," Michael recalled. Michael explained that the lyrics aren't about encouraging violence, but avoiding it by telling kids to step away before a fight breaks out.

After looking for suitable guitarists to play a solo piece on the song, Quincy decided to call Eddie Van Halen from the band Van Halen. "It was funny because when Quincy called Eddie, he thought it was a joke and hung up on Quincy," Matt Forger, who was present in Van Halen's studio session, recalls. "Quincy kept calling but Eddie kept hanging up. In the end, Quincy said, 'Look Eddie, this really is me!' He had to almost beg to be believed."

Michael and Quincy first presented Van Halen with a skeleton version of the song, so he could work on some ideas for the solo. "So then it was time for the main session," Forger said. "I said to Quincy, 'We should bring Eddie's engineer Donn Landee in for the session, so Eddie feels comfortable and can really be himself.' Quincy thought it was a great idea. So Friday came around, and it was time for Eddie to come in and do his bit. When they saw it was just me in the session Donn and Eddie looked around and said, 'So is Quincy not coming in?' I said, 'No, Quincy wants you guys to do the session like you usually would.' Donn said, 'I haven't worked on this console before'. But it was already set up and ready, and I was there if they needed anything."

Van Halen already had an idea in his head before arriving at the studio, so the session ran smoothly. "Eddie did four or five takes, and felt happy," Forger said. "So he says, 'Great, is Quincy coming in to pick the take?' To which I again said, 'No Quincy isn't coming in, he wants you to pick the take'. They seemed surprised at how in control they were of the session. In the end they chose part of one take and part of another, and the two were put together."

There have been many rumours over the years as to what the knocking sound is at the 2:45 mark, just as Van Halen is about to begin his solo. The most popular theory is that a technician knocked on the studio door and entered, unaware Van Halen was beginning a take, before quickly closing the door when realising his mistake. Forger put the record straight. "That was actually Eddie knocking on his guitar," he said.

Remarkably, Van Halen recorded the solo as a favour, free of charge, albeit without the approval of those around him. "I was a complete fool, according to the rest of the band, our manager and everyone else," he said. "I was not used. I knew what I was doing – I don't do something unless I want to do it." Van Halen described Michael in both musical and personal terms. "He was this musical genius with this childlike innocence," he said. "He was such a professional, and such a sweetheart."

Forger revealed that recording 'Beat It' was one of the biggest challenges the team faced in the entire *Thriller* production process. "Michael wanted a punchy sound to match the emotion of the track, so everyone was constantly being pushed to the limit," Forger said. "The studio equipment seemed to sense the struggle and fought back in its own way. At one time during a playback of the song the speakers actually caught on fire and smoke came pouring out of the wall. It's as if the studio was fighting back, but we prevailed and beat the song into form."

THE FINAL DAYS

The discovery of 'Human Nature' and 'Beat It' enabled Quincy and Rod Temperton to replace some of the songs they felt weren't strong enough for the album. Firstly, it was decided that 'Human Nature' would directly replace 'Carousel'. Quincy felt there was only space for one song with that kind of mood, and there was only one winner. The three 'poppy' songs, 'Hot Street', 'She's Trouble' and 'Got the Hots', were replaced with 'P.Y.T.', a song with a similar theme and tempo but clearly considered to be superior, as well as the rock song that was missing, 'Beat It', and Temperton's slower and less sugary 'Baby Be Mine' and 'The Lady in My Life'.

Michael said some of the material left on the shelf was 'just as strong or stronger' than what was eventually chosen for *Thriller*. Much to his disappointment, there was no space for 'Hot Street'. "I loved that one, Quincy and Rod didn't think it was good enough, I thought it was wonderful," he said. Another of his favourites was 'The Toy', written for the December 1982 movie of the same name at the behest of Quincy, but the song was 'canned' as Michael was too busy making *Thriller*.

Greg Phillinganes explained why the decision was made to omit some of these songs from the final tracklist, which is made up of 'Wanna Be Startin' Somethin'', 'Baby Be Mine', The Girl Is Mine', 'Thriller', 'Beat It', 'Billie Jean', 'Human Nature', 'P.Y.T. (Pretty Young Thing)' and 'The Lady in My Life'. "Quincy wanted a certain category of songs for that album," he said. "They were good songs, but there's a difference between good and great. And those that replaced them, especially 'Human Nature' and 'Beat It', were just great."

As a sign of Michael's increasing influence over the production of his albums he wrote four of these nine songs, up one from the three he wrote for *Off the Wall*. "I guess I had proved myself to him [Quincy] during our work on *Off the Wall*," Michael said. "He realised I had the confidence and experience I needed to make that record [*Thriller*] and at times he wasn't in the studio with us for that reason."

CBS put an enormous amount of pressure on the team to finish the album in time for a Thanksgiving 1982 release. They worked so hard in those final days in late October that they practically lived at the studio. "We went through a period where we were breaking our backs to get the album done by their deadline," Michael said. When the deadline crunch put the team in a tight position for time they used both Studios A and B at Westlake, keeping them booked full time until the album was completed. Bruce Swedien worked on mixes in Studio A while another engineer, Humberto Gatica, worked in Studio B. Work went right up until 9am on deadline day, with elements of 'Beat It' being the last thing recorded.

That morning, after working through the night, Michael went to Quincy's house for a short three-hour sleep. The team had to return to Westlake at noon for a listen of the final album mix. Bruce Swedien said when they first finished mixing the completed album they had too much playing time for two sides of a vinyl LP. He was quick to point out that this would affect the sound quality, but as nobody took much notice he delivered the tapes to Bernie Grundman's studio for mastering regardless.

Back at Westlake the head of black music at Epic Records, Larkin Arnold, was popping champagne, eagerly waiting to hear the final mix. Eventually Michael, his managers Freddy DeMann and Ron Weisner, Quincy, Swedien, Rod Temperton and the rest of the crew sat down to listen to the result. Just as Swedien had warned, it turned out to be a disaster, bringing tears to Michael's eyes.

"We listened, and the sound on the LP is dog doo-doo – it was horrible," Swedien recalls. "Quincy remembers we had 28 minutes on each side. I felt like shouting, 'I told you so'! The Epic dudes were popping corks, but out of the corner of my eye I saw Michael sneak out of the control room and go to the other studio across the hall. Quincy saw him too, and followed him. I was next…I remember that Michael was crying; he was heartbroken. Again, I felt like shouting, 'I told you so'."

Larkin Arnold wanted to get his hands on the album that afternoon, but Quincy broke it to him that they had to cut down the running time and mix the album all over again. "Already I did not have the master in time to meet the release schedule, so it was kind of nerve wracking," Arnold recalls. "I was already behind schedule."

Michael's managers suggested they take a two-day break and recuperate. After returning to the studio, they began to edit and mix one song a day over an eight day period (the album has nine tracks, but 'The Girl Is Mine' had already been released to the public at this stage). A lot of compromises had to be made as they attempted to cut down the playing time. Rod Temperton cut one verse from 'The Lady in My Life', and Michael agreed to trim the long intro to 'Billie Jean'. Eventually they cut it down to just over 21 minutes per side, losing a staggering 14 minutes.

On November 8, after eight long days, the album mix was finally completed. Three days later Swedien was back at Bernie Grundman Mastering, and Larkin Arnold was able to push the album through the system in time for a pre-December release date. Michael was relieved it was all over. "It felt so good when we were finished," he said. "I was so excited I couldn't wait for it to come out." What happened next was beyond everybody's wildest dreams.

CHAPTER 5:
THE *THRILLER* PHENOMENON

LATE 1982 – LATE 1984

In late October 1982 Michael's duet with Paul McCartney, 'The Girl Is Mine', became the first single to be released from *Thriller*, before the album was even fully completed. Michael said the label had no choice but to release it first and 'get it out of the way', otherwise it would have been overplayed due to the high profiles of both artists. When Bruce Swedien performed the final mix back in August, the rock group Fleetwood Mac visited the studio. "Michael hid with me in the control room, with a huge smile on his face," Swedien recalls. "Everyone was singing and dancing to the song. It looked like about 100 people had quietly slipped in while I was making safety copies of the master tapes."

Thriller was released on November 30, 1982, and became Michael's first album to hit number one in both the United States and the United Kingdom. Michael was set to have two albums near the top end of the charts at the same time, but MCA Records was forced to withdraw the *E.T.* storybook from sale for breaching the conditions of its agreement with CBS. Instead of waiting until after Christmas to release the album MCA released it in November, and promo copies of 'Someone in the Dark' were also issued to radio stations. MCA was forced to withdraw the album from sale after a $2 million lawsuit was filed by CBS, and the label was also prohibited from releasing any other material featuring Michael.

The *Thriller* album cover photo session was conducted by celebrity photographer Dick Zimmerman, who hired one of the best fashion stylists in Los

Angeles to gather a large variety of wardrobe. But Michael couldn't find anything he liked, apart from the white suit Zimmerman was wearing. "I was starting to get concerned because Michael didn't like anything that we brought in and time was running out," the photographer recalls. "Then he looked at the suit I was wearing. He liked that look but we didn't have anything similar, so I asked him if he would like to try on my suit. Luckily, it was the perfect fit."

Michael wore a variety of clothes throughout the six-hour photo shoot, including a leather jacket and a black shirt. "That leather jacket image was the alternative option," Zimmerman said. "Michael also held a light, because he liked magic, and we gave him a bunch of things to play around with." Zimmerman took around 300 photos in the session, including shots of Michael with a six-week old tiger cub named 'Little William'.

Once the photos were ready a few days later, Zimmerman met Michael at Westlake to pick out the final cover image. "Michael said, 'There are so many good ones here, how can I ever make a decision?' He told me to hold on a minute, and then ran back into the studio. After a moment, he came back out with Quincy Jones. Quincy took one look at the transparencies and with a confident smile, without any hesitation, pointed to one, and said, 'That's your cover, Michael'!" And so arguably the most iconic and recognised image in entertainment history was born.

MTV TROUBLES

The *Thriller* promotion campaign well and truly got underway in January 1983, when Michael filmed a video for the album's second single, 'Billie Jean'. CBS Records funded the $50,000 production costs, and the single went to the top of both the *Billboard* 100 and the United Kingdom singles chart.

'Billie Jean' was Michael's first real chance to experiment with what are commonly known as music videos, although he preferred to call them *short-films*. Before *Thriller*, Michael would view the videos on music channel MTV – launched in August 1981 – and be disappointed with their concept. "My brother Jackie came to my house and said, 'Are you watching this show that's on TV? All they do is play music. It's MTV'," Michael recalled. "I put it on and thought the concept was very interesting. What I didn't like were the videos that were a collage of images; I thought that if I were to do one, I would do something with a little entertainment value. My dream was to make something with a beginning, a middle and an ending, like a *short-film*." Michael wanted his videos to be a 'stimulant' for other artists to make better videos.

Although the 'Billie Jean' video became a huge hit on MTV, the channel initially refused to play it. According to CBS president Walter Yetnikoff, the station didn't want to show black artists. "Before *Thriller* – and Bob Pittman [MTV founder] disagrees with me, but Bob Pittman is full of shit – when MTV first started, it held itself out as a rock station," Yetnikoff said. "And, when 'Billie Jean' and 'Beat It' came out, MTV didn't want to play it. They said, in effect, 'No, no, no, we're a rock kind of sensibility, and this is Michael Jackson and he's black'."

CBS president Walter Yetnikoff and Paul McCartney

Michael was devastated. "They came right out and said it – they wouldn't play my music," he said. "It broke my heart." But the ignorance lit a fire in Michael, and with the help of Yetnikoff, he secured a victory. Yetnikoff threatened to pull the videos of all of his artists, including Bruce Springsteen, from the station if Pittman didn't relent. "I've never been more forceful or obnoxious," he said. "With added pressure from Quincy Jones, they caved in, and in doing so the MTV colour line came crashing down."

McCARTNEY AND ANKA

Throughout 1983, Michael took time away from the *Thriller* campaign to make music with many different superstars. In early February, he returned to London to complete work on two songs he had been recording on and off with Paul McCartney over the previous two years, 'Say Say Say' and 'The Man'.

Michael arrived in England with a complete demo of 'Say Say Say', which he had created with musicians Bill Wolfer, Nathan Watts, Ricky Lawson, David Williams, Jerry Hey and Gary Grant back in Los Angeles. "Michael told me he wanted to make a demo so good that Paul would want to use it as a final version," Wolfer said. "He came to my apartment and played me a tape of the song, which was just Paul on acoustic guitar and the pair of them singing. So a few days later we recorded a demo at Cherokee studio, which was so elaborate that Paul agreed to use it as the final record, once they had recorded their vocals and mixed it."

Producer George Martin, famous for his extensive involvement on each of the Beatles' original albums, joined the sessions at London's Abbey Road Studio and was impressed with Michael in the studio. "He actually does radiate an aura when he comes into the studio, there's no question about it," Martin said. "He's not a musician in the sense that Paul is, but he does know what he wants in music and he has very firm ideas."

Although the collaboration was a real learning curve for Michael, he considered himself McCartney's equal in the studio. "Paul never had to carry me in that studio," he said. "The collaboration was also a real step forward for me in terms of confidence, because there was no Quincy Jones watching over me to correct my mistakes. Paul and I shared the same idea of how a pop song should work and it was a real treat to work with him."

Michael wasn't quite so interested in completing a handful of songs he began recording in 1980 with Canadian singer/songwriter Paul Anka, who is most famous for writing Frank Sinatra's signature song 'My Way'. In early 1983, Michael nearly got himself into a spot of legal bother after 'stealing' the tapes of the work the pair did together over two years earlier. Their collaboration first came about when Anka was working on a duets album, *Walk a Fine Line*, which Michael expressed an interest to be part of. Michael visited Anka at his home studio in Carmel, 330 miles north of Los Angeles, and over a period of two weeks they recorded at least three songs, with Anka playing piano and Michael on vocals. Two songs that came from those sessions include 'I Never Heard', released posthumously as 'This Is It', and 'Love Never Felt So Good'.

Anka was impressed with the way Michael went about the writing process, but also sensed a 'ruthless' element in his character. "He knew how to make his way around a song, not only because he had an incredible vocal quality, but he also had a capacity to make complicated singing licks from an initial one-finger tune played for him on the piano," Anka said. "He didn't seem at all like a disturbed character when he was working. He was just very tenacious, very focused on what he needed to do. But you could tell he was also wildly ambitious and capable of anything; I sensed an absolutely ruthless streak."

When Anka was trying to complete *Walk a Fine Line* in early 1983 he had trouble contacting Michael, who was suddenly no longer interested in finishing their songs due to the impending success of *Thriller*. Instead, Anka alleges that Michael sent somebody to Sunset Sound in Los Angeles, where *Walk a Fine Line* was being recorded, to 'steal' the tapes of their collaboration. "I'm trying to finish my album, and suddenly I couldn't get him on the phone," Anka recalls. "Then he sent one of his people over to the studio and they actually stole the tapes we'd been working on. When I heard about this, I went, 'What? Michael went in and just took them? Holy shit'! Then Michael disappears, and only after weeks of threatening did I get the tapes back – finally." Anka, who offered 'Love Never Felt So

Good' to American singer Johnny Mathis instead, said Michael was later apologetic over the incident.

'BEAT IT' AND *MOTOWN 25*

Michael turned his attention back to the *Thriller* campaign in March 1983, when he filmed a video for the album's third single, 'Beat It'. Producer Antony Payne was on the hunt for the next big music video when he arrived at the offices of Michael's managers with director Bob Giraldi. "Steve Barron, who directed the 'Billie Jean' video, was destined to do the next one as well," Payne recalls. "But Michael was interested to hear our idea of doing a mini-movie, something which is four or five minutes long but tells a story rather than just being a performance." Together, they came up with a treatment based around Michael acting as a peacemaker between two rival gangs.

While discussing the concept, Michael brought up the idea of casting real gang members. "Not knowing what that entails, I said, 'Yeah let's go down and see if we can get them involved'," Payne said. "I had to go to Downtown Los Angeles to meet Caesar, this ruthless African-American businessman who was the head of either the Bloods or the Crips. When word got out that Michael Jackson was interested in doing a video with the gangs, it became clear Caesar was willing to do it." The next step was to work out how to stop the rival gangs from fighting. "We had police on set, but what really brought them together, which seldom happens, was the chance to be in a video with Michael Jackson, who was the biggest star around," Payne said.

Filming took place in several locations across Downtown Los Angeles' Skid Row district, an area notorious for its large population of homeless people. Police may have been present on set, but that didn't stop the production crew experiencing crime first hand. "While filming the café scene, our choreographer, Michael Peters, was standing outside the building just as we were setting up the camera," Payne recalls. "Suddenly, this red stuff started dripping onto his white jacket. We all stood back and looked up, and there was this guy a few storeys above shouting down, 'I've been stabbed, help, I'm bleeding!' But no one was diving up there to help him, one of the policemen just shouted up, telling him to get back inside. It was almost like they felt he was holding up the procedure."

Antony Payne, Michael and Quincy Jones on the set of 'Beat It'

The production cost $150,000, which Michael footed himself as the record company was giving him problems with the small budget. "In those days the big stars held the creative cards and mostly paid for their own videos," Payne explained.

Epic's Vice President of National Promotion, Frank DiLeo, convinced Michael to release 'Beat It' as a single while 'Billie Jean' was still at the top of the *Billboard* 100 chart. The record label was concerned that the move would see 'Billie Jean' disappear from the charts, but both songs occupied top five positions at the same time, a feat matched by very few artists. A week after 'Billie Jean' was knocked off the top position by English pop group Dexys Midnight Runners' 'Come On Eileen', 'Beat It' also went to number one. It peaked at three in the United Kingdom.

Two weeks after the 'Beat It' video was filmed, Michael performed with all of his brothers – including Jermaine, who had re-joined the group after recently leaving Motown – for the first time in eight years. The performance was taped for a television special, *Motown 25: Yesterday, Today, Forever*, to commemorate Motown Records' 25 years of existence.

After singing a medley with his brothers, Michael performed 'Billie Jean' in public for the first time. During the performance he debuted the 'moonwalk' dance and stage costume, which consisted of a black fedora hat, sequined black jacket and a single sequined white glove (he had worn a single glove before, but it went relatively unnoticed).

To begin his routine, Michael planned to pick up the fedora, snap it to his head and strike what later became an iconic pose. Assistant Nelson Hayes was tasked with ensuring the hat was placed on the stage in time. "While Mike was speaking on close-up camera setting up his solo part after the performance with his brothers, I placed the hat on a pre-arranged spot after stagehands had cleared The Jackson 5 set off-camera," Hayes recalls. "He didn't want any errors and needed to know that the hat would be on the floor spot to pick up, put on and proceed with that historical dancing."

The show aired on NBC in America in May, and was watched by 50 million people. Michael's performance became folklore, earning him an Emmy Award nomination, which recognises excellence in the television industry, as well as increased sales of *Thriller*.

PETER PAN

Music wasn't the only thing on Michael's mind at this time – he also had a burning ambition to star as Peter Pan in a filmed musical version of J.M. Barrie's novel. Director Steven Spielberg, who held the rights to make a Peter Pan film, was impressed with Michael's work on the *E.T.* storybook, and the two discussed making a version with Michael in the lead role as a singing and dancing Pan.

As early as 1979, even before he finished recording his first major solo album, Michael believed his future lay in the movie business. When asked what he wanted to achieve in the next ten years, Michael said, "There's so much, but I do want to choreograph certain films that I do. I also want to do some directing." That desire increased in 1980 when he spent a few weeks with his friend, actress Jane Fonda, on the set of her movie *On Golden Pond*.

Michael once explained that you can 'capture the moment' with film, whereas a live stage performance is gone forever once it's finished. "You capture it, it's shown all over the world and it's there forever," he said. "When I perform, I feel like I'm giving a whole lot but for nothing. I like to capture things and hold them and share them with the world."

Michael had always identified with Peter Pan – the boy who never grew up. Fonda believed Michael would have been perfect for the role. "I remember driving with him one day," she recalls, "and I said, 'God, Michael, I wish I could find a movie I could produce for you.' And suddenly I knew. I said, 'I know what you've got to do. It's Peter Pan.' Tears welled up in his eyes and he said, 'Why did you say that?' with this ferocity. I said, 'I realise *you're* Peter Pan.' And he started to cry and said, 'You know, all over the walls of my room are pictures of Peter Pan. I've read everything that [J.M.] Barrie wrote. I totally identify with Peter Pan, the lost boy of never-never land'."

After the *Motown 25* performance – before any movie deal had even been signed – Michael began recording songs for a Peter Pan soundtrack album with good friend Buz Kohan, a writer, producer and composer whom he had known since he was 12 years old. Kohan had previously worked with Michael and The Jacksons on their variety show, as well as other projects. They composed two songs together in the home studio at the remodelled Hayvenhurst estate, 'Make a Wish' and 'Neverland Landing'. Kohan said Spielberg would later play 'Make a Wish' for his son at night to help him sleep. "Michael made a full orchestral demo of 'Make a Wish' and sang it and then sent it to Steven," Kohan said. "We also wrote a song called 'Neverland Landing' which was done completely, and there is a demo with piano that I played at the house. I have it somewhere but can't put my hands on it immediately."

But Spielberg chose to put the Peter Pan idea on hold, first because he was busy filming *Indiana Jones and the Temple of Doom*, and then again when his son was born in 1985. By 1986, the director had allowed his rights to make the film lapse.

In 1989, after production studio TriStar Pictures had acquired the rights, Spielberg was hired to direct a film by the title of *Hook*, which acts as a sequel to Barrie's novel by focusing on a grown-up Peter Pan who has forgotten his childhood. But Spielberg cast Robin Williams in the lead role, which Michael said left him 'heartbroken'. "I worked on the script, writing songs, for six months," Michael later explained. "And they let me down. I was so heartbroken. Steven Spielberg admitted later it was a mistake. I was torn. He put me through a lot. We're friends now, though."

In his version of events, Spielberg says Michael wasn't enthusiastic about the vision of Peter Pan as an adult. "Michael had always wanted to play Peter Pan, but I called Michael and I said, 'This is about a lawyer that is brought back to save his kids and discovers that he was once, when he was younger, Peter Pan'. Michael understood at that point it wasn't the same Peter Pan he wanted to make." *Hook* was released in December 1991.

'SAY SAY SAY'...SANTA YNEZ

In October 1983, Michael and Paul McCartney travelled to the Santa Ynez Valley in Santa Barbara County, California, to film a video to promote the upcoming 'Say Say Say' single, which became Michael's sixth number one hit in America. The video was directed by Bob Giraldi and produced by Antony Payne, the pair who made the 'Beat It' video with Michael earlier in the year.

Michael fell in love with the Santa Ynez area, especially Sycamore Valley Ranch, which McCartney and his wife were supposed to lease for the duration of their stay. "Paul doesn't like staying in hotels, he likes his privacy," Payne said. "Before the shoot, Paul's manager Steve Shrimpton and I went up to Santa Ynez and started looking for houses for Paul to rent. Now this is not a place where you can really rent houses, all they have there are these big ranches."

Payne and Shrimpton met with William Bone, a real estate developer who owned the 2,700-acre Sycamore Valley Ranch. "We explained our predicament and asked if Paul could rent the ranch," Payne said. "As soon as we mentioned the name McCartney, Bill Bone's eyes just lit up, and right away he said it would be an honour to have Paul stay at this house. He explained that Paul could have the run of the place and that he would leave the property after the initial introductions. It was almost too good to be true under the circumstances."

Two weeks later, all the parties met at Bone's ranch ahead of the start of the video shoot. The McCartneys flew into Santa Barbara Airport by private jet, and Michael arrived from Los Angeles in his Rolls Royce with his mother Katherine and sister La Toya, who made a cameo appearance in the video. The Jacksons rented an entire floor at the Ramada Inn in nearby Solvang. "After the introductions, Bill Bone left the ranch, and we all walked around and saw quite a bit of this wonderful property," Payne said. "But a few hours later I received this strange call from Bill's butler, who told us Bill had changed his mind about Paul staying at his house and that he wanted everybody off the property by 4pm that afternoon. Paul and his wife were supposed to stay in the guest house, but they didn't stay a single night. We had no plan B, but luckily we found another place for Paul." Michael's visit to the ranch may have been cut short, but it would leave a lasting impression.

The video, which sees Michael and McCartney play a pair of conmen who get away with selling a 'miracle potion', was shot over two days with a huge $325,000 budget. During a lunch break on set, McCartney began explaining to Michael how he earned approximately $40 million a year from his various music publishing investments.

"Everybody was sat around that table; the McCartneys, the Jacksons and some of the crew," Payne recalls. "And Paul started talking about how music publishing is the big thing, how he got involved with it when he married his wife Linda and how he owned the Buddy Holly publishing rights and many others. Michael was listening very intently. Usually he was very childlike, but when it came to music and business he became a real adult, he suddenly had his business head on." Michael took the advice and began investing in music publishing, spending about $1 million on rights his attorney John Branca found for sale, which included the Sly Stone collection. McCartney would later regret the conversation.

***THAT* VIDEO**

Although still huge, by mid-1983 sales of *Thriller* began slowing, and after four long months at the summit of the charts, it was replaced at the top by the *Flashdance* movie soundtrack. *Thriller* soon regained top spot, before being knocked off again in July by The Police's *Synchronicity* album. Whenever the album dropped to number two, Michael would phone Walter Yetnikoff. "He'd berate me for failing to pump up the promotion," Yetnikoff said. "Michael's passion for world conquest was singular. He lived, breathed, slept, dreamt and spoke of nothing but number one successes. He was possessed."

Michael and label promotion chief Frank DiLeo began thinking of ways to push album sales back up. After 'Billie Jean' and 'Beat It', CBS had no further plans for any more music video releases. At this stage the title track, 'Thriller', wasn't even considered as a single. "Who wants a single about monsters?" Yetnikoff said. But DiLeo told Michael the single would do well if he made a video for it. "It's simple – all you've got to do is dance, sing, and make it scary," DiLeo remembers telling Michael. Michael agreed and felt 'Thriller' was a long track with plenty of material for a director to work with. He singled out John Landis for the role, as he loved Landis's 1981 horror movie *An American Werewolf in London*. Landis accepted the offer. "It was a great opportunity to bring back the theatrical short," he said.

Shooting began in October after Michael completed the 'Say Say Say' video, by which time the album was knocked off the top of the charts once more. The video was shot in three separate locations; at the Palace Theatre in Downtown Los Angeles (opening cinema scene); at the junction of Union Pacific Avenue and South Calzona Street in East Los Angeles (the zombie dance sequence) and 1345 Carroll Avenue near Downtown (final house scene). The red jacket that Michael wore in the video was designed by Landis's wife Deborah, whose aim was to make him appear more 'virile'.

CBS was unprepared to fund the production, as the executives felt it was unnecessary to plough more money into an album which was already selling so well. Like 'Beat It', Michael had no choice but to fund the video himself, gaining ownership rights to both as a result.

The fourteen-minute 'Thriller' video would end up costing $500,000, double the original budget. According to Landis, the often cited sums of $1 million are exaggerated. Thanks to a few shrewd business ideas from John Branca, Michael would be reimbursed. The attorney suggested they film a 45-minute documentary about the making of the video to run alongside the video itself. MTV paid $250,000 for the exclusive rights to premiere the hour-long package, titled *Making Michael Jackson's Thriller*, and Showtime paid $300,000 for the cable television rights. Just like that, the production costs were covered. More money was then made when Vestron Video offered to distribute *Making Michael Jackson's Thriller* at a retail price of $29.95; in this era, home videos were only usually sold to rental stores rather than directly to consumers.

In November 'Thriller' – the seventh and final single from the album – was released in many countries, including the United Kingdom, although it wasn't released in the United States until two months later. *Making Michael Jackson's Thriller* was first shown on MTV on December 2, becoming the station's first world music video premiere. Two weeks later it was released on VHS, and within months it sold a million copies, making it the biggest-selling home video of all time.

The plan for the 'Thriller' single, video and documentary to boost album sales was working – at one point *Thriller* was selling at a rate of one million copies a week. Even Michael was stunned by the response, and only three weeks after the video's MTV premiere, *Thriller* was back at the top of the *Billboard* 200. 'Thriller' remains the only music video to have been inducted into the National Film Registry by the Library of Congress, and *Making Michael Jackson's Thriller* earned a Grammy Award in 1985 for Best Music Video (long form).

By the end of 1983, over a year after the release of *Thriller*, the album had sold over 22 million copies. It was only three million short of the biggest-selling album of all time, the 1977 movie soundtrack to *Saturday Night Fever*. Michael felt he was the only person who had envisaged how well the album would do; neither Quincy Jones nor the CBS chiefs had seen this coming.

THE PEPSI BURN

Michael was in dreamland, but an incident on January 27, 1984 would have an impact on him for the rest of his life. While shooting a Pepsi commercial with his brothers at Los Angeles' Shrine Auditorium, Michael's scalp was severely burned when his hair caught fire after a pyrotechnic device malfunctioned. The Jacksons had signed their record-breaking $5 million sponsorship deal with Pepsi for an upcoming tour only a few months earlier.

Michael suffered second and third degree burns to the back of his scalp, causing a palm-sized bald patch where his hair was singed. For the pain he was prescribed a narcotic pain reliever by the name of Percocet, an opioid which is similar to morphine. To save his hair he underwent reconstructive scalp surgery three months later at Brotman Medical Center by his plastic surgeon, Dr Steven Hoefflin. But he still had to wear a small hairpiece to cover the scar.

Debbie Rowe, the assistant to Michael's dermatologist, Arnold Klein, says he also developed thick, painful scars following the burn. Michael met Klein in 1983, when he was diagnosed with lupus, an autoimmune disease that caused red rashes on his cheeks. He would be diagnosed with vitiligo, the condition that causes depigmentation of parts of the skin, three years later. "Michael had a huge amount of scarring on the top of his head, on the crown," Rowe recalls. "Because he's black, he developed keloids. Keloids are extremely painful, thickening scars. We were injecting them which is extremely painful to have done." The incident would hamper Michael for the rest of his life, eventually triggering a prescription drug dependency when he had further scar revision surgery in 1993.

Pepsi made a $1.5 million compensation payment to Michael, who donated it to the burns unit at Brotman Medical Center. The unit was renamed in his honour after the incident, but closed in 1987 due to financial losses.

Michael recovered sufficiently to attend the 26th Annual Grammy Awards, also at the Shrine Auditorium, in late February 1984. This time he didn't feel ignored by his peers, winning a record eight awards in a single night (seven for *Thriller* and one for the *E.T.* storybook). The record was only equalled 16 years later by Latin rock band Santana.

In March, Michael finally hired a permanent manager to replace Ron Weisner and Freddy DeMann, whose contracts had expired 12 months earlier and weren't renewed. He summoned Epic promotion chief Frank DiLeo to the Beverly Hills Hotel, and offered him the job. DiLeo may never have managed a pop artist before, but Michael believed he was largely responsible for the astronomical commercial success of *Thriller* and turning his dreams into reality. Michael felt that together, the pair could make the next album even more successful.

VICTORY

In June 1984 The Jacksons released *Victory*, the group's first studio album in four years. Recorded sporadically over the previous 12 months, the album was structured as a collection of solos by the brothers.

One of Michael's two solo efforts was 'State of Shock', which he originally began recording the previous summer with Freddie Mercury of British rock band Queen. Mercury was invited to work with Michael at Hayvenhurst, and over a six-hour session they came up with three songs, which also included 'There Must Be More to Life Than This'. Michael later called Mercury to schedule a studio session so they could complete 'State of Shock' for *Victory*, but arranging a second session proved difficult for both artists. "They were great songs, but the problem was time – as we were both very busy at that period," Mercury said. "We never seemed to be in the same country long enough to actually finish anything completely."

Mick Jagger – also a client of John Branca and recommended by the attorney – sang 'State of Shock' with Michael instead. "It was a shame, but ultimately a song is a song," Mercury said. "As long as the friendship is there, that's what matters." Michael's other solo, the haunting 'Be Not Always', was written with Marlon, and he also sang a duet with Jermaine, 'Torture'. Jermaine had re-joined the group after leaving Motown in 1983, and *Victory* was the first Jacksons record to feature him since 1975.

In July the brothers hit the road, performing in Canada and the United States as part of the Victory Tour. Originally Michael fought against the idea, as he had planned to spend most of 1984 working on movie ideas. His advisors also believed he would be taking a backwards step by participating. Eventually he agreed to take part for his brothers, who were in need of the cash. But Jermaine denied the brothers were 'coat-tailing' Michael for their own financial gains. "We never viewed Michael as a robotic money making machine," he said. "We viewed him as a brother with whom we wanted to share more glory." Ultimately, Michael agreed to the tour because he was a 'stage addict', Jermaine said.

The tour was beset with problems from the off. The ticketing system was particularly controversial; a $30 ticket price, almost double the amount that stars like Bruce Springsteen and the Rolling Stones charged at the time, was compounded by the requirement to buy four. Michael was against the system, but his brothers outvoted him five to one. When the plan was made public, fans all over the United States were outraged. Michael successfully demanded that the system be changed, and to counteract the perception that he was being greedy, he donated all of his performance money – an estimated $7.5 million – to charity.

There were also issues with the tour promoters, including the notorious boxing kingpin Don King, and Michael was deeply disappointed with some of the show's staging. To make matters worse Jackie missed the first half of the tour, having broken his leg two weeks before the first concert when his wife ran him over after catching him with another woman.

But there were some positives. The tour grossed approximately $75 million, setting a new record for the highest-grossing of all time, at least until it was beaten by Bruce Springsteen a year later. It was also Michael's first opportunity to perform for his fans after the release of *Thriller* nearly two years earlier. He sang four songs from the album and four from *Off the Wall*, making up more than half of the entire set list.

The tour finally came to a close in December 1984 with a concert at the Dodger Stadium in Los Angeles, marking the end of the *Thriller* period. Michael's brothers were hoping to take the tour to Europe, but at the end of the final show Michael told the crowd they had just witnessed The Jacksons' final ever tour, much to everybody's surprise, including the rest of the group.

By the end of 1984 *Thriller* had sold more than 35 million copies, taking the record for biggest-selling album of all time in the process. It is estimated that the 'Thriller' single, video and documentary resulted in 14 million extra album sales within a six-month period. Today, *Thriller* is still the biggest-selling album of all time. Although estimated sales stand as high as 110 million, these figures are unreliable. Taking only total certified copies sold into account, *Thriller* is still positioned at number one. It's a record that is unlikely to ever be broken. According to a former advisor of Michael's, his total pre-expense share of the entire *Thriller* project, including the album, singles and videos, surpassed $125 million. For many, this monumental success changed him forever.

CHAPTER 6:
THERE COMES A TIME

JANUARY 1985

Although weary after spending four months on the road with his brothers, Michael wouldn't have much time to relax. Almost immediately after the Victory Tour, he was asked to put his energy into writing a major charity single, which became 'We Are the World'.

The 'We Are the World' project began as an idea singer and social activist Harry Belafonte had for a charity song similar to the 'Do They Know It's Christmas' Band Aid single, which was released in the United Kingdom in 1984. Belafonte felt something should be done about the 1983–1985 famine in Ethiopia and the on-going civil war there.

Belafonte contacted entertainment manager Ken Kragen, who had a history of successful fund-raising, to discuss putting together a star studded concert to raise funds for Africa. But Kragen didn't think a concert would raise enough money, and suggested that a group of artists record a song instead, much like 'Do They Know It's Christmas'. Kragen got his clients Kenny Rogers and Lionel Richie on board for the project, and asked Quincy Jones to produce the record. Quincy agreed, and the next task was to figure out who would write it.

The combination of Richie and Stevie Wonder was mentioned, but Wonder was busy recording an album, so Quincy gave Michael a call. "I was in my bedroom in Encino, and he [Quincy] said 'Smelly, we need a song for the children of the world, there are a lot of children dying and I want you and Lionel Richie to go in and write a song'," Michael recalled. "I said, 'Quincy…I just finished *Thriller*! I just spent all that time in the studio and I don't feel like it'. And he said, 'but it would be very important for the children'. And as soon as he said that, he knew how I feel about children and how important that is to me, so I said, 'I'll do it'."

Michael invited Richie to Hayvenhurst, where they began trying to write the song in Michael's bedroom. For four days, not a note was written. "We got together and goofed off, doing nothing, just making fun of each other and being silly, because we go way back since I was eight years old or something," Michael said. "We had a lot of catching up to do, so we talked and laughed and threw things at each other and joked around, we didn't get anything done."

While in Michael's bedroom, Richie had an encounter with Michael's pet snake, Muscles. "There's a bunch of albums around the wall, and there's a carpet and a little bench," Richie recalls. "I hear over my shoulder, hhhh-hhhhhhhh. It was a big-ass, ugly-ass snake. I'm from Alabama – what you do with a snake is you call the police and you shoot the damn thing. I was screaming. And Michael's saying, 'There he is, Lionel, we found him. He was hiding behind the albums. We knew he was in the room, we just didn't know where he was.' I said, 'You're out of your freaking mind.' It took me about two hours to calm my ass back down."

When the pair spent some time apart, Richie created what became the chorus melody, 'we are the world, we are the children…' Michael took Richie's tape and went into the studio to write the rest of the song, including the melody for the verse sections, 'there comes a time, when we heed a certain call', etc. "I strongly remember getting on my knees and praying to God, thanking him for the melody that came into my head, 'cos I was pleased with it when I woke up that morning," Michael recalled. He compiled a rough demo, before presenting it to Richie and Quincy. "They were in shock," Michael said. "They didn't expect to see something this quick. They loved it." Michael and Richie then completed the lyrics.

While the song was being written, Kragen lined up an all-star super group to sing it. Many members of the music industry signed on to help, including Stevie Wonder, Bob Dylan, Bruce Springsteen, Tina Turner, Billy Joel and Diana Ross. At one stage, so many artists volunteered that Kragen had to turn down 50 offers. Barbra Streisand initially agreed to take part, but was talked out of it by her advisors.

On January 22, 1985, Michael, Richie and Quincy entered Kenny Rogers' Lion Share Studio on Beverly Boulevard in Los Angeles to record a reference demo with guide vocals. At around 1.30am, Quincy called it a night. "If we get it too good, someone's gonna start playing it on the radio," he told the others. "Let's not put anything more on this tape." The demo was put on 50 separate tapes and sent out to all the stars involved, so they could learn the song. Quincy enclosed an accompanying letter, which read:

> The cassettes are numbered, and I can't express how important it is not to let this material out of your hands. Please do not make copies, and return this cassette the night of the 28th. In the years to come, when your children ask, 'What did mommy and daddy do for the war against world famine?' you can proudly say this was your contribution.

On January 25, organiser Ken Kragen held a production meeting at a bungalow off Sunset Boulevard, where 20 associates gathered to discuss various matters such as transportation, security and traffic control. Over at Lion Share, arranger Tom Bahler began working on the vocal arrangements, deciding who would sing what. One particularly interesting pairing was Michael and Prince. "I said to Quincy, 'This is like arranging in heaven'," Bahler recalls. Initially, Michael wanted to sing all of the lead vocals with Richie, while the other stars performed background vocals. Quincy had to talk Michael out of the idea, knowing full well they wouldn't accept bit-part roles.

The following night, the main recording session was planned 'like the Invasion of Normandy' at Richie's house. Quincy then went to A&M Recording Studio in Hollywood, where the session was scheduled to take place, and put tape on the floor with each artist's name on it to indicate their position. To help keep such a huge collection of stars in check, he also put a sign on the studio door which read, 'Check your egos at the door'.

The main session was held on Monday, January 28. The 'We Are the

World' music track had already been recorded, so it was just a case of recording the vocals. Michael arrived at the studio at 9pm to record some of his vocals alone. Over the next hour, the other 44 artists began to arrive. Many came directly from the 12th Annual American Music Awards, which were held that night at the Shrine Auditorium in Downtown Los Angeles.

While most of them arrived in limos, Bruce Springsteen parked at a nearby grocery store in a pickup truck and walked to the studio without a bodyguard. The original number of artists was 46, but Prince did not attend, ruining the tantalising prospect of a vocal match-up with Michael. According to Ken Kragen, Prince was too shy to perform in front of his peers. "He knew it was a mistake," Kragen said. "It was unfortunate that he didn't show." Prince's line was given to Huey Lewis.

The session got underway at 10.30pm. The group chorus, featuring all 45 artists, was recorded first so the soloists wouldn't disappear after singing their part. After more than four hours of recording, the group posed for the album cover photo. But Michael was nowhere to be found. "I went looking for him all through the studio until I found him in the bathroom curled up on the counter," Ken Kragen recalls. "He was so intimidated. He had never recorded with all these superstars. I said to him, 'Michael, you've gotta come out. You wrote the record'."

By the time the solo recordings started, it was 4am. With limited time on their side, the solos were recorded in the open with the artists standing side by side waiting their turn, rather than individually in a vocal booth. The session eventually wound down at 8am, and the song was mixed the next day by engineer Humberto Gatica at Lion Share.

The single was released on March 7, 1985, going to number one in both the United States and the United Kingdom. It was also included on a *We Are the World* album, to which Michael contributed no further. Global sales of the single are said to be at 20 million, and it is estimated that since its release, $63 million has been raised for humanitarian causes.

Creating the song was one of Michael's proudest musical achievements. "It has reached a lot of people; it has touched a lot of people," he explained.

"It was like a prayer when all of the radio stations played it, I had tears." A year later, Michael and co-writer Lionel Richie scooped a Grammy Award for 'Song of the Year'. It was a sweet victory for Michael, marking both the first and last time he won the coveted award.

Yet Michael still couldn't rest on his laurels; he now had the mammoth task of recording a worthy follow up to the biggest-selling album of all time. Over the next two-and-a-half years, the challenge became an obsession.

CHAPTER 7: FOLLOWING *THRILLER*

EARLY 1985 – MID 1987

Michael began working on song ideas and demos for the follow up to *Thriller* in 1983, at a time when he was also recording The Jacksons' *Victory* album. Michael was recording with his brothers at Can-Am Studio in the San Fernando Valley when he met engineer Brian Malouf. "The Jacksons came in every day for a few weeks, and one day Michael tapped my shoulder and asked if I would engineer for him while he worked on his own songs," Malouf recalls. "Of course I said yes, so we did quite a bit of work at Can-Am and also at Hayvenhurst. Sometimes he didn't like being at home, so we worked at other studios, wherever was convenient. We also worked at Westlake and Sunset Sound."

Malouf said Michael often brought his pet chimp, Bubbles, with him to the studio. The engineer admits he was shocked to see how Michael would keep the animal under control. "Michael was required to spend a certain amount of hours a day with the chimp, or he would never be his pet, so Bubbles would come to the studio at least twice a week," Malouf said. "Michael was such a gentle person, so it was shocking to see him physically reprimanding this chimp in the form of the hardest smack right on the top of its mouth. It was right in the face, but from the chimp's reaction it didn't seem like it hurt. Michael said he was given instructions from the chimp's trainer to do that to discipline it."

Whenever Michael worked in the studio, there was usually a musician present. During these sessions it was mostly John Barnes – who was also working on *Victory* – or guitarist David Williams. Malouf said Michael had an incredibly close relationship with the musicians. "Michael would sit right in front of David Williams and place his own fingers on the guitar strings, muting the notes he didn't want while David played an entire song," Malouf said. "This wasn't a common thing to do, but that's how involved Michael was in his work."

One of the earliest completed demos was called 'Scared of the Moon', which Michael worked on in early 1984 with his friend, Buz Kohan. During this period the pair would often have lengthy phone conversations, carrying on late into the night. "All kinds of things would come up in our conversations," Kohan recalls. "Michael was going with Brooke Shields at the time, and one night he called me and told me about Brooke's sister; he said she was scared of the moon. And I said to him, 'Michael, that's where the word lunatic comes from, a lunatic is someone who is scared of the moon'." Inspired by the conversation, Michael wrote a song about a girl being scared of the moon. He created the music with partial lyrics, before calling on Kohan to help him complete the song.

In early 1985, after spending more than six months out of the studio due to the Victory Tour and 'We Are the World', Michael continued working on his demos. His home studio at Hayvenhurst was in the process of being refurbished, so he experimented at other studios across Los Angeles. The album was scheduled for release in early 1986.

Michael became distracted again when the Disney Corporation asked him to come up with an idea for a new ride for the four Disneyland parks. Ultimately it was decided he would star in a 3D short-film produced by *Star Wars* guru George Lucas, which would show in specially designed theatres at the parks.

Disney came up with three concepts in February 1985, and pitched them to Michael and Lucas. They agreed to go with the one called *Space Knights*, in which Michael plays a space captain who goes on a mission to unlock the beauty within a planet's wicked Supreme Leader, through song and dance. The title was changed to *Captain EO* after *The Godfather* screenwriter Francis Ford Coppola was brought in to direct.

The project was perfect for Michael, who had intended to spend most of 1984 working on films rather than touring with his brothers. He began working on song and sound ideas for *Captain EO*, which would earn him around $3 million, with engineer Matt Forger and musician John Barnes. After *Thriller*, Michael and Forger struck up a great friendship. "I worked with Michael on several projects that he was developing, including the *Victory* album with The Jacksons, the Victory Tour and the song 'Centipede' for his sister Rebbie [a song which Michael wrote; released in November 1984]," Forger said. "I then transitioned into *Captain EO* in early 1985, working on ideas with Michael at Westlake studio."

Their musical ideas would develop into two songs; 'We Are Here to Change the World', written by Michael and John Barnes, and 'Another Part of Me', a song about global unity and love written by Michael alone.

Captain EO went into production at Laird Studios (now the Culver Studios) in June 1985, and principal photography was completed in August. But the special effects and editing would take nearly a year to complete.

That August, Michael also made a major business investment. Eleven months earlier, he had been informed by John Branca that a major music publishing catalogue, ATV Music Publishing, was up for sale. The catalogue contained the rights to nearly 4,000 songs, including over 250 of the Beatles' compositions. Lennon and McCartney had sold their copyrights to a publisher in 1963, a decision they later regretted. As songwriters they still collected 50% of royalties on their music – or 25% each – but the other half went to the publisher. McCartney had tried to buy ATV in 1981, and urged Lennon's widow, Yoko Ono, to join him in a bid. When Ono declined, McCartney refused to pay the $40 million asking price.

By late 1984, fresh from receiving over $100 million from the *Thriller* project, Michael had some serious money to invest. After learning that the ATV catalogue was available, he was desperate to acquire it. Following months of complex negotiations, John Branca closed the purchase for Michael, who paid catalogue owner Robert Holmes à Court, an Australian billionaire businessman, $47.5 million. Over the years, the huge, ever-increasing value of the catalogue would prove invaluable to Michael.

Of course, it was somewhat ironic that Michael's interest in music publishing was initiated by McCartney himself, when the pair worked together in 1983. After learning that Michael had acquired the songs, which he called his 'babies', McCartney felt betrayed by his one-time friend and collaborator. McCartney was especially hurt that Michael had not contacted him to forewarn him of his plan. "I think it's dodgy to do things like that," McCartney said. "To be someone's friend and then buy the rug they're standing on." He later acknowledged that Michael informed him of his bid, and that the purchase was carried out totally overboard, but their relationship never recovered.

In the following years, McCartney tried several times to contact Michael about the possibility of buying the catalogue from him, only to be 'stonewalled'. "He will not deal," McCartney said. "It was on my advice that he bought it, the fact that he stepped into publishing at all, and I've got only myself to blame really."

Michael's interest in music publishing and royalties only served to increase his desire to write more of his own material for his next album. "Michael saw how much money Rod Temperton made writing hits like 'Rock With You' and 'Thriller'," musician Gary Grant said.

THE B-TEAM

Once work on the Hayvenhurst studio refurbishment was complete in mid-1985, Michael, Matt Forger and John Barnes began working on demos and ideas in earnest for the album. Forger acted mostly as a recording engineer and sound designer, and Barnes worked as a musician and programmer, aiding Michael with developing his ideas.

Producer and programmer Christopher Currell was in charge of the studio's huge Synclavier, a state-of-the-art digital synthesiser, sampler and workstation which could imitate most instruments and would change the way Michael's music was recorded. Currell was initially invited to Hayvenhurst to teach Michael how to use the Synclavier, but he soon found himself working 15-hour days to create unique and unusual sounds for Michael's sound library. "When I was finished, I would run them off on a cassette tape and slide it under his bedroom door every night before I would go home," Currell recalls. "Many times, he would call my house at 2am and be all excited about some sounds or groove. I could hear the tape I had made blasting in the background!"

The pair soon developed a strong musical rapport. "It quickly got to the point where Michael would say to me, 'Make me a sound that makes me do this', and he would do a dance move," Currell said. "I got it right away, and I could make the sound that he was feeling."

In October 1985, engineer/musician Bill Bottrell was hired to work alongside Forger, Barnes and Currell at Hayvenhurst. Bottrell, like Barnes, had also previously worked with The Jacksons, engineering *Victory*, and recalls how he first met Michael. "I was doing remixes that [music executive] John McClain would bring me. It was early in his career and he became quite the cheerleader for me. He went to school with the Jacksons and convinced them, one at a time, that I was the best. I started with Jermaine's solo album [*Dynamite*] and moved into the *Victory* album, when I met Michael, who brought me the tapes of 'State of Shock' to mix." Soon Bottrell found himself working on the follow up to the biggest-selling album of all time.

The four-man crew of Forger, Bottrell, Barnes and Currell became known as the 'B-Team', a second-tier unit working with Michael without the influence of the 'A-Team', people such as Quincy Jones, Bruce Swedien and Rod Temperton. Although Michael began the project without Quincy, the plan was to team up with him at Westlake at a later stage for the main production. A couple of musicians believe Michael wanted to record and produce the entire album without Quincy, a claim which Matt Forger refutes. "Quincy signed a contract to produce a third album with Michael [executed in December 1985]," Forger said. "There was never any mention of doing it without Quincy."

Michael was simply at the stage of his creative life where he was ready to write most of the tracks for his next album himself, and experimenting and recording away from Westlake and Quincy would enable him to have more of a say in the overall production. "Michael was beginning to develop a real creative growth and gaining skills, not only in writing, but also in the production area and just taking more control over his music," Forger explained. "It was something Quincy actually encouraged, he felt

Michael should make his next album more his own." Bottrell described it like 'a teenager leaving the nest'. "Michael was growing and wanted to experiment free of the restrictions of the Westlake scene," he said. "This is how he started to express his creative independence."

Matt Forger and Michael in the studio at Hayvenhurst

Nobody needed to motivate Michael. He felt that, together with the promotion expertise of his manager Frank DiLeo, he could make the album even more successful than *Thriller*, which by now had sold around 40 million copies. Epic's then West Coast Publicity director Glen Brunman said Michael didn't see *Thriller* as a phenomenon, but a 'stepping-stone' to even greater things. Michael wanted the follow up to sell 100 million copies, and even wrote the figure on his bathroom mirror so he could constantly remind himself of what he felt he needed to achieve. Michael wasn't fazed; "I always do my best work under pressure," he said.

Over the course of the second half of 1985 and most of 1986, Michael and the B-Team created many demos that would later be brought to Quincy's attention at the main Westlake sessions. Michael came back from the Victory Tour with many new song ideas, several of which were socially conscious and touched on issues he wanted to address through his music. Matt Forger said his role during those sessions at Hayvenhurst was to draw or pull those ideas out of Michael's head. The songs would develop and grow over time; Forger said they were started and then worked on intermittently throughout the entire project, with no specific pattern.

Bill Bottrell said Michael was 'sonically designing' his songs for the album. "He was happy, loose and free," Bottrell said. "He could walk out of his bedroom door and into the studio day or night. He could call me up to do something with two hours' notice, and the same went for John Barnes." The studio at Hayvenhurst became known as 'The Laboratory'. "I recall the monitors were terrible," Bottrell said. "I kept trying to install something I could listen to, but the room was very small, and it wasn't to be."

Two of the earliest demos were called 'Dirty Diana' and 'Al Capone', and John Barnes worked heavily with Michael on the arrangements of both. Michael began writing the autobiographical 'Dirty Diana' over a year earlier. It tells the life story of a groupie, which refers to a particular kind of female fan assumed to be more interested in relationships with rock stars than their music. Michael was exposed to groupies throughout his years of touring and performing. "I've lived with that all my life," he said. "These girls, they do everything with the band, everything you could imagine."

Michael's mother, Katherine, admitted she found it difficult to watch as girls threw themselves at her son during concerts in the Jackson 5 days. "Sometimes the girls would get onstage and I'd have to watch them tearing at Michael," she recalls. "He was so small, and they were so big." One incident was so bizarre that it landed a young woman in a mental institution.

'Al Capone' would eventually evolve into a song called 'Smooth Criminal'; it was an example of where a part of a song inspired another version. "There have been many cases where Michael has done that, where he would dwell on a song and refine concepts, or lyrics or melodies," Matt Forger said. "The bassline in 'Al Capone' – you can see how it evolved into 'Smooth Criminal'. And the whole gangster theme carried over – though as it evolved it became less about a particular historical figure and more about a situation and a story."

Michael's brother Jermaine said the new version, 'Smooth Criminal', was inspired by the mid-eighties California serial killer Richard Ramirez, who was dubbed 'The Night Stalker'. Jermaine said there were two reasons why this inspiration was not revealed at the time. "First, so that the media didn't accuse him of glorifying such a heinous crime," Jermaine said, "and second, he didn't want the elders [Jehovah's Witnesses] to know that a worshipper of the occult partly inspired this song."

For Michael, the ideas would keep on coming. "He would never stop creating and he had an endless supply of song ideas," Forger said. Michael wrote several ballads, including 'Fly Away', 'Loving You', 'I'm So Blue' and 'Free'. Other demos include 'Tomboy', 'What You Do To Me', 'Cheater', 'Make or Break', 'Don't Be Messin' Round', 'Buffalo Bill' and 'Price of Fame'. 'Do You Know Where Your Children Are', which is about a runaway girl who was abused by her father and ends up as a prostitute in Hollywood, touches on some of the social issues Michael wanted to address. The potentially controversial 'Abortion Papers' is another.

Although these songs were never fully completed and wouldn't be brought to the A-Team at Westlake, they were a prime example of Michael's experimentation during this period. "The thing I love about these demos is the rawness," Forger said. "Michael had the freedom to just get the expression out there without thinking, 'Oh, Quincy is going to be judging the vocal, or it has to be perfect'. It's just Michael going for it, experimenting, having fun."

As well as 'Dirty Diana' and 'Smooth Criminal', the other songs that would eventually make it to Westlake include 'Hot Fever', 'Speed Demon', 'Liberian Girl', 'I Just Can't Stop Loving You', 'Leave Me Alone', 'Streetwalker' and 'Bad'.

'Hot Fever', later titled 'The Way You Make Me Feel', was inspired by Michael's mother, Katherine; she wanted him to write a song with a 'shuffling kind of rhythm'. When Michael recorded his vocals during the main sessions later down the line, he sang while dancing around the customary darkened studio, clicking his fingers and stomping his feet on the ground. "He'd sing his line, then he'd disappear into the darkness," Bruce Swedien recalls. But instead of editing those sounds out of the final version, Swedien kept them as he felt they enhanced the overall sonic value.

'Speed Demon' was reportedly written by Michael after he once received a speeding ticket. Matt Forger confirmed the story is true. "It happens," he said, smiling.

'Liberian Girl', originally titled 'Pyramid Girl', was also written more than a year earlier and was among those considered for The Jacksons' *Victory* album. "I wrote that in my house in the game room, I guess I was playing some pinball or something, and the song just popped in my head," Michael explained. "I think I ran upstairs, put it on tape and it became 'Liberian Girl'." Quincy Jones described the ballad as an 'amazing fantasy'.

Another ballad, 'I Just Can't Stop Loving You', was written by Michael during the middle of the night, according to John Barnes. "That's one of those you get the phone call to wake up and we need to record right now, and we were done probably in an hour and a half," the musician said. Michael revealed he had no one particular in mind when writing the song.

'Leave Me Alone' is ultimately about a relationship between a man and a woman, but it is also a response to negative stories about Michael that frequently appeared in the media from 1985 onwards. "What I'm really saying to people who are bothering me is: '*Leave me alone*'," Michael explained. The most infamous stories claimed Michael wanted to buy the bones of the Elephant Man, John Merrick, which he dismissed as a 'stupid story', and that he slept in a hyperbaric oxygen chamber so he could live to the age of 150. Out of curiosity, Michael had tested the chamber – which helps to heal burn victims – while visiting a hospital, but a picture leaked and ended up in the tabloid *National Enquirer*. The perception that Michael's only constant companion was his pet chimp Bubbles, as well as his ever-increasing use of plastic surgery, led to the British tabloid *The Sun* coining the term 'Wacko Jacko', one which he hated.

THE A-TEAM

Although Michael and Quincy hadn't yet entered the studio together, they stepped up their preparations in the spring of 1986. Michael was still writing songs, while Quincy geared up for the record by scouting rappers, hiring musicians and mapping out ideas. They were trying to figure out how to create a new, tougher image for the album, in order to keep changing. At the time, Michael admitted he hated his 'goody-goody' image.

Quincy wanted Michael to do a duet with his great rival Prince, so he set him the task of writing a song the pair could sing. Michael began writing and came up with a song called 'Bad', which would also fit perfectly with the new tough image. According to Michael, the song indicates that, "You're cool, you're alright, you're tough, but not criminally bad." He wrote the lyrics so the collaboration would appear like a confrontational standoff between the two. Quincy, delighted with the 'attitude' and 'feeling' of the song, subsequently set up a meeting between Michael and Prince, which took place in the study at Hayvenhurst.

The meeting proved to be unsuccessful; Prince didn't like the song when he heard it on tape, and felt it would be a hit without him regardless. In a later interview, he explained part of his decision. "The line of that song is, 'Your butt is mine'," Prince said. "Now, I was saying, 'Who is gonna sing that to who? Cos you sure ain't singing that to me, and I sure ain't singing it to you – so right there, you know, right there we got a problem'." After Prince passed on the opportunity, it was decided Michael would simply go it alone.

In August 1986, after more than two years of on-off work, Michael was ready to join forces with the A-Team again, as he felt he had enough material to present to Quincy. It was essentially the A-Team taking over from the B-Team, although Michael would continue to work at his home studio. Work had been scheduled to begin a few months earlier, but Quincy spent the month of June on an island in Tahiti recovering from a nervous breakdown, caused by exhaustion and overwork and the stress of a failing marriage to Peggy Lipton.

The A-Team was joined by newcomers Brad Sundberg, a Westlake staff engineer who became Swedien's understudy, and fellow engineers Craig Johnson and Russ Ragsdale. The sessions took place at Westlake's new Studio D on Santa Monica Boulevard in Hollywood, an unremarkable two-storey red brick building which blends in perfectly with the surrounding bland architecture. No signs announce its location, but if one were to have wandered down the tight alley behind the studio that August, they will have seen a horde of Mercedes, Rolls-Royces, Ferraris and stretch limousines belonging to Michael Jackson and company. The studio was built especially for the production of the album and was in full lockout, meaning no one except Michael and his team was allowed to record there.

At this stage, the album also still had a very unusual working title. "When we started at Westlake, the album did not have a definite title, so Quincy called the album 'Pee', like urine," Bruce Swedien explained. "'Pee' was a Quincy name… we still call it that now!"

Michael and Quincy picked out the demos they would re-produce and enhance for inclusion on the album, and chose 'Bad', 'The Way You Make Me Feel', 'Speed Demon', 'Liberian Girl', 'I Just Can't Stop Loving You', 'Dirty Diana', 'Smooth Criminal', 'Leave Me Alone' and 'Streetwalker'. Michael had written at least 60 songs; according to *Rolling Stone*, he initially wanted to use 33 of them on a three-disc set. Quincy opposed the idea, and suggested they stick to ten tracks. "There was the possibility that it could have been a three-disc set, but the time and effort alone to finish that much material made it impractical," Matt Forger said. "The idea was to make it a single disc of just the strongest songs for the best possible success in the marketplace."

The day before work began Michael had his huge Synclavier system, which was used to record the demos at Hayvenhurst, transported to Westlake. The Synclavier was new to Quincy, who planned to re-record the demo tracks with his A-Team session musicians. But Michael said he preferred the Synclavier versions. "This happened all the time, so soon, Quincy changed his way of working and we began to use the Synclavier for everything," Chris Currell said.

At the same time the Westlake sessions were starting, Michael and Matt Forger were also putting the final touches on sound work for the *Captain EO* short-film, which would be released in September 1986. Forger returned to the *Captain EO* project to conform music to picture and mix Michael's songs, 'Another Part of Me' and 'We Are Here to Change the World', for the film. Forger then oversaw the installation of *Captain EO* at the various Disney 3D theatres. Walter Yetnikoff, counting on Michael's album to come out in January 1987, was furious. When he discovered that Michael had written songs for the film, he reportedly threatened to sue him. They eventually reached a compromise – no songs from *Captain EO* would be released, and Michael would soon resume work on the album.

In November 1986, Michael flew to New York to film a video for 'Bad'. It was the first time he filmed a video while an album was still in production, keeping him out of the studio for many weeks. Movie director Martin Scorsese accepted Quincy's invitation to direct the 'Bad' film, and hired screenwriter Richard Prince to write the script.

The dance scenes in the 18-minute video, which features a young Wesley Snipes, were mostly filmed in New York's Hoyt–Schermerhorn subway station. The film reportedly cost over $2 million, breaking Michael's own record for the most expensive video of all time, which was 'Thriller' at over $500,000.

Engineer Craig Johnson said the song itself wasn't even fully completed when filming began. "Bruce Swedien and I flew to New York to work on edits of the soundtrack for the film at the Hit Factory studio in Manhattan, and we would send them to Michael at the rehearsal space," Johnson said. "It is safe to say things we were trying with the edits contributed to the final version of the song itself."

Michael was hearing a very specific bass sound in his head for 'Bad', and finding it became challenging for musician Christopher Currell. "He was looking for a certain feel," Currell said. "I tried many bass sounds. Michael liked them but there was always something missing. In the end, the solution was to mix all the sounds Michael liked into one bass sound. To accomplish this it took nine different bass sounds, which included synth sounds, organ bass pedal sounds as well as electric bass sounds."

TENSION

With the 'Bad' video complete and the Christmas break over, Michael and the A-Team resumed recording at Westlake in early January 1987. The record company had hoped to release the album sometime in 1986, and then either in January or February of 1987, but there was still a lot of production work to be done in the studio.

Even this far into the project, Michael was still concerned that the tracks were not sounding the same as when they were originally recorded into the Synclavier at Hayvenhurst. "He had discussed this with Bruce [Swedien], but he did not seem to understand Michael's concern," Christopher Currell said. "Michael was concerned that the punch of the music was being lost somehow. Michael called a meeting with me and his manager, Frank DiLeo, to listen to the original tracks at Michael's studio on the Synclavier. Frank agreed that there was a difference. Michael especially noticed this on the song 'Smooth Criminal'."

Although Michael and Quincy were producing the album together, they had conflicting ideas about the sounds. Michael was so unhappy with what was happening at Westlake that he even dared to make his own changes behind Quincy's back. "Something major happened during these sessions," one musician said. "When you wanted someone to work on a song for you away from the studio, you would make them 'slave tapes', and one day Michael took home slave tapes to work on at Hayvenhurst, away from Westlake and away from Quincy. Quincy couldn't believe it. No one took tapes away from a Quincy Jones production and made changes behind his back!"

With Michael wanting more of a say in the production of the album, there was inevitable friction between him and Quincy. "There was definite friction there," musician Larry Williams said. "Michael was very eager to prove he could produce, as well as sing and dance." Michael Boddicker shares this view. "Michael and Quincy began bumping heads a little on this album," he said. "Quincy had his way and Michael had his way. Michael wanted a big say on production and things were starting to get a little fractured. Michael felt that Quincy had made him the star, and realised he needed to write and produce more. But with two producers on an album, problems are going to arise."

Michael admitted there was tension, especially when it came to sound. "We fight," he said. "We disagreed on some things. If we struggle at all, it's about new stuff, the latest technology. I'll say, 'Quincy, you know, music changes all the time'. I want the latest drums sounds that people are doing. I want to go beyond the latest things."

Quincy was also trying to push Michael in the direction of rap, so he set up a meeting between Michael and hip-hop group Run DMC, who were at the height of their popularity. They were supposed to collaborate on an antidrug track, 'Crack Kills', but the plan fell through. According to Quincy, Michael was reluctant to move into the genre as he felt rap was 'dead'.

The pair also fought about credits. "On the song 'Speed Demon', Jerry Hey definitely contributed an element of writing, in terms of the track itself... the music," Larry Williams said. "So Quincy said to Michael, 'Look, you have to credit Jerry for what he did on that song'. But Michael refused to credit Jerry, and instead he took extra money for his work."

Some members of the A-Team became so disconcerted about Michael's idea of also recording the album after hours with the B-Team at Hayvenhurst, that they demanded the likes of Bill Bottrell and John Barnes stop working on it. Barnes left the project, while Bottrell was fired by Frank DiLeo with the promise that he would be re-hired for the next album. "We became friends, and Michael seemed to identify me as someone with a certain aesthetic that he knew he wanted to work with on that level," Bottrell said of his time working with Michael. "I worked with Michael at his home studio for some 14 months. Michael took this time for himself; he was available, ready, committed, and present. He had in mind what he wanted from the very beginning. My astonishment was to recall all the time we spent together, no business meetings, no musicians, no techs, no stubborn producers, self-important engineers or studio staff. Besides that, we also drove around, watched movies, talked philosophies, childhood, friends, and mentors. It was a great 14 months for both of us."

Bottrell also described what life was like working at the Jackson family home. "It was wonderful working there," he said. "We watched from the sidelines as all the family life happened, Janet in the hot tub with her husband Rene, Mom, Dad and brothers coming and going, entertainments like Elizabeth [Taylor] visiting, and Michael wanted twinkle lights in the trees like they had at Tavern on the Green. Some character came out with a tractor or crane to put them up, and tore up the grass, and then another character came out to quickly replace the grass with sod, just in time for the party…which went without a hitch. Michael would have kids over, and the best part…if you went from the control room through the Synclavier room and went through a door, you found yourself in the candy store. I watched *To Kill a Mockingbird* with Michael on a rainy winter day. This wasn't trivial, it required calling his professional projectionist and sitting in his custom theatre eating popcorn."

It was towards the end of Bottrell's time working with Michael when the pair recorded a cover of the Beatles song 'Come Together'. "Michael asked me to drive him home to Century City [to Michael's secret new condominium at 1101 Galaxy Way] one night," Bottrell recalls. "During the drive, we played lots of Beatles songs he had compiled on a tape. He was pretty interested in my opinion, and I told him we should pick 'Come Together'." Within a few days Bottrell created a music track using guitars and other instruments, and Michael then added his vocals. But the song would not come into consideration for the album.

FOCUS: MICHAEL AND SONGWRITING

PLANTING THE SEED

In terms of songwriting, Michael was gifted in a sense that his creativity was totally effortless. Rather than having specific writing sessions, an idea would just come to him naturally without thought. "If I sat here and said, 'Right, I'm going write the best song I've ever written', nothing happens," he explained. "Nowadays, artists seem to get in the way of the music. Get out of the way of the music! Don't write the music! Let the music write itself." For that reason, he never believed in the concept of writer's block. "He wasn't an artist who said, 'Oh, I've got an album coming up, I better start writing songs'," Matt Forger said. "The songs were constantly flowing from him, and if it wasn't a song it was a poem, it was an idea for a story or short-film…It was a constant creative process."

Michael felt that the creation of a song was very spiritual – as if the song was already written before it came to him. "It's hard to take credit for the songs that I write, because I just always feel that it's done from above," he once said. "I feel fortunate for being that instrument through which music flows. I'm just the source through which it comes. I can't take credit for it because it's God's work. He's just using me as the messenger."

Michael found that song ideas would come to him at any given moment. "I could be walking along on a road or I could be sitting on a bench at Disneyland or something eating peanuts and there it is – it's in my head, or I could be in the shower."

A certain phase in Michael's life or a particular emotion in a given moment would often influence his creative thought process. "I never categorise the music [I write] 'cause I never sit down and say, 'I'm gonna write a disco song, or pop or rock'," he said.

THE TRANSLATION FROM MIND TO TAPE

As Michael could not read music or play an instrument to an adequate level, his method of songwriting was different from that of many other writers. When an idea suddenly came to him, he would sing the entire arrangement of a song that he was hearing in his head into a tape recorder, including the bass and the melody, as well as aspects such as percussion and drums. "He can convey it [a song arrangement] with his voice like nobody," Bill Bottrell said. "Not just singing the song's lyrics, but he can convey a feeling in a drum part or a synthesiser part. He's really good at conveying those things."

Although the words to the chorus of a song would sometimes come to Michael at the same time that the melody was created, the lyrics for the verses were mostly written after the melody and instrumentation was completed. "I first hear the music and feel the dance, and then the words come spontaneously," he said. To Michael it was the melody, and not the lyrics, that was always the most crucial component of a song.

He explained that with lyrics, the listener is restricted to understanding English, whereas a melody is a universal language. "You have to be able to hum it [the song], from the farmer in Ireland to that lady who scrubs toilets in Harlem to anybody who can whistle to a child poppin' their fingers," he said.

Michael said great melodies are immortal. "Fashions change, culture changes, customs change. [But] we still listen to Mozart, Tchaikovsky and Rachmaninoff. Great music is like a great piece of sculpture or a great painting. It's forever. For generations upon generations to appreciate forever."

Michael collaborators soon learned how important melody was to him."The one thing with Michael: melody is king," future producer

Teddy Riley said. "That was his favourite slogan, that and 'settle for nothing less than great'. That's the one thing that's important with Michael, he doesn't care what the words say, he cares about the melody."

Michael admitted translating these ideas and sounds from his mind to tape wasn't an easy process. "It's very difficult sometimes, you only have one voice, but you're hearing full chords," he said. In another interview, he said, "In my head, it's [the song] completed, but I have to transplant that to tape. It's like [Alfred] Hitchcock said, 'The movie's finished'. But he still has to start directing it. The song is the same. You see it in its entirety and then you execute it."

TRANSLATION FROM TAPE TO TRACK

After translating his ideas to tape, the next step for Michael would be to bring in musicians to replace his voice with instruments. Together, they would create a demo composition of the song. "He has an entire record in his head and he tries to make people deliver it to him," Bill Bottrell said. "Sometimes those people surprise him and augment what he hears, but really his job is to extract from musicians and producers and engineers what he hears when he wakes up in the morning."

Some who worked with Michael felt that having musicians execute his ideas was a form of cheating. One musician, who worked with Michael for over 15 years and will remain unnamed, said: "The problem with Michael is that he would often have musical secretaries. He would sit down with a musician and have them play parts he had in his head. If a musician played a certain part, Michael would then say, 'No not like that', and then when the musician played it differently, he would say, 'Yeah like that, like that!' On the musician's part, this would sometimes be classed as writing."

Another musician, who also worked with Michael for over 15 years, shares a similar view. "Sometimes what musicians would do for

Michael would border on writing. Michael would sing a note to a musician, and he would play a chord, sometimes making writing decisions without getting credited for it."

Matt Forger totally disagrees with this viewpoint. "These were situations where Michael worked with different people to help him realise his ideas; sometimes the people working with him contributed ideas as well," he said. "It would have to be a case-by-case evaluation. I worked on many songs that Michael created from scratch. Others may have opinions of their own, but other people were not responsible for writing his hit songs. They may have played a part, but it was usually in support of him."

Bill Bottrell is also in Michael's corner. "Michael was better than most at knowing the difference between writing and everything else that goes on," he said. "We split our compositions clearly and fairly."

After the creation of a demo Michael would then take it to the main studio, such as Westlake, where the session musicians would record a final musical track. Michael would then add his vocals. After this, it was a case of sweetening the track before the engineers (usually Bruce Swedien) mixed it.

MAKE THAT CHANGE

Although Michael had written dozens of songs, Quincy still felt the album needed a big anthem to complement the works; a song with "a good feel to it and some sunshine on the world." During the first week of February 1987, the producer held a meeting at his house with the thirteen songwriters from his publishing company, informing them, as well as writers from other publishers, that he was looking for a certain type of song.

One of the songwriters was singer Siedah Garrett. At the time, Garrett was regularly writing music together with Glen Ballard, a staff producer for Quincy

Jones Productions who had already written material for Michael in 1982. The song Ballard wrote, 'Nightline', was not chosen for inclusion on *Thriller.*

When the pair worked together, Garrett would write the lyrics, and Ballard the music. "We have an initial writing session in which we come up with all these ideas and deviations of ideas from musical variations," Garrett explained. "And we also start a lyric idea from that point. Then I take it home and embellish the lyric and Glen embellishes the music."

The two met at Ballard's house in Encino in an attempt to write the song Quincy was looking for. Ballard began playing some music on his keyboard, while Garrett flipped through her lyric book looking at song titles she had written down. One particular title, which Garrett scribbled two years earlier, stood out during that session. It was 'Man in the Mirror'.

Armed with both the music and the title Garrett began writing lyrics, and almost instantly the pair came up with the first verse and chorus. They then made a quick demo of the song, with Garrett singing.

The demo was completed on a Friday evening, but knowing that Quincy's offices were going to be closed until Monday, Garrett called the producer and told him he had to hear it immediately. "Four hours later he called me," Garrett said. "He said, 'Baby, the song is great. It's really good. But…' I said, 'But what?' And he said, 'I don't know. I've been playing songs for Michael for two years. And he has *yet* to accept an outside song'."

Michael even rejected songs written by Rod Temperton, who had written six hits for *Off the Wall* and *Thriller*. One of the Temperton songs Michael turned down was called 'Groove of Midnight'. But this time, Quincy had no need to have doubts; three days later he called Garrett and told her that Michael loved the song and wanted to record it. Garrett was shell shocked, and screamed with joy.

After Michael heard the demo, Ballard was told to make the music track. "We were pleasantly shocked and thrilled that both Michael and Quincy responded positively to the song, based on a quick demo we had made with Siedah singing," Ballard said.

In mid-February, Michael began shooting a video for 'Smooth Criminal' at Universal Studios in Los Angeles. But Quincy admitted he didn't even want the song to be included on the album. "I gotta be honest, I was never a big fan of that song," he said. But Michael stood his ground and insisted on its inclusion. "Michael loved it to pieces, man," Quincy said.

Christopher Currell said the song was 'not even close' to being finished when the shoot began. "I remember messengers coming to the studio every couple of hours to get the newest mix of what I was doing on the Synclavier, so they could use it for the dance choreography over at the video sound stage," the musician recalls.

The dance sequence in the video pays tribute to Michael's hero Fred Astaire's 1953 musical comedy film, *The Band Wagon.* It was English director Colin Chilvers who suggested the 'film noir' look, a cinematic term used primarily to describe stylish Hollywood crime dramas from the early forties to the late fifties. "I showed Michael a movie that I felt would fit the theme of the piece, *The Third Man*," Chilvers recalls. "He loved that sort of film noir look, so we used that to get the camera man to light it in a similar way."

In the video Michael performs a gravity-defying 'lean', which arguably became his second most famous dance move behind the moonwalk. Chilvers, who won an Oscar for his special effects work on the 1978 *Superman* movie, said the move was performed using special heels and wires. "We had Michael on wires and fixed his feet to the ground so he could do that," the director said. "I fixed their heels to the ground with a slot, so that they were locked into it. If you look in the video, when they come back up from that lean, they kind of shuffle their feet back – they were unlocking themselves from the support they had in the ground."

As with 'Bad', shooting 'Smooth Criminal' kept Michael out of the studio for many days. "We got to shoot it for about two weeks; it was unheard of to be given this length of time to shoot a music video," choreographer Vince Paterson said. Chilvers said Michael was able to take his time and make the video as perfect as possible, because he was paying for the project out of his own pocket.

But Michael's schedule was beginning to concern Frank DiLeo, who scrambled an emergency meeting at Universal Studios. It was decided that the album had to be released before the beginning of a world tour supporting it, which was already scheduled to begin that September. DiLeo and John Branca announced a deadline of June 30 for completion of recording. "You need a dramatic deadline," Quincy said at the time. "I swear to you, it doesn't happen without that. We'd have been in the studio for another year."

Meanwhile, in the spring of 1987, 'Man in the Mirror' was recorded by Michael, the A-Team and its writers Siedah Garrett and Glen Ballard. The only modification from Garrett's original demo was a key change, as she originally sang it in a key that was one step too high for Michael. Garrett re-sang the demo in the new key, with the added pressure of being filmed by Michael.

As producer, Quincy sprinkled the song with a little bit of his magic. He helped Ballard with the rhythm arrangements and hired the Andraé Crouch Choir and The Winans to sing background vocals, giving the ending some drama. Garrett also contributed to the background vocals, and Michael asked her to attend his own lead vocal session so he could sing it the way she did. "That was such a high compliment," Garrett said. "It was great. I stayed. It was like I was producing."

Michael usually contributed to outside songs in a way the writers had not envisioned, and 'Man in the Mirror' was no different. "It had everything to do with Michael's vocal interpretation," Glen Ballard said. "In the last two minutes, Michael started doing these incantations, all the 'Shamons' and 'Oohs'. He went to that place on his own. We certainly couldn't have written that." Ballard said Michael took the song to a place that most songwriters can only dream of. "I have lived a charmed life," he said.

Michael loved the song because of the message it portrays. "If you want to make the world a better place, take a look at yourself and make a change," he said. "Start with the man in the mirror. Start with yourself. Don't be looking at all the other things. Start with *you*."

After 'Man in the Mirror' was recorded Garrett thought her work on the album was complete, but Michael and Quincy had other ideas.

'I Just Can't Stop Loving You' was originally intended to be a duet between Michael and a woman of his choice. Barbra Streisand and Whitney Houston were among those approached, but nothing materialised. According to Frank DiLeo, Streisand 'didn't like' the ballad. DiLeo was unfazed. "I didn't lose any sleep over it," he said. "I knew the song was a hit – with or without Barbra." As for Whitney Houston, her record label didn't want her to be overexposed, as her second solo album was due to be released that summer. Although she was relatively unknown outside the music industry, Michael chose to sing the song with Siedah Garrett, as he loved her voice.

Garrett was unaware she would be singing the song until the day of the main recording session, despite receiving a tape of it from Quincy beforehand. "It came as a total surprise," she said. "Quincy called me after I had worked with him doing the background vocals for 'Man in the Mirror' to come back to the studio to do more work. And the song they were working on wasn't 'Man in the Mirror'. It was a song that Quincy had given me a tape to learn. But I had no idea – I do lots of vocals on demos for Quincy, so this was nothing unusual."

Quincy asked Garrett if she had learnt the song from the tape, and told her to join Michael in the recording booth. Only then did it dawn on Garrett what was happening; the two were about to sing the lead vocals for 'I Just Can't Stop Loving You'. "It was exciting," Garrett said. "But see, Michael is funny. He has a real keen sense of humour. If I was talking to Quincy and we were serious for some reason, Michael would toss cashews and peanuts at us. I would be talking to Quincy and these peanuts would fly by. You know, the duet is a very serious love song. And when I was doing my verse, Michael was making these faces at me so that I would mess up. Quincy would say, 'Siedah – come on! You're holding up the whole album'! And I would get in trouble!"

At the beginning of the song, Michael performs a spoken part that was eventually removed from subsequent album re-releases. The part was recorded by Michael in a bed, after the engineers built a microphone into the head of a mannequin.

It had already been decided that the album would feature a duet between Michael and Stevie Wonder. Michael and Quincy were looking for the right song for the pair to sing together and chose 'Just Good Friends', written by British songwriters Terry Britten and Graham Lyle. Britten and Lyle had previously written many songs for Tina Turner, including 'What's Love Got to Do with It'. The pair hadn't intended for their song to be a duet, but Michael said he knew it would be perfect for him and Wonder to sing. With hindsight, Quincy felt the song was weak. "We couldn't get the right song, I know I didn't have the right song," he said. "So if someone says that didn't work, I know it didn't work!"

The 'Just Good Friends' recording session is one of engineer Russ Ragsdale's fondest studio memories. As well as vocals, Wonder also contributed the synthesiser solo in the middle of the song. "I was standing in the control room right next to Stevie as he laid down the most ripping solo, and watched Stevie tell Bruce [Swedien] to burn the first take, that he'd give him a better one, and that's what happened," Ragsdale said. "How could Bruce go wrong with Stevie Wonder at the keys to make him look good?"

It wasn't unusual for many celebrities to drop by the studio, but during this particular session, the team had a more unexpected visitor. "Right in the middle of a take, we noticed that a homeless guy had heard music coming from a studio cartage door which had apparently been left unlocked," Ragsdale recalls. "He wandered into the tracking room, crapped his pants probably, but remained quiet up against the wall. I remember this like yesterday, and once he was discovered he was escorted back outside."

WESTLAKE LIFE

Michael was now more famous than ever before, and he was weary of constantly being in the spotlight following the manic *Thriller* period. "Because of this, I resolved to lead a quieter, more private life," he explained. Dennis Hunt, a music critic for the *Los Angeles Times* who had known Michael for many years, said he was affected by the pressures of not having any privacy.

"People who know him well say it's finally gotten to him, and he's staying away from people," Hunt said at the time. "He's not dealing with the pressures the way he used to. There's no way that he will turn outward and live in the real world again. People thought that at some point he might outgrow it and open up, but now that's impossible. Because of the level of stardom that he has achieved, he is alone most of the time, except for dealing with members of his family, a few friends, and his menagerie of animals."

Many of those who worked with Michael believe the success of *Thriller* changed him forever. Steve Porcaro said there was a noticeable difference between Michael in 1982 and 1987. "He was very different, a lot more distant than before," Porcaro said. Saxophonist Kim Hutchcroft agrees. "I noticed that Michael was a lot more guarded and cautious in 1987 than he was when I last worked with him back in 1979," he said. "It must have been because of *Thriller*. People who knew Michael was in the studio were going through the garbage can outside, looking for photos, anything at all to do with him. There was just no privacy."

Porcaro also noticed another change. "Michael really liked to crank his music up in the studio when he was listening to something," he said. "It wasn't like that during *Thriller*. Michael really began to listen loud during these sessions."

Although his fame had gone to another level since the release of *Thriller*, Michael still drove himself to the studio. "For a while he drove a big Ford Bronco with dents and scrapes on it," Brad Sundberg recalls. "He was not a great driver. More than once he called into the studio to say he would be late after being in a fender bender."

There was a certain outfit that Michael would usually wear to the studio. Most days he would wear black shoes, a black hat and a red shirt, together with sunglasses, and other times, according to Quincy, he would wear 'this Captain Marvel stuff' or 'a beautiful chic suit'.

The staff at Westlake always tried to treat Michael as they would any other ordinary person. "Westlake was always buzzing, hence whenever a 'star' arrived to enter or leave nobody really took any special notice," Westlake staff engineer Raff Sanchez said. "I think Michael liked that so he could blend into it all the more discreetly."

Despite trying to maintain relative normality, at times it was nigh on impossible. Many celebrities would visit Michael at the studio, including Hollywood stars Steven Spielberg and Robert De Niro, John Lennon's son Sean, chat show queen Oprah Winfrey and actor and close friend Emmanuel Lewis.

Sometimes, more unusual guests would appear at the studio, and they appeared much more frequently than before. "The chimps were common guests in the studio, as was a giant snake, both of which I would wind up holding during Michael's vocals," Brad Sundberg said. It took three grown men to carry Crusher – the 300-pound, 20-foot snake which replaced Michael's previous snake Muscles, which died in 1986 – into the studio. According to Quincy, Greg Phillinganes 'freaked' when he saw the snake. "[He had a] Small heart attack, Greg Phillinganes could be an hors d'oeuvre for that snake," Quincy said. John Robinson also remembers Crusher. "Michael was watching me play the drums and said to everybody, 'let's take a picture'," he recalls. "So there were seven or eight of us posing for this picture while holding Michael's huge pet snake. It was so heavy, even the part I was holding. I certainly wasn't holding the head though!"

Musician Larry Williams wasn't so impressed with the animal guests. "In the studio, Bubbles [Michael's pet chimp] would be jumping around a lot, it was cute for a minute, but in the end he was getting in the way a little," Williams joked.

Although there was serious work going on, the atmosphere was very relaxed. Greg Phillinganes said there was always an air of fun in the studio. "Michael was very loving, very fun and loved to laugh," he said. "There were different sides to him that we would all see. The recording of 'Leave Me Alone' is one of my favourite memories of that entire time. I was putting down some strings and bass on that track, and Michael was there grooving next to me!"

Many of the musicians would regularly bring their children into work. "My children would come into the studio sometimes, and sit on Michael's lap," Larry Williams said. "They always wanted to see Michael. If the kids came in, everything in the studio would stop. It was very sweet." Kim Hutchcroft also remembers Michael's soft side. "It was my daughter's birthday, and I asked Michael if he could wish her happy birthday, which he did," he recalls. "I dialled the number and put Michael on, my daughter had her friends around and there was pandemonium. On the next weekend another one of my daughters came to the studio for the day; she was very shy, not jumping onto Michael's lap or anything. There was a friendly atmosphere; Jolie Levine's [Michael's personal assistant] kid would be there as well, running around with other kids. It was a friendly studio."

Michael also cared about the musicians and their families. "At one stage, my daughter was very ill and was in hospital," Larry Williams said. "Michael sent a room full of toys and dolls, which was a really nice gesture."

There were times when Michael wasn't required in the studio, and for these he had his own private lounge. "In between takes, most singers will try to stay in character in order to prevent the mood from changing, Michael included," Russ Ragsdale said. "At Westlake Michael had his own little private room upstairs with a window that looked out into the tracking room. If he needed to get away during times he really wasn't needed, he often went to this room, where he would trash it with popcorn all over the place. He was really quite messy, as he probably is used to having someone pick up after him; this was usually me!"

On occasion, Michael would display his eccentricities. "One day I looked over at Michael, and he was chewing on toilet paper," Larry Williams recalls. "I said, 'Michael, why are you eating toilet paper?!' And he said, 'Didn't you ever eat Kleenex when you were little?' I certainly did not!"

There was certainly no shortage of quality food at the studio. "Michael's cooks would make some great food, a lot of vegan stuff was for Michael, but I rarely saw him eat," Larry Williams said. Michael started a tradition where his chefs, Catherine Ballard and Laura Raynor, would cook dinner for the entire studio crew every Friday evening. Bruce Swedien said

Quincy nicknamed Ballard and Raynor 'The Slam-Dunk Sisters', because every meal they cooked was a 'winner'.

THE FINAL WEEKS

While the team worked on the album, there was also Michael's first solo tour to think about. The tour, announced in late June 1987 by Frank DiLeo, was scheduled to kick off in Japan in September. Engineer Russ Ragsdale, who worked only on the studio side, said the album and tour aspects were very much separate. "Of course all of us who had worked on the album wanted to continue the ride as long as possible, but we were denied access to many of the tour-related benefits like tour jackets," he said. "Damn it, I really wanted one! But nope, I was on the studio side. Sure, any prime seating that we wanted at the shows we did get, even tickets for friends in other cities."

In June, Michael took more time out from the studio to film a video for 'The Way You Make Me Feel' in Skid Row, Los Angeles, which sees him chase model Tatiana Thumbtzen through the streets in an attempt to win her affection. Choreographer and director Vincent Paterson, who worked on seven of Michael's videos across his career, said a moment on the set of 'The Way You Make Me Feel' is one of his favourite memories. "When we shot that video, there was silence on the set while Mike walked up to Tatiana," he said. "When he sang the first lyrics out loud, 'You knock me off of my feet, now, baby', then yelled out his 'OOOOOH', the entire crew freaked. It gave everyone goose bumps. His energy felt like it came from an outside alien source, it was so powerful."

When Michael and Quincy were choosing the final tracklist, they had difficulty deciding between 'Streetwalker' and 'Another Part of Me', a song that was originally written for *Captain EO*. There was space for only one more song; Michael wanted 'Streetwalker', whereas Quincy preferred 'Another Part of Me'.

Ultimately, it didn't make a difference to Michael as he had written both of them, but a decision had to be made. Unable to agree, Michael and Quincy held a meeting with Frank DiLeo. When DiLeo heard 'Streetwalker' he remained in his seat, yet when 'Another Part of Me' was played he began to dance. "DiLeo helped me get 'Another Part of Me' because he started shaking his butt on it," Quincy said. "I said [to DiLeo], 'You're not helping Michael at all'!" 'Another Part of Me' came out on top, and Matt Forger's 1986 *Captain EO* mix was remixed for the album by Bruce Swedien.

The final tracklist consists of 'Bad', 'The Way You Make Me Feel', 'Speed Demon', 'Liberian Girl', 'Just Good Friends', 'Another Part of Me', 'I Just Can't Stop Loving You', 'Man in the Mirror', 'Dirty Diana' and 'Smooth Criminal'. Due to space constraints, 'Leave Me Alone' only appears on the CD edition of the album as a bonus track. Michael wrote nine of the eleven songs and received a co-producer credit for the album. The most notable outtakes that have surfaced on subsequent album re-issues are 'Streetwalker', 'Cheater' and 'Fly Away'. 'Scared of the Moon' also failed to make the cut, as Quincy thought it sounded too 'Broadway' and too far from the genre Michael had been known to write and sing about.

Like the *Thriller* sessions, the final weeks of production required extra studio space. Although most of the recording took place in Studio D, it also migrated into other rooms as production edged towards the finishing line, with engineer Humberto Gatica mixing in Studio C. Final mixes were completed on July 9, and the next day Bruce Swedien took the tapes to Bernie Grundman's for mastering.

The team were at Westlake for a total of eleven months, compared with three months for *Thriller*, and the album also cost significantly more to produce; over $2 million compared with $750,000 for *Thriller*. It was Quincy's style to spend as little time in the studio as possible, and the producer later criticised Michael for the time it took to complete the album. "[It took] Too long," he said. "Paralysis through analysis. You make your mind [up] on the tunes you're going to do and you do it."

Michael Boddicker said Quincy was very budget conscious and aware of deadlines. "To Quincy, studio time was precious, we were there to work," Boddicker said. "There was no accepting phone calls, no meetings and no watching TV or videos. Even if your wife called and you took the call, you would be mocked. Session time was golden to Quincy. A bomb could have gone off outside the studio and no one would have noticed, because everybody was hard at work."

On July 13, Michael hosted a dinner party at Hayvenhurst for record label executives and sales people to preview the 'Bad' video and the album tracks. It was Walter Yetnikoff's idea to host the dinner; he felt that if the key promotion executives and retailers met Michael, they could 'make a difference'. Food that night was prepared by celebrity chef Wolfgang Puck.

At this stage, the album title was still being finalised. When Michael decided on *Smooth Criminal*, he called Epic's Senior VO of Marketing, Larry Stessel, and notified him of his decision. Shortly after Stessel received a call from Quincy, who told him he had a problem with the title. "Michael tried to follow the pattern set down by *Thriller*, with a really cool title," Stessel said. "So I originally called Quincy, who said, 'I'm not having a black artist call their album *Smooth Criminal*. He felt uncomfortable with the stereotype." Instead they opted for *Bad*, which also fitted in with the tough image Michael and Quincy wanted for the album. "'Bad' was the main track and I think Michael felt comfortable with that title too," Stessel added.

There were also issues with the original album cover, a headshot of Michael based on a *Vogue* photograph of Gloria Swanson that had been shot back in the 1930s. The photographers placed a piece of lace in front of the camera and shot Michael's face through the lace, so it looked like he was wearing a veil. But when Walter Yetnikoff saw the photo, he was far from impressed. "We created the album cover and sent it to Walter, who called and said, 'No fucking way is this the album cover, he looks like a girl'," Larry Stessel said. "So I was like, 'Okeydoke!' I called Miko Brando [son of Marlon], one of Michael's assistants, and said, 'We've got a problem, tell Michael to call me'. I told Michael we can't have the album cover. He wondered why, and when I told him what Walter said and he was surprised. So in the end, we went for the back-up."

The back-up was a photo taken by Michael's personal photographer, Sam Emerson, during the filming of the 'Bad' video in New York in November 1986. Emerson always photographed Michael during special occasions such as video shoots. Every day after shooting finished Emerson was ready to take the picture, but Michael complained that he was too tired. On the third day, Frank DiLeo urged Michael to finally have it taken. "I was set up for three days, but every day he was dancing and not up to doing it," Emerson recalls. "On the third day, Frank said, 'Come on Mike you gotta take this picture'. So he gave me a few minutes, and after three rolls and twelve shots, we were done."

Understandably, Michael was concerned about the comparisons *Bad* would get with *Thriller.* The closer he came to completing the album, the more terrified he became of that confrontation with the public. He wanted the album to be as close to perfect as humanly possible, and only declared it finished because factors such as the solo tour, sponsorship and record label schedules depended on it. "It's very hard to create something when you feel like you're in competition with yourself because no matter how you look at it, people are always going to compare *Bad* to *Thriller*," Michael said.

Michael was so obsessed with perfection that the musicians played their parts numerous times. "I was replacing parts that someone else had done previously, and I'm sure some of my stuff was replaced too along the way," Steve Porcaro said. "Quincy could afford to do that with the budget. Bruce [Swedien] just had so many options on what to use for each song." Guitarist David Williams said he performed the exact same part at least five different times on each song. "There was so much stress, and so much tension," he said. "They were trying to match the other one, the *Thriller* album, at least."

Michael admitted his obsessive perfection often angered the musicians. "I've had musicians get angry with me because I'll make them do something literally several hundred to a thousand times 'til it's what I want it to be," he said. "But then afterwards, they call me back on the phone and they'll apologise and say, 'You were absolutely right. I've never played better, I've never done better work, I out-did myself.' And I say, 'That's the way it should be because you've immortalised yourself. It's a time capsule.' It's like Michelangelo's work. It's like the Sistine Chapel, it's here forever."

CHAPTER 8: THE *BAD* CAMPAIGN

MID 1987 – MID 1989

Bad was finally released on August 31, 1987. But in the two year period prior to the release, Michael's image had changed dramatically. In its June 1987 issue, *Spin* magazine said Michael had gone from being 'one of the most admired of celebrities to one of the most absurd' in record time. Many wondered if Michael had deserted listeners by taking five years to come up with a follow up to *Thriller*, or if the eccentricities portrayed by the media had alienated his audience.

The big question in the minds of the media, and even Michael himself, was whether *Bad* could match the sales of *Thriller*. Perhaps Louis Kwiker, one of 60 key retailers who heard the album at a listening party thrown by the record company prior to its release, put the situation into perspective. "Clearly, the jury is still out as to whether it's going to match *Thriller*, but I don't think anybody can expect a world record every time somebody goes to the plate," he told the *Los Angeles Times* in July 1987. "The question is what are you going to measure it against – everything else that has happened in the marketplace in the last couple of years, or the greatest-selling album of all time?" Thomas Noonan, then the associate publisher and director of charts for *Billboard*, agreed. "The critics get too esoteric, and it's not fair to keep comparing it [with] *Thriller*," he said. "Did Michelangelo and Picasso trace over their best work?"

The lead single, 'I Just Can't Stop Loving You', received mostly negative reviews despite reaching number one on the *Billboard* 100 in September.

The song became the only number one single from *Bad* in the United Kingdom, and was released without an accompanying music video. Quincy called it the album's equivalent to 'The Girl Is Mine', the first single from *Thriller* which is also a ballad.

Auditions for the eagerly anticipated Bad Tour, Michael's first as a solo artist, took place at Leeds rehearsal studios in North Hollywood. Michael wasn't present at the auditions, but the musician's performances were filmed and later shown to Michael at Hayvenhurst.

Michael had a certain image in mind for the band, and wanted to hire a female guitar player with bright blonde hair. The Guitar Institute of Technology was notified and sent over its best female player, Jennifer Batten. "She did not look like a rock star [when she arrived at her audition], she looked more like an introverted librarian," Christopher Currell, who was already part of the band, said. "I showed her the stage. Jennifer asked what she should play. We said anything she wants. So she played the Eddie Van Halen solo on 'Beat It' perfectly, with no backing music. We were floored! Later that evening, at Michael's house, we were watching the videos. I told Michael that Jennifer was really good, and [that] he should really check her out. He watched and got very excited and said, 'Wow! She is really good but we have to do something about her look'! We all laughed. She was immediately in the band." Batten would continue to tour with Michael until 1997, but never worked on the studio side.

Currell, who worked on *Bad* in the studio, was brought on board to play Synclavier and digital guitar. "Since the Synclavier was such an important instrument for the *Bad* album in the studio, he wanted to use it live," Currell said. "Michael's idea of the show was to duplicate the record. He said people listen to the album and then they go to the shows expecting to hear those songs like they are on the album. So using the Synclavier was important to achieve his idea for the live shows."

Another of the studio musicians, Greg Phillinganes, became musical director and lead keyboard player. Rory Kaplan, who was part of the band for the Victory Tour, was also on keyboards, while Don Boyette was hired to play bass, with Ricky Lawson on drums and Jon Clark also on guitar.

Singer Sheryl Crow was hired as a backing vocalist after gate-crashing an audition only seven months after moving to Los Angeles from Missouri to try to break into the music industry. She was joined by backing singers Kevin Dorsey, Darryl Phinnessee and Dorian Holley.

Vincent Paterson was brought in to choreograph and co-direct the tour with Michael, while the four dancers were LaVelle Smith, Randy Allaire, Evaldo Garcia and Dominic Lucero. Costumes were designed by Gianni Versace, Dennis Tompkins and Michael Bush.

The delay in finishing *Bad* meant Michael had little time to rehearse for the tour. By the time he began rehearsals in August, the band, singers and dancers had already been working every day for a month, with a punishing schedule consisting of 6–10 hour days. Michael joined the rest of the team at a huge sound stage at Universal Studios in Los Angeles, where every element of the show came together. Although everything was rehearsed in separate parts, the team did not have time to do a full run-through of the show from A to Z. One day, Michael was paid a visit at rehearsal by Frank DiLeo and Epic marketing chief Larry Stessel.

"Michael was rehearsing for the tour, and when he was on stage singing, he kept taking his left hand and smacking it against his right arm and then pulling his arm up, which means 'Fuck You' in Italian," Stessel recalls. "So I was there with Frank DiLeo, who told Michael he can't make that move on stage. 'It's a bad move, you can't do that, it's a dirty expression', Frank told him. Michael asked him what it means, and when Frank told him he said, 'Frank I feel so bad, I'll never do that again', so he stopped doing it."

Before the start of the tour, DiLeo said it would be Michael's first and final solo tour, because he wanted to concentrate on making music and films. His arrival at Tokyo's Narita International Airport on September 9, three days before the first concert at Korakuen Stadium, caused pandemonium. The airport had to be shut off as hundreds of fans and over 600 journalists and cameramen waited for his arrival. The tour equipment was flown in on a specially chartered Boeing 747 and totalled 22 truckloads. Michael's considerable entourage included his pets Bubbles and Crusher the snake, which arrived on a flight that landed 30 minutes ahead of his plane. The pets travelled from the airport to the hotel on a bus with the band. "Bubbles was swinging around Tarzan style from all the poles and seats, creating his usual havoc," Christopher Currell said. "But the band loved it and we laughed all the way to our hotel."

When the tour began the set-list included just two songs from *Bad*, 'I Just Can't Stop Loving You' and the title track. According to Michael, the other new songs were too 'unfamiliar' at this stage, as only those two had been released as singles. Michael also decided to perform 'Thriller' for the first time, having agreed not to sing it on the Victory Tour following pressure from the Jehovah's Witnesses. But Michael was now free to do as he wished, having left the group in 1987 in response to their disapproval of the 'Smooth Criminal' video. "They thought the song ['Thriller'] was the devil's work and that under no circumstances should Michael perform it live," Christopher Currell said. "His intention was not evil. He said it was just kids' stuff, like Halloween, and was not a serious thing. But pressure from the church was great so he caved in and agreed not to perform it. He still believed in the church's basic teaching about being good and helping others, but he said he felt suppressed creatively, so decided to officially leave." During the entire tour Michael sang his songs 30% faster and two keys lower than the originals to save his voice, as he was singing close to every number live.

While in Tokyo, Michael had Disneyland shut to the public so the tour crew could all hang out alone. There was one particular moment that guitarist Jennifer Batten will always remember. "At one point at Disneyland I was hanging out with Sheryl Crow in a shop and Michael came up behind us, tapped me on the shoulder and said he liked how I was playing the 'Beat It' solo and started talking to us," she recalls. "It was a surprise because he was always surrounded by security whenever we were out and we never tried to get close to him."

Although the two spent over a year together touring the world, Crow said Michael never learned her name. "He didn't speak to me," she said. "Someone else would speak to you on his behalf. It was a Woody Allen type situation. It would be, 'Michael wants this, Michael thinks that'. But Crow later said she still spent 'a number of occasions' alone with Michael. "He invited me to his hotel room in Tokyo and we watched *Amos n' Andy* videos and the movie *Shane*, just completely unexpected," she recalls. "He was funny, he had a big laugh, he loved practical joking and I can remember vividly going to Disneyland and going on a ride with him and he wouldn't let the ride stop and by the end of it I was just absolutely ill. And he thought that was the funniest thing he'd ever seen."

Michael performing in Vienna on the Bad Tour in June 1988

After fourteen hugely successful dates in Japan, where Michael received favourable press coverage, the tour moved to Australia for a further six concerts. The leg finished in Brisbane in November, and Michael flew back to Los Angeles as the tour took a three-month break. On February 10, 1988 Michael arrived in the small city of Pensacola on Florida's Gulf Coast, where he chose to base rehearsals ahead of the next leg of the tour, which was due to start in Kansas City two weeks later. The set-list would include five more songs from *Bad* than the previous leg, for a total of seven. Michael loved Christopher Currell's tour version of 'Smooth Criminal' so much, that he told the musician they had to record the album version again with the Synclavier as soon as possible.

After only two concerts, Michael took a short break to rehearse for special performances of 'The Way You Make Me Feel' and 'Man in the Mirror' at the 30th Annual Grammy Awards at New York City's Radio City Music Hall on March 2. It was his first televised performance since *Motown 25* five years earlier. Engineer Brad Sundberg said Michael wanted to do something special for his performance, so they decided to record a new slow intro for 'The Way You Make Me Feel'. Michael's background vocals for this intro were recorded in his hotel room in Pensacola, with engineers running microphone cables up to his room from a recording truck below. "We put it all together in the truck, and jumped in the Hit Factory studio in New York a few days before the Grammy show for some final touches to the mix," Sundberg said. "The performance was amazing, and our little hotel studio worked like a charm."

After his performance Michael took his seat in the front row, and waited for the winners to be announced. But despite being nominated in four categories, including Album of the Year, he failed to win a single award. He was devastated and humiliated, but had to pick himself up quickly as the Bad Tour's three New York dates took place at Madison Square Garden in the days following the awards.

During all three shows Michael was joined on stage by special guest Steve Stevens, the guitarist who performed a solo on 'Dirty Diana'. Stevens says Michael isolated himself from the rest of the tour crew. "I didn't see him until I was onstage," the guitarist recalls. "The minute he finished the show, he was scuttled off into a van and then he was gone. At this time,

Quincy wasn't around, and I think that Quincy was almost like a father figure who kept things light and who had a way of putting people at ease. With Quincy not around, I began to see a different side. And that side showed me how isolated he was. I realised that he was really cut off, that he was really isolated. It made me really sad. It's never a good thing when somebody's that cut off."

Meanwhile, while in New York, Christopher Currell and Bruce Swedien went to the Hit Factory to re-record 'Smooth Criminal' for Michael. "The Synclavier was set up ready to go and Bruce had 'Smooth Criminal' all cued up," Currell said. "He turned to me and said, 'I have already recorded this twice. I don't know what Michael wants to hear'." Michael was clearly not satisfied with Bruce and Quincy's Westlake version; like many of the songs on *Bad*, he felt it sounded better when it was originally recorded with the Synclavier at Hayvenhurst. "Michael was supposed to come to the studio but changed his mind," Currell added. "He was off playing with some friends. I told Bruce that I know what Michael wants to hear. So Bruce said, 'You mix it then'."

They re-recorded the song with the Synclavier, and Currell performed the final mix before playing it to Michael at his penthouse. "Everyone was nervous about how Michael would respond to the new mix," Currell said. "I was confident that I got it the way he would like it, because of our work at his house. Bruce started the song, and immediately Michael started to dance. This was a good sign! He danced all the way through until the end. Then he said, 'This is great! It sounds the way it is supposed to sound'! Then he turned around and left. Everyone breathed a sigh of relief. This mix was used on later pressings of the *Bad* album. Basically it has more punch than the first version." Michael also had additional mixes performed on some of the other *Bad* tracks.

When the Bad Tour took a two-week break in May 1988 after a concert in Minneapolis, twenty-nine-year-old Michael finally moved out of Hayvenhurst to Sycamore Valley Ranch, his newly purchased estate near the small town of Los Olivos in Santa Barbara County, a two-and-a-half hour drive north of Los Angeles.

He fell in love with the ranch in October 1983, when he visited it while filming a video for 'Say Say Say' in the area. In February 1987 Michael bought the ranch from owner William Bone for $17 million, having first had a $13 million offer turned down seven months earlier. He renamed it Neverland Valley Ranch – Neverland for short, after the fictional setting of Peter Pan, the boy who never grew up.

The 2,700-acre estate is set in the hills of the lush Santa Ynez Valley at the foot of a 3,000-foot peak which Michael named Mt. Katherine, after his mother. The latter portion of the journey leading up to the modest oak gate occurs on the twisting Figueroa Mountain Road, and once inside, a half-mile long lane leads to the spot where the famous cast-iron front gates stood. "You would never think it was the driveway of a global celebrity," engineer Brad Sundberg, a frequent visitor to Neverland, said. "There were no lawns or flowers on the drive to the main ornate gate, as we called it, and the hills were usually dry and dusty with bushy shrubs and lizards.

"Before too long you would see the 'boy on the moon' logo welcoming guests from a sign on the side of the road, and finally you would pass over the last hill and start to round the corner. As you drove down that hill leading to the ornate gate you would see a huge parking lot for guests. Neverland wasn't really set up for a lot of traffic, as the primary roads are barely wide enough for two cars to pass each other without driving on the grass. Michael and most guests also drove customised golf carts on the ranch, so it was safer to keep cars and trucks in this lot."

After parking their vehicles, guests were then greeted by a uniformed ranch employee and escorted through the gate and onto a private amusement park train. "This was a great way for them to enter into Michael's world," Sundberg said. "Michael loved to create build-up and drama, he understood how to tell a story and how to set a stage, and it started with the arrival of the guest at this gate."

A further 500-metre long path, complete with a small railway track and dotted with bronze statues of children at play, leads to the main six bedroom French Normandy style mansion which Michael called home. Other luxuries in the vicinity include a four-acre lake and waterfall, a 180-foot swimming pool, outdoor Jacuzzi, tennis courts, a private golf course, ten garages, three separate guest quarters and a runway for small planes and helicopters. If that wasn't enough, Michael then spent a further $35 million renovating the ranch, creating a video game arcade, 50-seat movie theatre, a train station and railroad, an amusement park and a zoo.

The iconic Neverland train station with its huge floral clock

For Michael, the ranch was a secluded environment away from record executives, his immediate family and the bright lights of Hollywood. It meant he didn't have to be around people, and he never had to grow up. It was also a far cry from the grimy industrial city of Gary where he spent his first eleven years on earth. Michael said that when he created Neverland, he was creating a world the way he would like to see it, a place where he could have everything he never had as a child. "I can't go into a park," he explained. "I can't go to Disneyland, as myself. I can't go out and walk down the street. And so, I create my world behind my gates. Everything that I love is behind those gates." But over the years, maintaining this sprawling home of dreams would cost him as much as $7 million a year.

Michael may not have won Album of the Year at the Grammys, but he made history in July 1988 when *Bad* became the first album to have five number-one singles in America; 'I Just Can't Stop Loving You', 'Bad', 'The Way You Make Me Feel', 'Man in the Mirror' and 'Dirty Diana'. The record wasn't equalled until 23 years later by Katy Perry's *Teenage Dream.*

Michael spent over $10 million making his music videos for *Bad*, and this figure increased to $40 million with the release of his anthology film *Moonwalker* in October. Rather than featuring one continuous narrative, the 90-minute film is a collection of short-films about Michael, several of which are long-form music videos from *Bad*. *Moonwalker* cost a massive $27 million to make but was a big box-office success, grossing $67 million. Although never released theatrically in the United States, it was released there on home video. Michael's first and only autobiography, *Moonwalk*, was also finally released in 1988; talks about the project first began in late 1983.

Meanwhile, in 1988, as promised by Frank DiLeo a year earlier, Michael rehired musician and engineer Bill Bottrell. At this stage, Michael wasn't entirely sure of the concept of his next project – he was still engaged in the *Bad* campaign, so Bottrell simply began experimenting at Smoketree Studio in the San Fernando Valley, while Michael was away on tour. It was here where Bottrell began experimenting with an unused song from the *Bad* sessions, 'Streetwalker'.

"While Michael was on the Bad Tour he called and asked me to work on 'Streetwalker', which we had demo'd at Hayvenhurst and Quincy had produced for *Bad*, but which didn't make the album," Bottrell said. "So I was at Smoketree, all set up, starting from scratch on 'Streetwalker' and I fooled around with sounds and samples."

Using 'Streetwalker' Bottrell wrote the music for another song Michael would eventually record. He made a simple demo and then sent it to Michael, who liked it but wasn't sure what to do with it. "I wasn't completely satisfied with it, I was frustrated that it wasn't exactly what it should be," Michael said. "I have a lot of songs like that, that are kinda unfinished. So I gave the song to Billy, and he fooled around with it, put some drum sounds [on it], and put it through computers and things, and he gave the tape back to me, with the bass lick, and the drums, and everything on it. And I would listen to this quite often, and I liked what I heard, but I didn't really have the melody yet, a vocal melody." Eventually, the melody would come.

The Bad Tour ended with five concerts at the Memorial Sports Arena in Los Angeles in January 1989. The tour grossed $125 million at the box office, of which Michael reportedly netted $40 million, making it the largest grossing tour in history. It also had the largest audience in history, with 4.4 million people attending the 123 shows.

That January, Frank DiLeo confirmed that Michael would be retiring from touring in order to fulfil his movie dreams. "It's time to pursue this in earnest," DiLeo said. "We have stacks and stacks of scripts and proposals. We'll sort through them and see what's right for Michael." But Michael's older brother Marlon didn't buy it. "I think he's going to tour again," he said. "I mean, you say something like that and then three or four years pass and you get the urge again."

After an exhausting 16 months on tour Michael spent some time at his new property, the Neverland Ranch, and evaluated the *Bad* campaign as a whole. The tour may have been a huge success, but Michael was disappointed with the commercial performance of the *Bad* album. His target was 100 million sales, yet by early 1989 *Bad* had 'only' sold one-fifth of that. The record label was 'ecstatic' when *Bad* shot past the 20 million mark, but Michael wasn't – *Thriller* sold 15 million more copies in its first 18 months on sale.

Frank DiLeo said everybody did 'the best' they could. "We made the best album and the best videos we could, we don't have anything to be ashamed of," he said in January 1989. But for Michael it wasn't enough – a month later, DiLeo was out of a job. Somebody had to take the blame. It is estimated as many as 45 million copies of *Bad* have been sold worldwide, placing it among the most successful of all time. But Michael wanted it to be *the* most successful. He also felt DiLeo had taken his wish to make his life 'the greatest show on earth' a little too far, with too many strange and false stories appearing in the press after 1985. As Michael was refusing to be interviewed during the *Bad* era, much of his PR came through DiLeo. Michael's hair/ make-up artist, Karen Faye, claims Michael fired DiLeo because he was stealing from him. Faye says John Branca provided proof to Michael that his own manager was stealing ticket revenue money from the Bad Tour.

DiLeo himself claimed Michael was 'talked into' hiring another manager with a more established background in the movie industry, so he could fulfil his Hollywood dreams. By 1989, Michael was becoming more and more influenced by his business advisor, David Geffen. Michael looked up to Geffen, a hugely successful entertainment mogul, and listened to him carefully. At the end of the Bad Tour Michael also fired his accountant, Marshall Gelfrand, and replaced him with Richard Sherman, who worked for Geffen. DiLeo believed Michael's decision to fire him wasn't about the performance of the *Bad* album (or the stealing of money, at least not publicly), but one instigated by his key advisors.

In April 1989, the eighth and final video from the *Bad* album, 'Liberian Girl', was filmed, although Michael only makes a very brief appearance at the end. The video was designed so Michael's celebrity friends, including Steven Spielberg, John Travolta, and David Copperfield, were shown waiting on the set to get ready to film, only to discover that Michael was filming them all along. Michael's short appearance shows him filming the set with a camera.

Larry Stessel believes Michael only made a cameo appearance because he got tired of making videos by the end of the *Bad* campaign. "I was talking to Walter Yetnikoff about it and he said, 'You gotta get him in the video'," the former Epic marketing chief recalls. "So I called up Michael and I said, 'You gotta be in this video someplace…' He goes, 'OK I have an idea', and he goes, 'You got one take, you got 15 minutes'."

When the single was released later that summer, it marked the end of the *Bad* campaign after two long years. Frank DiLeo estimates that between *Thriller*, *Bad*, the tour and sponsorship deals, Michael earned as much as $350 million. Now the hugely successful *Bad* campaign was over, it was time for Michael to ponder his next career move.

CHAPTER 9: *DANGEROUS* DECISIONS

MID 1989 – LATE 1991

For his next project, Michael made the decision to dispense with the services of Quincy Jones, even though the three albums the pair recorded together had sold over 70 million copies to date.

One of the reasons Michael no longer wanted to work with Quincy was because he felt the producer was taking too much credit for his work. Walter Yetnikoff recalls Michael telling him he didn't want Quincy to win any awards at the Grammys in 1984 for his role in producing *Thriller*. "People will think he's the one who did it, not me," Michael told Yetnikoff. Quincy believes that key members of Michael's entourage were whispering in his ear telling him that he had been getting too much credit.

Quincy also felt Michael had lost faith in him and his knowledge of the market. "I remember when we were doing *Bad* I had [Run] DMC in the studio because I could see what was coming with hip-hop," he said. "And [Michael] was telling Frank DiLeo, 'I think Quincy's losing it and doesn't understand the market anymore. He doesn't know that rap is dead'." Michael was also said to be unhappy after Quincy gave him a tough time over the inclusion of 'Smooth Criminal' on *Bad*.

Most significantly, Michael wanted complete production freedom for his next project. On *Bad* Michael wasn't always able to produce the way he wanted to, especially when it came to working with the Synclavier, because co-producer Quincy had his own methods. Future producer

Brad Buxer said Michael wasn't angry with his one-time mentor. "He has always had an admiration for him and an immense respect," Buxer said. "But Michael wanted to control the creative process from A to Z. Simply put, he wanted to be his own boss. Michael was always very independent, and he also wanted to show that his success was not because of one man, namely Quincy."

Making *Bad* was a stressful period for Michael; he was competing with himself in an attempt to make the album as successful as *Thriller.* John Branca attempted to take some pressure off by persuading him to release a two-disc greatest hits collection (with up to five new songs included) to follow *Bad*, rather than an album of entirely new material.

The collection was to be titled *Decade 1979–1989* and completed by August 1989, in preparation for a November release. In addition to the new songs, the original plan was to include four tracks from *Off the Wall* ('Don't Stop 'Til You Get Enough', 'Rock With You', 'Off the Wall' and 'She's Out of My Life'); seven from *Thriller* ('Wanna Be Startin' Somethin'', 'The Girl Is Mine', 'Thriller', 'Beat It', 'Billie Jean', 'Human Nature' and 'P.Y.T.') and six from *Bad* ('Bad', 'The Way You Make Me Feel', 'I Just Can't Stop Loving You', 'Man in the Mirror', 'Dirty Diana' and 'Smooth Criminal'). 'Someone In The Dark' (from the 1982 *E.T.* storybook album), 'State of Shock' (the 1984 duet with Mick Jagger), The Jacksons song 'This Place Hotel', 'Come Together' (a Beatles cover recorded during the *Bad* sessions) and adult versions of two Jackson 5 classics, 'I'll Be There' and 'Never Can Say Goodbye', were also set to be included.

With the *Decade* format in mind, Branca began renegotiating Michael's contract with CBS Records. CBS was now under new ownership; the label was sold to the Japanese Sony Corporation for $2 billion in November 1987. The deal meant that artists contracted to CBS subsidiaries, in Michael's case Epic Records, would see their music distributed by Sony. The company wouldn't be renamed as Sony Music Entertainment until January 1991.

In the summer of 1989, after a few months of rest at Neverland, Michael returned to the studio to begin recording new material for *Decade*. With the ranch over 100 miles away, Michael would mostly stay at his secret three-storey condominium in Century City – which he called the 'Hideout' – whenever he was working in Los Angeles.

Now Quincy was out of the picture, Michael began working with Bill Bottrell and Matt Forger, just as he had done at the beginning of the *Bad* sessions in 1985. Inspired by seeing the world, Michael had been writing songs while spending time at his ranch after the Bad Tour. Forger said Michael returned from his tour with certain impressions. "His social commentary kicked up a notch or two," he said. "Most of the early songs we worked on were more socially conscious. His consciousness of the planet was much more to the forefront." The most prominent of these were later titled 'They Don't Care About Us' and 'Earth Song'. Michael and Forger began working on these tracks in Westlake's Studio C on Santa Monica Boulevard in June 1989.

In addition to his engineering work, Forger was very much in charge of sound design. "Michael was getting me to get new sounds, all with different qualities, and there were some very unusual things," Forger recalls. "One day, Michael said to me, 'Hey Matt, my brother Tito collects old cars'. So we ended up using some of Tito's old cars to make certain sounds. Michael loved metallic sounds, and sounds of nature. Another day, Michael had Billy [Bottrell] take a microphone to the back area of the studio, the loading area. They began smashing a metallic trashcan, and Michael had Billy record it. With Michael, you either had the sounds he wanted, or if not he would make you create those sounds. You never knew what sounds he would want."

While Forger was based at Westlake, Bottrell worked over at Ocean Way Recording, a short distance across Hollywood on Sunset Boulevard. Bottrell had recently finished working with Madonna on her album *Like a Prayer*, mixing and also helping to produce the title track. During their sessions, Michael would hum melodies and grooves and then leave the studio while Bottrell developed these ideas with drum machines and samplers. But none of the ideas they worked on at Ocean Way would develop much further, and after a short period Bottrell joined Forger at Westlake, taking over Studio D while Forger remained in Studio C. The pair worked together in both rooms and also operated independently.

In July 1989, Bottrell brought in keyboardist Brad Buxer to join the team. Buxer had been in Stevie Wonder's band for three years at that point and also worked with Smokey Robinson and The Temptations. "The first thing I remember is seeing Michael right in front of me in the studio wearing a black hat and looking like the ultimate star," Buxer recalls. "I had been working with a lot of celebrity artists by this time, but what really blew me away was this was the first time I was truly star struck. I had a huge smile on my face and so did he. We hit it off immediately. This first session was for drum and percussion programming. Michael's favourite colour was red and in the studio there was a bright red Linn 9000 drum machine. If a mistake was made in the session while we were programming I would look at him and he would look at me, and we would both laugh. We instantly took to each other." It was the beginning of a close personal and working relationship that would continue for another 20 years.

HEAL THE WORLD WE LIVE IN

As soon as Bottrell moved to Westlake, he and Buxer began working with Michael on a song called 'Black or White', which Michael wrote in early 1989 in his 'Giving Tree' overlooking the lake at Neverland. Climbing trees was always one of Michael's favourite pastime activities and often sparked creativity. "My favourite thing is to climb trees, go all the way up to the top of a tree and I look down on the branches," he explained. "Whenever I do that, it inspires me for music."

The first thing Michael did was hum the main riff of 'Black or White' to Bottrell, without specifying what instrument it would be played on. Bottrell then grabbed a Kramer American guitar and played to Michael's singing. Michael also sang the rhythm before Bottrell put down a simple drum loop and added percussion.

Once Michael had filled out some lyrical ideas (the theme is about racial harmony) he performed a scratch vocal, as well as some background vocals. Bottrell loved them and strove to keep them as they were. "Of course, it had to please him or he would have never let me get away with that," he said. Unusually for Michael, the scratch vocal remained untouched and ended up being used on the final version. The total length of the song at this stage was around a minute and a half, and there were still two big gaps in the middle to fill. Production of 'Black or White' would continue at other studios in Los Angeles later on.

Bottrell was also asked to work on an idea Michael had previously started with Matt Forger, an environmental protest track which eventually became 'Earth Song'. "I originally started that one with Michael, and then Bill continued working on it and developed it further, actually recording another version," Forger said. "I don't know if he used my version as a starting point or not. Sometimes Michael would work that way to get another person's take on how they would interpret a song. But many of the elements were exactly the same as my version, so it seems he did at least hear it."

Michael was on the Bad Tour in Vienna in June 1988 when he created the idea for 'Earth Song in his hotel room. "It just suddenly dropped into my lap," he recalled. "I was feeling so much pain and so much suffering of the plight of the Planet Earth. This [the song] is my chance to pretty much let people hear the voice of the planet."

Michael originally envisaged the song in the format of a trilogy, starting with an orchestral piece, then the main song and finishing with a spoken poem, which was later released as 'Planet Earth'. He wanted a particularly powerful bassline, so Bottrell brought in Guy Pratt, a British bassist who was touring with Pink Floyd. "I basically stole the bassline from 'Bad' because I figured Michael would like it, but wouldn't know why," Pratt admitted. Andraé Crouch, who had previously worked on 'Man in the Mirror', brought in his choir to sing on the song's epic finale. "They came in with the most wonderful arrangement," Bottrell said.

Bottrell remembers the very beginnings of another of his collaborations with Michael, a song which became the paranoid and despairing 'Who Is It'. "'Who Is It' was Michael's idea; he brought it to me, sang me parts and I produced them," Bottrell recalls. "But I didn't do as much arranging on this as the other songs." Bottrell hired a soprano, Linda Harmon, to sing the main melody, which was recorded at his own studio in Pasadena, Los Angeles. 'Monkey Business' was another notable song the pair wrote together. "Michael talked like it ['Monkey Business'] was purely fictional, a feeling, really, of poor southern country folk doing mischief to each other," Bottrell explained.

In the fall of 1989, Michael and his team began working on another environmental awareness anthem, 'Heal the World', which was originally called 'Feed the World'. Michael was inspired to write 'Earth Song' and 'Heal the World' because he was concerned about the plight of the planet and global warming. "I knew it was coming, but I wish they [the songs] would have gotten people's interest sooner," he said. "That's what I was trying to do with 'Earth Song', 'Heal the World', 'We Are the World', writing those songs to open up people's consciousness. I wish people would listen to every word." Famed primatologist Dr Jane Goodall said Michael was also inspired by the endangerment of chimpanzees. Goodall said Michael asked her for tapes of animals in distress because 'he wanted to be angry and cry' as he wrote.

Michael created the lyrics and music for 'Heal the World' at the same time, which, like keeping his first 'Black or White' vocal, was another unusual way for him to work. "With 'Heal the World', it was just Michael and me at the piano and in that single two-hour session that song came into existence," Brad Buxer said. "Billy [Bottrell] was in the control room recording the piano. Michael wrote the song and I executed it. The entire song was completed in that one session."

As part of his sound design work, Matt Forger was asked to help create the song's intro. Michael wanted a spontaneous intro involving a child speaking about the state of the planet, so Forger went out to record 'children just being children'. After recording over a hundred youngsters, Forger interviewed Ashley Farell, the daughter of his wife's friend. "I just began asking her questions about planet earth without coaching her, and she said these lines so sincerely," Forger recalls. "It was totally spontaneous and innocent, but after I started editing it to take out some of the hesitation and stammering, Michael said he wanted to leave it as it was. It was exactly what he wanted."

When Michael was once asked which three songs he would choose if he could only perform those for the rest of his life, 'Heal the World' made his list. "The point is that they're [the three songs] very melodic and if they have a great important message that's kinda immortal, that can relate to any time and space," he explained.

Keyboardist Michael Boddicker, who performed on 'Heal the World', believes the song says a lot about Michael. "It really represented his innocence when it came to his creations," he said.

After a few months of work at Westlake, producer/songwriter Bryan Loren, who was only 23 at the time, joined the team and worked in a third room at the studio. Michael liked Loren's work in producing the 1987 Shanice album *Discovery* and invited him to join the sessions.

It was after songs such as 'Black or White' and 'Heal the World' were developed when Michael began entertaining the idea of recording a full album of new material, rather than a greatest hits package with only a handful of new songs. Michael was indecisive about the *Decade* project and unsure about which songs to include on it, and had already missed the August deadline for its completion. Yet no definite decision was made; Michael would keep creating and see how he felt later down the line.

'YOU WERE THERE'

In early November Michael received a visit at the studio from a long-time friend, Buz Kohan, who was trying to persuade him to perform at an all-star tribute to Sammy Davis Jr's 60 years in show business. Kohan was co-producing and writing the show, which was being taped for broadcast on November 13 at the Shrine Auditorium in Los Angeles. Kohan was joined on his studio visit by the show's executive producer, George Schlatter.

"George had promised the network four big stars to actually sell them the special and one of them was Michael," Kohan said. "I don't think we discussed what he would do that night we visited him at the studio, but Michael did commit to make every effort to appear and we would discuss what he was to do later. At the time, Michael was in extreme pain from the Pepsi commercial accident when his hair caught on fire."

Kohan and Schlatter hadn't realised just how much distress Michael was in. "He took us into a back bathroom at the studio and asked us to feel his head," Kohan recalls. "He told me he was in constant pain and on painkillers. Because of this, he truly didn't know whether he would be able to perform at all."

Kohan went home and began thinking of the easiest, most gentle way of accommodating Michael's needs and those of Sammy Davis and the show. "Suddenly this phrase popped into my head, 'You Were There'," Kohan said. "It applied so perfectly to Sammy and what he meant to so many young performers like Michael who were spared some of the pain and torment he went through to make things happen."

'You Were There' was originally just a poem, but could easily be turned into a lyric if music were added. Shortly after, Kohan wrote Michael a letter to tell him about the piece he had written. "I told Michael, 'If the words strike a resonant chord in you; if they express how you feel about Sammy, and if you think you would like to spend an hour with me putting a melody to it before the show then give me a call'. And I said to him, 'If you feel you just want to say the words without actually singing them I can arrange to have some lovely underscore under your voice'. Knowing how busy he was, I took it upon myself to write a tune to it and make a song out of it."

At around midnight the night before the show, Michael showed up at the Shrine Auditorium. Together with Kohan he went into the adjacent Shrine Exposition Hall, which was completely empty except for a grand piano and one light in the far corner. The producer, the arranger and a number of others involved in the show all stood outside – the arranger would have to do a chart by the next morning if Michael agreed to perform the song.

"So Michael sat on the piano bench next to me," Kohan said. "He used to call me 'Buzzie Wuzzie'. I played the song for him on the grand piano, and Michael said, 'Buzzie that's beautiful'. We sat there for a while and made some adjustments to the melody line and changed a few words and chords, but Michael still wasn't sure if he would be able to learn the song, agree to the arrangement, set his lighting and feel physically up to performing it. So I said to Michael, 'This man, whether you are aware of it or not, has done so much for you, and if you pass up this last chance to say thank you, you will never forgive yourself'."

Michael told Kohan he understood and that he would try, so at least the producers finally had a commitment of sorts. Everything then went into gear to prepare for the dress rehearsal, which by then was less than 12 hours away.

"I knew Michael…he was such a perfectionist, he would spend days and weeks honing a performance or a song," Kohan said. "But here he was, going on stage before an audience of millions to perform a song he had never sung before, which had an orchestration he would hear for the first time on the afternoon of the show. It was so out of character for him, but to his everlasting credit, he set the wheels in motion and went home with a piano track I made on a small cassette recorder to learn the song."

After rehearsing the song on the afternoon of the show, Michael went to his dressing room to rest and prepare. That evening he performed 'You Were There' for the first and only time, joining other stars such as Clint Eastwood, Mike Tyson, Whitney Houston, Frank Sinatra, Dean Martin and Stevie Wonder in honouring Davis. Michael's tribute brought tears to Davis, who was battling throat cancer. After Michael finished performing, he walked over to his idol and hugged him warmly. "Michael was brilliant, simple, eloquent and so powerful," Kohan said. "The connection was made, the debt was paid, and it was one of the most memorable moments in a night that was overflowing with exceptional performances."

PROBLEMS, CHANGES

Between November 1989 and January 1990, Michael and the crew switched from Westlake to the Record One studio complex, located in Sherman Oaks in the San Fernando Valley. They had exclusive 24-hour access to the studio, costing an estimated $4,000 a day. Matt Forger said the move was made because of studio scheduling; at the time they required two studio rooms full time for a year, as Michael was entertaining the idea of recording a full album of new material rather than releasing *Decade*.

Bruce Swedien, who had recently finished working on Quincy Jones's album *Back on the Block* and was now available for Michael, joined the production at Record One along with engineer Brad Sundberg. Swedien, who engineered *Off the Wall*, *Thriller* and *Bad*, was given a production role by Michael, alongside Bill Bottrell and Bryan Loren. Incidentally, Michael rejected the chance to contribute a song to *Back on the Block*. "I asked Michael to be on it," Quincy said, "but he said he was afraid to do it because Walter Yetnikoff would be mad at him. But I think that if Michael had really wanted to be on the record, it would have been OK."

Shortly after moving to Record One, Michael received a visit at the studio from American Football star Bo Jackson. "I remember that day," Matt Forger said. "I was working in the Studio B control room and Michael brought Bo in to meet us. He was impressive to meet in person, so muscular; you could feel his athletic prowess. After a few pleasant words we continued with our work. Just another day in the studio, you didn't know what might happen or who might drop by. It was great fun."

Working at Record One at the time was a staff engineer called Rob Disner. "Michael didn't say much to me at first, until one day he ran in screaming that there was a 'vagabond' sitting in the alley behind the studio," Disner recalls. "I took a look, expecting Charlie Chaplin to pop out or something, but there was just some homeless guy sipping malt liquor out of a bag on the back steps."

Meanwhile, in late 1989 Michael's earnings figures were released by *Forbes* magazine. It is estimated that the *Bad* campaign, as well the income from his music catalogues, saw Michael earn over $225 million between 1987 and 1989, a figure which made him the highest-paid entertainer of all time.

As soon as the team moved to Record One and Bruce Swedien joined the production, many new song ideas were started. But by March 1990 Michael was still unsure about whether to go through with the *Decade* project – now due in the fall – or record a whole new album. "I'm not sure yet whether I'll release a Greatest Hits album or a new album, it depends how I feel," he told Adrian Grant, a journalist who visited him at the studio.

Over the course of the first half of 1990 progress on Michael's new project was very slow, with the uncertainty surrounding its format a major factor. Michael was also going through personal difficulties. In April a close friend of his, Ryan White, died from AIDS complications at the age of 18. His grandmother Martha Bridges also died a month later, as did one of his idols, Sammy Davis Jr. On June 3, Michael was admitted to St. John's Hospital in Los Angeles with chest pains, which his publicist Bob Jones said were likely to have been brought on by his struggles. Tests later traced the pains to inflammation of rib cage cartilage. Although Michael was released from hospital five days later, the illness kept him out of the studio for several weeks. Michael was also unhappy with his CBS contract, which John Branca had been renegotiating for many months.

By 1989 and 1990, Michael was becoming increasingly influenced by his close friend and business confidant, entertainment mogul David Geffen. After the Bad Tour he fired his accountant in favour of one who was working for Geffen, as well as his manager, Frank DiLeo. Michael finally hired a replacement for DiLeo in the summer of 1990. The new man, Sandy Gallin, who was brought in along with his management partner Jim Morey, was also a Geffen associate.

Gallin recalls the first time he spoke to Michael at Record One. "John Branca called me and took me to the studio, and we clicked right away," Gallin said. "We had conversations about his music, and where he could go with selling records and touring. That night, we got talking about how big a star he could become, and he felt we were on the same wavelength. Michael knew how to seduce people better than anybody, and he just told me how much he liked me, and that I made him feel good in the meeting." Michael played some of his new music to Gallin, who was blown away. "It was unbelievable, spectacular, and I got really turned on. He really was, at that time, at the top of his game."

One thing the pair didn't discuss was movies. "Our conversation was much more about Michael continuing to be the biggest record seller in the world," Gallin said. "In his mind, he might have thought, 'Sandy has produced many television shows and he'll be able to get me into the movie business'. But we didn't actually discuss that until later on." Yet DiLeo believed it was the 'promise' of a movie career under Gallin's stewardship that led to his own dismissal.

Advising Michael to replace DiLeo with Gallin was said to be part of Geffen's wider agenda of avenging his enemy Walter Yetnikoff, the CBS president. The two were formerly close friends, but their relationship soured at the tail end of the eighties. They often fell out as Geffen headed his own rival record label, Geffen Records, but Yetnikoff started to take matters to another level.

"He was pissed at me for a couple of reasons," Yetnikoff explained. "At Michael Jackson's whining insistence, I told Geffen he couldn't use a Michael track [the unreleased 'Come Together' from the *Bad* sessions] for the *Days of Thunder* soundtrack; and I kept circulating the story that I wanted David [who is openly gay] to show my girlfriend how to give superior blow jobs. In short, I showed him contempt at every turn." Another bad move by Yetnikoff was making enemies of Geffen's powerful attorney, Allen Grubman. Yetnikoff said he treated Grubman, who also represented many CBS artists, "like a schlemiel".

Yetnikoff said an infuriated Geffen then went on a 'power tear' after selling his label to MCA Records in March 1990 for $550 million (although he would carry on running it until 1995). One way of wreaking havoc for Yetnikoff would be to turn his most prized asset, Michael Jackson, against him by making Michael want to leave the label, which would alarm its new Japanese executives. Although Michael always had a good relationship with Yetnikoff, he listened to Geffen carefully because he looked to him like a father and admired him as a hugely successful business magnate.

Geffen discussed with Michael his relationship with CBS, convincing him that the label was making more money on his albums and videos than he was making himself. Geffen said one of the reasons he didn't have the best recording contract possible was because John Branca had a close relationship with Yetnikoff, much like Frank DiLeo did. "Rightly or wrongly, Michael was apparently unhappy – or at least concerned – with the way Branca was handling the renegotiation," a 'top level executive' told the

Los Angeles Times. "He seemed to feel he needed someone who wasn't so closely associated with CBS as Branca." Michael was also beginning to grow anxious over Branca's representation of other artists, such as The Rolling Stones.

Geffen's supposed plan worked, as Michael was so annoyed that he began to think about leaving CBS altogether, with Geffen/MCA Records a possible destination. But Michael was unable to simply walk away because he still legally owed CBS four more albums, and the label would be able to sue for damages if he reneged on his contract.

Michael told CBS he wouldn't be delivering his new album until his contract was improved, and felt the solution was to fire Branca and hire a new attorney to secure a better deal. Convinced it was the right decision, Michael dismissed Branca in the summer of 1990 after ten hugely successful years of working together. Much to Yetnikoff's dismay, Michael replaced him with a three man team including Bert Fields for litigation, and for negotiating his new record deal...Allen Grubman.

Grubman began putting together a contract which Yetnikoff considered to be 'outrageous', but Michael refused to deliver his album until the label agreed to it. Word got back to the Japanese executives that Michael was unhappy, with Yetnikoff the reason. For Yetnikoff, the writing was on the wall. Michael had transferred his loyalty to Geffen, and with Yetnikoff's relationship with other CBS artists – including Bruce Springsteen – also souring, his position as CBS president looked extremely vulnerable. Having lost the support of his key artists, and with his eccentric behaviour also worrying the executives, Yetnikoff was fired in September 1990 after 15 years in charge. He was replaced by his understudy, Tommy Mottola.

Yetnikoff believes it was Geffen who influenced Michael to fire DiLeo and Branca, two of Yetnikoff's close allies, and replace them with his own associates, in an attempt to turn Michael against him. One of Michael's new attorneys, Bert Fields, admits it was Geffen who brought him and Michael together. Perhaps tellingly, Branca's law partner Kenneth Ziffren also severed his ties with Geffen and his company in the wake of Branca's dismissal. Geffen, however, said Michael made the decisions with his own best interests at heart. “Michael changed lawyers because he wanted to,” he said. “He felt John Branca was too close to Walter.” He also denied being behind a coup to get Yetnikoff fired. “People want to make me out as having more to do with all of this than I had,” Geffen said. “He shot himself in the head. None of us had anything to do with it.”

NEW ALBUM, NEW SONGS

In the summer of 1990, Michael finally decided to shelve the *Decade* project in favour of an album of new material, due to an avalanche of song ideas. “Michael simply wasn’t interested in old material, he wanted to keep creating,” Matt Forger said. “We just had too many new ideas.” David Geffen was also said to have influenced the decision. The album was pencilled in for a January 1991 release.

Once he recovered from his illness, Michael resumed work in the studio. After starting work on ‘Black or White’, ‘Earth Song’, ‘Who Is It’ and ‘Monkey Business’ at Westlake, Michael and Bill Bottrell developed more song ideas at Record One. Bottrell offered Michael something the other producers didn’t. “I was the influence that he [Michael] otherwise didn’t have,” Bottrell said. “I was the rock guy and also the country guy, which nobody else was.”

With ‘Beat It’ and ‘Dirty Diana’ featuring on the last two albums, Michael wanted to write another song with ‘a rock edge to it’. The idea for ‘Give In to Me’, a hard rock ballad, came when Bottrell played a tune on his guitar in the studio one day. Michael loved what he was hearing and added a melody, before the two performed a live take together with Bottrell on guitar and Michael singing.

Michael added lyrics, and Guns ’N’ Roses guitarist Slash was invited to perform on the song as a special guest. “He [Michael] sent me a tape of the song that had no guitars other than some of the slow picking,” Slash recalls. “I called him and sang over the phone what I wanted to do. I basically went in [to the studio] and started to play it – that was it. It was really spontaneous in that way. Michael just wanted whatever was in my style. He just wanted me to do that. No pressure. He was really in sync with me.”

'Give In to Me' was originally drafted as a dance track rather than hard rock, with a drum beat programmed to play while Michael sang and Bottrell played the electric guitar. The song evolved and ended up as a rock track, but Bottrell regrets changing it from its original concept. "We took that song too far," he said. "It was me who got insecure and started layering things. Eventually, he [Michael] had Slash come in and add loads of guitars, and the song was transformed; not for the better, in my view. And that had nothing to do with Slash, but by virtue of the production that went into it."

It was at Record One where Michael and Bottrell also filled in the two large gaps that still existed in the middle of 'Black or White'. Michael had the idea for a heavy guitar section, and Bottrell suggested they insert a rap.

Michael sang the riff to the heavy guitar section to Bottrell, who then hired his friend Tim Pierce, as he couldn't play that kind of guitar. "Tim laid down some beautiful tracks with a Les Paul and a big Marshall, playing the chords that Michael had hummed to me – that's a pretty unusual approach," Bottrell said. "People will hire a guitar player and say 'Well, here's the chord. I want it to sound kinda like this', and the guitarist will have to come up with the part. However, Michael hums every rhythm and note or chord, and he can do that so well. He describes the sound that the record will have by singing it to you… and we're talking about heavy metal guitars here!"

Pierce recorded his parts for 'Black or White' at Record One in one day, and also played on 'Give In to Me'. "Firstly we did the bridge for 'Black or White', and Michael was present for that," Pierce recalls. "He wanted a heavy metal guitar part and that's what I brought in. After we finished that part, I then did my part on 'Give In to Me'. It was just Bill and me… Michael had gone by then. Michael was really sweet, nice, and looked me in the eye whenever we spoke. I liked that. He looked good as well, like a real superstar. He was definitely a fourteen-year-old wrapped in a thirty-year-old body."

The rap for 'Black or White' was now the only section left to record. "All the time I kept telling Michael that we had to have a rap, and he brought in rappers like LL Cool J who were performing on other songs," Bottrell said. "Somehow, I didn't have access to them for 'Black or White', and it was getting later and later and I wanted the song to be done. So, one day I wrote the rap – I woke up in the morning and, before my first cup of coffee, I began writing down what I was hearing, because the song had been in my head for about eight months by that time and it was an obsession to try and fill that last gap."

Although Bottrell wasn't a fan of white rap, he performed it himself and played it for Michael the next day. "He went 'Ohhh, I love it Bill, I love it. That should be the one'. I kept saying 'No, we've got to get a real rapper', but as soon as he heard my performance he was committed to it and wouldn't consider using anybody else. I was OK with it. I couldn't really tell if it sounded good, but after the record came out I did get the impression that people accepted it as a viable rap." In the credits, the rapper is named LTB. "LTB stood for 'MC Leave It to Beaver', an obvious reference to my cultural heritage," Bottrell explained. "Lesson learned – never joke around with credits."

Matt Forger helped to design the 'Black or White' intro, with Slash playing guitar and Bottrell playing the dad. A young actor named Andres McKenzie was brought in to play the son. Many believed it was the voice of *Home Alone* star Macaulay Culkin, although he wasn't involved until the video shoot.

Michael wasn't present for the recording session, much to Slash's disappointment. Bottrell himself was frustrated that the credits portrayed Slash as playing the main guitar section throughout the song. Slash only played the 'intro' section, whereas Bottrell played the whole song. "I was frustrated by the printed credits on the album for 'Black or White'," Bottrell admitted. "Because of the way it worked grammatically, most people thought Slash played guitar on the song. Bad luck for my legacy."

By the fall of 1990, Michael had also come up with an idea for the music track Bottrell originally crafted from 'Streetwalker' two years earlier. The track Bottrell made had no title, melody or lyrics, but Michael listened to it many times, and one day a melody came to him.

The song, about a predatory lover, would be called 'Dangerous'. Seconds before Michael was about to record vocals for a demo in the studio, he attempted to move a makeshift recording booth wall behind him, but the legs became unstable and the wall fell straight on his head. "All the lights were off, and right before I started singing – I think it was seven feet tall – this huge wall fell on my head, and it made a loud banging sound," Michael recalled. "It hurt, but I didn't realise how much it hurt me till the next day, and I was kinda dizzy. But it's pretty much on tape, if you played the demo of us working on 'Dangerous', it was even recorded."

After the incident, Michael continued to record for over an hour. When the session finished engineer Brad Sundberg called a doctor, who advised him Michael should be assessed for concussion, so Sundberg took him to hospital.

Although Bottrell would continue to tweak the song over the coming months, Michael still wasn't fully satisfied with it.

Over the course of 1990, Michael also worked with Bruce Swedien on a number of new songs. The majority of these were written by Michael and co-produced by Swedien. The pair brought in former 'A-Team' musicians Michael Boddicker, David Paich, Steve Porcaro, Greg Phillinganes, Paulinho Da Costa and Jerry Hey to play on the tracks, and newcomer Brad Buxer also contributed heavily.

The idea for 'Jam' – which was originally called 'Time Marches On' – came from Swedien and his writing partner Rene Moore, a Los Angeles musician. "In the late eighties, we began experimenting with extremely high-energy drum and rhythm tracks," Swedien said. "We worked on one of these ideas to use on Rene's solo album for Motown Records." Swedien even used sleigh bells from his grandfather's farm in Minnesota as a rhythm element. "After a while we realised that we had a toe-hold on a genuinely killer groove, and the song was really beginning to shape up. We were working in Rene's home studio and one afternoon we both looked at each other and said, 'Wow! This is really great, maybe we had better play this one for Michael'. The next day Rene came with me to the studio, I asked Michael if we could play a track for him, and he said 'Absolutely, call me when you're ready'."

Brad Sundberg, Michael and Bruce Swedien at Record One

A couple of hours later, they entered the studio. "Michael came into the control room with his pal, Emmanuel Lewis," Swedien recalls. "I played the track really loud and Emmanuel and Michael danced all over the control room, he absolutely loved the concept."

Another track Swedien co-produced was called 'Gone Too Soon'. In April 1990, Michael's close friend Ryan White died from complications from AIDS. Michael had previously discussed this friendship with another close friend, Buz Kohan, and confided that he wanted to do some kind of special tribute to White to honour his life.

Upon hearing of White's death Kohan had his friend, archivist and videographer Paul Seurrat, put footage of Michael and White onto a video cassette, with Dionne Warwick's rendition of 'Gone Too Soon', a song written by Kohan and Larry Grossman, playing over the footage. "Paul owed me a favour, as I had introduced him to Michael years before and he became his 'go-to-guy' for gathering footage for projects, keeping records of Michael's appearances on TV and in general becoming the 'keeper of the files' for his personal footage as well," Kohan said.

'Gone Too Soon' was a song Kohan and Grossman had written for a TV special in 1983 called 'Here's Television Entertainment', a special honouring variety TV performers from the past. Dionne Warwick sang it on the show as a tribute to those who had passed on, and after Michael saw the show, he immediately called Kohan. "He told me he loved the show, especially the song 'Gone Too Soon' and that someday he was going to record it," Kohan recalls. "I thanked him but having been there before with Michael, I didn't put much stock in the idea that he ever would."

Fast forward to 1990, and Michael called Kohan once more after receiving the tape from Seurrat. "He said he watched the video, that he loved it, and that 'Gone Too Soon' was going to be his tribute to Ryan," Kohan said. "The only thing was, he said he never does cover records, so he asked me if anyone else had ever recorded the song. I told him that when Dionne Warwick sang that song back in 1983, she said, 'I love it, I want to record it'. But she never did. Other performers, including Patti LaBelle and Donna Summer, also sang it at charity events and said they definitely wanted to record it, but also never did."

Kohan told him that no one had ever recorded it, and that his people have a word, 'bashert'. "That word, it means, 'It was meant to be'," Kohan said. "I told him, 'Michael, this song has been waiting for you, it was meant for you', and he agreed. I had written other songs for and with Michael that never made the final cut, so I was leery when he said it would be on the album he was preparing. He knew I had been disappointed before, and assured me it would be on the album, as promised."

Other tracks Swedien co-produced include the epic 'Will You Be There', which is another song Michael wrote in his 'Giving Tree' at Neverland, and 'Keep the Faith', which is about overcoming barriers. At the very end of 'Will You Be there', which is nearly eight minutes long, Michael performs a spoken part with words that would later take on a much deeper meaning than when he originally wrote them. 'Keep the Faith' was written by the 'Man in the Mirror' songwriting team of Glen Ballard and Siedah Garrett. Garrett said Michael received a songwriting credit on 'Keep the Faith' as he made changes that became an 'integral part' of the finished product. "It seemed only fair to include him as a writer on the song," she said.

When young producer Bryan Loren began working with Michael, he hoped to return to the 'organic' feeling of *Off the Wall* and *Thriller*. The pair recorded more than 20 songs together, including 'Men in Black', 'Superfly Sister', 'Verdict', 'Call it Off', 'Truth on Youth', 'Stay', 'Fever', 'Serious Effect', 'To Satisfy You', 'Work That Body', 'She Got It' and 'Seven Digits'. "Sadly, many of these we never finished," Loren said. "But when we did do vocals, beyond his lead work it was always a pleasure to listen to this man lay background harmonies. His voice was truly unique. Really pure tone, and great intonation."

The pair also created 'Do the Bartman' for the album *The Simpsons Sing the Blues*, released in December 1990 on Geffen Records after David Geffen had the idea to record an album based on the hit animated sitcom. Loren wrote the song, while Michael came up with the title. The vocal was performed by Bart Simpson's voice actor Nancy Cartwright and went to number one in the United Kingdom, although it was never released in the United States.

Michael and Loren spent much time together outside of the studio; the producer was a regular visitor to both Neverland and Michael's Hideout in Century City. "I remember once being on the 101 freeway coming from the Hideout on the way to the studio in my car, with Michael in my passenger seat," Loren recalls. "At some point, a man driving on the passenger side of my car looks in the window at Mike, curly hair and fedora in tow. Does a double-take and shrugs his shoulders as if to say 'Nah, couldn't be'. Now that was funny."

Loren also remembers the fun times in the studio. "I still have the fedora I took off his head while he was annoyingly poking at a plate of food I was eating at the studio one day, making him recoil because he had 'hat-hair'."

ENTER: TEDDY RILEY

By late 1990, Michael had been working on new music for 18 months, but he still wasn't satisfied with the sound of some of the material. To complement the best of what he had recorded so far, he was looking for something more contemporary and modern, something with 'fire' and a 'driving snare'. As Bruce Swedien put it, Michael's desire was to "present something very street that the young people will be able to identify with."

Michael identified another young producer, Teddy Riley, as the man who would be able to bring that sound to the project. Riley is credited as one of the pioneers of the new jack swing sound that came out of New York in the late eighties. New jack swing combines the sweet melodies typical of R&B with the tough, driving beats and instrumentation typical of dance and hip-hop. A founding member of Guy, Michael loved Riley's work with the group, and the producer was also working with Heavy D, Big Daddy Kane and Bobby Brown, co-writing and producing the latter's smash hit 'My Prerogative'.

Michael had actually met Riley before; Riley co-produced the song '2300 Jackson Street' from The Jacksons' 1989 album of the same name. It was the only song on the album that featured Michael, and the two subsequently met on the set of the video. As well as Riley, Michael's brothers also enlisted Guy manager Gene Griffin and Riley's band member Aaron Hall to write and produce on another track from the album, 'She'.

Michael was also familiar with the new jack swing sound as it features prominently on his sister Janet's 1989 album *Rhythm Nation 1814*, the style and sounds coming courtesy of Minneapolis-based super producers Jimmy Jam and Terry Lewis. Michael was particularly impressed with the album's bass sounds. "I always tell her [Janet] my favourite song of hers is 'Rhythm Nation' and 'The Knowledge'," he said. "I love the bass lick, it really just makes me crazy; makes me wild." Michael wanted Jam and Lewis to work on his album, but the pair turned him down due to their loyalty to Janet.

Michael contacted Riley over the phone in late 1990, and asked him if he could fly out to Los Angeles the next week. But before flying out, Riley wanted to work on some tracks that he could present to Michael. "We talked regularly before I produced the album and he described everything he was looking for, sound-wise," Riley said. "He pulled out one of my songs ['Spend the Night'] from the Guy album, which I sing, and he said he wanted that sound. He wanted something driving like that."

Riley rented out a studio from rapper Q-Tip at Soundtrack Studio in Queens, New York, and began working on grooves for Michael with his engineer Dave Way. "Before we came out to work with Michael we spent one or two weeks just getting some beats together to get the ball rolling," Way said. "Teddy just started writing and making beats, and prepared around 12 tracks. No melodies, no lyrics, just beats. Teddy said he really wanted to bring something new to the table for Michael."

At this point, Way had been working with Riley for around two years, and engineered Guy's album *The Future*, which was released in November 1990. Way remembers the day when Riley told him they were going to be working with Michael. "We were working on Heavy D's album at the time, *Peaceful Journey*, which Teddy was producing," Way recalls. "One day Teddy said to me, 'Michael wants to work with me, and I want you to come out to Los Angeles with me'. I was very excited and was never going to say no."

When Riley first arrived in Los Angeles in early 1991, he travelled up to Neverland to meet Michael. "His staff greeted me at the gate and brought me inside the house but Michael was nowhere to be found," Riley recalls. "So they put me in what I'd call his trophy room that had all kinds of awards, but the one thing that captured my eyes was the chess set. It was gold and platinum. I went to mess with it and picked up one of the pieces and turned to see Michael standing right behind me. He scared the living heck out of me. He fell on the ground laughing and couldn't stop because he saw how my eyes lit up, scared as heck!"

The pair started talking for a while, and Riley became anxious to play the music he had prepared, but Neverland was only equipped with a dance studio and not full recording facilities. "He said we'd go to the studio [in Los Angeles] the next day and took me on a tour of Neverland, the zoo and the park where he had his rides," Riley said. "Then we sat down and talked some more until I got tired. Michael convinced me to ride the helicopter back to L.A., where he had booked a room for me at the Universal Hilton."

The hotel is only a short distance away from the Record One studio where production was taking place. "He [Michael] thought I should be close to his studio and you know, I'm going to listen because he's the teacher," Riley said. "'Stay close to your music', he said. So that's what I did."

Engineer Dave Way was delighted to be in Los Angeles. "I had recently started playing golf and I'd brought my clubs with me," he said. "I was thrilled that I could run down to the Par 3 Studio City golf course on Whitsett before heading to the studio in the middle of February!"

Meanwhile, as Michael had missed the January 1991 release date, the album was pushed back to the summer.

Before long, it was time for Michael to finally hear the music Riley had created. Way recalls his first encounter with Michael on day one at the studio. "Myself and Teddy were working in a room at Record One, and Michael came in not realising there was work going on in the room. He just goes, 'Oh sorry, I didn't know anyone was in here'! And I was like, 'Yeah! That's Michael Jackson'!"

The three of them later gathered in one of the studio control rooms to listen to the dozen beats, which were played from a Digital Audio Tape (DAT). "I'll never forget pressing that play button – the first track came slamming out of the monitors...it was so loud it nearly made the ears bleed," Way said. "Teddy liked it loud, but Michael liked it louder. The tracks were typical Teddy – hard-hitting, new jack style."

When the tape finished playing, Riley and Way were anxiously waiting for Michael's first reaction. "Of course we were nervous," Way said. "We were thinking, 'Would Michael like them?' But he loved them. We felt that the first beat was the best one. As it turned out, it was Michael's favourite too. He said, 'Play it again!' That track would later become 'Blood on the Dance Floor'. Michael loved all of them, but he became fixated with that first beat and played it many times."

The only way Riley knew his music was right was if Michael was dancing to it all over the studio. "He starts going, 'Yeah, whoa'," Riley recalls. For the young producer, that first session was extra special. "Our first day at the studio – just watching Michael listen to my music – was the biggest experience in my life," he admitted.

Even when producers came up with a music track for Michael, he always wanted to ensure that he created the melody. Michael was eager to add a melody to one of the beats he had just heard and asked Riley to join him in a back room, where there was a piano. Michael then asked Riley to play the chords to the track. "I thought he was testing me," the producer said.

While Riley played the piano, Michel suddenly came up with the melody and chorus hook for a song that would become a cornerstone of the new album, 'Remember the Time'. Riley had no idea what inspired Michael to create the hook, which goes, 'Do you remember the time, when we fell in love'. "I don't know how he thought of it, what came out of him, [but] that's what he felt, so we rolled on that," Riley said.

Dave Way recorded Michael singing the hook, which was all that was written of the lyrics at the time. After Michael sang it once, Way stopped recording. "Michael was bemused as to why we stopped the tape," Way said. "So I explained that Teddy and I usually record the chorus once and then fly it in to all the other chorus sections. But Michael wanted to sing the chorus sections all the way through. So we started the song from the beginning, and Michael sang each note and harmony and doubled, tripled and quadrupled the hook. Each time, everything was matched to perfection, vibratos perfectly matched, perfectly in tune. It was done in 20 minutes, quicker than if we had flown them in."

Riley later brought in producer/musician Bernard Belle, whom he had been working closely with since 1986, to write the rest of the lyrics. Riley told Belle to make sure the words closely matched Michael's melody. "That's one thing that's important with Michael," Riley said, "he doesn't care what the words say, he cares about the melody."

Riley admitted he was so in awe of Michael at first that he found it difficult to produce him. "It worked itself out when he shook me," Riley said, "with words like, 'Listen, you're going to have to really produce me like you've produced a new artist. I need you to talk to me, I need you to criticise me, I need you to comment, I need you to give me all of you. I want the Teddy Riley that got that record out of Guy and the records out of your previous artists'."

Michael also worked on ideas for his favourite beat, which was the first one Riley and Way played from the tape. He came back with the title 'Blood on the Dance Floor', which was created two years earlier by Bill Bottrell for another song. Using the title, Michael then came up with lyrical ideas for his own song, which is about a predatory woman by the name of Susie.

Now it was clear Riley and Way would be staying in Los Angeles for the foreseeable future, the pair set up their gear, before playing the beats for Michael again. But because Record One had a different mixing console from the one they used to originally create the tracks in New York, some of them now sounded a little different.

"Michael was happy with the sound of the 'Remember the Time' beat, but the first track he initially loved so much, 'Blood on the Dance Floor', didn't excite him as much as the one on the tape," Way said. "He said, 'Why doesn't it hit as hard anymore?' I said to him, 'I think it's because of the console, in New York we used an SSL, that's why it's harder hitting'."

Riley and Way had only been at Record One for a few weeks when they moved to a newly built studio five miles down the road, Larrabee, where they would stay for the remainder of production. With Bruce Swedien, Bill Bottrell and Bryan Loren already sharing two rooms at Record One, there was simply no space for a fourth producer. "There was a lot going on at Record One, so it was decided to find an additional room," Matt Forger said. "I believe Teddy already knew Kevin Mills who owned Larrabee. It was a matter of finding a good studio not too far from where the centre of operations was located at Record One. Larrabee was only about a 10- or 15-minute drive away. It also gave a separation of work spaces, and I know Michael liked that." The studio's SSL mixing console was also perfect for Riley's style of music.

Michael booked three rooms at Larrabee; two studios and a personal lounge. The cost of exclusive use of Larrabee was an estimated \$3,000–\$4,000 a day; in addition to the \$4,000 it was already costing each day to hire all the rooms at Record One.

After Riley and Way settled at Larrabee, they worked on the 'Blood on the Dance Floor' beat using the SSL mixing console to make it sound like the original, but without success. Michael wasn't convinced it was the same, and that was as far as work on the song would go. "That was the last I saw of it," Way said. "Even though it was everyone's favourite track from day one, we barely touched it again. That's the way it goes sometimes."

THE BIG CONTRACT

In March 1991, Michael and his record label, which was now called Sony Music, finally announced a huge new six-album, 15-year deal. The contract, which took over a year to negotiate, was structured mainly by John Branca and improved and finalised by Michael's new attorneys, Bert Fields and Allen Grubman.

The contract gave Michael the highest royalty rate of any artist in the world, at 25% of retail sales, which equates to between $2.5 and $3 per retail sale. Michael would also be paid on every album sold – most artists at the time were paid on only 85% of total albums sold.

The deal was fairly complicated. Firstly, Michael was given a non-recoupable bonus of $4 million. He also received an estimated $18 million straight advance for the upcoming album, which Sony would recoup from his royalties before he could make a profit, plus more than $10 million in advances to fund the videos. However, Michael would only receive a guaranteed $5 million advance for his next five albums. He sacrificed a bigger guarantee in return for profits beyond his royalties; half of the profits that normally go to Sony, which was unprecedented at the time.

The deal also extended beyond his own music. Through the creation of the Jackson Entertainment Complex, Michael and Sony became business partners. Michael was given his own record label, initially titled Nation Records and later changed to MJJ Music, and Sony agreed to cover the running costs. Together they would share the label's profits equally in a 50-50 venture, and if it were ever to be sold, Michael would be entitled to half the stock. "He will be developing new, young and budding talent, and he will be the magnet to attract superstars to leave their current recording company to come to Sony," Tommy Mottola, the new Sony Music chief who had replaced Walter Yetnikoff, said at the time.

The complex would also have film and music video divisions, allowing Michael to realise his true passion – starring in movies. One of Michael's attorneys, Bert Fields, said the change of administration at Sony during the contract negotiations added to Michael's bargaining power. It was in Mottola's interest to keep Michael happy after what happened to Yetnikoff. "My reading is that they were close to losing Michael Jackson," a senior executive of a rival entertainment company said. "So you start by saying, 'What do you have to do to keep him?' He doesn't need the money. So you say we have this fantastic company that has all these avenues for you. Give us your albums and you can do movies, TV shows." The first movie under the deal was supposed to be a science fiction musical extravaganza called *MidKnight*, distributed by Sony's Columbia Pictures. But the whole project was put on hold after the director, Oscar-winning *Batman* set designer Anton Furst, committed suicide in November 1991.

Although Yetnikoff considered the contract 'outrageous' while it was being negotiated, Sony executive Michael Schulhof described it as 'economic' for his company. "If Michael continues to perform the way he has in the past, both he and we will do very well," Schulhof said. "He's thirty-three years old. I don't think anybody, including Michael himself, can predict how he is going to exercise that creativity. It may be in music, it may be in film, it may be in totally new areas of entertainment. The fact that the contract with him is unique reflects the fact that he is a unique talent."

Michael's business adviser David Geffen agreed. "I don't see the Sony deal as a sign that other record companies are going to start tearing up contracts of other artists and adding zeroes – at least not until someone else comes along who can sell almost 70 million records [over the previous decade]," he said. "Michael is a unique artist, and therefore his contract is unique." Although Geffen had a huge amount of influence over Michael during this time, they would later drift apart.

At the time of the announcement, the deal was portrayed by the media as being worth $1 billion to Michael. Even though Michael was happy with the final negotiation, he wouldn't sign the contract unless the accompanying press release announced it as a billion-dollar deal. "By no means were we paying Michael a billion dollars," Tommy Mottola said. "But if that was the press release Michael wanted, we figured out a way to do it for him. Yes, if his albums sold along the lines of *Thriller* and *Bad*, a case could be made that the sales of those albums would total a billion dollars. So we were able to spin it in a way that pleased Michael."

In March, it was also revealed that the album would be titled *Dangerous*.

MADONNA

After beginning work on 'Remember the Time' with Teddy Riley, Michael wrote a note with a list of songs he had at this stage, as he often did. On the note, he wrote 'MA & MJ duet', referring to his desire to collaborate with Madonna.

Michael dined with Madonna on a few occasions across March and April 1991. After being seen together on at least three occasions, the press rumoured that the pair were an item. During one conversation, Michael offered her to sing with him on one of his new song ideas, 'In the Closet'. Like 'Remember the Time', Riley had already prepared the music track for what became 'In the Closet' before coming to Los Angeles. It was Brad Buxer's favourite beat. "Teddy did some incredible work," Buxer said. "I was in the studio with Bruce Swedien working on a song – it might have been 'Will You Be There' – and Michael and Teddy came in with a tape of 'In the Closet' and played it at top volume in the studio. It just blew Bruce and me away. It was just so good." Michael added the missing melody and lyrics to Riley's beat.

Madonna said what followed was 'an experiment'. "He wanted to write a song with me and I was curious," she said. "He played me a bit of music, it was a very unfinished track and he said that he wanted to call the song 'In the Closet', and I said, 'Really'?"

Madonna was shocked that Michael wanted to write something with such a provocative title, and began writing words and getting ideas. "I presented them to him, and he didn't like them," she said. "I think all he wanted was a provocative title, and ultimately he didn't want the content of the song to live up to the title."

Engineer Rob Disner remembers Madonna visiting Michael at the studio on one occasion. "They spent a little while in his 'private' room in the back and then she left," he recalls. "When I asked Michael later about her visit he said that she 'scared' him. I think we all speculated that she tried to make a 'move' on him but Michael never said. In any event, we never saw her again after that..."

In May 1991, Madonna gave an interview to a magazine that seemed to all but end any hope of the pair ever collaborating. "I have this whole vision about Michael," she said. "We're considering working on a song together. I would like to completely redo his whole image, give him a Caesar – you know, that really short haircut – and I want to get him out of those buckly boots and all that stuff. What I want him to do is go to New York and hang out for a week with the House of Xtravaganza [a group of voguers]. They could give him a new style. I've already asked Jose [Guiterez] and Luis [Camacho] if they would do it. They're thrilled and ready. I said, 'Could you give this guy a make-over for me?' Because I think that's really what he needs."

When asked if Michael was 'up for it', Madonna said, "I don't know. He's up for a couple of things that surprise me. The thing is, I'm not going to get together and do some stupid ballad or love duet – no one's going to buy it, first of all. I said, 'Look, Michael, if you want to do something with me, you have to be willing to go all the way or I'm not going to do it'." Madonna seemed to be implying that if they were ever to collaborate in the future, the song would have to be more provocative than a ballad. The comments about Michael's image, however, seemed to put an end to the idea for good.

The woman who eventually collaborated with Michael was Princess Stéphanie of Monaco, daughter of the former Prince of Monaco and American actress Grace Kelly. Stéphanie, who is credited only as 'Mystery Girl', was forging a career in music and Michael liked the sound of her spoken voice. Young Larrabee studio engineer Thom Russo remembers the session. "She couldn't really sing that well, so Michael was like, 'Hey guys, can you fix the pitch a little'," Russo recalls.

Russo, who had only arrived in Los Angeles a few months earlier, was thrown straight into the sessions when Michael and his team began working at Larrabee. "People were running around the hallways there and I was just in the right place at the right time," Russo recalls. "Bruce Swedien recognised my qualities and the knowledge I had and gave me responsibility. Michael may have been the biggest star in the world but working with him was no big deal to me. He liked me and we became good friends."

STUDIO LIFE

Russo remembers the fun times in the studio. "Michael was goofy, he was giggly, innocent and so much fun," he said. "One night at Larrabee, Teddy [Riley] and Dave [Way] had gone and it was just Michael and me at the studio. I was busy doing something on a console. Suddenly, I looked over to the corner, and there was Michael practising some dance moves. I caught him popping. He smiled and realised I caught him. It was a really cute moment that I'll always remember."

Russo also recalls the day Nancy Reagan, the former First Lady of the United States, visited Michael at the studio. "Nancy and Michael were good buddies," he said. Fellow engineer Brad Sundberg said the Secret Service had to search the building for a few hours before Reagan could visit.

Sometimes the engineers would be sent out on shopping trips by Michael. "He started sending me out on errands, like going out with his credit card one afternoon to fill his huge Blazer up with gasoline," Rob Disner said. "If I remember correctly, he had an auxiliary gas tank mounted so he could get up to his ranch without having to get out and fill up along the way."

One particular day, Disner was asked to do Michael 'a special favour' – to buy him some underwear. "Of course I agreed, which was when he told me flat-out that he had just run out of underwear," Disner said. "For pretty much the whole two years that I worked with him, Michael came in every day wearing black dress pants and a red button-down shirt. He had a whole rack of just these two items in his office, which I assume he either had cleaned and returned to him, or just threw away at the end of the day. But on this particular day, I guess he was running low on drawers. At first, he just said that he wanted underwear. When I asked him what kind, he just repeated 'underwear'! When I told him I wasn't his mother and didn't know what to get, he kind of laughed, and then said, 'Hanes thirty please.' However when I was almost out the door he came running up and yelled, 'Make them thirty-twos, I don't want them to be too tight'!"

Another memorable experience for Disner was calling a Tower Records retail store an hour before closing time and having them shut early, so he and Michael could go shopping. "Even though it was just up the road, I was glad to get out of Michael's car and into the safety of the store," Disner said. "I think he dropped about $1,500 on CDs that night."

Disner was also asked to run down the street to McDonalds to grab some lunch for Michael. This was a rare request, as Michael usually had a personal chef to prepare his meals. "When I asked him what he wanted he admitted that he had no idea what they served, and that he had just heard from people that the food was good there! I ended up getting him one sample of nearly every item from the menu. He took a small bite of each, and then told me what he liked and what he didn't. If I remember correctly, he really liked their fish sandwich."

One day, Michael had some $900 remote-controlled motorcycles delivered to the studio. "He asked me to come out to the parking lot to try them out, and when we were messing around with them, he drove his motorcycle out of the lot and into the alley, when a car came by and ran it over," Disner recalls. "He thought that was really funny. I couldn't believe that he could laugh so much at losing a thousand-dollar toy!"

Michael may have been spending thousands of dollars a day on studio time and turning a blind eye to his expensive toy being crushed by a car, but when it came to borrowing an ink pen from Disner in the studio, he wanted to leave a note. "Michael left me this note on my desk one day just telling me that he took a pen off my desk, he was really concerned about doing anything that would inadvertently upset anybody around him," Disner said. "It pretty much tells you everything you need to know about him as a person and an artist."

During the *Dangerous* sessions, Michael also continued to blast music from the studio speakers at ear splitting levels. "I mean Teddy Riley really liked his music loud, but Michael was just at another level," Thom Russo said. "His level was rock star loud; he liked blowing up headphones, he had no problems going through a pair for each listening session. He would burn 'em up!" Despite this habit, none of Michael's collaborators ever noticed any loss of hearing in him.

Rob Disner also remembers actress Brooke Shields – whom Michael said he dated a lot – often calling the studio. "This was the pre-cell phone era so I would usually answer his calls and then have to go find him in the studio," Disner said. "She was always really nice to me." Michael once described Shields as 'one of the loves of my life', and would even speak with her about the two marrying and raising adoptive children together. But ultimately, they would remain friends.

"TEDDY, I NEED YOUR HELP ON THIS"

In the summer of 1991 Michael enlisted the help of top producers Antonio 'L.A.' Reid and Babyface, real name Kenneth Edmonds, much to the dismay of his brother Jermaine, who was also working with the pair. But nothing they worked on with Michael, including 'Slave to the Rhythm', would make the album. Later in the year, a song Jermaine had recorded which takes a swipe at Michael, 'Word to the Badd', was leaked to several radio stations. Jermaine said he wrote the song because his younger brother had frozen him out of his life. "I understand he's a very busy person, but after you repeatedly try to contact your own brother and he doesn't call you back, you begin to wonder if he hasn't just completely lost touch with reality," Jermaine said at the time. The two later settled their differences.

There was also a personnel change in the Teddy Riley production team. After a few months of working on *Dangerous*, Riley took a break and returned to the East Coast to tour with his band, Guy, to promote their new album. He was also in the midst of building a new studio in Virginia. Riley wanted Dave Way to join him, but the engineer chose to stay in Los Angeles. "Teddy wasn't too happy," Way recalls. "So when he returned he brought another engineer out with him, Jean-Marie Horvat. He took over my job as his assistant and I didn't end up working on the album again for a few months. For the last month, I was brought back in because of my knowledge of the project."

When Horvat joined the team, he wasn't even a mixing engineer. He was extremely nervous at first, but soon impressed those around him. "Lord I was shitting in my pants at first," Horvat admitted. "I actually thought I was gonna get fired because one day I messed up on the encoding and decoding. It turns out that it was a mistake that made me stand out and Bruce Swedien was saying, 'What a great mistake'!"

After working on 'Remember the Time' and 'In the Closet', Michael wanted to keep creating new music with Riley. In a memo written during a recording session, Michael noted that he wanted two more 'killer Teddy Riley dance grooves' that were 'better than Knowledge', referring to his sister Janet's song.

Riley created the music track for a song called 'She Drives Me Wild' using sounds from sample CDs he owned, and Michael wrote the lyrics around the music. Riley's whole percussion track revolves around motor sounds; trucks, cars starting and screeching, motorcycles idling and revving and car horns. Even the bass is a car horn. "It came out perfectly," Riley said. "I didn't go out into the field and record actual car sounds and take back to the studio – I had a sample CD that was really cool. It wasn't something I'd done before; it was the first time I went for unusual sounds in the place of drums."

Engineer Brad Sundberg thought the track was pretty ordinary, until Michael made it come to life. "I would walk into the control room and listen to it, but it never really grabbed me," Sundberg admitted. "Day after day that groove would play, and it was cool, but we had a lot of cool grooves. Finally Michael sang a scratch lead vocal and started building the chorus harmonies. It's hard to describe what was going on in my head, but it was like a camera coming into focus – in 90 seconds that song went from a repeating, almost boring groove to a piece of music. It stopped me in my tracks, even after hearing so many of his songs come to life."

The rap lyrics were written and performed by Aqil Davidson of the new jack swing/hip-hop group Wrecks N' Effect. Riley had a close affiliation with the group – he produced all three of their albums, and his brother was also a member.

Riley and his production partner Bernard Belle also wrote 'Why You Wanna Trip on Me' for Michael in response to people who, in Riley's words, were 'going after' him. "We anticipated a lot of people saying a lot of stuff about Michael," Riley said. "Jermaine going after Michael. We anticipated that. That's why we wrote songs like 'Trippin''. We know that people are after him, people are talking about him. But we didn't get too direct; we didn't say anybody's name. 'Cause when you're too direct, it gets boring." The element of the song Riley is most proud of is his guitar playing. "I thought he [Michael] was going to get another person to play on it but he wanted my good self playing, that was something special to me," he said.

The music track to what became 'Can't Let Her Get Away' also came mostly from instruments on sample CDs. Riley said it reminded him of the James Brown sound. "I could feel it," he said. "I thought I'd bring a shadow of some of the greatness of the James Brown production sound to this. Throughout the album I was drawing off a lot of CDs I had hanging around, all played by myself. I'm a multi-instrumentalist."

Another track the pair recorded, 'Joy', wouldn't make the album and was later recorded by Riley's new band Blackstreet in 1994. Engineer Jean-Marie Horvat said Michael's version was 'simply overwhelming'. "His vocal performance made me speechless," he said. "That was just great art."

As well as contributing his own tracks to the project, Riley was asked to re-produce 'Jam' and 'Dangerous', which were started by other producers. Michael felt they weren't 'contemporary' enough and wanted Riley to update the sounds.

'Jam' was originally given to Michael by Bruce Swedien and his writing partner Rene Moore. "One day Bruce came up to Teddy and said, 'Michael would love you to do your thing on that track'," Dave Way recalls. "Teddy really went to town on 'Jam'."

'Jam' was brought to Riley as a drum beat and needed major work. "Rene Moore and Bruce Swedien came up with the idea and gave it to Michael as a beat, so you can't take that credit away from them," Riley said, "but it was just a stripped tune until Michael did his vocals and I came in with the icing. I actually added most of the keyboard parts, all of the percussion elements, all of the horn parts, and all of the guitar parts to make the tune what it is today." Riley also brought in Michael's favourite rapper, Heavy D, to perform on the track.

Michael had already produced 'Dangerous' with Bill Bottrell, and the song was even chosen as the album's title track. But for Michael, it still wasn't quite right. "I wasn't satisfied with it, to me it wasn't contemporary enough," he said. "So I had Teddy go in, and kinda update the sounds." Riley remembers getting the call to work on the song. "I was at the hotel and he woke me up with a call. [Michael said] 'Teddy, you got to get over here right now. I need your help on this'."

The fact 'Dangerous' was originally Bottrell's production could have caused problems between him and Riley. As engineer Thom Russo put it, "No producer likes his track being re-produced by another producer, whoever it is." But Bottrell had no issue with Riley doing a version of the song. "I never felt competition with Teddy, and when Michael suggested Teddy do a version, I had no problem," Bottrell said. "Hey, it's all about the writing, Teddy's version rocks and sounds like the nineties, whereas mine was stuck in the eighties. Everything was in divine order."

Riley was equally gracious about the situation. "'Dangerous' had already been recorded by Bill Bottrell, but the music didn't move Michael," he said. "I told Michael, 'I like Billy; I like his producing, and everything about him. But this is your album, Michael. If this is the right tune, I can utilise what you have in your singing'. He said, 'Try it. I guess we gotta use what we love'. And we did. I'm quite sure if anyone else had come up with a better 'Dangerous', he would have used that – so it's not actually about me or Billy, it's about the music. I always say the music is the star."

Bruce Swedien described Riley as 'very professional'. "He'd come in with a groove, we'd say it wasn't exactly right, and there would be no complaining," Swedien said. "He'd just go back and then come back in and blow us away with something like 'Dangerous'." Concerned that his songs wouldn't make the album, Riley worked so hard that he actually slept at the studio more than his hotel, which was less than a mile away. "He [Michael] asked me to stay at the studio," Riley said. "Literally to see if I wanted a bedroom there because he thought it would be a great idea. So he took over the entire studio, chose a room all the way in the back and made it his bedroom. I found an empty lounge close to the kitchen. They [Michael's staff] made it into my bedroom."

Riley brought sounds to the project that had never featured on a Michael Jackson album before. Michael's mastering engineer Bernie Grundman described them as 'aggressive, mechanical and hard edged'. But ultimately it was the new jack swing combination of sweet melodies and driving beats that Riley wanted to present to Michael, with 'Remember the Time' being his best example. "That [song] was the sound I was thinking of for this album and he loved it – loved it from the beginning," Riley said.

Former Epic marketing chief Larry Stessel says that with Riley's production, *Dangerous* became the first album where Michael tried to follow the lead of other artists around him. "Michael looked up to the Beatles, realising they were leaders, they never looked around at what everything else was doing, they made what they made and he and I talked about that," Stessel said. "Michael was a go-to artist as well; people were looking at what he was doing. A lot of artists in the eighties and nineties tried to make music that would fit in, and I think when you look at *Dangerous* that's what Michael trying to do with the rap. He was looking at what others were doing rather than being the leader."

PRESSURE

By the summer Michael had again missed his deadline, reportedly because he was unhappy with some of the tracks, especially the dance cuts. It was likely that he needed more time, especially since Teddy Riley had only joined the team a few months earlier , changing the direction of the album. But it had now been two years since recording began, and Sony began to put pressure on Michael to finish the album in time for a pre-Thanksgiving release.

"That's when the intensity tripled, because we were running out of time and there wasn't much time left to finish the project," Brad Buxer recalls. Thom Russo also remembers the pressure building. "By the summer, Sony was ready and really wanted that album," he said. "The executives came in and said, 'Let's start cooking'."

Michael's relentless desire to create an album as perfect as humanly possible was the main reason behind the delay in completing *Bad*, and this was no different. His aim, once more, was to create a masterpiece that people would listen to for generations and generations. "I would like to see children and teenagers and parents and all races all over the world, hundreds and hundreds of years from now, still pulling out songs from that album and dissecting it," he said of his hopes for *Dangerous*. "I want it to live."

This perfectionism meant nothing was ever rushed, and Michael wouldn't submit an album to his record company until he was totally satisfied. Michael worked extremely fast during the *Off the Wall* and *Thriller* sessions, but this approach changed completely as his influence over his own music production grew. With *Bad*, and now *Dangerous*, the executives had to force him to hand over his work. Teddy Riley noted that if Michael had the chance, he would keep working on his songs forever. "He was demanding and we'd work on songs for a long time," Riley said. "We always had to get the mix right, we had the elements, but we had to get the mix right."

Thom Russo also experienced Michael's perfectionism first hand. "Michael was very slow doing vocals," he said. "He was such a perfectionist, and so detailed. It would frustrate many people, including the record label, but that was Michael, and he wouldn't settle for anything but perfection." Dave Way reiterated this. "Michael wouldn't do a vocal until he felt ready, certain things had to be right; the lyrics, his mood, and the vocal warm up with Seth Riggs."

As production of *Dangerous* neared the end, Michael and Riley kept coming up with new ideas. "Michael loved the work he and Teddy did together," his manager Sandy Gallin said. "Michael was really on a roll, and he came up with one masterpiece after another. He would record something, and he thought it was better than anything else on the album, so he would replace one track with another. This went on for quite a while. Sony thought he would never finish the album. Towards the end I had Mickey Schulhof and Tommy Mottola calling me constantly. I told Michael, 'You cannot start another song'. He would still be working on it today if he could."

By August, the team knew they really had to dig in. "By then it was all go go go," Thom Russo recalls. "Michael was singing mostly at night, it always seemed to be late when he did his vocals. He had no problem being up until 3am singing."

When production intensified in the late summer, Michael and Bruce Swedien moved to the Universal Hilton to be closer to Record One and Larrabee, travelling to and from the studios in Swedien's Big Bronco. "We'd drive to the studio and work until we couldn't work anymore, then we'd drive back to the hotel, go to sleep and then go back in the morning and hit it again," Swedien recalls.

Swedien's wife Bea would also drive Michael to and from the studio. "One day there were these fans camped outside of the studio, and Michael said to us, 'Put the window down, I want to speak to them'," she recalls. "We said, 'Michael you can't trust them', but Michael said, 'Yes, it's OK, after the Pepsi accident they were camped outside the hospital for days waiting for me'."

Over the years, Michael became close friends with both Bruce and Bea. "We always had such fun with Michael, we spent so much time together, we were with him forever," Bea said. "I drove him to his Hideout in Century City once, it was a three storey complex and the Reagans also had an apartment nearby. So we got inside, Michael had all these pinball machines and this lifelike figure of Shirley Temple. He went off somewhere and said, 'I'll be right back, go and enjoy yourself'. Then when he came back I just saw this person, and I said, 'Who is that?!' And it was Michael wearing this scary mask made for him by his 'Thriller' video make-up artist, Rick Baker. I was so scared and Michael was really embarrassed that he had frightened me."

Sometimes engineer Thom Russo would also drop Michael back to the hotel if the two were working on vocals late into the night. "Michael would come in, work for five or six hours, and then I would drive him home to the Hilton in my little Honda Civic," Russo said. "When we got to the Hilton, there was a secret entrance we could use so Michael didn't get mobbed."

Before Michael moved into the Hilton, he would often drive himself to the studio from his Century City condo. "He was a bad driver," Dave Way said. "I remember when he drove into the studio one day he bumped his light against a wall or metal pole, and then on another day, he really got himself into trouble. He drove into the back of someone on the 101 freeway. Both cars immediately stopped. The driver in front got out of his car and started yelling and waving his arms and was telling whoever was in the car to get out. He didn't know it was Michael, the windows were tinted and you couldn't see inside. So Michael didn't get out of the car. A few minutes passed, and Michael still didn't emerge! You can imagine what it was like, no one coming out of this car! So Michael was frantically on the phone to his people saying, 'You gotta help me'!"

Engineer Rob Disner too described Michael as 'an awful driver'. "He hit everyone's car in the studio lot at least once, including mine," he said. "Eventually, he gave up and got someone to drive him in to work every day."

In September, at the same time as trying to finish the album in the studio, Michael began shooting his most ambitious and extravagant music video to date. The 11-minute video for the lead single, 'Black or White', cost $4 million to create, making it the second most expensive of all time, behind Madonna's $5 million effort for 'Express Yourself'.

'Thriller' director John Landis teamed up with Michael once more to work on the video. Landis was initially reluctant to work with Michael again, as he was still owed money for the 'Thriller' project, but eventually he was swayed. "Michael called, and he kept coming over to my house, pleading, 'John, come on, come on'," Landis recalls. "So finally I said, 'All right. But I want to be paid weekly'."

The video kept Michael out of the recording studio for many days over the course of more than a month. On some occasions, when Michael was due on set, he would be busy with other projects; once Landis was told that Michael was doing a commercial for Sony Television, Japan. Director Vince Paterson, who worked with Michael on the 'Smooth Criminal' video and choreographed 'Black or White', said it was difficult to shoot while the studio work was still ongoing. There were days when work on the video was put on hold so Michael could work on the album. "The album had to take precedence," Paterson said. "So the video got scrambled. And if Michael was in the studio for eighteen hours, there was no point in then bringing him out to the set and trying to shoot him. He would have been dead, he would have been exhausted, and we would have just had to re-shoot it anyway."

The huge budget reflected Michael's desire for extravagance. The brief segment in which he dances with Native Americans in full tribal dress, filmed at Vasquez Rocks north of Los Angeles, took five days to rehearse. A freeway was re-created in Sun Valley for the scene in which he dances with a female partner in the middle of a busy road, and 50 stunt drivers were hired. The Red Square set was constructed on a Culver Studios sound stage. Michael's friend, eleven-year-old child star Macaulay Culkin, also made a cameo appearance.

At the end of the song, several people of differing races and nationalities, including model Tyra Banks, dance as they morph into one another. The morphing technique had only been used previously in a handful of films, such as *Terminator 2*. "We've pushed this one step further than what has ever been done before," Jamie Dixon of Pacific Data Images in Los Angeles, which created the visual effects, said. "Michael wanted to put just about everything in the whole universe in this thing."

When the song finishes, Michael appears as a black panther before morphing into himself and dancing alone in a city back street. He then morphs back into the panther, before the video ends with a specially created scene from *The Simpsons*, in which Homer tells his son Bart, who is wearing a Michael Jackson t-shirt, to turn off the television.

THE FINAL WEEKS

The month of October was a manic one for Michael in the studio. In addition to his work with Teddy Riley, he was also finishing his productions with Bruce Swedien and Bill Bottrell. In the final weeks, the building pressure on Michael was beginning to take its toll. The day had come for him to sing the lead vocal on 'Keep the Faith'. But after singing the first two verses, he rushed out of the recording booth. "It was very unlike Michael, I found him standing in the corner of his office, crying his eyes out," Swedien recalls. "He was absolutely heartbroken – cut to the quick."

Michael's voice cracked while he sang, meaning he was no longer able to reach the higher notes. The studio staff quickly changed all the configurations so Michael could sing the vocals in a lower pitch. "I told him, 'Michael, it's not that big a deal, I'll just record it in the other key'," Swedien said. "We'd tried two keys and, unfortunately, picked the wrong one. He was really upset. I told him, 'Michael, we've got to face this right now'. I called the synth player and programmer. I felt we had to get the right key and get Michael to face it before it turned into something ugly. I thought we'd have a major, major problem. I was visualising headlines. I told him, 'Pull yourself together, face this now'. And it was late. I said, 'We're not going home until you've sung this all the way through. Then we'll go home and be able to sleep and continue'. That was scary. But he did it. He pulled himself together. We went in the studio, cut a whole new demo and recorded a scratch vocal all the way through. A situation like that could have been a real block. We didn't leave the studio till dawn."

Walking out of the studio was often an indication that Michael was unhappy. "He doesn't like to be negative, he has his own indications [that he is unhappy], and you just learn what they are," Bill Bottrell said. "Walking out of the room is one way."

So much music was recorded for *Dangerous* – Michael wrote over 60 songs for the project – that he had a hard time picking the final tracklist. "Michael kept coming back with lists of his 'final' selections but they almost always added up to over 74 minutes – the maximum running time for the disc," engineer Rob Disner recalls. "I remember them going back and forth on this for weeks."

Michael used to write song titles on stickers and place them on a board, but every day the titles would change. "He takes a song off, replaces it with another, changes the order of the titles…Every time I look at the board, something has been changed," Bruce Swedien recalls.

Eventually, Michael and Swedien chose 'Jam', 'Why You Wanna Trip on Me', 'In the Closet', 'She Drives Me Wild', 'Remember the Time', 'Can't Let Her Get Away', 'Heal the World', 'Black or White', 'Who Is It', 'Give In to Me', 'Will You Be There', 'Keep the Faith', 'Gone Too Soon' and 'Dangerous'. Michael had a hand in writing 12 of the 14 songs, and solely wrote and composed four.

The arrival of Teddy Riley, who received a reported $2 million for his work on *Dangerous*, significantly changed the production and direction of the album. Many songs produced with Bill Bottrell and Bryan Loren were left off the final tracklist in favour of Riley's material. Riley himself was shocked when Michael told him how many of his songs would make the cut. "One day he [Michael] told me it was cool if I wanted to start doing interviews about the album," Riley recalls. "I said, 'Well, what about songs? What should I mention?' He said, 'Okay, we're going to sit down and I'm going to tell you all your songs that made the album'. I felt confident that 'Remember the Time' would make the cut but I was blown away when he mentioned the names of six songs we'd done together. 'These are all great', he said."

Michael got a co-production credit on all of the songs, but Riley had no issue. "On every album Michael does, he has some sort of input so I didn't mind him getting a co-production," he said. "Well, you can't exactly tell the King of Pop he can't, can you?"

Two of Bill Bottrell's main productions which failed to make the album were 'Monkey Business' and 'Earth Song'. "I was disappointed when 'Monkey Business' and 'Earth Song' didn't make the record, but I got over it," Bottrell said. At this stage, Michael wasn't quite satisfied with 'Earth Song'. "It was a song Michael was just not sure of, something about the bassline," Bottrell said. "I was sure of it and said so." Dave Way heard 'Monkey Business' a few times in the studio and was surprised it was left on the shelf. "I couldn't believe 'Monkey Business' didn't make the record, Bill played me that song a few times and I loved it," Way said.

Not a single Bryan Loren production made the cut. "*Dangerous* was a rough period for me as we'd recorded so much music and none of it was used for that project," Loren admitted. "But I will say that I spent a great deal of enjoyable time with Michael and made some great music with him as well. There are some songs that, even in their unfinished format, you can hear their potential." Loren still features as a musician on three of the tracks, 'Black or White', 'Heal the World' and 'Who Is It'. Michael gave a special mention to Loren in the album credits. "Bryan Loren... you have brought so much to the project as a musician," Michael wrote. "You are brilliant and a wonderful human being to work with. All my love, Michael Jackson."

Other songs left out include 'They Don't Care About Us', 'Don't Be Messin' 'Round', 'Joy' and the ballad 'For All Time'. Contrary to popular belief, 'For All Time' wasn't recorded for *Thriller.* The song was actually written by 'Human Nature' writer Steve Porcaro and his writing partner Michael Sherwood for *Dangerous*, and a demo was recorded at Record One in 1990. "Michael recorded it but it wasn't quite finished," Porcaro said.

Another ballad, 'Someone Put Your Hand Out', was also overlooked. Michael wrote the original version, which failed to make *Bad*, and then reworked it with Teddy Riley during the *Dangerous* sessions. After it failed to make the cut once more, the song was completed in April 1992. It was released a month later as an exclusive Pepsi promotional cassette-only single; 500,000 copies were made available by collecting a winning token from certain Pepsi products. "I wrote it originally years ago and Teddy loved it, I loved it, and we made some changes, just changed the verse and I gave him co-writer's credit," Michael said.

In the very final week of production, the team worked feverishly to get the album completed. Swedien estimates that during the last three days of the project, he and Michael slept around four hours. "Michael said, 'We bumped the pumpkin'," Swedien said. The last day of mixing was on October 29, 1991.

At 4am on Halloween, Michael, clad in all black and donning a surgical mask, visited Bernie Grundman's mastering facility in Hollywood to supervise the group of engineers – including Swedien – putting the finishing touches on *Dangerous*. Whenever Michael visited Grundman's mastering studio he would head straight into one of the rooms at the back, which would be made into his own lounge. "Nobody would be allowed to go back there," Grundman said. "For a superstar, I was amazed by how impressed he was by little things. When he first walked into one of our rooms, he would say, 'Wow', and seemed in awe of things."

Sony employees were also present, preparing to hand deliver the master copies of *Dangerous* to eight pressing plants around the world. Given the number of days it took to make the CDs, cassettes and LPs and ship them to stores around the world, Michael had cut it extremely fine for Sony's pre-Thanksgiving release date.

To promote *Dangerous* – which cost a whopping $10 million to record – Michael was about to embark on what was set to be the biggest album launch campaign of his career so far. "Everything was ratcheting up; when *Bad* came out, although it sold phenomenally, it didn't approach the numbers of *Thriller*, and Michael was less than happy," Epic's Senior Vice President of Marketing Dan Beck, who worked heavily on the *Dangerous* campaign, said. "With *Dangerous* the stakes were higher, Michael wanted it to return to the levels of *Thriller*. But that's very difficult, once in a career is pretty amazing."

Michael would give it his best shot.

CHAPTER 10: THE *DANGEROUS* CAMPAIGN

LATE 1991 – EARLY 1993

The hype surrounding the release of *Dangerous* was enormous, perhaps even bigger than *Bad*, which was overshadowed by a media focus on Michael's recently acquired eccentric image and the looming shadow of *Thriller*. Considering the challenges he was up against, Michael came through the *Bad* campaign with flying colours; the accompanying world tour also increased his appeal outside of the United States, and therefore the appetite for the next album. The promotion and marketing campaign for *Dangerous* began early in November, when 30-second album teaser adverts created by director David Lynch aired on television.

On November 14, the 11-minute video for 'Black or White' premiered simultaneously in 27 countries, amidst unprecedented hype. Michael was so determined to get it right that it was still being edited the night before, nearly three months after shooting began. The networks, including Fox, MTV, Black Entertainment Television (BET) and VH1, had little time to review the product before broadcasting it during its prime time slots.

The response was extraordinary, with an estimated audience of 500 million worldwide, the highest ever for a music video. But the video's four-minute ending, in which Michael morphs from a black panther into himself before dancing alone in a back street, created much controversy in the days following the premiere. In these dance scenes, Michael simulates masturbation, zips his pants up, destroys the windows of a car and throws a garbage can through a shop front. The networks were besieged with calls from angry parents, and media all over the world covered the controversy. *Entertainment Weekly* even devoted its cover story to 'Michael Jackson's Video Nightmare'.

Michael chose to cut the four-minute scene from subsequent broadcasts, and issued an apology. John Landis says the controversial ending was Michael's idea. "He wanted it to be even more sexually explicit [than it was]," the director said.

Michael used his bargaining power to convince the networks to refer to him as the King of Pop on screen when premiering the video. By 1989, Michael was perhaps the biggest pop star the world had seen. But while Elvis Presley was dubbed 'The King' and Bruce Springsteen 'The Boss', Michael had no such nickname. He was desperate for his own moniker, so his publicist Bob Jones came up with 'the King of Pop, Rock and Soul'. Both the *New York Post* and the *Chicago Sun-Times* first used the shortened name 'King of Pop' in articles in 1984.

Jones said he had written a speech for his namesake, Quincy, to read when presenting Michael with an award at the Black Radio Exclusive Awards in March 1989, referring to him as the King of Pop, Rock and Soul. But Quincy didn't use the name, and it was left to Elizabeth Taylor to use in another speech at the Soul Train Awards a month later. Taylor said: "Ladies and Gentlemen, the 1989 Heritage Award and Sammy Davis Jr. Award recipient and in my estimation, the true King of Pop, Rock and Soul, Mr Michael Jackson."

Fast forward to late 1991, and the PR offensive to call Michael the King of Pop had truly started. Fox, MTV and BET received memos shortly before its premieres of 'Black or White' directing all on-air personnel to refer to Michael as the King of Pop at least twice a week over the next two weeks. "Michael loved the King of Pop name, just loved it," his manager Sandy Gallin said. "He became obsessed with it. I found myself negotiating with several people about how many times they would mention the name King of Pop on all sorts of platforms. It was of prime importance to Michael."

Once news of the memos leaked to *Rolling Stone* Michael received criticism for 'self-proclaiming' himself as the King of Pop, even though media outlets had used the name before. Regardless, the public took to the name, and its origins soon became irrelevant.

In the days following the 'Black or White' premiere, Michael filmed a two-song performance ('Black or White' and another song from *Dangerous*, 'Will You Be There') inside Santa Monica's Barker Hangar for MTV's 10th Anniversary Special, which was aired later in the month. After filming was completed, producer Joel Gallen only had 24 hours to edit Michael's performance. "Michael came into the edit room and sat with me for all twenty-four hours," Gallen recalls. "There was a moment when he wanted a certain edit, and I said, 'Michael, if we do it that way, your mic will be in your right hand in the first shot and then in your left the next'. And he said, 'But the children will think it's magic'."

Dangerous was released on November 26, 1991, and went to the top of the charts on both sides of the Atlantic. The anticipation was so high that three armed robbers stole pallets containing 30,000 copies of the album from a warehouse at Los Angeles International Airport six days before the release.

The mesmeric album cover is a piece of work which took fine artist and illustrator Mark Ryden six months to complete. It includes images of Michael as a young boy, his friend Macaulay Culkin, his pet chimp Bubbles and one of his inspirations, American showman and businessman P.T. Barnum. But Ryden said Michael was most concerned with his depiction of Bubbles. "He [Michael] commented on my first attempt, 'You made him too wrinkled. He's cuter than that'. Eventually Michael preferred I paint him from life to capture his true inner soul. Bubbles was secretly brought to my studio by limousine at midnight for a one-night painting session and Michael liked how in the new depiction Bubbles's eyes seemed to follow him around the room."

In the space of seven weeks the album would sell a staggering ten million copies worldwide, becoming Michael's fastest-selling album to date. It was a blistering start.

The *Dangerous* campaign continued after the Christmas break when the nine-minute video for 'Remember the Time', filmed in mid-January 1992, was premiered simultaneously on three television networks on February 2. Set in ancient Egypt, the $2 million video features ground-breaking visual effects and appearances by actor Eddie Murphy and NBA star Magic Johnson. The single peaked at number three in the United States and in second spot in the United Kingdom.

A day after the video premiere, Michael held a press conference in New York to announce that he would be hitting the road again to raise funds for charity, despite 'retiring' from touring after the Bad Tour. "The only reason I am going on tour is to raise funds for the newly-formed Heal the World Foundation, an international children's charity that I am spearheading to assist children and the ecology," Michael said. "My goal is to gross $100 million by Christmas 1993." He would also have been aware that sales of *Dangerous* wouldn't reach his desired levels without a tour to promote it. The announcement coincided with a new tour sponsorship deal with Pepsi, estimated to be worth $10 million. Pepsi had also sponsored the Bad Tour.

Armed with huge advances from Sony, Michael filmed four music videos in the space of three months before the start of the Dangerous Tour, which was set to kick off in Munich on June 27. In late March he filmed 'In the Closet' with British supermodel Naomi Campbell in the Salton Sea desert near Palm Springs, California. 'Who Is It' was originally scheduled to be the third single release from the album, but Michael decided on 'In the Closet' when he saw director Herb Ritts's treatment for the video. Campbell described Michael as a 'prankster' and said the two had water pistol and whipped cream fights on set. "We had a lot of fun," she said. "We were like two children."

Three weeks later Michael travelled to Chicago to film a video for the fourth single, 'Jam', with basketball superstar Michael Jordan. The video is set in an abandoned indoor basketball court in a neglected neighbourhood in the Windy City, and footage exists of the pair teaching each other how to dance and play basketball. "They're arguably the best physical performers in each of their areas of performance," director David Kellogg said. "And that was sort of the charm of it, really. How can these two guys that are really great physical performers be so inept at the other's form?

Michael Jackson was not a particularly good basketball player, Michael Jordan wasn't a particularly good dancer."

Next up was 'Who Is It', which was filmed in June, although the video is relatively simple by Michael's standards. Reportedly unhappy with the editing and angry about its early release, Michael withdrew the video almost immediately after it premiered in the United Kingdom, where the single peaked at number ten. At this stage, the single was not released in the United States. On June 25, two days before the start of the Dangerous Tour, Michael arrived in Munich to shoot a video for 'Give In to Me' with Guns 'N' Roses guitarist Slash. Set as an indoor rock concert, Michael said it was filmed in just two hours. "We had no time at all to shoot it," he recalled. "We wanted it to be exciting and fantastical, it's a rock concert and that's how it ends up." The single wasn't released until February 1993.

Before the tour kicked off at Munich's Olympiastadion, the concert equipment was flown from Los Angeles to London on the world's second largest operating aircraft, the Russian cargo Antonov An-124. It included a stage 80 feet wider than the largest in the United States at the time, which was New York's Radio City Music Hall at 190 feet. The equipment was then loaded onto 65 trucks, which hauled it around Europe from venue to venue.

On October 1, after 36 concerts around Europe, the tour arrived in the Romanian capital, Bucharest, where Michael performed in front of 70,000 fans at the national stadium. American cable network HBO paid a record $20 million to film and televise the show live. The concert received the highest TV ratings in the history of HBO, and was also broadcast live on radio and shown on television across 61 countries.

The next day Michael flew to Istanbul, where he was set to play another show. But due to a vocal cord ailment he had to cancel it, plus the two remaining dates of the European leg in Izmir and Athens. Michael flew to London to see a specialist, and although no serious damage was done, he had to rest for several weeks before the beginning of the short second leg in December, which consisted of eights concerts at the Tokyo Dome in Japan.

December also saw the release of 'Heal the World' as a single; it was the biggest hit from *Dangerous* in the United Kingdom, staying in the number two position for five weeks. After Michael played the Tokyo concerts, the Dangerous Tour took a long break.

When Michael returned home in early January 1993, he celebrated his first ever Christmas at Neverland with best friend Elizabeth Taylor and her husband Larry Fortensky. It wouldn't be long before he was back at work. In mid-January a member of Michael's law team, Bert Fields, announced in a press conference that his client was going to be more 'receptive' than ever before. "He was reclusive before, but the nineties demand more reality and accessibility," Fields said.

Michael's manager, Sandy Gallin, felt Michael needed to reconnect with the American public. "I knew that we had to do something drastic and show Michael as a living human being, because his image was just so bizarre," Gallin said. "I came up with a plan, and when I presented it to Michael, he thought I was insane. He said, 'No way, you're crazy, you're trying to make me the boy next door.' And I said, 'Michael, I could work with you for a thousand years and I could never make you the all American boy next door. I just want people to know that you're human and that you don't walk around with a snake around your neck'. People thought he couldn't talk, that he couldn't carry a conversation, and that he was from Mars."

Gallin's strategy was to place Michael in front of the largest television audiences possible. This began with a performance at President Clinton's Inaugural Gala in Washington D.C. on January 19, and was followed by the American Music Awards at the Shrine Auditorium a week later. But the most high profile performance was made on January 31, when Michael sang a medley of songs at the Super Bowl XXVII halftime show at the Rose Bowl in Pasadena, Los Angeles. Although smaller acts had performed on the halftime show for decades, in the early nineties executives decided to up the game and recruit the biggest acts in the world, starting with Michael. The 1993 Super Bowl was the first in history where audience figures actually increased during the halftime show, and it became the most watched American television broadcast ever.

Michael's time in the public eye continued when he gave a rare interview to chat show queen Oprah Winfrey on February 10 at Neverland. After at least six years of whispers and rumours that Michael was deliberately changing the colour of his skin by 'bleaching' it with creams so he was no longer black, he revealed to Oprah that he was suffering from vitiligo. Michael denied to Oprah that he was bleaching his skin, but when police searched his rented Los Angeles home after his death, they found dozens of tubes of skin whitening cream.

The creams are medically prescribed to treat vitiligo by permanently removing colour from normal skin located around the skin with vitiligo, explaining how Michael's entire body became pale. His dermatologist Arnold Klein confirmed that this was the only way of dealing with the issue, as using make-up to even out the darker parts was ultimately unsustainable. "His [vitiligo] became so severe, that the easier way is to use certain creams that will make the dark spots turn light so you can even out the pigments totally," he said. "That's ultimately what the decision had to be, because there was too much vitiligo to deal with."

The Oprah show, which was telecast live around the world to an estimated 90 million viewers, was a monumental success for Michael. Along with the Super Bowl show, it helped *Dangerous* rise back up the *Billboard* 200 chart to number ten, over a year after its initial release. Geoff Mayfield, who managed the *Billboard* chart, said he couldn't remember such resurgence at the end of an album's life, and the *Los Angeles Times* described the shock media blitz as 'the sudden coming-out of Michael Jackson' in the United States. Sandy Gallin's plan to 'humanise' Michael had worked. "It made him much more accessible, and made him appear more like a real person," Gallin said. "Michael was thrilled with the results. I knew I would have been fired immediately if it didn't work."

Michael wasn't finished there; two weeks after the Oprah show he attended the 35th Annual Grammy Awards at the Shrine Auditorium. Michael had nominations in three categories for 'Black or White' and 'Jam', and although he came away with no wins, his sister Janet did present him with the Grammy Legend Award. Michael gave a lengthy speech lasting more than six minutes, which was well received by the audience. "In the past month I've gone from, 'Where is he'? to 'Here he is again'," Michael joked, bringing laughs from the crowd. "But I must confess it feels good to be thought of as a person, not as a personality."

In February, 'Give In to Me' was released in Europe, reaching number two on the United Kingdom chart. In the United States Sony released 'Who Is It' instead, due to phenomenal demand after Michael's beatbox performance of the song during the Oprah interview, although it could only peak at 14 on the *Billboard* 100. At this point, Sony wrapped up its marketing campaign for *Dangerous*. "We all breathed a big sigh of relief when it was over," former Epic marketing executive Dan Beck said. "Michael had done the Oprah interview, the Super Bowl, and the Grammys, and we felt that through *Dangerous* we had accomplished a great deal with Michael from an image stand point."

Everything would change only five months later.

CHAPTER 11: TURMOIL

MID – LATE 1993

The summer of 1993 saw Michael take on several projects. After a theme tune and music video by rapper MC Hammer proved a good promotional tool for the 1991 *Addams Family* movie, Paramount Pictures coaxed Michael into creating a horror-themed song and short-film to support the sequel, *Addams Family Values*. He teamed up with legendary horror author Stephen King to write a script for the short-film, which was given the title *Is This Scary*.

When writing the script, Michael told King he wanted the storyline to reflect how he felt the media had 'monsterised' him in recent years. Michael plays the role of a maestro with supernatural powers, who lives alone in a creepy-looking mansion at the top of a hill overlooking the town of 'Normal Valley'. After residents of 'Normal Valley' find out the maestro has been entertaining some local children by showing them his scary supernatural tricks, they storm the mansion carrying torches and bearing signs demanding that the 'freak' leave town. The maestro then performs some of his tricks in front of the parents, much to the delight of the children.

King recommended filmmaker and screenwriter Mick Garris, best known for his screen adaptations of King's stories, to direct *Is This Scary*. After completing the script, Michael began preproduction work with Garris and the Academy Award-winning special make-up effects creator Stan Winston. "Michael had become enamoured with scary things ever since doing 'Thriller' with John Landis," Garris said. "His goal was to top that and make this the biggest and scariest music film ever. Stephen and Michael worked together on the script and this phrase from it, 'Is This Scary', became the title. It was going to be a 12-minute music video with a song in the middle, and the story around it. But it directly related to the *Addams Family Values* movie, and we shot scenes with members of the cast, including Christina Ricci and Jimmy Workman. Michael wanted it to be really special and unique, and, as he liked to say, 'to do the best thing and the most amazing thing possible'."

Shooting took place at CBS Studio Center in Los Angeles, with a budget of around $5 million. For the song, which was set to be released as a single ahead of the movie's November 1993 release and played during the end credits, Michael worked with *Dangerous* producer Teddy Riley at Larrabee studio in Los Angeles. "The song was also titled 'Is This Scary'," Garris said. "It was going to play in the middle of the short-film, with extended instrumental parts surrounding it for the dance stuff. Michael told me about this dancing called popping [a street dance], and he really wanted this to be the first video where people see it. Michael and his producer [Riley] worked on the music, and he would bring that to the set, but nothing was finished, it was just basic rhythm tracks. Michael rehearsed all the dance routines and the extended musical portion, but we never filmed them or got the point of Michael actually singing."

Is This Scary wasn't the only film related project Michael worked on that summer. Following the collapse of the *MidKnight* venture, he began developing other film ideas with screenwriter, director and producer Rusty Lemorande, who he had known since they worked together on *Captain EO* in 1985. But first, Lemorande explained to Michael that he couldn't just play any role. "I think people didn't understand how to relate to him," Lemorande admitted. "I used to say to him, 'You're a little like Arnold Schwarzenegger. You can't do any part. The part has to be tailored to you. He became a star because of *Terminator*.' Michael said, 'Well, you come up with some ideas.' And I came up with two fairly quickly."

One idea was to remake the 1964 film *7 Faces of Dr. Lao*, and the other was a remake of the 1938 gangster film *Angels with Dirty Faces*, which starred James Cagney. "Michael was a huge James Cagney fan," Lemorande said.

"Michael loved both projects. Part of it was the way I explained it to him, talked him through it. One [*Angels with Dirty Faces*] was set up at Warners [studio]. And the other [*7 Faces of Dr. Lao*] was set up at Turner – who owned the remake rights. And everything was going great. Fantastic."

Sandy Gallin also met with director Stanley Donen, whose most notable works include *Singin' in the Rain* and *On the Town*, to discuss a role for Michael in a movie musical adaptation of Robert Louis Stevenson's novel *The Strange Case of Dr Jekyll and Mr Hyde.*

The lead role in a film adaptation of English composer Andrew Lloyd Webber's 1986 musical *The Phantom of the Opera* was another Gallin tried to secure for Michael. Warner Bros. purchased the film rights to the musical in 1989. The plot centres on a beautiful soprano who becomes the obsession of The Phantom, a mysterious musical genius who wears a mask on one side of his face to cover a disfigurement. Webber believes Michael felt a connection to the 'lonely, tortured musician'. "That was the only role I thought he could play," Gallin admitted. "I met with Andrew, who thought Michael should audition for the role in London. Michael had lots of ideas about how to do the dance numbers. But I don't think Andrew was really interested in Michael for the role." Various factors, including Webber's divorce, meant the production was postponed until 2004 regardless. Gerard Butler was cast in the lead role.

As if Michael wasn't busy enough, he was also signed up to compose music for a Sega Genesis video game, *Sonic the Hedgehog 3*. Furthermore, he was due to begin work on a handful of new songs for his next album, a greatest hits package which was scheduled for a November 1993 release. It was Sony's idea to release the collection – according to Dan Beck, it was the fastest way to generate more revenue from the Michael Jackson brand. "The discussions for bringing out a greatest hits album went way back into 1992, 1991 even," the former Epic marketing executive said. "Dave Glew [Epic Records Chairman] raised the idea, the senior management wanted to keep the release cycle happening. The formula for many greatest hits packages was for the artist to record a couple of new songs that could be released as drivers for sales of the album. That was the idea that was presented to Michael at this point."

Then there were the rehearsals for the upcoming third leg of the Dangerous Tour. Michael even cancelled two concerts, scheduled for August 15 and 16 in Hong Kong, so he could concentrate on the numerous projects he was working on. The concerts, which were due to be held at Sha Tin Racecourse, couldn't be rescheduled because of conflicts with the start of the horse racing season. The third leg would instead begin in Bangkok on August 24, but Michael would leave Los Angeles having been unable to complete any of his projects.

Michael's busy schedule that summer became all the more difficult because he was suffering from severe pain. In March, he had surgery to reduce scarring on the scalp injury caused by the Pepsi commercial incident in 1984. He didn't want to wear the small hairpiece any more, and his painful keloids also needed treating. Michael had balloons implanted under his scalp, designed to stretch the skin, and when it reached the proper elasticity the surgeon would cut the scar tissue away, remove the balloons and stitch the scalp with the re-grown skin together.

Although pain from such surgery usually lasts no longer than six weeks, it continued to affect Michael into the summer due to his busy work schedule. The wound was supposed to be exposed to air, but Michael continued to wear a hairpiece to cover it for rehearsals and filming. "His schedule was so busy that he never had time to heal from the surgery," Michael's hair/make-up artist Karen Faye said. "His scalp was healing from the operation, but he was getting chronic migraine headaches from this operation. It caused incredible pain." Faye, who was first hired by Michael in 1984, became more than an employee; she was one of Michael's closest confidants.

To relieve his pain Michael was prescribed narcotic medications which are similar to morphine; one was Percocet, which he used when the incident originally happened in 1984, and another was Demerol. Following the surgery, Michael's pain management plan was placed in the hands of two of his long-time doctors – plastic surgeon Dr Steven Hoefflin and dermatologist Dr Arnold Klein.

Dr Klein's then assistant Debbie Rowe said the two doctors, who did not get along, took advantage of Michael's low pain threshold by competing with each other in an attempt to prescribe the better drug. Rowe described it as 'a pissing contest', and believes they saw treating Michael as a method to generate money. "Michael respected doctors immensely, that they went to school, that they studied and to do no harm," she said. "Unfortunately, some of the doctors decided that when Michael was in pain they would try to outbid each other on who could give him the better drug and so he listened to those doctors." Yet Dr Hoefflin firmly denies ever overprescribing drugs to Michael, and says he only administered narcotics in a hospital setting.

Rowe said one of the doctors even prescribed Dilaudid – which is about eight to ten times more potent than morphine and about three to five times more potent than heroin on a per milligram basis. When Rowe saw it in Michael's possession, she immediately took it from him.

On behalf of Dr Klein, Rowe often took medication directly to Michael at his condo in Century City, where he was staying during the summer of 1993 in order to work on his projects and tour rehearsals. By early August she became concerned about his continued use of the narcotic medications, and explained the dilemma to his primary physician Dr Allan Metzger, without her boss's knowledge. Rowe was concerned Michael would still be using the narcotics by the time he departed for Bangkok at the end of the month to begin the tour.

As a result, Dr Metzger, who Rowe believes is the only doctor that had Michael's best medical interest at heart, designed a programme to change his medication from narcotics to non-narcotics, which are not habit forming. But when Michael left Los Angeles on August 21, the programme hadn't been fully completed. Despite Dr Metzger and Rowe's best efforts, Michael's treating doctors continued to administer narcotics to Michael when he asked for them on tour, eradicating any progress that had been made. One of the tour physicians said stress only increased Michael's urge for these medications. This stress was caused by certain allegations that would change his life forever.

THE ALLEGATION

On August 23, the day before Michael's first Bangkok concert, news broke around the world that a criminal investigation of him had begun. Rumours spread that the subject was of child molestation, although the media could not officially confirm it.

On the day of the concert, Michael's private investigator Anthony Pellicano held a press conference to confirm that Michael had been accused of molestation, and that these allegations were the result of a failed $20 million dollar extortion attempt. It would soon be revealed that the child was a thirteen-year-old boy named Jordan Chandler, whom Michael had met in May 1992.

Michael befriended Jordan and his mother, June, who became regular guests at Neverland and also joined him on vacations around the world. Jordan's father, Evan Chandler, a Beverly Hills dentist who was divorced from June, became jealous of the friendship and claimed Michael was breaking up the family.

In June 1993 Chandler confronted his ex-wife, who had custody of Jordan, with suspicions that their son had been in a sexual relationship with Michael, but the mother dismissed his worries. Instead of going to the police, Chandler hired an attorney and threatened to go public with the evidence he claimed he had against Michael. When Michael was told of the plan, his attorney Bert Fields hired Anthony Pellicano to deal with the situation.

In early July, at a stage when Jordan hadn't even accused Michael of wrongdoing, his stepfather secretly taped a phone conversation with Chandler, who admitted he was getting ready to execute a master plan which was going to 'destroy' Michael if he didn't get what he wanted. On the tape, Chandler was recorded as saying: "If I go through with this, I win big time. There's no way I lose. I've checked that inside out. I will get everything I want, and they will be destroyed forever. They will be destroyed. June will lose [custody of Jordan] and Michael's career will be over. It will be a massacre if I don't get what I want." Only days after the conversation, Jordan's mother and stepfather played the tape to

Pellicano. "After listening to the tape for ten minutes, I knew it was about extortion," the investigator said.

After a meeting in early August, Chandler's attorney Barry Rothman presented Pellicano with a demand for $20 million to not take the allegations further. The problem for Chandler was the fact his son still hadn't accused Michael of anything. That changed when Chandler took the boy to a dental anaesthesiologist, where he was administered the controversial sedative sodium amytal. A 1952 study showed that the drug can implant false memories. Chandler would say that he used the drug to sedate his son during a dental procedure, although the drug is rarely used for that purpose and has only been approved for anxiety, insomnia and epilepsy. It was under the influence of sodium amytal that Jordan came out with the allegation that Michael had molested him.

In mid-August Chandler took his son to a psychiatrist, and during the three-hour session the boy repeated his assertion. Under law the psychiatrist was required to report the allegations to a social worker, who then informed the police.

On August 18, Michael was told by his attorneys that a criminal investigation of him had begun. In response, they filed extortion charges against Chandler and his attorney. Michael was due to fly to Bangkok three days later for the tour, but he no longer felt like hitting the road. Bert Fields, fearing Michael would be arrested, called Sandy Gallin and told him they needed to get Michael out of the country as soon as possible. "Bert told me that if they didn't get him out of the country, Michael would be arrested," Gallin recalls. "And then whole tour would have been cancelled at a huge financial loss. Michael was in bad financial shape [he already had debts of $30 million by 1993]. He was pouring money into Neverland, he would go on shopping sprees, and he would cancel video shoots. He was also extremely generous to his young friends. Michael did not want to go on the tour, but somehow, Anthony Pellicano got him on the plane. How, I don't know. He went to his apartment in Century City; he may have drugged him, tied him up, or talked him into going quietly. I don't think Michael understood that if he didn't do this tour, he had a chance of losing Neverland."

On August 21, the day Michael arrived in Bangkok, Neverland was searched by police officers, before the allegations became public knowledge two days later. After his first concert on August 24, Michael received a continuous 24-hour drip of morphine. He cancelled the next two Bangkok concerts, scheduled to take place on August 25 and 26, before going back on stage on August 27. The official reason for the cancellations was given as dehydration due to performing in hot weather, but one of the tour doctors said the use of narcotic medication was also a factor in the decision. On August 30, Michael cancelled another show in Singapore. According to Karen Faye, Michael appeared to be dazed from his medication and stumbled into his dressing room just before the concert was due to start, falling over a potted tree. The reason given for the cancellation this time was a collapse due to a severe migraine.

In mid-September Evan Chandler filed a $30 million civil lawsuit against Michael, alleging sexual battery, seduction, wilful misconduct, emotional distress, fraud and negligence. By October the criminal investigation involved over a dozen detectives from both Santa Barbara (location of Neverland) and Los Angeles counties. Convinced of his innocence, Pellicano and Bert Fields began collecting evidence to be used at the civil trial, which was scheduled for March 21, 1994. "They had a very weak case, we wanted to fight," Fields said. "Michael wanted to fight and go through a trial. We felt we could win." By now the boy's mother had also switched sides, fearing she might be charged with parental neglect for allowing the friendship between Michael and Jordan in the first place. With the criminal investigation ongoing, Fields, primarily an entertainment attorney, hired criminal-defence attorney Howard Weitzman.

'STRANGER IN MOSCOW'

The latest single from the *Dangerous* album, 'Will You Be There', was making its way up the charts when the allegations became public, and peaked at seven on the *Billboard* 100 in early September. At the very end of the song, Michael performs a spoken part which includes the words; 'In Our Darkest Hour/In My Deepest Despair/Will You Still Care/Will You Be There/In My Trials/And My Tribulations', which seemed poignantly appropriate at this time in his life.

In September, news reports also confirmed that Michael's *Addams Family Values* project, *Is This Scary*, had been shelved. Production stopped when Michael went to Thailand for the tour. Director Mick Garris recalls: "We had been shooting for two weeks, and the next day it was like, 'Where's Michael'? He was out of the country." Garris said Paramount Pictures pulled the plug on the project as soon as the allegations surfaced. It was somewhat ironic that the storyline – written before the scandal – was mainly based around parents demanding that Michael's character stop scaring their children.

After Paramount pulled out, Michael decided to take on the project himself; he had spent a huge amount of money on the film, as the studio would have paid for it on delivery. After concerts in Bangkok, Singapore and Taiwan Michael performed in Japan, where he had the *Is This Scary* set shipped so he could finish it. "After Paramount backed out over the legal issues Michael thought, 'Ok this is mine now'," Garris said. "Even after shooting stopped, I would get calls from Michael all the time. He would say, 'You've gotta believe we're gonna finish it and it's gonna be amazing'."

After the set was shipped to Japan, the budget had ballooned to around $7 million. "I was never paid for any of my work, but that's ok because I was most concerned about Michael," Garris said. "Some of the crew, including producer Peter McIntosh, went to Japan with the set. I think Peter was there for a week, and others for two, but because it was on Michael time it was very difficult to arrange a schedule. Later on Michael brought me to Mexico City, where he was performing, to talk about it. He would still say, 'Mick you've gotta believe it's gonna be fantastic'. He never let his enthusiasm flag."

After Japan the next tour stop was Moscow, where Michael arrived on September 12. News of his arrival sparked scenes of near-hysteria among young Russians, who embraced him as a symbol of all things American. The Soviet Union had fallen only two years earlier; until then it had been illegal simply to purchase Michael's music. But Michael was a man who liked to make history.

Michael and Brad Buxer at the piano

While on tour, Michael was writing music with Brad Buxer, who had taken over from Greg Phillinganes as the tour's musical director for the third leg. The pair often worked on material in their hotel rooms. "I always had musical gear in my hotel room so I could work on ideas both for and with Michael," Buxer said. "The gear was called a 'Hotel Room System', studio gear that the crew would set up in my hotel room so I could work on stuff with Michael." One of the songs the pair worked on while in the Russian capital became a song called 'Stranger in Moscow'.

The idea for the song came about when Michael called Buxer to his room in the Presidential Suite at the city's Hotel Metropol at 10.30am one morning. "I had a cassette player with me of the *Sonic the Hedgehog 3* cues that I had been working on for him and Sega, I thought he called to see me so he could hear how the cues were coming on for the Sega game," Buxer said. "Instead, he said, 'I want you to sit at the piano and just play'. There was an upright piano in the room and I just started playing stuff, and one of the things I played was one of the cues I had done for the Sega game. He loved it and this became the verse for 'Stranger in Moscow'."

Buxer then moved on to other chords, which became the chorus, and in an hour and a half, 'Stranger in Moscow' was born. "When I left the room it was noon time and I remember standing underneath the doorway saying goodbye to him – it was so obvious that we had just written a beautiful song together that I said nothing," Buxer said. "I almost said, 'Did we just write a song together'?"

The lyrics came to Michael on the day of his show at Moscow's Luzhniki Stadium. The night before, he received the news that his accuser's father had officially filed a $30 million civil lawsuit against him. Michael said the idea fell into his lap because of the emotions he was feeling. "The lyrics are totally autobiographical," he said. "When you hear lines like, 'Here abandoned in my fame…Armageddon of the brain' – at the time that's how I really felt. It kinda created itself."

As for the Sega project, although Michael's tracks feature in the *Sonic 3* game, including the chords for what became 'Stranger in Moscow', there is no mention of his name in the credits. "It's because he was not happy with the sound coming out of the console," Buxer explained. "At the time, game consoles did not allow an optimal sound reproduction, and Michael found it frustrating. He did not want to be associated with a product that devalued his music." Those who collaborated with Michael on the project, including Buxer, Bobby Brooks, Doug Grigsby, Darryl Ross, Geoff Grace and Cirocco Jones, are all credited. However many observers believe Sega made the decision to drop Michael's name from the project in the wake of the allegations.

DANGEROUS COMES TO AN END

During the remainder of September Michael performed shows in Tel Aviv, Istanbul and Tenerife. In October he had eight scheduled dates in South America, where he cancelled one concert in Chile and another in Peru, reportedly due to back problems. Neither concert was rescheduled. Michael was still taking strong narcotic medication to deal with his scalp pain and the stress from the allegations.

Michael's next stop was Mexico City, where he again had to reschedule three concerts, this time due to a severe tooth problem. On November 8 and November 10, while in Mexico, Michael was further stressed when an attorney spent seven hours taking a deposition from him for a copyright infringement case, which he later won.

By now Michael's use of narcotic medications, mainly Demerol, had intensified. Debbie Rowe, who visited Michael in Mexico City, described him as 'a hot mess' when she first saw him. "He was depressed," she recalls. "He had taken something. I don't know what he had taken or who he had got it from. He wasn't making eye contact, he wasn't speaking, he didn't make sense when he did, and he said he was having problems with his scalp again." Rowe said Michael was uncharacteristically unkempt, and his five room suite on the 42nd floor of Mexico City's Hotel Presidente was 'a complete mess'.

After a three-day argument with Michael, Rowe said she convinced him to end his tour early and enter a drug rehabilitation programme. Rowe said one of the issues was the fact the next tour date was in Puerto Rico, which is an unincorporated territory of the United States. "You cannot go to Puerto Rico," she told Michael. "It's like being in the United States, and you can't go looking and acting like this. You need to straighten up, you need to face whatever it is that's going on, and we'll get through it. You can't just do this." Rowe said Michael "knew he had screwed up."

Michael's manager, Sandy Gallin, remembers receiving a call from one of the tour doctors. "The doctor said to me, 'Sandy, Michael is in a huge amount of trouble, and if somebody doesn't get him into rehab, either he'll kill himself, or the drugs will kill him. Somebody has to get Michael off the road and into a hospital'."

On Thursday, November 11, Michael performed the last of his five concerts at Mexico City's Estadio Azteca. Instead of returning to his hotel suite that night to rest ahead of travelling to Puerto Rico for the next show, Michael was whisked away on a private jet by close friend Elizabeth Taylor and her husband Larry Fortensky. Taylor had been called in to perform the intervention by Sandy Gallin and Howard Weitzman. After Michael left the Hotel Presidente, staff entered his suite and discovered carpets stained with vomit and chewing gum, dented walls scrawled with 'I Love You' messages and trash all over the floor.

Late that night, Michael was taken to London via brief stops in Canada and Iceland. After landing at Luton on the Saturday morning, he was driven to the Charter Nightingale rehabilitation facility in Chelsea to be treated by a specialist recommended by Elton John, Dr Beauchamp Colclough.

Dr Colclough said that when he first met Michael, he was intimidated by the circle of people surrounding him. "It was an entire organisation," he said. "But once I'd got past them and met Michael himself, it was fine. In the end, he was just a person to me. He responded to me wonderfully. We were together for about 31 days and we just went through a whole process together. It worked out all right."

Dr Colclough even took Michael to a Kentucky Fried Chicken restaurant in London's Shepherd's Bush, as he wanted to do something 'normal'. "Amazingly, nobody noticed because nobody expects to see somebody like him in a place like that," Dr Colclough said. "He really enjoyed it."

The day after the final Mexico City concert, Michael's team released an audiotape statement announcing that he was cancelling the rest of the tour to seek treatment for a prescription drug dependency. Michael said it was triggered by the scalp surgery and worsened by the stress of the allegations.

In the statement, Michael said: "My friends and doctors advised me to seek professional guidance immediately in order to eliminate what has become an addiction. It is time for me to acknowledge my need for treatment in order to regain my health. I realise that completing the tour is no longer possible and I must cancel the remaining dates. I know I can overcome the problem and will be stronger from the experience.

"As I left on this tour, I had been the target of an extortion attempt, and shortly thereafter was accused of horrifying and outrageous conduct. I was humiliated, embarrassed, hurt and suffering great pain in my heart. The pressure resulting from these false allegations coupled with the incredible energy necessary for me to perform caused so much distress that it left me physically and emotionally exhausted. I became increasingly more dependent on the painkillers to get me through the days of the tour."

Four days later, Bert Fields told the media that Michael 'was barely able to function adequately on an intellectual level'. Fields later said it was important to tell the truth. "The press took the position that Michael was trying to hide and that it was all a scam," he said. "But it wasn't."

The decision was made much easier because the next concert was on American soil. If he entered Puerto Rico at this time, there was a chance he could have been arrested because of the allegations. Concerts in Venezuela, Monterrey (Mexico), Australia, Malaysia and India, where the tour was due to finish in December 1993, were also cancelled. The numerous cancellations over the course of the tour would cost Michael untold millions.

Karen Faye was surprised Michael even managed to continue performing for nearly three months after the allegations surfaced. "Michael had to go on stage every night knowing that the whole world thought he was a paedophile," she said. "He had to stand up in front of all these audiences with the physical pain that he had and knowing that everybody in that audience is thinking that he was the vilest paedophile on earth. To this day I don't know how he did that."

Shortly after Michael cancelled the tour, Pepsi announced it was severing its ties with him, although the company minimised the significance of the decision. "All we're saying is that if the tour is over, as we understand from media reports, then that would end our sponsorship agreement because that would mean there's nothing to sponsor," a spokesman said.

Michael's greatest hits album, due to be released before Christmas, was postponed following the allegations, and a new release date of June 1994 was set. "Initially the allegations put everything on hold, we [the record company] had not had a lot of contact with Michael since we stopped the marketing for *Dangerous* in March 1993," Dan Beck said. "Then Michael was away on tour, and the next thing we knew these allegations arose. And although many people thought we knew something, we were really out of the loop as record companies don't speak to their artists every minute of the day. It was a sad time for many of us."

In December, the ninth and final single from *Dangerous*, 'Gone Too Soon', was released, but could only reach number 33 on the United Kingdom chart. A tenth single, 'Dangerous', was scheduled for release in January 1994, but was cancelled due to the molestation scandal and the disappointing performance of 'Gone Too Soon'.

Two years after the album's release, the *Dangerous* campaign was now closed. By the end of 1993 the album had sold 20 million copies worldwide, and in the United Kingdom seven of its singles all reached the top ten, a record only broken by British dance artist Calvin Harris 20 years later. Three quarters of sales were made outside the United States, making Michael the most international music star ever. It is estimated that 45 million copies of the album have now been sold worldwide. "It would be hard for anyone to call that album less than a colossal success," Sony Music chief Tommy Mottola said.

After the *Dangerous* campaign Michael was expected to turn his attention to other projects under his comprehensive deal with Sony – including making movies. But the allegations destroyed all of his dreams, including the two film projects he began developing with director Rusty Lemorande. "The truth of the matter is, very simply – and in fairness to Hollywood and the big studios – they have huge investment obligations to their shareholders," Lemorande explained. "So they got very nervous. They didn't know if the audience would still be there for Michael. Suddenly, nobody wanted to touch him."

Sandy Gallin says Michael's appearance was also a hindrance when it came to securing movie roles. "I don't think the studios saw Michael as a leading man in a movie," Gallin admitted. "Part of it was to do with his appearance on stage, the surgery to his face. I think it was something that was not going to be overcome."

Michael wasn't deterred – he even called Joel Schumacher, who was directing 1995's *Batman Forever*, and asked if he could play the Riddler. But Schumacher, whom Michael had known since the director wrote the screenplay adaptation of *The Wiz*, told him there was 'no role' for him.

Ambitious plans to open a series of Michael Jackson theme parks in Asia were also abandoned. The different rides and attractions would have been based on all things Michael, including Neverland, his music and his videos. Business magnate Ong Beng Seng planned to open the first park in his home city-state of Singapore. If successful, the parks would have extended to other countries across Southeast Asia.

THE SETTLEMENT

Shortly before Michael returned to the Unites States from London on December 10, his legal team changed. Disagreements between Bert Fields and Howard Weitzman led to Fields's resignation, and top Los Angeles attorney Johnnie Cochran was brought in. Cochran's close relationship with Los Angeles district attorney Gil Garcetti meant the attorney was able to secure a promise that Michael wouldn't be arrested on his return from London. Investigator Anthony Pellicano also left the defence team, and John Branca, whom Michael fired in 1990, was brought back to work alongside Weitzman and Cochran.

On December 22, live from Neverland, Michael made a four minute statement to the world proclaiming his innocence, before travelling to Las Vegas eight days later to spend the New Year holiday in the desert. By January 1, 1994, $2 million had been spent on the criminal investigation by prosecution departments in California and 200 witnesses had been questioned, but the Chandler family's allegations could not be proven.

In the end, some members of Michael's law team advised him to settle the civil case out of court, due to concerns about the delivery of justice and possible political and racial issues with a jury. Bert Fields, who by now had left the case, said he was 'very strongly' of the opinion that Michael should not settle. He believes it was Michael's close friend, Elizabeth Taylor, who tipped the balance in favour of a settlement. "I was convinced that Michael was innocent, and I had the opportunity to observe him as a father," Fields said. "I thought that paying a substantial amount of money would forever tarnish his reputation, and injure him professionally. But he was listening to Elizabeth Taylor, and I suspect that she had the attitude where she told him, 'Michael you've got all the money in the world, why do you need a trial.' He had a very good lawyer in Johnnie Cochran, who was convinced he would have won an acquittal. It's very tough to lose a case in which you are innocent."

When Michael chose to settle the civil suit out of court, his team dropped the extortion charges against Evan Chandler. Cochran began negotiating with Chandler's representatives, and on January 25, Michael signed the settlement papers at the Mirage Hotel in Las Vegas, where he was staying. The settlement totalled over $20 million, with $15.3 million going to the boy and $1.5 million apiece to his parents. The family attorney received over $3 million in fees.

Michael said the uncertainty over the guarantee of justice swayed his decision. "I talked to my lawyers and I said, 'Can you guarantee me that justice will prevail?' And they said, 'Michael we cannot guarantee you that a judge or a jury will do anything'. And with that I was catatonic, I was outraged, totally outraged. So I said I have got to do something to get out from under this nightmare. All these lies and all these people coming forth to get paid and all these tabloid shows, just lies, lies, lies. So we got together again with my advisors and they advised me. It was hands down, a unanimous decision – resolve the case. This could be something that could go on for seven years."

Tom Mesereau, Michael's future defence attorney, described the settlement as 'the worst decision' he ever made, as many would view it as an admission of guilt. But Michael only actually settled the civil suit, and contrary to reports insisting the settlement halted criminal proceedings, the boy was not prevented from testifying if the case was tried in a criminal court. Los Angeles district attorney Gil Garcetti confirmed the settlement would not affect the criminal prosecution of the allegations. "The criminal investigation of singer Michael Jackson is on-going and will not be affected by the announcement of the civil case settlement," Mr Garcetti said. Despite this, the boy refused to testify even though the settlement did not prevent him from doing so. "Remember, this case was always about money, and Evan Chandler wound up getting what he wanted," Anthony Pellicano later said.

The Santa Barbara County investigation would continue until May 1994, when a grand jury disbanded without indicting Michael, while a Los Angeles County grand jury too closed its case four months later. After the questioning of 200 people, including 30 children, not a single valid witness could be found, and the search warrants executed at Michael's properties didn't result in any findings that could support a criminal filing.

In the end the sole allegation would come from one boy, questioned by his father Evan – who committed suicide in November 2009 – while under the influence of a controversial sedative after Michael refused to make a $20 million payment.

Michael knew it would be difficult for his career to recover from such image shattering allegations, but it was a challenge he would not shirk.

CHAPTER 12: MAKING *HISTORY*

EARLY 1994 – MID 1995

While the civil suit was being settled out of court, Michael's team of producers and engineers spent a week in mid-January 1994 preparing the Record One studio in Sherman Oaks, so work on new material for the delayed greatest hits package could resume. The situation changed when the Northridge Earthquake struck in Reseda, Los Angeles, on January 17. The epicentre was only nine miles away from the studio, which seemed to alarm Michael. "I was terrified – almost out of my brains, I thought the world was ending," he said.

Michael chose to move production to the other side of the country, to New York City. "We were reviewing tapes for the greatest hits that would be on the album and then, when the earthquake happened, Michael wanted out of town," Matt Forger recalls. His production team, including Forger, Bruce Swedien and Brad Buxer, all relocated and began setting up for preproduction at the Hit Factory studio on West 54th Street in central Manhattan around two weeks after the earthquake. At the time, Swedien described the studio as 'the best in the world'.

"Bruce and his wife Bea were older and found the idea of moving to New York very attractive," Forger said. "Brad Sundberg and I had more difficulties, we both had families, so we took turns to work two-week shifts in New York, while the other would stay in Los Angeles. Whoever was in California would act as the Los Angeles consultant if the team needed tapes or equipment sent over. Brad did the first two-week shift."

Working at the Hit Factory at the time was a young staff assistant named Rob Hoffman, who became a freelance engineer after Swedien and co arrived. Hoffman was soon in the thick of the action. "The idea was to work on anything between one and four new songs for a greatest hits package," he said. "Bruce occupied Studio 4, the big mix room, and another room was a writing room where Bruce and his writing partner Rene Moore began writing and churning out song ideas for Michael. One of those songs became '2 Bad'. Bruce and Rene had put a lot of track ideas together by the time Michael later arrived in New York."

Michael wouldn't join the team until March. "Maybe he was waiting for the weather to warm up so he could avoid the cold weather," Forger said. In the meantime, Michael was communicating with Brad Buxer from the west over the phone. Buxer flew to New York a few weeks before Michael, so he could start working on 'Stranger in Moscow' with engineer Eddie Delena. "Eddie was the engineer who I brought to the project and who was in the studio working with me, and all I was working on this entire time was 'Stranger in Moscow'," Buxer said. Before arriving in New York, Buxer recorded Michael beatboxing in the dance studio at Neverland. Buxer then made drum sounds out of the beatbox samples, which were used for the song's intro, and completed the piano, string and drum elements before Michael arrived on the East Coast.

Not long after arriving in New York, Michael booked into a 12-room duplex apartment near the top of Trump Tower in midtown Manhattan, a short drive a mile from the Hit Factory. "Michael's apartment at Trump was over the top, with dramatic views and gold fixtures in the bathrooms," friend Frank Cascio recalls. "On the second floor there were three bedrooms. He transformed one of them into a mini dance studio by having all the furniture removed and putting in a dance floor." Frank is the son of Dominic Cascio, who was the manager of New York's Helmsley Palace Hotel when Michael stayed there in February 1984. From that point Michael became close to the Cascios and always considered them to be a second family.

Initially, Michael worked mostly with Brad Buxer at the newly built Sony Music Studios while the others remained at the Hit Factory. The two studios were a matter of feet apart on West 54th Street. "There was a lot of political rambling, so Michael did most of his early work over at Sony with Brad," Rob Hoffman said. "It was to appease Sony, so they could keep an eye on things."

Although the idea was to record just a handful of new songs, this didn't play on Michael's mind; he just started working. The last time he entered a studio to record some new tracks for a greatest hits collection, he was so prolific he came up with the *Dangerous* album. "At this stage, we weren't thinking one way or another about what the overall concept of the album should be," Buxer said. "We simply began working on songs – many songs, it was far more important for Michael just to work on new songs. The material was what was important, not so much a pre-conceived idea of what the album concept was going to be."

'Stranger in Moscow' was the first song Michael and Buxer worked on. "When Michael finally came out to New York and heard my work on 'Stranger in Moscow', the strings, piano, drums and the beatboxing samples that make up the rhythmic backbone of the track, he literally shrieked with joy," Buxer recalls. Although Buxer is the co-writer of 'Stranger in Moscow', as he created the music, Michael would not credit him. "That song, more than anything I've ever done with him, was a true collaboration to say the least," Buxer revealed. "It is absolutely my most important contribution to him." But Buxer doesn't hold a grudge. "Of course I'm disappointed that I didn't receive a songwriting credit on it," he admitted. "But Michael chose not to credit me; there is nothing I can do about it."

Before long, the pair left the Sony studio and joined the others over at the Hit Factory, as Michael wasn't enthused by the idea of being constantly pressured and observed by the record label bosses. Hit Factory's Studio 3, on the first floor, is where Michael recorded most of his vocals. When he sang his scratch vocals, he usually wanted the room empty. "Vocals were mostly recorded by Brad Buxer and Eddie Delena," Rob Hoffman said. "When Michael left the studio, Andrew Scheps [another engineer] and myself would help and assist Brad. A lot of the time, we would stay up all night working. Eventually Bruce [Swedien] would get whatever we were working on so he could change things and mix."

Having Swedien on the team always made things easier for everybody. "One great thing about Michael's sessions was that Bruce would mix as he went," orchestrator Geoff Grace, who was flown to New York to work on the album on two occasions, said. "This would make things sound good all the way through. So when the musicians came in to do their parts, instead of hearing skeletal demos or whatever, they would hear close to the real thing. The musicians would hear a more inspiring version."

MICHAEL OVER-RECORDS...AGAIN

Soon after starting work on 'Stranger in Moscow' Michael resurrected 'They Don't Care About Us', a protest song from the *Dangerous* sessions. Michael liked some of the unfinished songs from those sessions and wanted to complete them. "Although the idea for this song existed from the earlier sessions, I think Michael and Matt Forger started on the song again from scratch," Rob Hoffman said.

Hoffman may have joined the team as an engineer, but he soon found himself playing instruments. Michael liked the song 'Owner of a Lonely Heart' by Yes, so when the rock band came to New York, guitarist Trevor Rabin was invited to the studio to play on 'They Don't Care About Us'. "We had many programmers and guitarists come in and play the main bridge guitar riff, including Trevor, Slash and Jeff Bova," Hoffman said. "After Trevor and Slash played their parts, someone came in and said they played the wrong notes on the riff, so they got me to replay it. I prayed they would keep my take, and they did. That was my first ever guitar credit, on a Michael Jackson record!"

Over the course of the late spring and summer, Michael began working on more and more songs. These included five completely new songs: 'Money', 'Innocent Man', '2 Bad', 'D.S.' and 'Morphine'. This newly written material was inspired by Michael's recent troubles, much like 'Stranger in Moscow'. He also decided to resurrect two songs he began writing over ten years earlier, 'Little Susie' and 'Much Too Soon'.

'Money' is most probably an attack on the Chandler family, which Michael accused of extortion after the molestation allegations. The song features American guitarist Nile Rodgers. "That was one of the really fun parts about working with Michael, you could call anyone and get them down there," Rob Hoffman recalls. "We needed a funk guitar player [to play on 'Money'], and some names were being tossed about. I finally said, 'Hey what about Nile Rodgers'. Michael was excited for that because they had toured together in the seventies. Of course Nile played some of the funkiest shit ever, however, Michael had a very specific part in mind for 'Money'."

'Innocent Man', much like 'Stranger in Moscow', captures Michael's mood at the time the allegations were made. It includes haunting lyrics such as, 'Let the whole world be against me long as God knows I'm an innocent man' and 'Sometimes I feel just like a fugitive, I'm running for my life and deep inside I ask the question why, but I'm not running at all I'm just healing a lonely wounded heart, I wish I could fly away'.

'2 Bad' is one of the music-only tracks that Bruce Swedien and Rene Moore wrote for Michael, who added the melody and angry lyrics. Michael offered a surprise rap cameo to basketball star Shaquille O'Neal, who released his debut hip-hop album in October 1993. Michael visited O'Neal at his Florida home to discuss the collaboration, and after the NBA star came on board he recorded his rap verse at a studio in Orlando.

'D.S.' is a thinly disguised attack on Tom Sneddon, the late Santa Barbara County district attorney who led the molestation investigation against Michael. The only concession Michael would make to the Sony attorneys is to allow them to change Tom Sneddon's name to Dom Sheldon, the initials to which became the song's title. Bruce Swedien brought in musician Larry Williams to play a guitar solo on 'D.S.'. "They flew me to New York, and I played my solo, and they then kept me there until Michael heard it and signed it off," Williams recalls. "This took a month. Michael would be out of town or doing some other stuff and I was being paid $2,000 a day just to sit there and wait for Michael to hear the solo!" In the end, a solo by Guns 'N' Roses guitarist Slash was used instead. "I remember Slash coming in," Williams recalls. "Put it this way, there was a lot of Jack Daniels and a lot of cigarettes."

'Morphine' was almost certainly written by Michael in 1993–1994 in relation to his troubles with prescription drugs, mainly Demerol, which is mentioned in the lyrics. Rob Hoffman said the music was inspired by industrial rock band Nine Inch Nails. "Michael was a big fan of the Nine Inch Nails album *Downward Spiral*," Hoffman said. "Obviously I was shocked to learn this, but it was clear that Michael loved the sounds, and 'Morphine' was an example of this."

'Little Susie', a unique song about a neglected and mistreated young girl, had been worked on for previous albums, but was always a bit of an orphan. 'Little Susie' is one of the songs orchestrator Geoff Grace was brought in to work on. "Michael wanted some orchestrations re-done on 'Little Susie', and my version was at least the second time it had been orchestrated," Grace said. "To have orchestrations re-done cost a lot of money, it was almost unheard of. But Michael was not afraid to cut orchestra, despite the costs involved. In the end, he cut my orchestra as well, and replaced the orchestra parts with keyboard." The music box intro was created by Rob Hoffman and fellow engineer Andrew Scheps. "We bought a bunch of music boxes, tore them apart and created a sample set," Hoffman said. "Brad Buxer then played the part in the intro. A little girl [Markita Prescott] was called in to hum the melody of the music box."

'Much Too Soon' was another song Michael decided to resurrect from previous sessions. "It's totally different to the posthumous release," Hoffman said. "Although it was dropped fairly quickly after work began on it, it was simply one of the greatest things I had ever heard."

HAVE YOU SEEN MY CHILDHOOD...

As well as working on his own compositions, Michael wanted to write a song with Grammy-winning singer, producer and composer David Foster, and the Canadian hitmaker answered his call. Foster had previously co-written 'It's the Falling in Love' for *Off the Wall.* Michael wanted to ensure Foster was comfortable, and rented him and his family a five-bedroom suite at the luxury Plaza Hotel by Central Park.

One night Foster's children decided they wanted to take Michael to the movies, and dressed him up in their own clothes to disguise him. "They put a scarf on him, and some jeans, and they tucked his hair under a cap and turned it to the side, gangster-style," Foster recalls. "Michael wasn't wild about hiding the curl, though; he wanted it right out there on his forehead, for the whole world to see. The kids told him he had to hide the curl because it was a dead giveaway, but he was adamant. 'No, no, I've got to have my curl out,' he said. I thought that was very telling. He didn't want to be seen, but he kind of wanted to be seen – which I guess is often the issue if you're famous. Then they argued about what movie to see. My kids voted for *Speed*; Michael was more interested in *Little Big League*."

The engineers set up a writing rig in the live room in Hit Factory's Studio 1 so Michael and Foster could work on ideas, but their sessions didn't begin as smoothly as expected. "What was fascinating was that two of the most talented persons out there were sitting at the piano, trying to write a song, but nothing came of it," Rob Hoffman said. "Everyone left the room, apart from [engineer] Andrew Scheps, who was in there with a DAT, waiting to capture anything that came. When Andrew came out, we all said, 'Well, have they got anything?' And Andrew turned around and said, 'Nothing at all'!" It was further evidence that ideas simply came to Michael in any given moment; if he sat down with the intent of writing a song, nothing would happen.

Hoffman remembers one of the pair's writing sessions in particular. "They bounced ideas back and forth, but at one point David wasn't getting the chords Michael wanted to hear, so he said, 'You play it'. Michael said, 'I can't, I'm a terrible piano player'. David said, 'Show me anyway'. Apparently after a few minutes of plinking David stopped him, and said, 'You really are terrible'."

During another session, Michael and Foster sat at the piano and spoke about their favourite old songs. Michael told Foster one of his favourites was Charlie Chaplin's 'Smile', which is about smiling through adversity. Like James Brown, Sammy Davis Jr., Jackie Wilson, Fred Astaire and Gene Kelly, Chaplin was one of Michael's major influences. "How could you not admire his genius," he once said of Chaplin. "He was the king of pathos;

he knew how to make you laugh and cry at the same time. I relate to him. I sometimes feel I am him."

It was after the conversation with Foster when Michael decided to record a version of 'Smile'. Chaplin originally composed the music for his 1936 movie *Modern Times*, and the song only became 'Smile' some 18 years later in 1954, when lyricists John Turner and Geoffrey Parsons added lyrics and a title. Nat King Cole first sang the song that same year.

Michael also wanted to work with Foster on an orchestral track he had written, 'Childhood'. Like other songs before it, 'Childhood' was written by Michael in his 'Giving Tree' at Neverland, and was yet another extremely personal creation. "Our personal history begins in childhood and the song 'Childhood' is a reflection of my life," Michael explained. "It's about the pain, some of the joys, some of the dreaming, some of the mental adventures that I took because of the different lifestyle I had, in being a child performer. I was born on stage and 'Childhood', it's my mirror – it's my story."

Michael said those who want to learn about him as a person should listen to 'Childhood' above all other songs. "If you really want to know about me, there's a song I wrote, which is the most honest song I have ever written, it's called 'Childhood'," he said. "[People] should listen to it. That's the one they should really listen to."

Both 'Childhood' and 'Smile' were recorded live with an orchestra at the Hit Factory on the same day, with the majority of Michael's live vocals from the sessions used on the final versions. But Michael was so unhappy with his vocals for 'Smile' that he recorded over a dozen takes. "Michael did a bunch of takes live with orchestra that would be called amazing by most standards," Rob Hoffman said. "He then did more later that day, and I think some the next as well. In all I think there were 14 takes."

Michael may not have been satisfied, but the orchestra was blown away by the performance. "When we finished recording with the orchestra, Michael asked me if he could go out in the studio and meet the musicians," Bruce Swedien said. "During the recording, the entire orchestra had been listening to Michael sing through their individual headphones. When Michael walked out in the studio to meet the orchestra, they gave him a standing ovation. Every member of the 50-piece orchestra stood up and tapped their music stands with their bows, as loud as they could! Michael was thrilled."

Once Foster was on board, Michael also asked him to help finish another song from the *Dangerous* sessions, the environmental protest track 'Earth Song'. Besides some additional vocals, Michael completed a version of 'Earth Song' in 1990 with Bill Bottrell, but he wasn't fully satisfied with it and it failed to make *Dangerous*. Not every song Michael liked was completed for an upcoming album; if he didn't feel something was right, he would move on to something else. Some songs took him years to perfect, and 'Earth Song' came into that category. "Michael has always felt better really fleshing out something over a long period of time to discover everything that he can about it," Bottrell explained.

When Michael pulled 'Earth Song' out of the vaults in New York, he made some slight changes with the help of Foster. Bottrell said his version was completed by August 1990, and that the Canadian only changed the outro vocals at the end from falsetto to full voice, and added the guitar riff in the second verse. Foster also brought in composer Bill Ross to add some drama to the orchestration. Bottrell was unhappy to hear that Foster was working on his production. "Foster became frustrated with Michael because he kept going back to my version," he said. "I was not happy to find David Foster's name on what I considered my best production ever." Michael also wanted to re-record parts of his vocal, but this task was not so straightforward for the engineers, who had to find a microphone that matched the one originally used by Bottrell.

***HIS*TORICAL THINKING**

Michael missed his deadline to complete the new material in time for a June 1994 release, a practice which was becoming the norm. Like the *Dangerous* sessions, he kept bringing new ideas to the studio and simply couldn't stop creating music. The album was initially supposed to include up to five new tracks, but by September reports claimed the number of new songs had grown to eight. "Michael went into the studio and recorded the five new tracks for the [greatest hits package] and felt that the whole piece was not enough," former Epic Records chairman Dave Glew recalls. "So he came to us and said, 'I need to cut two or three more tracks', and it just got stronger and stronger." Sony gave Michael a new deadline; the album had to be completed in time for a pre-Christmas release.

The record company held a meeting in the summer of 1994 in an attempt to get Michael to finish the album before the Christmas sales rush. "We held a major meeting with about 40 people; it was Michael, his managers, producers and individuals from every facet of the record company," Dan Beck said. "Everyone gave Michael a presentation of what their area of the record company could do if this record was released before Christmas. Michael loved the meeting, and it was essentially our way of begging him to finish. But he just continued to record and record."

Beck was the man behind the album title, which was leaked in the media in June. One day, Beck asked Sandy Gallin if Michael had come up with a title for the new album yet. Gallin told Beck that he hadn't, and suggested the record company conjure up some ideas. "I had a meeting with two of my colleagues at Epic, Dave Glew and Polly Anthony, and we really felt that the album title should come from Michael, it was his album, and an important one in his career," Beck said. "But we thought if we came up with some ideas, maybe it would stimulate Michael into coming up with something in response. At the end of the meeting Polly said how great it would be if Michael's album title was as good as Madonna's *The Immaculate Collection*. I agreed, Michael's greatest hits deserved to have a name that was such a clever play on words."

Beck had just heard some of Michael's songs in the studio, and noticed the 'darker' theme of the new material. "Michael didn't speak out in the media at all about what he had been through, and he seemed to be speaking out through the lyrics in his music, he was responding through these new songs," Beck said. "It seemed to be 'his story' about the past year or so, and the double-album also included the greatest hits, which was his musical history. So I wrote it down and played around with it, and came up with *HIStory*." Michael loved Beck's idea and the play on words, and later thanked him for his 'HIStorical thinking'.

In early August, Michael flew to Budapest to shoot an album teaser video, in which he marches past delirious fans in full military attire with hundreds of Soviet style soldiers. The video cost an estimated $4 million to make and didn't feature any of his upcoming music, much to the bewilderment of Sony executives. "This was how Michael saw history, and it was enough to make you wish he hadn't picked your idea," Beck said. "This was not a concept we really felt was going to help us, we didn't see it as something that would drive the album. But Michael was a dreamer. He got very excited about certain ideas, and would get lost in these concepts. We felt something with Michael and his music was all we needed, but I think sometimes he just wanted to surround himself with so much stuff. I think at times we believed in the power of his recorded music more than he did."

Some of the studio staff weren't even aware Michael was flying to Europe. "When Michael left the studio, he said to Eddie Delena, 'See you tomorrow'," Rob Hoffman recalls. "The next thing we hear is that Michael is in Hungary doing a video commercial! He would disappear at times unexpectedly."

Accompanying Michael on the trip was his twenty-six-year-old wife Lisa Marie Presley, Elvis's only child. Michael married Presley in secret in late May, but remarkably, the news only became public in mid-July. The two first became close in late 1992, and Presley later offered emotional support after the allegations surfaced and Michael became dependent on prescription drugs. "She was very, very supportive the whole time," Michael said. "She would call and be crying. She was angry and really wanted to choke people." Presley became a regular visitor to the studio in New York. "They acted like two kids in love," Hoffman recalls. "They held hands all the time, and she hung out at the studio for quite a while. I never questioned their love for each other."

Having completed the teaser video, it appeared Michael was serious about releasing the album before Christmas.

A WHOLE NEW JAM

As Michael continued to come up with new ideas, super producers Jimmy Jam and Terry Lewis were also asked to contribute a track, as Michael wanted to record a first ever duet with his sister Janet. Jam and Lewis had been working with Janet since 1985, and by 1994 they had produced her last three solo albums – including *Rhythm Nation 1814*, which Michael loved.

Jam and Lewis first met Michael in Minneapolis in 1988, when he played a show there during the Bad Tour. "We actually recommended the hotel in which he was staying and he loved his suite," Jam said. "He invited us to the show, which was great, and then for dinner after at the hotel. It was just surreal to be in his presence."

Fast forward to 1994, and the pair were contacted by Janet. "Janet called us and said, 'My brother wants to do a duet'," Jam recalls. "So we asked her how she felt about it, because obviously we were very loyal to her and didn't want to create a conflict of interest. But she was fine with it and said Michael wanted us to produce the song. Because Janet was fine with it, we were fine with it."

After accepting Michael's invitation, the pair began to create some tracks at their Flyte Tyme studio in Minneapolis ahead of flying to Manhattan. "Michael didn't really give us any direction," Jam said. "He just said, 'Come up with a bunch of tracks and I'll listen to what you come up with'. So over a period of three or four days we began creating about five different tracks at our studio in Minneapolis. We had Janet come over because we wanted her here for inspiration; we felt it was important for the tracks to have a Janet vibe. So Janet listened to the tracks and for one of them, she said, 'This is the one he will like'. So Terry and I were like, 'How do you know?' And Janet just said, 'I know my brother'. And then after listen- ... another one of the tracks, she said, 'I hope he doesn't like this one, ... nt it'!"

... Jam and Lewis flew to New York and met Michael at ... ys that when they joined the project, the two-disc album was to contain 23 greatest hits and seven new tracks. "Now the Hit Factory studio had great speakers, but Michael brought in his own speakers, which were even bigger, he had an entire wall of speakers," Jam recalls. "It was literally the loudest thing I have ever heard. Ever. So Michael greeted us... Janet was there and we began listening to the tracks, which we had narrowed down from about eight to six. They were all just music, no lyrics. I thought Michael would listen to each track for about a minute, but I was surprised because he listened to each song the whole way through. He really liked what he heard, he was like, 'Wow I like them all, you guys really listened to me'."

Michael chose his favourite track, and sure enough, it was the one his sister said he would like. "Michael said, 'This is the one I want, it's angry, aggressive, that's what I wanted'," Jam said. "Janet just started laughing and said, 'Told you so'. She was just glad he didn't like the track she wanted for herself, which actually ended up being 'Runaway' from her album *Design of a Decade*, and she recorded it about a year later. I actually thought that would be a great choice for them to sing together. But Michael had other ideas, and the track he chose was perfect for what he wanted to do."

Having picked his favourite track, Michael met Janet, Jam and Lewis the next day at his apartment in Trump Tower to begin writing. "So Michael said, 'I have an idea', and began coming up with a melody and rhythm for the track, but no words," Jam said. "Then he started singing the melody, but we realised it was too low for Janet. It was more to his strengths than hers and we needed to make sure Janet fared well, but she just said, 'It's his album, his song and his feeling, and I'm just the guest'. She had no expectation beyond helping her brother."

In the meantime, Michael and Janet worked on the lyrics separately. Michael wanted to write about how angry he had been feeling over the past eighteen months, which would continue the lyrical theme of the album so far. "Michael came up with most of the actual lyrics, he knew exactly what he wanted lyrically, something aggressive," Jam said. "Because he knew what he wanted, he wrote everything very quickly. He was very fast, very intense." Although Michael came up with most of the lyrics, Janet created the title, 'Scream', and also wrote the lyrics to the bridge. When they entered the studio to record the vocals, the plan was to record Michael's first, and Janet's immediately after.

"So we were sat there, Terry, Janet and myself, and Michael is wearing these hard shoes and some kind of jewellery, which you're not really supposed to in case it interferes with the vocal," Jam said. "Everything is fine...Michael said his headphones are OK, and his voice is smooth after he drank his usual hot water with Ricola cough drops. So he says, 'Let's give it a go'. The music comes on, and for about ten seconds, Michael just starts dancing around, stomping...snapping his fingers...clapping, which is really unusual. And suddenly, he just started singing."

Jam says they were simply blown away. "I had never seen or heard anything like it in my entire life. We had to almost hold onto our chairs due to the sheer energy and force of his singing. And when it was over, Terry and I were speechless. So Michael's like, 'How was it?' And we're like, 'Yeah...great', and Michael then asks us if we want him to do another vocal, and we're like, 'Sure!' And he nailed it in about four or five takes. Then Janet turns to us and says, 'I think I'll do my vocals in Minneapolis!' I mean, how do you follow that?! When Janet was leaving, Michael said to her, 'Are you not doing your vocals now?' And Janet says, 'No, I'm doing them in Minneapolis'."

What was supposed to be a three-day session had now stretched to a week and a half. Jam and Lewis returned to Minneapolis where they recorded Janet's vocal, before sending Michael a rough mix. Happy with the mix and Janet's vocals, Michael then told Jam and Lewis that he wanted to re-record his lead vocal over in Minneapolis, as he thought he could make improvements. "It really showed his competitiveness and his perfectionism," Jam said. "Of course we told Michael that he was welcome to come to Minneapolis."

The pair did record their background vocals together. "The two of them singing together was amazing," Rob Hoffman recalls. "Super tight, no bad notes, one part after another. When they took a break they sang the show tunes they used to sing as kids. Again, perfect harmony. Michael refused to sing the 'stop fuckin' with me' part [of 'Scream'] because he would not curse!"

A WHOLE NEW ALBUM

In the fall of 1994, mastering engineer Bernie Grundman was invited to New York – Michael was seemingly at the final stage of production before handing over the album to Sony. Grundman told Bruce Swedien he would have to shut down his mastering studio in Los Angeles and bring over all of his own equipment in order to make the trip. "Of course, this wasn't cheap," Grundman said. "But Bruce just said, 'Ah, send me the bill – I'll take care of it'. I was flown to New York on a first class ticket, and they put me up in The Pierre hotel in Manhattan, which was extremely expensive. So I walked in on a Monday, and everybody was there…music chiefs, producers and engineers, but I was never given anything to work on. I think I only touched one song while I was there, and that was 'Smile'. I said to Bruce, 'I'm not getting anything done…I need to see more songs'. So in the end I went back to Los Angeles. It was obvious they were nowhere near finished!"

Grundman believes he was only flown in to keep Sony satisfied. "I think it was simply a plan to make Sony feel better, to make them feel like they were near completion," he said. "Sony would have thought, 'Hey, they are mastering this record! It must be complete!' It seemed like a stunt to appease Sony."

Grundman says Michael was more private than ever before. "He booked out a few of the top floors at the Trump Tower and had a couple of empty floors below him, it seemed like he wanted to be isolated from other guests," Grundman said. "Having to dress up in disguise all the time to get some privacy…always being recognised…that takes its toll and only increases the desire and need for privacy. It was fascinating to see Michael arrive at the Hit Factory every day. There were hundreds of fans outside the studio every day, but nobody ever saw him! He would arrive in a huge chauffeured van that had blacked-out windows. The van would drive into an elevator at the studio and bring him to the floor he needed to be on."

It soon became apparent that Michael wouldn't meet the deadline for a pre-Christmas release. After the influx of new material, Michael and his team made the decision to record an entire disc of new songs, together with a separate disc of greatest hits. "So many new ideas came in, so after Michael spoke to Bruce Swedien, the decision was made to have a whole disc of new songs," Matt Forger said. Michael explained the reasoning for the decision. "In truth, I really didn't want the album to be about old songs," he admitted. "To me, greatest hits albums are boring. And I wanted to keep creating."

According to friend Frank Cascio, Michael didn't want to release a two-disc album, but was overruled by his record company. "That added to the price and Michael wanted to keep his music affordable for his fans," Cascio said. Sony, however, insisted on the inclusion of the greatest hits. "His loyal followers were sure to be happy with this bonus," Tommy Mottola explained. The next release date set by Sony was February 1995.

As the project grew and grew over the course of 1994, several different producers were hired. One of those was Teddy Riley, who had produced seven songs on *Dangerous*. "I came up [to New York] for the album but Michael wasn't in the studio," Riley recalls. "He wasn't really doing any work so I was just sitting there and I didn't want to waste his money or his time, he was wasting his money by me sitting there, so I said, 'Let me go home and then when you need me, call me'. And then Jimmy Iovine didn't want me to work on that project so he scratched me from the project." Iovine was the head of Riley's record company, Interscope Records, and wanted him to concentrate on the next album for his new band, Blackstreet. Riley considered giving Michael what became the band's 1996 hit collaboration with Dr. Dre, 'No Diggity', but Iovine wanted Blackstreet to record it.

Another producer Michael called in was Babyface, who had worked briefly on *Dangerous* in the summer of 1991. Babyface wrote a song called 'Why' for the project, but according to Rob Hoffman, Michael felt it 'sounded too much like a Babyface song'. Instead he offered it to his three nephews, Tito's sons Taj, Taryll and TJ, who were in a band called 3T.

Michael signed the band to his new record label, MJJ Music, and ensured his nephews' careers stayed on track after the death of their mother, who was murdered in August 1994. "My world crumbled, and my uncle

[Michael] saved it," 3T's youngest member, TJ, said. "He was there. He kept me inspired, kept me ambitious, and he was just there for me. He took us under his wing and became an important part of our success."

3T recorded 'Why' around a year later for their debut album, *Brotherhood.* "He gave it to us, under one condition; that we keep his vocals," TJ said. "So we kept his vocals for the chorus, and redid the verses in our own voices. Uncle Michael was there with us for the recording. He helped us out on the placement of our verses and just the whole feeling of the song."

Musician Steve Porcaro, who had been working with Michael since 1979, was also asked to work on ideas. "My involvement on *HIStory* started when myself, David Paich and Steve Lukather were flown to New York to work on 'Stranger in Moscow'," Porcaro said. "We were supposed to be there for one day. David and Steve did their bits [Lukather on background guitar and Paich on keyboards/synth/bass] and then flew out to Europe for the Toto tour. I wasn't going on that tour so I was asked to stay, and I ended up staying for a month!"

Porcaro soon realised just how big and expensive the project was. "They were so nice to me," he said. "They even gave me my own studio and my own assistant engineer, and I was being paid $2,500 a day to just sit in a room and write. They wanted to see if I could come up with ideas and write some demos for Michael. It was unreal that they had people in different studios just writing, I had never seen anything like it. And I saw a lot of money wasted. Every day they had the best food brought in from the best restaurants in New York for us to eat, steak, lobsters, everything. There was so much money flying around. The best hotel rooms for everybody; every studio at the Hit Factory was booked out; the best food was brought in; you name it. It was a huge thing."

Michael was big on hearing sounds which neither he nor anybody else had ever heard before, and hired synthesists especially for the purpose of creating them. One day Michael asked Bruce Swedien if he knew anybody who could create original synthesiser sounds, and Swedien suggested musician Chuck Wild. "He is indeed original, his sounds are the greatest," he told Michael. Wild will never forget his first conversation with Michael.

"He [Michael] said, 'Chuck, I want you to manufacture sounds that the human ear has never heard. I want them to be fiery, aggressive, unusual and unique'."

Wild said Michael's instructions raised the bar and changed the way he looked at sound design. "On and off over the next three years, working with about 25 synths, three samplers, and a couple of Macintosh computers, I created a library of sounds and soundscapes," he said. Michael then distributed these sounds to members of the production team for use on some of the album tracks.

Michael also hired several other synthesists; every day several packages would arrive at the Hit Factory via FedEx, consisting of different tapes full of synths and sounds. "Michael wasn't even listening to these tapes," Steve Porcaro recalls. "These musicians must have been working their asses off making these sounds. I played one of the tapes and there was some incredible stuff on there, but they weren't being used or even listened to. What I would do to get hold of those tapes now."

NEW YORK LIFE

Michael always made sure everybody on the studio team was taken care of, and he often shared his privileges. "He got one of the first PlayStations from Sony in his lounge," Rob Hoffman recalls. "We snuck in late at night to play the games that hadn't been released yet." Michael's private lounge at the studio was filled with candy, drinks and toys. A few crew members also hadn't seen the movie *Jurassic Park* when it was released the previous summer, so Michael arranged a private screening for them at Sony.

In July 1994, Michael invited everybody from the studio to watch his sister Janet in concert at Radio City Music Hall. "The studio crew got free tickets to the Janet show so we all went right from work one night," Hoffman said. "About halfway through the show we see this dude with a long beard, dressed in robes dancing in the aisle behind. I mean really dancing…it was Michael in disguise, kind of like the costume Chevy Chase wears in *Fletch* while roller-skating."

Hoffman also saw Michael's childlike side. "We recorded a Christmas song during the summer of 1994 that needed a children's choir," he said. "Michael insisted that the entire studio be decorated with Christmas lights, tree, fake snow and a sled for their recording. And he bought presents for everyone."

Working with Michael in the studio was never short of funny and memorable moments. During one session, Michael called producer Brad Buxer to his lounge and threw a pie in his face. "That pie that Michael nailed me in the face with so completely covered me that I had to go back to the hotel to change clothes because I was such a mess," Buxer said. "I was covered from head to toe, and it was the nastiest pie, some kind of Boston cream pie with chocolate and custard whipped cream and whatever else. Michael of course couldn't stop laughing."

Even in the studio, Michael couldn't always escape the negative attention in the media. "Once, while we were taking a break, I think we were actually watching the O.J. Simpson case on TV, there was a news program talking about him being in Europe with some little boy," Hoffman recalls. "I was sitting next to the guy while the news is making this crap up. He just looked at me and said, 'This is what I have to deal with'." Hoffman also remembers how Michael yearned for everyday normality while in the Big Apple. "Bruce [Swedien] and I were talking about walking to the studio every day in NYC, and what routes we took. Michael looked at us and said we were so lucky to be able to do that. He couldn't walk down the street without being harassed. It was a sad moment for all of us."

'YOU ARE NOT ALONE'

Now Michael had made the decision to record a whole new album he was still searching for more songs from outside producers and writers, so he contacted R. Kelly's manager to see if the singer would write a song for him.

Kelly said he was 'psyched' once he entered the studio to work on material for Michael. "I feel I could have done his whole album," he admitted. "Not being selfish. I was just that geeked about it." Kelly sent Michael a tape of an R&B ballad about love and isolation, titled 'You Are Not Alone', which he had written after the loss of people close to him, including his mother. On the tape, Kelly sang the song imitating Michael's vocal style. "I think I am him," he said. "I become him. I want him to feel that as well."

Another song Kelly sent to Michael was called 'Life', which would later be recorded by American R&B duo K-Ci & JoJo. Although Michael liked both songs, he actually preferred 'Life' to 'You Are Not Alone', but Kelly said he didn't feel 'Life' would be as big a hit and had to argue his case. He recalls telling Michael, 'This song is for you, trust me, it's gonna be big'.

When Michael's team received the tape of 'You Are Not Alone' they saw great potential in the song, but they knew it needed more work. Michael re-produced the track and added a choir in the final portion, which he said gave it 'a sense of climax and structure'. But Kelly said Michael later proceeded to give himself a co-writer's credit. "Naturally that got me a little upset," Kelly admitted, "but the minute I put a call in to Mike, he got right back to me." Michael told him it was a mistake, and the credits were amended.

As Kelly didn't like to fly, his programmer travelled to New York to help Bruce Swedien with the music track. Michael and Kelly then spent the final week of November 1994 recording in Kelly's home city of Chicago. "Wherever Michael Jackson went, the world knew about it," Kelly said. "It was like there were secret agents putting out the word. So, days before he landed in Chicago, the city knew he was coming. The whole town was wired for his arrival."

Kelly was excited to be working with Michael, but also extremely nervous. When Michael first arrived at the Chicago Recording Complex Kelly was afraid he wouldn't be able to finish the project, but in the end passion took over. Kelly ordered Chinese and vegetarian dishes for Michael, and put Walt Disney items all over the studio. "I knew he was a big kid, everyone knew that," Kelly said. "And I also got my little dog because I knew he loved animals, I couldn't afford giraffes, but I did have a dog. It broke ice and we talked. And I went to the bathroom and my manager came with me, and I remember that I fell to the floor because I just couldn't believe it, but I got back up and straightened myself out because I realised that I had to be professional."

While in Chicago, Michael and Kelly visited the city's Water Tower Place shopping mall. Michael headed straight for the Disney store, where he became fascinated by a larger-than-large life statue of Donald Duck located above the entrance. Michael enquired about buying it, so he could take it back to Neverland. Kelly recalls: "When the manager appeared, Michael couldn't have been sweeter, 'Is there any way I could buy that Donald Duck?' he asked. [The manager said] 'I'm afraid not, Mr Jackson. It's permanently built into the front of the store.' [Michael replied] 'Oh, that's a shame, but thank you anyway, sir'."

Every night after Michael left the central Chicago studio and got in his van, people were hanging out of office buildings and hotels to get a glimpse of him. "He'd always stop and wave," Kelly said.

MINNEAPOLIS

In early December, after working with Kelly in Chicago, Michael flew to Minneapolis to record his extra vocals for 'Scream'. But Jimmy Jam said the new vocal lacked the initial energy of the original. "It was good, but it didn't have the same feel or anger that his New York vocal had," Jam said. "The final vocal pretty much ended up being the vocal he recorded originally."

Jam recalls how Michael went to the Mall of America nearly every day when he was in the Twin Cities. Michael loved to go in a disguise with moustache and hat when the mall was crowded because he enjoyed experiencing the social scene. "He'd always go at peak times, that's when everybody's having fun," Jam said.

Jam has happy memories of Michael and Janet working together. "Them in the studio together was probably the highlight of the whole record," he said, "because they were reminiscing about the old songs Michael had written a long time ago, and Janet would start singing, and Michael would go, 'Oh, you remember that song', and they'd start singing it together."

The producer said the siblings' approach to making music was completely different; Janet works very simply and very quickly, whereas Michael was a little more methodical. "He's a perfectionist and tends to cut a million songs, then pick the best of what he has," Jam said.

While in Minneapolis, Michael also told Jam and Lewis about the lyrics and melody for a ghost-themed song, 'Is It Scary' [title changed from 'Is *This* Scary']. The song developed from the ideas Michael had while working on music for the shelved *Addams Family Values* short-film in the summer of 1993. "He asked us to write the music track for this song he had in mind, and we just created this sort of sinister track," Jam said. "We weren't sure if Michael was going to include the song on the album or what he wanted to do with it."

Work on the track continued later in the project, but it was decided it wouldn't complement the rest of the songs on the album. "To my knowledge, 'Is It Scary' was in the running to be included on *HIStory*, but at a meeting with the entire crew two weeks before finishing the album it was not considered close enough to being finished," Rob Hoffman recalls. Brad Buxer said Michael strongly considered the song for the album. "He really liked 'Is It Scary', it was a trashy kind of sound that was kind of cool, a really interesting track," Buxer said. "It was very different from the other stuff Michael had done." Another idea which developed from the *Addams Family Values* sessions became a song called 'Ghosts'; producer Teddy Riley originally created the music track for the short-film. The team worked a little on 'Ghosts' while in New York, but not to any great extent.

In November 1994, Michael decided it was time to move production back to Los Angeles. It had been nearly a year since the Northridge earthquake, but other factors also influenced the decision, the weather for one. "Winter had arrived in New York, and I think Michael was getting tired of the cold," Matt Forger said. "He wanted to come home, and most of the team lived in Los Angeles too." Production was moved back to California while Michael was away in Chicago and Minneapolis.

HISTORY IN CALIFORNIA

After the Christmas break, which Michael spent with Lisa Marie, recording resumed in the warmth of Los Angeles. Michael booked out two rooms at both Record One and Larrabee studios; Bruce Swedien worked in the main room at Record One, with Brad Buxer in the back room, while Larrabee became Jimmy Jam and Terry Lewis's studio.

The *HIStory* team at Larrabee: Top row: Craig Johnson, Andrew Scheps, Rob Hoffman, Brad Sundberg and Matt Forger. Bottom row: Bruce Swedien, Michael and Eddie Delena.

On Michael's first day back in the studio, the members of his production team weren't the only familiar faces to greet him. "In New York, there were dozens of fans sat outside the Hit Factory every day waiting to get a glimpse of Michael," Rob Hoffman recalls. "But there were these two women in particular. They were amazing; they were there *every* day. They seemed to know as much about our whereabouts as we knew ourselves. When we moved to Los Angeles, the first day back in the studio, they were already waiting outside for Michael. How they knew we were moving operations back to Los Angeles I do not know, but they were there before us!"

Jimmy Jam and Terry Lewis figured their work was complete after 'Scream', but Michael enquired about another of the music tracks the pair had initially proposed back in October. "We were originally brought in just for the Janet duet, but Michel really liked another of the tracks that we played for him in New York," Jam said. "He said it sounded similar to Janet's song 'The Knowledge', which he loved."

The track in question became the foundation for 'Tabloid Junkie'. "The song was really simple, Michael had a concept for it already and wrote the melody and the lyrics, and we brought in the completed track and did all the blurbs that feature on it," Jam said. The song was initially going to be called 'Tabloid Jungle'. "We felt like the tabloids were the hunters and Michael the prey, he's the biggest prize in the jungle, and the media's on this mission to capture him," Jam explained.

During the sessions for 'Tabloid Junkie', Michael mentioned to Jam that he needed to write a title tune, 'HIStory' (the album title was chosen months before the song was created). So Jam and Lewis stayed on the West Coast a little longer, and wrote and composed the song with Michael. Jam said Michael wanted a big anthemic song. "I think he gave it a couple of tries himself but then asked us to give it a go," he said. "So we went back to Minneapolis and made the music track, and then Michael did his thing on the melody."

The song became a huge production. It features an 80-piece orchestra, a choir and background vocals by Boyz II Men, not to mention Michael's own vocals. Numerous tape clips from historic news dispatches and speeches were also used. Everything came to about 160 tracks, which had to be mixed into one single recording. This would be far from easy, and wouldn't take place until the final week of recording.

Michael and Bruce Swedien insisted the choir be recorded at Westlake's Studio D, where 'Man in the Mirror' was recorded. "Michael and Bruce were both nostalgic, and maybe a bit superstitious," Rob Hoffman said. "We needed to add choir to a couple songs while we were in L.A., so they immediately said it had to be recorded at Westlake D. Bruce sent me over there with his prized M49 microphones, and everyone on the session was like, 'You know he's never let them out of his sight, and no one has ever put them up or taken them down but him'. Yes, I was scared!"

During the final minute of the song, various people reciting famous dates in time can be heard. These people are actually members of the production team. The collage was put together by Matt Forger, who recorded each person using a portable recording rig. "I must say it's an honour to hear my own voice on a Michael Jackson record, along with the many others who worked on the project," engineer John Van Nest said.

Apart from producing and songwriting, Jimmy Jam also had other roles on the project. "At that stage I was just around, I felt I could be trusted," he said. "It was mostly me there and not Terry, I wasn't an advisor as such, just a confidant. I could make musical decisions and Michael was always inquisitive as to how I did certain things."

Jam was impressed with Michael's work rate. At times the team would look at the clock only to realise it was three or four in the morning, but Michael would still be in the studio first thing the next day. "He was a guy who loved being in the studio, he would work all hours; he didn't care," Jam said. "I've never seen anybody work any harder than he does, and that's coming from somebody who has worked with Prince – now Prince is a hard-working guy."

Jam feels working with the very best producers throughout his career was both a gift and a curse for Michael. "The gift was that Michael grew up with Motown, and learnt from the best of the very best, such as Berry Gordy, Freddie Perren, Gamble and Huff, and then after that Quincy Jones," Jam said. "So he would have absorbed their ways of production like a sponge and made mental notes. That meant production wise Michael learnt from the very best, but that quest for perfection was the curse, and as a result Michael was not good at making definite decisions. Michael would always say, 'We need to really challenge ourselves, push ourselves as far as we can go'. He just did not want to commit – he could not let go of a song or an album. In his eyes it was never ready."

Berry Gordy said Michael had 'a knowingness' about him as a child, and paid close attention to every single thing he said. "Even when my back was turned, I knew he'd be watching me like a hawk," Gordy said. "The other kids might have been playing or doing whatever they were doing, but Michael was dead serious. And he stayed that way."

Michael, in turn, said he always used Gordy's principles in his adult years. "Berry insisted on perfection and attention to detail," Michael said. "I'll never forget his persistence. This was his genius. Then and later, I observed every moment of the sessions where Berry was present and never forgot what I learned. To this day, I use the same principles."

Jam says Michael needed a producer around him who could put his foot down and make quick and definitive decisions. Jam said that stopped when Michael no longer chose to work with Quincy Jones. "Michael would work meticulously, whereas Prince would be more prolific and record whole songs in a single day, and you can't argue with either approach. But Michael never had natural constraints – who is going to tell him that his budget is restricted or that he only has a certain amount of time when he keeps making record-breaking albums?"

As always, Michael continued to have fun in the workplace despite the pressure he was under to complete his album. "He's a kid at heart," Jam said. "His office [at the studio] is not like a normal office. He has all the kids' toys. A lot of times we'd be in a session, in the middle of playing a video game, and he'd be like 'Well, we got to do this. But go ahead and finish your game, though – I don't want to mess your game up'." Jam says Michael used to love snacking on sunflower seeds and Frosted Flakes in the studio. "One night he told me and Terry that he was gonna show us how to grub on some Frosted Flakes," Jam recalls. "He ordered some milk and threw those flakes in a bowl and it was 'on' after that!"

Jam fondly remembers the long conversations he used to have with Michael. "Once Michael said to me, 'Jimmy, how do you want to be remembered when you die?' I said to him, 'I want to be remembered as a nice guy'. So Michael goes, 'No, I mean *how* do you want to be remembered?' He meant how many number ones I made, what kind of producer I was, just statistics. And I said, 'Michael, they're just statistics. They aren't *who* I am.' He just didn't get it…he was totally puzzled.

A year later, Jam needed to get permission from Michael for a song sample. "So I called him but before I could ask him anything, he said, 'Remember what you said about how you want to be remembered? Every time someone asks me about you, I just say, he's the nicest guy.' And I said, 'Michael I'm glad you understood.' And he just got it in that one moment. It's a conversation that I'll always remember. Although Michael had all those groundbreaking hits, albums, tours and videos, he was simply one of the nicest people I've ever met and worked with."

In Los Angeles, veteran horns musicians Jerry Hey, Kim Hutchcroft, Larry Williams, Gary Grant and Bill Reichenbach were brought in to add the icing on the cake to some of the tracks. But Hutchcroft, who last worked with Michael on *Bad* in 1987, noticed yet another change in him. "By 1995, he seemed even more secretive than when I worked with him in 1987, and Michael was pretty secretive then after *Thriller*," Hutchcroft said. "In early '95 I came in with the others and worked on the song '2 Bad' at Larrabee and there were bodyguards at the studio every day – there just wasn't that interaction that there was before. It was much more fun back in 1979, and 1987 even. Somebody always seemed to want something from Michael in those later years and he was very wary of that. But he would still come out and greet us all, and he remembered everybody, he was a real gent as always."

Another hitmaker Michael asked to contribute a track was Atlanta-based producer/songwriter Dallas Austin. Austin, who co-produced four songs for Madonna's 1994 album *Bedtime Stories*, arrived in Los Angeles with around a dozen music track ideas for Michael to choose from. Michael picked out his favourite and added lyrics, which touch upon the allegations and his issues with the media. Austin admitted he wasn't used to the 'mad freedom' Michael gave him. "You're pressured by time, but not by creativity or money," the producer said. "You'd think he'd be very controlling, but if he likes you enough to work with you, he wants your expertise." Michael invited up-and-coming hip-hop star Notorious B.I.G. to rap on the song, which he called 'This Time Around'.

Engineer John Van Nest was excited to hear the rapper would be coming to the studio. "Michael used to call people to ask them to participate on albums, it was interesting knowing that nearly anyone on the planet would come to the phone if it were Michael calling," Van Nest said. "So, Dallas [Austin] and I were expecting him any minute, and pretty much on time, Notorious strolls in. He was quite an imposing figure when he walked in, as he was quite popular at the time. I had no idea what to expect from him in terms of attitude, but he seemed nice when he walked in. No problem. But almost immediately, he blurted out, 'Yo, Dallas, can I meet Mike?' To which Dallas replied that he thought so. Biggie went on to talk about how much this opportunity meant to him, as Michael was his hero. Anyway, Dallas tells him that we're going to lay down the rap first, so Biggie heads in the booth, we get some headphone levels and get ready to start recording."

Notorious recorded his rap in two takes, before waiting to meet his hero. Once his security checked that it was just Van Nest, Austin and Notorious in the room, Michael entered the studio. "Biggie nearly broke out in tears…I could tell how much this meant to him," Van Nest recalls. "Well, Michael could have this effect on anyone, even the most hardcore rappers! Biggie was tripping up on his words, bowing down and telling Michael how much his music had meant to him in his life. Michael was, as always, very humble and kept smiling while Biggie just went on and on how much he loved Michael. I watched Biggie just become this big butterball of a man, and it was really very sweet to witness. After all, we are all just people."

Michael loved the rap and thanked Notorious for coming all the way from Philadelphia to attend the session. "Biggie asked rather sheepishly whether he could get a photo, and Michael agreed," Van Nest said. "Michael said goodbye and stepped out, leaving Biggie standing there looking completely stunned."

THE FINAL DAYS

One of the very last songs to come into the equation was 'Come Together', a cover of Michael's favourite Beatles hit. Michael completed a rough version of the song with Bill Bottrell during the *Bad* sessions in 1986. "I just went in and in one take started singing it," Michael recalled. "We kept it kinda raw and funky. It was just spontaneous, but I knew I wanted to do something with it." Somewhat surprisingly, he decided to pull it out from the vaults nearly ten years later. Apart from some slight alterations, the song was left in its original state.

Bottrell, who played all the instruments and produced the track, admits he was shocked when Michael decided to include it on *HIStory*. He didn't think it was good enough to be released, and described it as 'crude'. "I never intended that track to be released that way, they put it out without informing me," Bottrell said. "It's all a bit overwhelming and hard to remember. He legally didn't have to credit me, but he did."

The inclusion of 'Come Together' completed the final tracklist, which also includes 'Scream', 'They Don't Care About Us', 'Stranger in Moscow', 'This Time Around', 'Earth Song', 'D.S.', 'Money', 'You Are Not Alone', 'Childhood', 'Tabloid Junkie', '2 Bad', 'HIStory', 'Little Susie' and 'Smile'. The team worked on around 40 songs during the project; those which failed to make the cut include 'Much Too Soon', 'Morphine', Innocent Man', 'Is It Scary', 'In the Back' and 'Michael McKellar'.

As with his two previous albums, Michael was again heavily involved in the production and writing process, writing nine of the tracks alone and co-writing a further three. *HIStory* is therefore the album Michael had the must influence over in his entire career, which is reflected by the personal themes of the majority of the songs. Michael described them as 'very autobiographical'. "They come from the heart – they are about myself," he said. He later described the album as a 'musical book'. "If you want to know how I feel, you can check out *HIStory*," he said. It is safe to say it would have been a completely different album had the child molestation allegations not arisen.

Jimmy Jam said that if an artist's personal feelings are reflected in their music, it gives it a completely different energy. "Everything on Michael's mind is on the album – positive and negative," he said. "He sang what was on his mind and it's a very aggressive, very personal album, and to me it's his finest album just because of that part."

Bruce Swedien described the lyrics of 'Stranger in Moscow' and 'Childhood' as the 'most personal' and the 'most beautiful' Michael had ever written. "He went above and beyond himself," Swedien said at the time. "The horrible things he went through lately inspired him a lot."

But Michael didn't deliberately write such personal songs. "I just kind of write according to the emotion, according to what I'm going through in the moment," he explained. "I get caught up in the moment wherever the moment is, wherever the emotion is." Michael said his favourite songs on the album were 'Stranger in Moscow', 'Earth Song', 'You Are Not Alone' and 'Childhood' as he liked songs with emotions, a message and a sense of immortality.

At the end of March 1995, it was finally time to wrap up production. But in the final week the team still had to mix 'Tabloid Junkie' and 'HIStory', among other things. Jimmy Jam knew 'HIStory' would take four or five days to mix, because it came to a massive 160 tracks. The production was so big that when the time came for Jam's engineer to mix the song, both studios at Larrabee were required. Each mixing console was only big enough for around 100 tracks, so the engineers had to wire two consoles together.

"We wanted to pare it down to 96 tracks so mixing would be easier but Michael did not want to sub mix anything," Jam said. "It was a logistical nightmare and we were running out of time. We were saying to each other, 'How do we sync these machines together?' So somebody suggested we link the boards together. The problem of course became the time constraints, but we needed to get it done, so we stayed at the studio and barely slept."

Although they managed to mix the song in time for the deadline, Jam wasn't happy that the process had to be rushed. "You shouldn't rush a production like this," he said. "And then Michael began altering the mix, turning up claps and snaps again. There were elements of that song that I just didn't feel were right. We needed more time, but it is what it is, in the end we just gave up and let Michael have his way."

The hectic final sessions took place over the last weekend of March. The Jam and Lewis songs were mixed at Larrabee, and everything else was mixed at Record One. On the Thursday, Michael informed engineers Rob Hoffman and Eddie Delena that the team wouldn't be getting much sleep over the weekend, as the tapes had to be taken to Bernie Grundman's for mastering on the Monday morning.

"For the whole weekend, we were camped out at Record One," Hoffman recalls. "Michael was singing, and there was a lot of mixing going on. The final night of recording was late on the Saturday night into Sunday morning, and this was when Michael sang the huge ad-libs at the end of 'Earth Song'. It was the last vocal of the record as Michael knew it would kill his voice. Before that vocal, we all thought 'Earth Song' was finished. Michael turned around and said, 'I have to do the ad-libs on Earth Song.' So we turned around and said, 'What do you mean? What ad-libs?!' We were all so busy during those few days I think Michael just forgot about it."

As Michael was gearing up to sing that final vocal, he and Hoffman began talking about John Lennon. "I told him the story of John singing 'Twist and Shout' while being sick, and though most people think he was screaming for effect, it was actually his voice giving out," Hoffman said. "He loved it, and then went in to sing his heart out."

Later that night, everyone left the room so Michael could turn up the music while some of the songs were being mixed. "This was a common occurrence during the mixes, and I was left in the room with ear plugs, and hands over my ears, in case he needed something," Hoffman said. "This particular night, all the lights were out and we noticed some blue flashes intermittently lighting up the room during playback. After a few moments we could see that one of the speakers was shooting blue flames. Michael liked this and proceeded to push all the faders up!"

On the Sunday night and into the early hours of Monday, the team were literally printing the last few mixes so Bruce Swedien could drive the tapes over to Bernie Grundman's for mastering. The album was mastered that Monday, March 28.

Even after the frantic final weekend, there was still a twist in the tail during the mastering process. Engineer John Van Nest was given the task of sequencing the album and editing it down to a size that could fit onto a CD. "This was no small undertaking, as about seven minutes needed to be trimmed somewhere," Van Nest said. "I laid this all out in Sound Tools [a digital audio workstation] and came to know every bar of every song very intimately. I found places where songs could be tightened up and came up with many suggestions. On the night of mastering, I was put in a room at Bernie Grundman's with my Sound Tools rig, and in this room, I would have to 'negotiate' with Michael about what to take out. I'll never forget this night."

Michael was told by Bruce Swedien that they had two options – either to remove one whole song or shorten and edit the others. They chose the latter. "I started with song one and played Michael my edits," Van Nest said. "[He said] 'Oh no, we can't take *that* out…it's my favourite part of the album!' Okay. Let's try another. 'Oh no, we *must* keep those four bars.' OK…let's go to the vamp, which carries on for two minutes…how about removing these eight bars…'Oh no, that's my favourite part of the vamp!' Well, you get the picture."

Jimmy Jam told Michael the edits were actually improving the album, but he wasn't budging. "What saved us all was Bruce coming in, appearing somewhat as an authority figure and simply telling Michael that I either had to make the cuts or we would have to cut one song off the album," Van Nest said. "The CD format was simply not capable of handling 80 plus minutes. And over the course of about five hours, we got it down." Dawn was approaching when the engineers finally finished.

During the mastering of albums such as *Dangerous* and *HIStory*, Bernie Grundman would see Michael more often than before. "It seemed like Michael was more hands on for his last few albums," Grundman said. "Maybe before then Quincy would be in charge and take care of things. After we did our mastering bit, we would give him a disc of the album to take home and listen to, so he could suggest any changes. Most of the mastering in Michael's era took $200,000 per record to master. Most artists don't get that kind of budget to produce an entire record now. Times have changed – the budgets will never be the same as they were in Michael's era."

After the album was mastered, Michael played it for the record label executives at Larrabee. Michael did not enjoy playback sessions, but he was persuaded to attend on this occasion by his managers, Sandy Gallin and Jim Morey. The entire album was played in front of around 30 people, but after the last note sounded the executives left the studio without uttering a single word. "No applause, no comment, no reaction – I was absolutely mortified," Bruce Swedien said. "How can people that are supposed to be in the record business be so dumb? Sandy Gallin was jumping up and down, and waving his arms and screaming at them, 'Are you all brain dead?' There were tears in Michael's eyes. Bea [Swedien's wife], Michael, and I went out to the parking lot and got in my Big Bronco. Michael said to me, 'I'll never do this again'!"

Michael invited everyone associated with the production for a finish party at Neverland, which took place on Sunday, April 2. Jimmy Jam was at the party when he received a call from Janet, who was in Europe. "Janet called, and she said, 'Jimmy, have you heard the mix of 'Scream' they put on the master tape?' I said, 'Yes, what's wrong with it?' After hearing the new mix they put on the masters, it was clear someone had gone in on Michael's behest and turned down Janet's vocals, because they were now lacking their original power. So I said to Michael, 'This isn't the right mix.' And he said, 'Oh really? I didn't know.' But I think he knew – there was just a real element of sibling rivalry. Michael was really competitive with Janet, even though she was his sister. He wanted perfection. So we went back in and corrected the problem, tweaked her vocals and put some handclaps in."

Making *HIStory* cost at least $10 million. For every aspect of production, Michael wanted the very best. His team were put up in the very best hotels, and in the studio they ate the very best food. Michael also worked with the very best producers – the likes of Jimmy Jam and Terry Lewis, David Foster, R. Kelly and Dallas Austin commanded some of the highest fees in the business. Top producers such as Teddy Riley, Babyface and Wyclef

Jean also worked on the project, but none of their work was even used. Michael also had his own production teams, including Bruce Swedien, Rene Moore and Brad Buxer.

Michael also flew in top musicians and special guest artists, the likes of Slash, Notorious B.I.G., Shaquille O'Neal, Boyz II Men, Nile Rodgers and Trevor Rabin. Musicians such as Steve Porcaro and Larry Williams, who spent longer periods working on the project, were also paid around $2,000 a day for their work. If Michael was away on business or vacation, everybody on the team would still have to be paid.

At times, Michael also had all four studios at the Hit Factory booked out, not to mention having exclusive access to two recording studios in Los Angeles once production was moved back to California. Incidentally, Michael's presence in New York would single-handedly turn around the fortunes of the New York studio scene. "When Michael went to New York, the studio scene there was suffering a bit of a recession," orchestrator Geoff Grace said. "But Michael came, used studios like the Hit Factory and Sony and 1994 ended up being one of the best studio years in New York for a long time."

With technology advancing (digital recording would replace the traditional analogue method by the new millennium) and young up-and-coming hip-hop producers becoming ever popular, *HIStory* would end up being the last Michael Jackson album for many of the original 'A-Team' session musicians. Most of them wouldn't work with Michael again. "It was the tail end of working with him; the big finale," trumpeter Gary Grant said. "I said to Michael, 'We've done all these records together, but we've never had a picture taken together.' So Michael said, 'Well, let's get one!' It was a really nice touch."

Now recording was completed, Sony faced the monumental task of promoting and marketing *HIStory*.

CHAPTER 13: THE *HISTORY* CHALLENGE

MID 1995 – LATE 1996

By recording and finishing the *HIStory* album, Michael had seemingly done the easy part. The world's biggest superstar had just made a settlement against the most serious and image exploding charges an artist could face, meaning Sony was faced with arguably the most challenging album promotion and marketing campaign of all time.

But despite the events of 1993, the label was backing Michael all the way with a huge $30 million promotional offensive, which the *Los Angeles Times* compared to one usually reserved for the Super Bowl or a royal wedding. Tommy Mottola said the label did 'everything' it could to promote *HIStory*, putting into it about ten times the marketing emphasis that went into *Thriller*. "At our end, the feeling was that we had to put all image questions to the wall and drive home the importance of the album," Dan Beck said. "It was all about doing everything possible, because this album was huge for Michael's career."

As well as overcoming image issues, Beck said the record company also faced other challenges. "By the mid-1990s more than 70% of Michael's album sales came from outside the United States, so when the world is your market, it's a different thing," he said. "We knew that his audience amongst teen males was weak; they were mostly into hip-hop or grunge, and by the time you are 16, it's not cool to like something you liked when you were 10. That was what we faced, and the media were tough on Michael; today everybody is up against it, but back then Michael seemed to be singled out, rightly or wrongly." Market analysis appeared to show that the allegations had little impact on Michael's reputation outside of the United States.

For the first time since *Thriller*, Michael didn't shoot a music video while recording was still ongoing. This certainly contributed to production being completed quicker than the previous two albums.

In May 1995, Michael and Janet filmed a video for the lead single, 'Scream', which was part of the huge 18-month promotional campaign Sony was about to unleash. The video, set on a large spacecraft, cost an enormous $7 million to produce, and is still the most expensive music video ever made. The effort did garner Michael a Grammy Award for Best Music Video (Short Form) in 1996, his first Grammy since 'Leave Me Alone' won in the same category in 1990.

Jimmy Jam was invited to watch the siblings in action on the set in Los Angeles. "Michael and Janet were very competitive, and I was the only person accepted by both camps," Jam said. "It was funny, because I would be asked to go into Michael's trailer, and then somebody would tell me that Janet wanted me in her trailer, and I would be going back and forth. When I went into Michael's trailer, he had a new video game, he thought he could beat me but I kicked his ass! Then the next thing I know, I'm back in Janet's trailer." Several media outlets were present on set, and Jam was asked to act as Michael's spokesperson.

Jam felt the lead single should have been 'You Are Not Alone', but Michael and Sony opted for 'Scream', which was released worldwide at the end of May with 'Childhood' on the B-side. "Firstly, Michael was very much in love with Lisa Marie and they were happy," Jam explained. "I thought they should have let people see that they were in love and 'You Are Not Alone' was the perfect song for that and perfect for a big 'Welcome Back'. The public were excited about Michael's new music and I think what had happened with the accusations was beginning to drift away. I just felt that the nature of 'Scream' would bring everything that had happened back up, just as it was slowly being forgotten about. But Michael was angry about what had happened and wanted 'Scream'. I'm not the record company, but I just felt it reopened the wounds a little." Jam pointed out that the first singles from *Thriller* and *Bad* were also ballads.

'Scream' became the highest new entry in the 37-year history of the *Billboard* 100 after crashing onto the chart at number five, where it peaked. But Jam's instincts appeared to be correct as radio stations soon began dropping it from their playlists in favour of 'You Are Not Alone' – before it was even announced as a possible single. Meanwhile, the $4 million album teaser video also began airing on MTV at the end of May.

In the days leading up to the album's June 16 release, Michael faced a backlash over the lyrical content of 'They Don't Care About Us'. Critics who obtained pre-release copies of the album highlighted that the lyrics in question, 'Jew me, sue me, everybody do me, kick me, kike me, don't you black or white me', could be interpreted as anti-Semitic.

Some Jewish groups condemned the lyrics and considered them offensive, although Sandy Gallin, himself a Jew, said it was 'the most ridiculously misconstrued interpretation' of a song he ever heard. Michael said he was 'angry and outraged' that he could be so misinterpreted. "My intention was for this song to say 'No' to racism, anti-Semitism and stereotyping," he explained. "Unfortunately, my choice of words may have unintentionally hurt the very people I wanted to stand in solidarity with." To quell the controversy Michael made the decision to modify the lyrics slightly and re-record that part of the song.

Two nights before the release of the album, Michael and Lisa Marie appeared on ABC's Primetime Live, which was Michael's first interview since the molestation allegations. Described as 'the TV event of the summer', the broadcast, hosted by Diane Sawyer, was watched by some 60 million people and included the full network debut of the 'Scream' video. Sandy Gallin says he spent three days carefully preparing Michael and Lisa Marie for the show. "It was me who convinced Michael to do the Diane Sawyer show," Gallin said. "Deepak Chopra [an Indian-born American author and public speaker] and I spent three days with them, prepping them for the show and asking every possible question that Diane could have asked them."

One of nine 32-foot statues placed strategically around Europe to promote *HIStory*

When the album – *HIStory: Past, Present and Future Book I* to give it its full name – was released to the public on June 16, it hit number one in both the United States and the United Kingdom. Sony set a target of 20 million sales worldwide; an ambitious figure given the album was twice as expensive as a typical CD, as it contains two discs and a 52-page booklet.

Michael's vision was to appear as a giant marble statue on the album cover, which is said to have been inspired by a 280-foot monument in the Russian city of Volgograd. In early 1994, sculptor Diana Walczak created a four-foot clay sculpture of Michael, based on a photo shoot she supervised of Michael posing as he did when he exploded out of the stage at the start of each concert on the Dangerous Tour. The clay sculpture was then digitised to create the cover image. The idea Dan Beck envisioned for the cover was much simpler. "The original idea that I had for the history concept was a very textured cover that really embraced the fans, with symbols like Michael's shoes and white socks, and maybe a hand written lyric sheet," he said. "But Michael saw history in a different way, his vision of history was of statues and generals and he ran away with that idea."

As part of the promotion campaign, Sony built nine huge 32-foot steel and fibreglass statues of Michael based on the sculpture created by Walczak, which were placed strategically around European cities in mid-June. A day before the album's release, one of the statues was floated on a barge down the River Thames through London; the city's Tower Bridge was even raised to let the statue pass through. Statues were also placed in the Netherlands, Berlin, Milan, Paris, Madrid, Prague, Zurich and Vienna, which reflected the fact the majority of Michael's target audience was now outside the United States.

In July Michael filmed a video for the album's second single, 'You Are Not Alone'. It was the obvious choice for Sony, as the song was already popular with radio stations. The video was different from anything Michael had ever done before; it features semi-nude scenes with Lisa Marie and a performance in front of an empty hall in Hollywood's Pantages Theater.

Michael literally made history – again – when 'You Are Not Alone' became the first song to enter straight at number one on the *Billboard* 100, breaking the record set by 'Scream' only weeks earlier. It also topped the charts in the United Kingdom.

In the space of three months – between September and November – Michael sang some of his new songs during four one-off performances in America and on the hugely popular German Saturday night entertainment TV show *Wetten Dass*. At the MTV Video Music Awards in New York, Michael performed a 20-minute medley with stunning routines of 'Billie Jean' and 'Dangerous'.

In October Michael filmed a video for 'Earth Song' in the town of Warwick, New York, where a safe forest fire was simulated in a corn field. The video, which cost $2.6 million, has an environmental theme, featuring images of animal cruelty, deforestation, pollution, poverty and war. Before Michael filmed his parts, director Nick Brandt and his team travelled as far as the Amazon basin, Africa and Croatia to shoot scenes over a six-week period. The single was released in Europe in December, hitting the number one spot in the United Kingdom and staying there for six weeks, although it was only released to radio in America.

At the tail end of the year it was announced that Michael had merged his ATV Music Publishing catalogue, better known as the 'Beatles catalogue', with Sony for a return of $115 million. Michael had taken a big financial hit over the previous four years; the Dangerous Tour was hugely expensive due to high production costs and the abrupt cancellation, he paid over $20 million to settle a civil lawsuit, the costs of running the Neverland Ranch were increasing yearly, and he was spending tens of millions on making his albums and videos. But Michael denied the deal was made due to money issues. "This acquisition had nothing to do with needing funds," he said. "It's smart business."

Although Michael lost 50% ownership of ATV it was a merger not a sale; the deal merged it with Sony's own catalogue, creating Sony/ATV Music Publishing and becoming the third largest music publisher in the world in the process. Through the agreement, Michael became one of the most important shareholders in Sony. "We have been working on this for over a year and, now, with the two of us together, the sky is our only limit," Michael said at the time.

Tommy Mottola described it as 'a great deal' for Michael. "He basically had given up control of only half the catalogue in exchange for twice the money that he's paid for it," Mottola said. "Plus, the way Sony/ATV would market the overall catalogue, it would be highly profitable and in Michael's best interests over the long run. Further, Michael as a partner would participate in Sony's publishing interests. If Michael had been only a businessman, it would have been a dynamite win-win for everyone. The only problem was the deal connected Sony and Michael at the hip at a time when Michael the artist was in decline and would spend any amount of money to prove that he wasn't."

ONE NIGHT ONLY

In early December, Michael flew to New York to begin rehearsing for a highly anticipated cable concert special, which was set to be screened on HBO at 8pm on Sunday, December 10. The special, called *One Night Only*, was due to be filmed at the historic 2,800 capacity Beacon Theater on Broadway over two successive nights on December 8 and 9, with the highlights edited together.

Michael hired top television producer Jeff Margolis, whom he had known for many years, to produce and direct the show. One of the projects the two had worked on together previously was the Sammy Davis Jr. 60th Anniversary Special in November 1989.

Margolis said the decision to perform in such a small Broadway theatre was made by Michael and his managers. "They thought it would be really nice to see Michael in an intimate venue as opposed to the giant stadiums and arenas he was used to performing in, so both Michael and the fans could be closer to one another," he explained.

As well as his classic hits, Michael was planning to perform some of the new material from *HIStory*, including 'Earth Song', 'You Are Not Alone', 'Smile' and 'Childhood'. Michael had planned a special pantomime performance of 'Childhood' for the show with internationally acclaimed French actor and mime artist Marcel Marceau. The performance was set to feature a courtyard scene, with Michael on the left-hand side of the stage and Marceau on the right, both bathed in pools of light. While Michael was singing the song, Marceau would mime its themes. "From the very beginning, he wanted me to display, in this song, the yearning of his youth," Marceau said.

But at around 5pm on December 6, only two days before the first performance, Michael suddenly collapsed on stage while rehearsing 'Black or White' at the Beacon Theater. Jeff Margolis recalls the moment Michael fell face-first, hitting his head on a metal section of the stage flooring. "It was very frightening to all of us involved, we only hoped that he was OK," the producer said. After paramedics arrived, Michael was rushed to Beth Israel Medical Center on the Upper East Side.

Many believed the incident was a publicity stunt or a way for Michael to get out of the commitment, because he was unhappy with aspects of the show. Michael's estranged sister, La Toya, told the press the collapse was 'a little scheme' to get attention. After production began, Michael called in director Kenny Ortega – who had worked on the Dangerous Tour – because he was unhappy some of his classic choreography was being re-choreographed. Ortega said Michael seemed 'anxious' about what was happening around him. "I think that there were new choreographers that were brought in and the attempt was to put on a show with Michael's music and to do choreography that was fresh and new and different," Ortega said. "And Michael felt that the choreography was classic, timeless, and didn't need to be changed, and he was unhappy about that."

Michael said he was under a huge amount of pressure. "I worked so much to prepare that show, there was such a pressure, people pushing me to do this show no matter what," he said. "Then finally, nature took its course and said, 'Stop'. She decided I shouldn't do that show."

Sandy Gallin says Michael simply decided he wasn't going to do the show. "He didn't think it was good enough, and he didn't want to do it. He felt very insecure about it. He didn't like the choreography, and had a real anxiety and fear about it. He just didn't like what he was doing."

But Margolis, who witnessed the collapse, says it was 'definitely' not staged. The doctor who treated Michael also said his patient was in a 'critical' condition. "He was dehydrated," Dr William Alleyne said. "He had low blood pressure. He had a rapid heart rate. He was near death." Within an hour of Michael's arrival at the hospital, Dr Alleyne had him stabilised with intravenous fluids and other treatment, and transferred him to intensive care.

In the meantime, the world's media and hundreds of fans began to gather outside the hospital. Michael's visitors included Lisa Marie, his mother, his sister Janet, nephews 3T and long-time friend Diana Ross.

Even though the show was ready to go it was never rescheduled, costing both Michael and HBO a large sum of money. HBO officials had predicted the special would reach 250 million people worldwide. Jeff Margolis said the audience would have seen a side of Michael they had never seen before. "It would have really helped to move his career forward to the next chapter," he said.

Michael described the version of 'Childhood' he was due to perform with Marcel Marceau as 'wonderful'. "I adore this version of 'Childhood', it's strange, nobody ever saw it…there are things like that which nobody will ever see," he said.

After a week in hospital and further recuperation in his suite at the Four Seasons Hotel, Michael flew to Disneyland Paris for a break with the Cascio family.

It was an unfortunate end to what was a prolific year for Michael. Despite the marketing challenges he and Sony faced following the allegations, the *HIStory* campaign had started successfully.

THE CAMPAIGN ROLLS ON

In January 1996, Lisa Marie filed for divorce after only 20 months of marriage, citing irreconcilable differences. The two had a major falling out while Michael was in hospital a few weeks earlier. According to his hair/make-up artist Karen Faye, Michael planned to file for divorce first, but Lisa Marie called him and begged him not to. "She begged and begged, saying please don't file," Faye said. Michael promised not to file, only to see in the press the next morning that she had beaten him to it.

Michael continued with the *HIStory* campaign in February when he flew to Brazil to film a video for 'They Don't Care About Us', directed by Spike Lee, in the Dona Marta shantytown in Rio de Janeiro. Unhappy with the final edit, Michael had Lee put together a full 'prison version' of the video, shot in a studio in New York a few weeks earlier. The two versions were initially going to be edited together into a single video. After the 'prison version' was then banned by many music channels due to violent, true-to-life images such as the Rodney King beating, genocide and execution, Michael replaced it with the Brazil version.

'They Don't Care About Us' was released as the fourth commercial single from *HIStory* in March, and the first in the United States in seven months. Sony had considered releasing 'Money' instead, but Michael wanted 'They Don't Care About Us'. 'Money' would surely have been a wiser choice, at least in the States, where radio stations were reluctant to play 'They Don't Care About Us' due to the lyric controversy. As a result it only peaked at number 30 on the *Billboard* 100, although it managed to reach number four in the United Kingdom.

In March a press conference was held in Paris to announce the launch of Kingdom Entertainment, a surprise joint business venture between Michael and Saudi multi-billionaire business magnate Prince Al-Waleed bin Talal, dubbed 'one of the world's most powerful investors'. The two first met aboard the Prince's yacht in Cannes in September 1994, and later developed plans to create an entertainment empire. "Through Kingdom Entertainment the Prince and myself will combine human and financial resources to be successful in all phases of the global entertainment revolution," Michael said. "As an example, we intend to be active in theme parks, hotels, animation, feature films, interactive educational entertainment, and of course character licensing and merchandising."

The company also acquired 50% ownership of the Landmark Entertainment Group; a Hollywood-based diversified entertainment company with divisions in motion pictures and television, licensing merchandise, live entertainment and attractions, and theme parks and resorts. Kingdom Entertainment's first major project would be the sponsoring of Michael's third solo tour, the *HIStory* Tour, which was scheduled to start in September 1996.

MICHAEL JACKSON'S GHOSTS

Although the *HIStory* campaign was in full swing, Michael was still thinking about the scary themed short-film he began shooting in mid-1993 to promote the *Addams Family Values* movie. He had invested a large amount of money in the project, which was shelved in the wake of the child molestation allegations. Michael's love of film and directing meant he adopted the project for himself, and at 12–15 minutes it became an extension of the original idea. Initially titled *Is This Scary*, Michael renamed it *Michael Jackson's Ghosts* (shortened to *Ghosts*).

None of the original footage was retained when filming resumed in the spring of 1996 in a hangar at Van Nuys airport in Los Angeles. Michael had now lost his original director, Mick Garris, who was about to begin shooting the TV mini-series *The Shining*. Garris recommended Stan Winston, who did the special effects for the 1993 production, to take over the reins. "I wish I could have completed it with Michael but I had to do the mini-series with Stephen [King]," Garris said. "So I suggested to Michael that he do it with Stan, who directed the movie *Pumpkinhead*. I knew he was a good director. Stan didn't want to do it, but he saw the error of his ways after we talked about it with Michael, and he was so glad that he did it." Apart from some minor details, the new concept barely changed from the original. "Michael wanted to keep the theme [of the outcast stranger], which was very important to him," Garris said. "Although they did do some rewriting they kept Stephen King's name on it, because he has a lot of value in the horror community. I was no longer involved with it by then, but Michael would still call me about it late at night. 'Mick, it's going to be amazing', he would always say."

In the light of the events of 1993, which stopped production of the original in the first place, finishing *Ghosts* became even more important to Michael. The most significant script change saw the introduction of a town mayor, likely based on the figure of Santa Barbara district attorney Tom Sneddon. Originally a regular resident – played by actor Ken Jenkins – led the townspeople to the mansion of the maestro, but the mayor took over the role. "There's some pathos in this and I insisted on it," Michael said. "Well here's a guy, he doesn't really like to hurt anyone or offend anyone, but they find him to be strange and eccentric and weird, the older people do, the grown-ups because they're kind of bigoted." The film ends with the maestro scaring the mayor out of the mansion and winning over the people of the town. "When they start to challenge me, they make me territorial, and I start to challenge them back," Michael explained.

The dance choreography was the biggest change from the original. For *Ghosts*, Michael chose '2 Bad' from *HIStory* for a dance routine his character performs with his family of ghouls. Although the song was completed in 1995, it still had to be edited to fit into the film in the way Michael wanted, so a version that he could dance to was chopped up by Brad Buxer and engineer Eddie Delena. Buxer said *Ghosts* wasn't designed to promote '2 Bad', which was never released as a single. "Michael just always envisioned all of the dance scenes in the short-film to be centred around the groove in that song," Buxer said.

Michael, Buxer, Delena and fellow engineers Andrew Scheps, Matt Forger and Rob Hoffman camped out at Record One studio in Los Angeles to develop the film music; Michael split his time between the studio and the *Ghosts* set. "I worked on *Ghosts* for quite a while," Hoffman said. "Michael would have ideas, much the way he makes a record, and he would dictate to one of the crew what he wanted – singing, and beatboxing. As the film progressed those ideas would be refined, often while filming was taking place. We would get video from the set and need to edit and make changes, sometimes with Michael there, sometimes without."

Michael also resumed work on 'Ghosts', a track which developed from the *Addams Family Values* sessions in 1993 and was pulled up briefly during the *HIStory* sessions. Unlike '2 Bad', there were no plans to incorporate the song into the actual *Ghosts* dance routines. Instead, it would be played in its entirety over the end credits in a promotional format. "The song 'Ghosts' was never meant for the *Ghosts* short-film, Michael wanted to develop the song for future album release," Buxer said.

Ghosts was completed in the summer of 1996 after six weeks of production. Originally it was only supposed to run for 12–15 minutes, but in true Michael style it grew and grew during filming and ended up being over 39 minutes long. Although Michael saw it more as a film, in 2002 the Guinness Book of World Records honoured it as the longest music video ever, a record that was broken by Pharrell Williams in 2013. The entire project cost Michael a reported $15 million, but he wouldn't see much of a financial return. Television stations were offered the film as part of an hour-long special, but were put off by the high price.

Given the issues raised in the film it was very important to Michael, but for his record label, it was an idea that didn't serve a purpose. "It wasn't connected to the *HIStory* album, and it wasn't a film, and it wasn't a music video, it was kind of in the middle," Dan Beck said. "Sometimes we needed to ask him, 'Why are we doing this', and sometimes it allowed him to refocus, but this was a situation where Michael rolled on with something and we couldn't stop him, it was happening."

After *Ghosts* was completed Michael began rehearsals for the upcoming *HIStory* Tour in Los Angeles, and filmed a video for 'Stranger in Moscow'.

THE GIFT

In early September, Michael left California to kick-start the tour with a concert in Prague. Even by his standards the production was enormous – a private jet, a Boeing 707 and two Antonov An-124 cargo planes were required to ferry a 190-man crew and equipment weighing 200 tons across the Atlantic. The opening concert at Letná Park in the Czech capital became one of the single largest concerts of Michael's career, with approximately 125,000 people in attendance. To open the show, Michael emerged onto the stage from a rocket dressed in a futuristic gold space suit, before beginning a rendition of 'Scream'.

Michael Jackson's Ghosts premiered at the Motion Picture Academy of Arts in Beverly Hills in October, alongside Stephen King's horror movie *Thinner*, although Michael didn't attend as he was away touring. His new track 'Ghosts', which was completed in studios in Amsterdam and London during the tour, debuted during the end credits.

In November, the *HIStory* Tour arrived in Australia. While in Sydney, Michael surprisingly married close friend Debbie Rowe, an assistant to his dermatologist who was barely known in media circles. The service took place before a handful of friends at the Sheraton-on-the-Park Hotel in the hours following a concert at the Sydney Cricket Ground. The pair never had a romantic relationship, and only wedded because Michael's mother was unhappy that her son was fathering a child with a woman to whom he was not married – it had been revealed 11 days earlier that Rowe was six months pregnant. Rowe admits she agreed to carry Michael's children as 'a gift'. "Michael was divorced, lonely and wanted children," she explained. "I was the one who said to him, 'I will have your babies'."

The first leg of the *HIStory* Tour ended in January 1997 with the second of two concerts in Hawaii, Michael's first full shows in the United States in eight years. His drawing power in his homeland was thought to have diminished greatly since then, mainly due to the press circus that surrounded the child molestation investigation and subsequent settlement.

But Michael needn't have worried about a backlash, as he made history by becoming the first musical act to sell out the Aloha Stadium in Honolulu. At the time, promoter Tom Moffatt said he had never seen anything like it. "I've been doing these things since Elvis," he said, "and there's been nothing even close to this – the Rolling Stones, Elton John, Julio Iglesias, the Eagles."

Yet the marketing focus wasn't about to shift back to the United States, where sales of *HIStory* had fallen short of expectations. By the end of 1996, the album had long disappeared from the *Billboard* 200 chart and the American pop consciousness. But it was a completely different story overseas, where the promotion campaign was still in full gear and about to outlast Sony's 18-month plan. The record label was shipping as many as 100,000 copies of *HIStory* a week outside the United States, and it remained a top-seller in dozens of European and Asian countries. With nearly a year of the *HIStory* Tour remaining, Sony was also on course to achieving its target of 20 million album sales. Despite being twice as expensive as a typical CD, sales eventually exceeded that figure, making it the biggest-selling double album ever.

Michael's appeal outside of the United States was reflected in his next project, which came as something of a surprise to both his fans and collaborators.

CHAPTER 14:
BLOOD ON THE DANCE FLOOR

1997

Michael had considered following *HIStory* with a sequel album, *HIStory Book II*, which engineer Rob Hoffman said would have followed a similar format, with both new songs and greatest hits. "It would have included more old hits because there were songs such as 'Human Nature', 'Dirty Diana', 'Smooth Criminal' and 'Dangerous' that weren't on part one, and then there were the big songs from *HIStory*, like 'You Are Not Alone' and 'Earth Song', that they were going to add," Hoffman explained.

But recording a whole new album at this stage would have been time consuming, and Michael was interested in a shorter project. "The *HIStory Book II* concept was talked about but never that big of an idea in Michael's mind," Brad Buxer said. "Michael's desire was for an album with a limited amount of new tracks and one that wouldn't be that complicated or take that long to do."

Instead, Michael decided to record four new songs for a 'maxi single' to promote the forthcoming European leg of the *HIStory* Tour, which was scheduled to kick off in the German city of Bremen on May 31. Sony liked the idea, but believed a full album would perform better commercially. The label's idea was to fill out the album with nine club remixes of songs from *HIStory*, which Matt Forger said were aimed at the international market. "The practical thing was a record to support the second leg of the *HIStory* Tour, which was international," he said. "So the album filled that purpose as the remixes had a much more international dance sound."

Michael would get back into the studio to work on the new songs after the conclusion of his two Hawaii concerts, when the *HIStory* Tour took a five-month break. "It was then that we set out to complete the album," Forger said. "I was there to make sure the album got finished – the idea was to have it ready and released in time for the second part of the tour." With limited time on his side, Michael chose to finish four of his favourite songs which had failed to make the previous two albums, *Dangerous* and *HIStory*, rather than write and record completely new material from scratch.

In mid-January 1997, recording began not in California but on the shores of Lake Geneva in Switzerland – it was said that Michael loved the calmness and beauty of the location. "I think the trip enabled him to get away from Los Angeles," Forger said. "It was quieter there."

Michael travelled to Europe with a four-man team of Forger, Brad Buxer, mixing engineer Mick Guzauski and programmer Matt Carpenter. His usual engineer, Bruce Swedien, couldn't join them because of other commitments. They spent two weeks in the picturesque town of Montreux, staying in the Tower Suite in the Hôtel Montreux-Palace. During the trip Michael viewed a former residence of long-time idol Charlie Chaplin, now owned by the late English comic's family. It was reported that he enquired about purchasing the property, only to be told it was not for sale. Regardless, he visited Chaplin's grave to pay his respects and also dined with the family.

The team recorded at Mountain Studios, located inside Montreux Casino and owned by rock band Queen until 1993. Queen recorded several of their classic albums at the studio, and the Rolling Stones, AC/DC and David Bowie had also worked there.

It was at Mountain Studios where work resumed on a track which was started six years earlier during the *Dangerous* sessions with producer Teddy Riley, 'Blood on the Dance Floor'. During those sessions Michael had a hard time getting the song to sound the way he wanted. But like many other songs he often left on the shelf, he felt he could get it right eventually. The team took Riley's original demo with them to Switzerland, but as it existed only on a Digital Audio Tape, the track had to be completely recreated. "I played every single part, including all music and all drums for that new master, simply by copying exactly what Teddy had already done on the demo," Brad Buxer said. "In the end we had recreated a master that could now be used on an album and one that Michael could now do vocals to. Michael absolutely loved what we had done, and we had an absolute blast in Montreux."

Riley admitted he was disappointed that Michael didn't call him to 'vacuum clean this old master'. "When I heard it finished, I wished I could've been the one to [complete it]," Riley said. "But Michael knows what he wants, and he was happy with it."

Michael returned to California in early February to shoot a video for 'Blood on the Dance Floor', which was directed by Vince Paterson. That same week Michael's first child, Prince Michael, was born, so naturally he was a little distracted on set. But Paterson said the two still had an 'incredible time' working together. "Mike gave me so much freedom and trusted in me," Paterson said. "He loved the idea of dancing with a girl and loved the whole concept. We also shot a Super 8 [camera] version that Michael loved but Sony didn't want to use. I think it is very hot, perhaps the sexiest Michael ever looked."

After shooting was completed Michael attended a gala in Hollywood to celebrate Elizabeth Taylor's 65th birthday. He sang a song he wrote especially for his best friend while in Switzerland, called 'Elizabeth I Love You'. Michael composed the song over the phone with Buz Kohan, who co-wrote 'Gone Too Soon' from *Dangerous* as well as 'You Were There', which Michael sang at another gala in honour of Sammy Davis Jr. in November 1989. With its simple but powerful nature, the performance of 'Elizabeth I Love You' resembled the one Michael gave for Davis.

DARK THEMES, DARK MOODS

In February and March, Michael and his recording team camped out at Record Plant studio in Hollywood to resume working on tracks for the album, which was given the title *Blood on the Dance Floor/HIStory in the Mix* to reflect the hybrid format of new material and remixes. Michael and the four-man Montreux team were joined by producers Bryan Loren and Bill Bottrell, and engineers Dave Way and Keith Cohen. In true Michael form he also had other studios booked out, including Larrabee West and Ocean Way, which was used for orchestra.

Finishing touches were put on 'Blood on the Dance Floor' by the engineers, and Michael pulled a handful of songs out of the vault which had failed to make *Dangerous* and *HIStory*, including 'Morphine', 'In the Back', 'Seven Digits' and 'Superfly Sister'. Another song considered for inclusion was 'On the Line', written by Michael and produced with Babyface. It was originally recorded in July 1996 for the Spike Lee movie *Get on the Bus*, but wasn't included on the movie soundtrack.

Although 'Morphine' was mostly completed in New York in 1994 during the *HIStory* sessions, a few changes were made in 1997. Brad Buxer, Bill Bottrell and engineer Jon Mooney all sang background vocals on the track with Michael. "I do remember Michael and me driving over to Larrabee West in West Hollywood where there was an engineer [Keith Cohen] working on 'Morphine'," Bottrell recalls. "Michael and I sang a loose, rowdy chorus, and it was the most fun I had during those weeks." Slash and the Andraé Crouch Choir feature as special guests.

Brad Buxer describes 'In the Back', a song about betrayal, as 'one of the greatest songs Michael has ever done'. But instead Michael chose to include the sexual 'Superfly Sister', which was recorded with Bryan Loren during the *Dangerous* sessions. Another option was 'Seven Digits', also created with Loren, but it was still in a very incomplete state. Loren resumed work on 'Seven Digits' at Michael's behest, but with the tight time restrictions they chose 'Superfly Sister' as it needed the least amount of work.

Loren said he created the music and title for 'Superfly Sister', while Michael wrote the lyrics. "I remember giving Michael a tape with the basic track, from there we wrote the melody together," he said. "A few days later, Michael came back with the lyrics to the song, and we basically recorded it right away." When work on 'Superfly Sister' resumed in 1997 it still had to be mixed and arranged; Loren added a guitar solo and piano parts and Michael recorded some additional vocals and ad-libs. Although Michael received the sole production credit, Loren said they produced the track together.

The four new songs eventually chosen for inclusion on the album were 'Blood on the Dance Floor', 'Morphine', 'Superfly Sister' and 'Ghosts'. A version of 'Ghosts' had already been completed a few months earlier so it could be promoted at the end of the *Ghosts* film during its fall 1996 release.

Engineer Dave Way, who put the finishing touches on 'Ghosts' and 'Superfly Sister', said the sessions were completely different to what he experienced when he worked on *Dangerous*. "It seemed with this album like they were really searching for songs, scrounging almost," Way admitted. "All the songs were from previous sessions and they were doing anything to find songs. I really felt a contrast between *Dangerous* and those sessions. During *Dangerous* there was a real buzz, and Michael was in great spirits. There was a lot going on, people were in and out of the studio all the time, including several different producers and Michael's celebrity friends. This was before those allegations that had such an effect on him. But *Blood on the Dance Floor* was different, it was quiet. By the time I worked on the record, it was just Michael, Matt Forger, a few others and me. And Michael seemed unhappy; he was very secretive, something just wasn't right with him."

Producer Bill Bottrell also recalls a strange atmosphere. "I kicked around a bit and found the atmosphere chaotic and out of control," he said. "There were no adults, and lots of people working in different rooms. And Michael was in trouble. He was angry and abusive, and I shall forever regret leaving him that way. Forever." Bottrell said he did not know what was causing Michael to behave in such a way, but the dark themes of the new songs, especially 'Morphine', were perhaps reflective of his mood at the time. Neither Bottrell nor Way worked with Michael on the next album, and neither did Matt Forger. It was the end of an era.

After completing his studio work Michael jetted across the Atlantic to spend a few weeks in Paris, where he rehearsed throughout April ahead of the forthcoming second leg of the *HIStory* Tour. While Michael was in the French capital, *Blood on the Dance Floor* was being mastered back at Bernie

Grundman's studio in Los Angeles, and Matt Forger had the task of flying nearly 6,000 miles so Michael could hear the mixes.

Dave Way, who was mixing some of the tracks with Forger, remembers the incident well. "One day, we had just finished fine-tuning a mix over the phone with Michael while he was in France," Way recalls, "and he said, 'Dave, that's great. Can you put Matt on the phone please?' So Matt talked to him for a while. When the conversation ended, Matt said to me, 'Dave I need that DAT, a pair of Auratone speakers and an amplifier.' I said, 'Where are you going?' Matt said, 'To France!' He left immediately and caught the first available flight from LAX. He said he had already done the same thing a couple of times!"

HEARD ABOUT MICHAEL'S NEW ALBUM?

By the time Michael attended a screening of *Ghosts* at the Cannes Film Festival on May 9, 1997, the film had changed from the one released in the fall of 1996. Michael revealed that director Stan Winston thought the dance sequences should contain more music. As a result a short segment of 'Ghosts', originally played only over the end credits, was edited into one of the sequences. A portion of 'Is It Scary', a song with a similar theme which was mostly recorded during the *HIStory* sessions with Jimmy Jam and Terry Lewis producing, was also used.

"We needed more music and neither me, Stan Winston or anyone else could understand why we were not using 'Ghosts' or 'Is It Scary' in the short-film," Brad Buxer said. "We talked Michael into what seemed an obvious choice – why not use 'Is It Scary' and 'Ghosts' in a film about…ghosts?"

But as the dance scenes had already been filmed, incorporating the songs wouldn't be an easy task. "No dance scenes were ever shot to the music of 'Ghosts' or 'Is It Scary' during the entire course of making the film," Buxer said. "The work we did was before all the plugs were available that make work like this easier these days."

At the last minute, over a course of three days – a Friday through to a Sunday – Buxer, Matt Forger and programmer Matt Carpenter had to change the tempo of 'Ghosts' and 'Is It Scary' to fit the pre-shot dance segments. "We made new music work with pre-existing Michael Jackson choreography that was much slower than the original music, and it worked beautifully," Buxer said. "We did all the work at my house and when Stan Winston came over to view and listen to the work we had done, he loved it."

Michael, however, was satisfied with the original version, which featured only '2 Bad'. "Stan thought we should put more songs in the film, so we did, but I thought that the first version was good, I was satisfied," he said.

Michael attends a screening of *Ghosts* at the Cannes Film Festival

A late decision was made to include 'Is It Scary' on *Blood on the Dance Floor* as another soundtrack song, in addition to 'Ghosts'. To accommodate it, a remix of 'Tabloid Junkie' was removed. The eight remaining remixes, 'Scream', 'Money', '2 Bad', 'Stranger in Moscow', 'This Time Around', 'Earth Song', 'You Are Not Alone' and 'HIStory', were performed by artists such as Pete Heller, David Morales and Wyclef Jean. But Michael wasn't overly enthusiastic about their inclusion. "The least I can say is that I don't like them," he admitted. "I don't like it that they come in and change my songs completely, but Sony says that the kids love remixes."

Blood on the Dance Floor/HIStory in the Mix was released on May 20 to coincide with the next leg of the *HIStory* Tour, which would begin in Germany eleven days later. Both the album and lead single, the title track, went to number one in the United Kingdom, and were hits all over Europe.

The second and final commercial single release from *Blood on the Dance Floor* was a double A-side offering of 'Ghosts' and the Tony Moran remix of 'HIStory'. Released in July, the single reached number five on the United Kingdom chart but was less of a hit elsewhere. Both songs were promoted with videos; the video for the 'HIStory' remix uses archived footage of Michael, and the video for 'Ghosts' was taken from the *Ghosts* film, but edited down to five minutes.

The album and lead single had little promotion in the United States, where they failed to trouble the top 20. Support from both radio stations and music video channels was almost non-existent. The situation was perhaps best summed up by a headline from the *Los Angeles Times* two weeks before the release, which read: 'Psssst–Heard About Michael's New Album?' *The New York Times* said the promotional effort created 'hardly a sound'.

American critics panned Michael for the commercial performance of the album; *The Daily Gazette* said Michael 'is witnessing an erosion' of his fan base in the States, while *The Associated Press* said 'the thriller is gone for Michael Jackson'. But there was praise in most quarters for the actual music – at least the new tracks anyway.

Both Matt Forger and Sony executives themselves said the album's modest performance in the States was due to a deliberate marketing focus on Europe, Australia and New Zealand. "The album was deliberately aimed at the international market as Michael was going to tour Europe as part of the second leg, the idea of the album was to further boost the tour," Forger explained. Sony reiterated this, saying it was 'completely behind the album'. "Michael is certainly one of our superstars and is treated as such, we just went into this one with our global hats on," Melani Rogers, a spokeswoman for Epic, said.

Due to a lack of promotion in some corners of the world the album 'only' went on to sell around six million copies worldwide, but the figure is still the highest ever for a remix album. The commercial performances of both *HIStory* and *Blood on the Dance Floor* overseas showed Michael effectively no longer needed the United States market to have a hit record, something which Sony was well aware of.

The album cover image is an oil painting by artist Will Wilson. To paint the image, Wilson observed still shots of Michael dancing in the 'Blood on the Dance Floor' video. After speaking to Wilson on the phone to discuss the finished piece, Michael asked him to add a black armband to his right arm. "I did talk to Michael on the phone just as the painting was finished and ready to be shipped," Wilson said. "He asked if I could add a black armband on his right arm, but I have no idea what its meaning is." Michael regularly wore an armband to remind people of children suffering around the world.

HISTORY IS...HISTORY

By the time the *HIStory* Tour resumed in Germany on May 31, Michael was under different management, having fired Sandy Gallin and Jim Morey, who had been representing him since 1990. Gallin, a Jew, says he was dismissed because he refused to go on television to defend Michael over claims he was anti-Semitic in the wake of the 'They Don't Care About Us' lyric controversy.

Michael wanted Gallin to persuade high profile Jewish figures Steven Spielberg, David Geffen and Jeffrey Katzenberg to defend him publicly.

in the press. "But they weren't going to do anything," Gallin said. "All of them said, 'Michael, you wrote the lyric, and now you have to stand by it and defend yourself.' He also wanted me to go on television to defend him. Let me make this clear, I never thought he was being anti-Semitic. But I said to him, 'Michael, nobody is going to know who I am, and secondly, it's like having a husband or wife defend you. What else would a manager do? No one is going to pay any attention to it. I think it's going to be a joke, and it will backfire on you.' He wanted me to do it in the worst way, and it would not have served the purpose and would have made me look foolish. I knew that he was going to fire me over it. And by that time, I really didn't care that much. There were so many crazy things going on, and he wasn't thinking clearly at the time. Something was really not right."

Gallin and Morey were replaced with Tarak Ben Ammar, a media advisor to Al-Waleed bin Talal, with whom Michael had started the business company Kingdom Entertainment a year earlier. Ben Ammar was brought in mainly to oversee Al-Waleed's investment and cut the costs of the *HIStory* Tour – the first leg had lost $26 million due to the huge costs of staging the shows and Michael's considerable entourage. For the second leg operational costs would be cut by 50%, reducing the overall loss.

Over the course of Michael's 35-date tour around Europe in the summer of 1997, fans and those close to him became concerned over his apparent substance abuse. On several occasions concerts were in danger of being cancelled as Michael was still in bed in his hotel room minutes before the beginning of the show.

It would later be revealed that he was using the powerful anaesthetic Propofol during the tour to sleep, as sedatives had failed to work. Michael would receive the intravenously administered drug, usually used in a hospital setting, in his hotel room. Michael was never a great sleeper, but his insomnia would only become a serious issue during a tour phase. He would struggle to sleep after a show because of the adrenaline rush, and felt a real pressure to get enough rest in order to be fully energised for upcoming shows. "Michael was so buzzed by his own adrenaline after a show it would take him 24 hours to relax his body, and sometimes it would take two days to be able to sleep," Michael's hair/make-up artist Karen Faye explained. "He tried to find ways to deal with it."

Michael's wife, Debbie Rowe, said he turned to Propofol only after the sedatives failed to work. "I think they tried it and it hadn't worked and if he couldn't sleep, he couldn't perform," she said. "Michael was at the end of his rope. He didn't know what to do." Rowe tried to warn Michael about using such a dangerous drug. But after asking him about the possible fatal consequences, Michael told her he was more concerned about not sleeping than what could happen.

Alimorad Farshchian, a Miami-based doctor who treated Michael several years later, believes Michael's chronic sleep issues were caused by surgery to his face. "You have an area inside your nose called the turbinates, and if you remove the turbinates, it's possible that you produce what they call empty nose syndrome, producing insomnia," Dr Farshchian said. "To me, that was the cause of it."

The final show of the tour took place in Durban, South Africa in October, signalling the end of both the *HIStory* and *Blood on the Dance Floor* campaigns. It was a gruelling tour with a total of 82 shows, but Michael received criticism in some quarters for only singing the Jackson 5 medley and one full song, 'Wanna Be Startin' Somethin'', live during each concert. While singing those numbers his voice appeared hoarse and not at the level it had been in previous years.

Despite the substance abuse, the only concert Michael cancelled during the entire tour was the Ostend date in Belgium on September 1, following the death of Princess Diana. The rescheduled date took place two days later, although the cancellation cost Michael $170,000. The tour grossed a total of $165 million – the most any solo performer had ever grossed – but Michael still lost $11.2 million due to the huge costs incurred during the first leg.

In December, Sony planned to release a double A-side single comprising 'Smile' and 'Is It Scary', which would have been the final act in the *HIStory/Blood on the Dance Floor* promotion campaigns. Michael wanted to promote the release with a $2 million video for 'Smile'. But instead of shelling out millions of dollars when the campaign had essentially come to an end, Sony wanted Michael to promote it by singing 'Smile' live at the Royal Variety Show in London and on the popular German Saturday night entertainment TV show *Wetten Dass* in early November. But Michael was tired of performing, as the gruelling *HIStory* Tour had only just finished. The label did not believe the single would perform well commercially without the live performances, so, much to Michael's frustration, the release was cancelled.

Little did he know at this stage that a full-blown fallout with his record label would sabotage the final studio album of his life.

CHAPTER 15: THE FINAL ALBUM

LATE 1997 – MID 2001

Michael's last two projects were a combination of new songs and previous hits and remixes, but the next one was going to be a studio album with new material only. Upon its completion, Michael had plans to finally realise his movie dreams after years of setbacks.

Almost immediately after the *HIStory* Tour came to an end, Michael began composing music for the album with Brad Buxer at the producer's Los Angeles house. This is where the pair started the working titles for 'Hanson', 'That', 'Bio' and 'Monster' (not the posthumous release version). 'Hanson' was originally written for the American pop band of the same name, which had worldwide success in the summer of 1997 with the hit single 'MMMBop'. The song would later develop into 'The Way You Love Me'. Michael also sounded out new producers.

Although Michael began working on music again, for the first seven months of 1998 he mostly concentrated on raising his son Prince and second child Paris (born April 1998), as well as an array of business ventures.

In May he began looking into entertainment projects with his new business partner, African-American mogul Don Barden, who had opened a casino in Michael's Indiana birthplace two years earlier. They viewed potential sites in the U.S. Virgin Islands, Las Vegas and the African country of Namibia, but by July the pair's attention had turned to Detroit, where they announced plans to build an ambitious $1 billion hotel, casino and theme park complex named Majestic Kingdom. Barden believed Majestic Kingdom had the potential to grow into the largest African-American company in the world within two years. But following a campaign to convince the people of Detroit to approve the scheme, Michael discovered in August that it had been rejected.

Michael's affiliation with Barden came at a time when his relationship with Saudi Prince Al-Waleed bin Talal was on the wane. Although Michael had ambitious plans for their joint entertainment venture, including movie and theme park projects, it yielded only the sponsoring of the *HIStory* Tour and the distribution of the *Michael Jackson's Ghosts* home video. Al-Waleed also invested in Michael's record label, MJJ Music, which eventually folded.

During this time Michael turned to music executive John McClain to manage his career, replacing Tarak Ben Ammar, a media advisor to Al-Waleed who had been brought in a year earlier mainly to oversee the prince's investment. Whereas Ben Ammar was more of a business figure, McClain had a history in music management. A childhood friend of the Jackson brothers, McClain launched his executive career at A&M in the early eighties and later crafted the career of Michael's sister, Janet. McClain became a key figure in black music and was also part of the original founding team of Interscope Records in 1989.

After his business ambitions failed to materialise, Michael returned to the recording studio in August 1998. For the next project he wanted a more 'street' sound, which would involve working with the best young hip-hop, R&B and new jack swing producers around. Rap star Sean 'Puff Daddy' Combs wrote a song for the album, and producer Kenneth 'Babyface' Edmonds was also approached. Michael worked with Babyface during both the *Dangerous* and *HIStory* sessions, and the pair also collaborated on a song called 'On the Line' in 1996, which was recorded for the Spike Lee movie *Get on the Bus*. Thanks to this collaboration, the two got together again and worked on at least two songs, including 'Angel', supposedly inspired by the birth of Michael's son and described by Babyface as 'simply fantastic'. Michael also expressed an interest in working with DeVante Swing, lead writer and producer of the band Jodeci. Despite all proposing ideas to Michael, none of that material would develop much further.

Puff Daddy said his and Michael's ways of working were totally different. "He takes an insane amount of time to record a track, but that's just him, it's the way he works," the rapper said. "We weren't really suitable together, and I got some harsh looks I must say. You know when Michael Jackson's not happy – he pulls this funny face, but doesn't vocally tell you. He wanted to work his way, and I couldn't do that. I am never going to be a yes man to anyone. And I had an album coming out, had a tour, I couldn't really invest that amount of time."

Michael's main work at this stage was with long-time collaborator Brad Buxer and Dr. Freeze, real name Elliot Straite, a relatively unknown new jack swing producer. Michael had rooms booked out at both Record Plant and Record One in Los Angeles, with different sessions and production teams based across both studios. Whether at Record Plant or Record One, Buxer would typically occupy one room, while Freeze would work in the other.

Buxer continued to help Michael develop his own song ideas, and they also worked on songs R. Kelly had written for the project. Kelly, who contributed 'You Are Not Alone' to *HIStory*, submitted at least two tracks, including the R&B ballads 'Cry' and 'One More Chance'. The former, which highlights problems with the planet, became one of the earliest songs fully completed for the project.

Freeze, looking for his first big hit since co-writing and producing R&B group Color Me Badd's song 'I Wanna Sex You Up' in 1991, was brought to the project by Michael's new manager, John McClain. "I did not believe it at first and I thought it was crazy," Freeze admitted. The producer put together some demos, including 'Break of Dawn', 'Blue Gangsta' and 'A Place with No Name', all of which Michael loved.

"'Break of Dawn' is just a romantic ballad that I wrote one day," Freeze said. "For 'Blue Gangsta' I wanted to make a new 'Smooth Criminal', something more modern and rooted in the 2000s. That was the idea. 'A Place with No Name' is itself a kind of escape, a song where you just close your eyes to find yourself instantly transported into a wonderful world. In fact, this song was inspired by 'A Horse with No Name' from the group America. The lyrics of this song are very deep."

Of the three, 'Break of Dawn' was Michael's favoured choice. "That was his baby," Freeze said. "He just had to record vocals and add his magic, he did not want to change anything, and he wanted to keep the magic of the song absolutely intact." Michael even wanted to keep Freeze's chorus. "He found it very beautiful, and he wanted to leave everything as is," Freeze explained. "He liked my singing and would not spoil the chorus – he loved how I had preserved it." 'Blue Gangsta' and 'A Place with No Name' were eventually left on the shelf, but work on 'Break of Dawn' would continue for several years. "The process in the studio was as long as if we were filming a movie," Freeze said.

Assistant engineer CJ deVillar – who was on the staff at Record Plant when Michael began recording there – was one of several engineers working on the album at the time. Others included Mike Ging, Humberto Gatica and Michael Durham Prince, who worked mainly with Buxer. DeVillar recalls how Freeze's vocals could sound very similar to Michael's. "I think that's partly why Michael wanted Freeze to sing the chorus of 'Break of Dawn'," deVillar said.

DeVillar, who left the project in early 1999, has nothing but fond memories of his short time working with Michael. "Michael was very calm, he liked to chat and hang out, and he was totally at home in the studio because we engineers were his playmates," deVillar said. "No one wanted anything from him in the studio, and you could see how relaxed he was there. He would come in with wrinkled, dirty clothes because he didn't have to dress up, he could come straight from his house or hotel to the studio and didn't have to worry what he looked like. I always tried to make him feel safe and at home and I never asked him for anything, like photos or signatures."

DeVillar said one of most memorable moments was when singer Brandy Norwood came by the studio to meet Michael. "I went to the studio front door and saw Brandy there, she knew Michael was in the studio and really wanted to meet him. So I was like, 'Mmm OK, I'm not so sure but I'll ask him.' So I went to Michael and said, 'Brandy is here and she wants to meet you. She knows you're in here!' So he said, 'Ohh CJ, but I'm so stinky! I'm not dressed up, I'm a mess!' But she got her way and came in."

For some sessions, Michael would drive himself to the studio. "He would drive in his big red truck and come in with his son Prince," deVillar recalls. "Some sessions it was just me, Michael and Seth Riggs, his vocal coach. Prince would be running around the studio somewhere, and there were three sessions when I actually ended up holding Prince while Michael was recording his vocals. I would be at the console, working with one arm and Prince in the other."

During breaks, when Michael wasn't recording vocals, he liked to sit and watch cartoons with his son. "He would sit there and watch them, laughing, stirring a cup of hot water or tea with a spoon," deVillar said. "Then when I needed to record him he would be ready, and when we were done, he would go back to watch the cartoons."

ENTER: RODNEY JERKINS

After the Christmas break recording sessions were mostly held at Record One, where Michael continued to work with Dr. Freeze and Brad Buxer. He also began writing with Carole Bayer Sager, who wrote the *Off the Wall* track 'It's the Falling in Love' over 20 years earlier with producer David Foster. Michael was impressed with the pair's most recent effort, a duet by Celine Dion and Andrea Bocelli which won a Golden Globe for Best Original Song.

Michael, Sager and Foster came up with a millennium anthem, 'I Have This Dream', which Sager described as 'a song to take us into the year 2000 with hope'. "Our song will be a celebration of the changing times, a song for the future, which I suspect will be bright," she explained.

Sager also introduced Michael to twenty-one-year-old Rodney Jerkins, who was arguably the most in-demand R&B producer in the world at the time. "Everyone wants to work with Rodney," Atlantic Records executive Darren Higman said in February 1999. "A Rodney Jerkins song is the pedigree you want in R&B music. Right now, Rodney is in the position to do anything he wants."

Sager called the New Jersey-based producer and invited him to her house to join a writing session she was holding with Michael. Although Jerkins had sessions planned with other artists, it was an opportunity he could not turn down. Jerkins said there was a mysterious element about his first meeting with Michael, because of his reclusive nature. "You're not seeing him constantly at the industry events, and you're not seeing him at the parties, and so the mystique of it was just amazing," he admitted.

After a couple of meetings Michael offered Jerkins the opportunity to become his new Teddy Riley, and set him up at his Record One base. The producer recalls Michael telling him he wanted to 'shock the world' with his new music. "He [Michael] just sat down and said, 'I want you to give everything you got. Reach for something deeper. Go for it. Just go. Just go'."

And that's exactly what Jerkins did. He camped out at Record One to work on beats with his 'Darkchild' production team, which included songwriting partners LaShawn Daniels and his brother Fred Jerkins. Their engineer, Brad Gilderman, recalls exhausting sessions which often lasted for 30 straight hours. "At Record One Rodney started getting beats together, and it was all about writing," Gilderman said. "Rodney must have compiled around 30 beats and wrote a lot of stuff together with LaShawn. We didn't stop working, and we didn't go home at night. We literally slept in beds at the studio."

Although Michael wasn't in the studio much when the Darkchild team began work, he would still call in the middle of the night to check on their progress. Jerkins recalls: "Michael would call me at four o'clock in the morning and say, 'Play me what you got', and I'm like, 'Um, I'm about to go to sleep'! But that's how he was." LaShawn Daniels said the preparations that went into Michael's first visit to the studio were fit for the arrival of President Bill Clinton. "The place was swept, security came in, it was going crazy, it was going berserk," Daniels said.

At this stage Jerkins worked exclusively for Michael, turning down projects with LeAnn Rimes, N'Sync and Lil' Kim. He was also due to fly to London to work with British pop group the Spice Girls. "I was slated to do about seven or eight [other] artists in a single quarter," Jerkins recalls, "and Michael said, 'No, no, no. You have to really focus on my project.' And I was like, 'Yeah, but I got bills to pay.' And he said, 'I'll take care of those. Tell me what they're gonna pay you and how many songs and I'll take care of it'."

"THIS WILL BE MY LAST ALBUM"

In late March 1999, Michael left his production teams behind in California to work on a song in New York with producer Cory Rooney, who was also Sony's Senior Vice President. It was Sony Music chief Tommy Mottola who initiated the collaboration by proposing that Rooney, who had success making hits with artists such as Jennifer Lopez and Destiny's Child, produce a song with Michael. Rooney accepted the challenge and made a demo of a song called 'She Was Lovin' Me', which was sent to Michael in California. When he heard the tape, Michael loved it so much he decided to fly to the East Coast almost immediately to work on it with Rooney.

The pair then spent around three weeks 'tweaking' the song at the Hit Factory studio. "We spent almost a month of just talking and he was educating me on so many different things," Rooney recalls. "We barely got a lot of music done. It was a completely different experience than I thought it was going to be." At one point they left the studio, with Michael in a partial disguise, to watch magician David Blaine's latest stunt. Rooney was never able to complete 'She Was Lovin' Me', as he was busy helping to nurture the relationship between Michael and Rodney Jerkins, among his many other projects, and the idea was put on hold.

Work with Rooney stopped in mid-April when Michael flew to London, where he met with friend Mohamed Al Fayed. While in the city he gave a revealing interview to *The Daily Mirror*, telling the tabloid that this album would probably be his last. "I have an album coming out for the millennium, which I'm half way through," he said. "It's going to be the best thing I've ever done. I'm putting my heart and soul into it because I'm not sure if I'm gonna do another one after this. This will be my last album, I think. I may do the odd movie soundtrack, but this will be my last proper album." A few months later Michael confirmed that he would like to go into other areas, and not 'keep doing album after pop album'.

After returning to the United States, Michael decided he wanted a change of scenery and moved the album production from Los Angeles to New York. So the entire team, including Brad Buxer, Dr. Freeze, Rodney Jerkins and all the engineers, packed up and moved to the East Coast. It took them days to make copies of all the tapes and hard drives, label them, and then ship them to the Big Apple. Michael and his children checked into a suite at the luxury Waldorf Astoria hotel in Midtown Manhattan.

Michael spent most of May 1999 recording at both Sony Music Studios and the Hit Factory, which were a matter of feet apart on West 54th Street. At Sony, the Darkchild team finally presented their demos to Michael, a session which Fred Jerkins will never forget. "He [Michael] was standing in the control room, just kind of listening," Jerkins recalls. "He'd use his hands to punctuate a beat or chord change in the song, and at one point he just broke out dancing. I was trying to be cool and not stare, but all the time I was thinking, 'Wow, here's Michael Jackson right here, dancing to our music.' That was something."

The very first demo that was played to Michael was called 'You Rock My World'. After hearing the track, Michael asked who was doing the melodies. "It was me," recalls LaShawn Daniels, "and he [Michael] says, 'Shawn can you sing the melodies in my ear?' And I'm like, 'Are you serious dude?' He's like, 'Yeah just sing it in my ear.' I go right next to him and I gotta pull towards his ear and I start singing. Then he puts his hand on my shoulder and says, 'No. Let's change this part.' And I was like, 'Oh, my god!' I couldn't even continue and I had to stop. I said, 'Mike, listen, I appreciate you being so cool, but you can't be this cool with me because I don't really know how to take it. I don't even know what to do right now. And I can't concentrate on the melodies because I'm singing to Michael Jackson.' And he burst out laughing and just made us comfortable."

Other demos became 'Escape', 'Privacy' and the anti-war track 'We've Had Enough', one of three songs Jerkins co-wrote for the album with Carole Bayer Sager. Although Michael didn't create the initial demos, he contributed to the melodies and lyrics. Engineer Brad Gilderman said Michael seemed focused on his work during this time. "He was really on it, and he was now singing," Gilderman recalls. "He would come in at

10am every single day, and be in the studio until 6 or 7pm. It was very organised."

The Darkchild team worked to the point where they stopped showering and changing clothes. "In the end, the people at Sony studio were buying us new clothes because we weren't changing," Gilderman said. "Everything was over the top at Sony's studio. There were big screen TVs everywhere and there was so much food, every day there was at least $100 worth of fresh food lying around for people to eat. There was a couch and even a couple of beds. I could see then that Michael had sleeping problems, he would be awake at 3am reading a magazine in the corner of the room."

It became obvious to Gilderman that the album was costing millions of dollars to produce. "When we were in New York, I had a $700 a night hotel suite booked up, but I never even slept there," he said. "Nobody would cancel the rooms, but was it up to Michael to cancel hotel rooms? Of course not. I slept at the studio on an air mattress, most of us did, even Michael at times. I remember once when Michael and Rodney stayed in the studio overnight – it was like a pyjama party." Gilderman's abiding memory of working with Michael was watching him record his vocals. "He would dance, moonwalk, click his fingers – it was a nightmare to record but great to watch," he said.

In New York, Michael also worked with singer Robin Thicke and producer Walter Afanasieff on a song called 'Fall Again'. But while Michael was working on the song his son Prince became sick, so it was never completed. Michael also enquired about a track written by Dru Hill singer Mark 'Sisqó' Andrews, 'Do You Want Me', but that collaboration was also postponed due to Prince's illness. The incident also forced Michael to cancel an appearance at the 'Pavarotti and Friends' Kosovo benefit concert, which took place in Italy on June 1.

NO MILLENNIUM ALBUM

Work on the album ground to a halt in early June, when preparations began for two benefit concerts Michael was performing in South Korea and Germany later in the month. The first show took place in the South

Korean capital Seoul on June 25, and the second at Munich's Olympiastadion two days later. But both were full of technical problems and artist cancellations.

In Munich, Michael was performing his penultimate number, 'Earth Song', when a bridge he was standing on fell to the ground. The bridge was suspended in the air and was supposed to be lowered slowly, but due to a cable malfunction it fell much faster than it should have, injuring Michael's lower back in the process. "I thought he was dead," Karen Faye recalls. "I was devastated. Then I saw an arm go on stage. Then another arm. And then his leg. And he got up – and he finished that song."

At the end Michael collapsed into the arms of his assistants, before going back on stage to sing the final number, 'You Are Not Alone'. "My father told me no matter what, the show must go on," he told his worried entourage. Although Michael suffered no serious injuries, he would be plagued by back problems for the rest of his life.

After the concerts Michael was expected to return to New York to resume work on the album, but he chose to spend most of July on vacation in Paris and South Africa. In the French capital he was the subject of a secret album cover photo shoot, conducted by Parisian photographer Arno Bani. Despite the delay, Sony still hoped to receive the tapes in time for a November 9, 1999 release date, which was set in June.

When Michael finally returned to New York in August, he booked himself into a lavish townhouse on the Upper East Side in Manhattan, which he transformed into a mini-Neverland. "Up on the fifth floor was a game room, with video games, a pool table, a movie projector, a popcorn machine, and a fully stocked candy counter," friend Frank Cascio, who was now one of Michael's assistants, said. "Michael asked for some mannequins, which I picked out at show rooms. They were delivered, assembled and dressed in sportswear. We posed them around the first floor. Another whole floor was full of elegant art and china."

Michael once explained why he surrounded himself with mannequins. "I'll talk to them," he admitted. "I think I'm accompanying myself with friends

I never had. Being an entertainer, you just can't tell who is your friend. And they see you so differently. A star instead of a next-door neighbour. That's what it is. I surround myself with people I want to be my friends."

One person he could count as a friend was Rodney Jerkins. By now Michael had dropped his work with most of the other producers to focus on working with the Darkchild team, splitting his time between New York and Jerkins' studio in south New Jersey. As the pair continued to record together, they developed a close bond. "Sometimes he would come to my house for dinner, or I'd go out with him and his kids, it's really trust," Jerkins said. "He used to tell me all the time, 'You're a true loyal friend.' And he knew that when certain situations arose, I had his back. Plus we would have bets, like whoever wins gets like 100 DVDs. He beat me the first time and I took him to Virgin Megastore in Times Square and got him the DVDs. We went late at night. The first time he went to the store, he was in disguise, but a fan noticed him and blew the whole cover."

Jerkins also recalls a brave moment when he decided to take Michael out for a drive. "I picked him up at his townhouse in New York. When we got downstairs, he said, 'Where are you parked?', looking for a limo or something. But it was just me driving. When we drove off, he seemed a little nervous at first, with no security. But once I cranked up the music, he relaxed. People who saw him were going crazy, pointing and waving. I mean, you're stopped at a light, you look over and in the car next to you is Michael Jackson, but he was cool with it. He was waving. I think he enjoyed himself."

On another occasion, President Bill Clinton called the studio to speak to Michael. Much to Jerkins's amazement, Michael said he was too busy to talk. "He [the engineer] said, 'We got the president of the United States on the phone to talk to you', and he [Michael] said, 'I'm busy right now, tell him I can't talk'. I was like 'What'!" Just another day in the life of Michael Jackson.

Although Michael spent the majority of the second half of 1999 working on the East Coast, he was still out of the studio for lengthy periods, taking vacations abroad and returning to Neverland. In October Michael and Debbie Rowe also mutually agreed to end their marriage, remaining friends.

In New York, Michael's drug use began to escalate. In order to perform in the studio, he used the powerful anaesthetic Propofol to get to sleep. The drug was administered intravenously by several different New York-based doctors at Michael's townhouse.

For his back pain he also used Demerol, the narcotic he had become addicted to in 1993. "This was a measure of the depth of Michael's pain, and the sleep problems that went along with it," friend Frank Cascio said. "When his schedule called for him to begin work early in the morning, without the option of sleeping in, he found it hard to fall asleep early enough to get the rest he needed in order to perform."

Progress on the album slowed down to the point that Sony was forced to cancel the scheduled November 9 release date. In December, the label announced that it finally hoped to have the album out by the early summer. Two years had now passed since recording began, but Michael was not even close to finishing.

By Christmas, Michael had decided to move back to Neverland and resume recording in California. At the time he was embroiled in a few legal cases, including one surrounding the cancellation of two New Year's Eve millennium concerts he was due to perform in Hawaii and at Sydney's new Olympic Stadium. After the Australia show he would have flown to Hawaii, making use of the 24-hour time difference to perform two shows in one night. But engineer Michael Durham Prince said Michael was worried about the 'millennium bug', a computer problem that threatened the operations of business, finance, government agencies and science. The fear was that on the stroke of midnight between December 31, 1999 and January 1, 2000, all computers had the potential of shutting down, although few problems actually arose. Cancelling the shows cost Michael a cool $5.3 million.

Michael's studio schedule in California remained sporadic throughout most of 2000. Much to the frustration of his fans and the record company, the album release date was put back time and time again through the year, first until September, and then March 2001. Numerous factors contributed to the delays; Michael continued to take vacations, spending most of May in London and Monaco, where he attended the World Music Awards to collect an award for 'Male Artist of the Millennium'. At the end of his acceptance speech, Michael promised the world that there would be much more to come from him. "You ain't seen nothing yet," he told the audience. Michael was also a two hour drive away from the studio, as he was living mainly at Neverland with his children rather than in Los Angeles. At one point production stopped completely when Sony, concerned about the escalating costs, stopped paying staff and booking studios.

Early in the year Rodney Jerkins spent some time working with other artists, including Whitney Houston. The producer worked on a new version of Houston's 1998 song 'If I Told You That' for her upcoming greatest hits album. Although the updated version became a duet with George Michael, Michael Jackson was Jerkins's first choice. Jerkins said a duet between Michael and Houston would have been 'one of the biggest records ever', but the ambitious plan failed to materialise.

Although progress was slow, it was during this period when Michael created a song that would instantly become one of his favourites from the entire project. In March 2000, he spent some time in Germany's second city of Hamburg with the family of Sony executive Wolfgang Schleiter, close friends of his. Michael said it was on this trip that a water balloon fight with two children from the family became the inspiration for a song called 'Speechless'. "There are these two sweet little kids, a girl and a boy, and they're so innocent; they're the quintessential form of innocence, and just being in their presence I felt completely speechless, 'cause I felt I was looking in the face of God whenever I saw them," he said. Michael admitted it was the fun that inspired him. "I hate to say that, because it's such a romantic song, but it was the fight that did it. Out of the bliss comes magic, wonderment, and creativity."

After returning from Germany Michael was eager to record the song, so he called producer Brad Buxer at 4.30 in the morning from Neverland to sketch out the idea over the phone. "We put the entire song together in two hours," Buxer recalls. "I was at my house in Sherman Oaks and Michael was calling from the ranch. We frequently worked on songs over the phone for marathon amounts of time, sometimes days straight, and 'Speechless' was just one of those songs that came together immediately. Two hours later, at 6.30 in the morning, the song was complete."

Just days later, Buxer and engineer Michael Durham Prince travelled to Neverland to record vocals with Michael in the dance studio, using portable equipment. Frank Cascio stood outside the studio listening to the session. "I remember thinking it was the most beautiful song I'd heard in a very long time," he said.

A NEW SOUND

Under pressure from Sony, Michael agreed to wrap up production in September 2000 and start the mixing process, which was supposed to last one month. For this he brought in arguably his most trusted collaborator, engineer Bruce Swedien, who hadn't worked on a project with Michael since 1995. Mixing began at Marvin's Room studio on Sunset Boulevard in Hollywood. The studio, founded by Marvin Gaye, had been bought in 1997 by Michael's manager, John McClain, who saved it from being converted into a photo lab. Recording at McClain's own studio was a way of keeping production costs down, although the facilities weren't up to the standard of other top Los Angeles studios.

Swedien brought in an assistant by the name of Stuart Brawley, as he wanted someone who was familiar with the mixing console. Swedien reached out to two people for recommendations, and Brawley was the one person on both lists. Songs the pair started mixing in the first couple of weeks at Marvin's Room include 'Break of Dawn' and two Rodney Jerkins tracks, 'You Rock My World' and 'Privacy', the latter of which is another attack on the media. Swedien said the team knew 'You Rock My World' was going to be an album cornerstone. "It set the mood and the feel for the rest of the music," he said. The R. Kelly track 'Cry' was already completed and a certainty for the album.

Everything was pointing towards a March 2001 release, but it quickly dawned on the team that Michael was only satisfied with half a dozen songs, even after three years of recording. Jerkins, who had joined the mixing sessions, was about to be sent back to the drawing board as a result.

Although Michael liked the music tracks that became 'You Rock My World' and 'Privacy', he wasn't overly impressed with the other vintage beats he'd recorded with the Darkchild team over the previous 18 months. Engineer Brad Gilderman said those unused tracks captured the mood of some of Michael's older material. "There was some truly amazing stuff – I'm not sure why it didn't move him," Gilderman said.

Michael simply wasn't interested in his past. "He kept 'Rock My World', but he wanted to go more futuristic," Jerkins revealed. Much to the producer's amazement, Michael even told him he wanted to start writing and recording from scratch. "He was like, 'I think we can beat everything we did'," Jerkins recalls. "That was his perfectionist side. I was like, 'Man, we been working for a year, we gon' scrap everything?!' But it showed how hard he goes."

The producer soon found himself at junkyards, hitting various objects to create these rare sounds. "Michael called me and he says, 'Why can't we create new sounds?' I said, 'What do you mean?' He was like, 'Someone created the drum, right? Someone created a piano. Why can't we create the next instrument?' This is a guy [who is] forty years old, who has literally done everything that you can think of, but is still hungry enough to say 'I wanna create an instrument.' It's crazy."

Michael said he had never seen so much perseverance in a producer as Jerkins, and knew he could push him to the limit in his pursuit for innovation. "You can push him and push him and he doesn't get angry," Michael said. "We go out and make our own sounds, we hit on things, we beat on things, so nobody can duplicate what we do. We make them with our own hands, we find things and we create things. And that's the most important thing, to be a pioneer, to be an innovator. I pushed Rodney. And pushed and pushed and pushed and pushed him to create, to innovate more. To pioneer more. He's a real musician and he's very dedicated and he's real loyal."

By now Jerkins's engineer Brad Gilderman had left the project, and Bruce Swedien was brought in to mix the existing songs rather than record new ones, so Stuart Brawley assumed most of the engineering duties when Jerkins recorded new songs with Michael.

One of the new tracks Jerkins created became 'Heartbreaker'. The unique, innovative sounds Michael was looking for can be heard throughout the track, which was recorded at Marvin's Room studio. Michael told Jerkins he wanted a rapper on the song, but one that wasn't well known, so the producer called upon one of his protégés, 'Fats'. Michael liked the rap on 'Heartbreaker' so much that he had Fats perform on another new song, 'Invincible'. When describing these new songs, Jerkins said, "You may have to turn it down 'cause it's banging so hard, that's what I went for." After Sony executives heard Jerkins' new material they decided it was time for album mixing to resume, and production was moved down the road to Record Plant, off Santa Monica Boulevard.

FINISHING ON THE EAST COAST

Although Michael had recorded dozens of songs, he felt fewer than ten were strong enough to make it onto the album. The solution; bring in old friend and collaborator Teddy Riley and ask him to come up with half a dozen worthy tracks. "He called me and he said, 'Listen, I want you to help me finish this record'," Riley recalls. Reports claimed Riley would receive $1 million if he could come up with a chart-topper.

But there was further upheaval in November 2000, when label executives insisted that production move back to New York so they could keep an eye on operations after a relatively unproductive year. So Michael and his team found themselves back at the Hit Factory, recording mostly in Studio E, while Teddy Riley worked inside a remote recording truck parked outside the studio.

In Manhattan Michael and his children checked into the Four Seasons Hotel, booking out an entire floor. Michael had a portable recording studio set up in one of the rooms, where Brad Buxer would often work. It was in this studio where Michael and Buxer began working on a song called 'The Lost Children', which, as well as 'Speechless', was mostly completed at the Hit Factory. Both songs were very personal to Michael and among his favourites from the project. Buxer said 'The Lost Children' was Michael's anthem and his contribution to children that were lost, in need and uncared for. But the song wasn't well received by Sony or the critics.

There was another setback at the end of November, when Michael presented six of his songs to Sony executives. According to Michael, they were 'walking on air' when they heard the music. But in reality, they were far from impressed and told him to return to the studio and come up with better material. Insulted and humiliated, Michael decided to stop showing at the studio shortly after Christmas. "Bruce [Swedien] had gone home and told me to let him know when Michael returned," engineer Stuart Brawley recalls. "I made myself as busy as possible, doing new mixes, editing and cleaning vocals, running back ups, and waiting. Eventually I returned to Los Angeles to wait for Michael to return to the studio."

In the New Year, instead of working on his album, Michael put his energy into a foundation for children called 'Heal the Kids'. The foundation was a joint project with Rabbi Shmuley Boteach – whom Michael first met in New York in the late summer of 1999 – with the aim of bringing families closer together. The initiative meant several trips to Boteach's home in New Jersey, press conferences in New York as well as a speech at Oxford University in England, where Boteach spent years serving as a rabbi to its students. The pair parted ways at the end of March 2001, when Michael decided to regain focus on his career, put his frustration with Sony to one side and complete the album once and for all.

A few months earlier, songwriter and producer Andre Harris – affiliated to the production company A Touch of Jazz – was working on a ballad called 'Butterflies', among others, with Marsha Ambrosius of British R&B duo Floetry. Michael was made aware of Floetry's work by his manager John McClain, and decided to give A Touch of Jazz a call after loving what he heard. Michael left a message, which owner DJ Jazzy Jeff Townes played for Ambrosius. The singer recalls: "So he hits play, and this really light voice comes out of the answering machine, 'I'm really interested in that stuff coming out of A Touch of Jazz. That Floetry stuff is really cool'. It was Michael Jackson!"

After hearing a few potential demos, Michael fell in love with 'Butterflies' and asked if he could record the song. Townes, Harris and Ambrosius were more than happy to hand it over and recorded the music track for Michael at Touch of Jazz studio in Philadelphia. In March 2001, when it was time for Michael to record his vocals, Ambrosius and her Floetry colleague, Natalie Stewart, were invited to the Hit Factory to join the sessions.

Ambrosius vividly remembers the moment she walked through the front glass doors at the Hit Factory on day one. After showing identification to the staff at the front desk she was escorted to Michael's studio, which had a note saying 'Michael Jackson & Friends' taped to the door. "My heart is literally beating out of my chest and I'm two breaths short of a panic attack," Ambrosius recalls. "All I recall is the sound of a grand piano playing a harmonic scale, someone singing and seeing who that voice was coming from eye to eye. It was him. From the live room, he smiled at me and threw up a peace sign. He continued to warm up his vocals as I stood in awe and then made his way to me. He said my first name and gave me a welcoming embrace. 'Thank you,' he said."

Once the session got underway, Ambrosius and Stewart were asked to help guide Michael through the song. As the demo was made with Ambrosius singing, it was difficult for Michael to hit the high notes. "It was incredible," Stewart said, "because he continually asked, 'Marsh, what's the next harmony? Girls, does this sound right? What do you think? Is this what you were looking for?' He was so open."

Ambrosius became calmer in Michael's presence as the session went on. Like many before her, she found him charming and fun. "Michael was a practical joker, he was just funny," she said. "And his laugh just made you laugh. When we were in the studio, his engineer kept calling me a singing heifer. And [Michael] would tell the engineer, 'You know a heifer is a cow, that's a cow'. I'll never forget that. So I'll always be Michael Jackson's singing heifer."

By April, Teddy Riley had seemingly grown weary of working out of a remote recording truck and returned to his home in Virginia Beach. Michael decided to join him, and stayed in a two-bedroom condo belonging to the producer. Getting away from New York enabled Michael to focus for the first time in many months, and he spent two weeks recording with Riley at his Future Records studio.

One of the songs that stood out for Riley at this time was called 'Whatever Happens'. The song, which is about a girl who discovers that she is pregnant, came from an artist signed to Riley's label. "We were going to sign him to Interscope, but this guy started tripping out," Riley said. "So I ended up going to the writers of that song [Gil Cang and Geoffrey Williams] and asked them could I produce the song for Michael. They let me do it." Michael also received a writing credit, even though he did not write the song. For decades, less established songwriters have been forced to give up a slice of their publishing rights as part of the condition of having their song recorded by the superstar artist.

Riley wanted a 40-piece orchestra to perform strings on 'Whatever Happens', and Carlos Santana to play guitar. "Michael was like, 'Okay, we will make that happen,' I wanted 'Whatever Happens' to be special," Riley said. But Santana was spending time with his family and didn't want to leave his San Francisco home to travel to the East Coast, so he recorded his parts at his home studio. The musician admitted he was honoured to receive the call, and the respect was mutual. "He [Santana] was the nicest man," Michael said. "He's so kind and so spiritual. I found him to be so humble, so I said to myself, 'We have to make this work'." Michael also loved the improvisation of Santana's whistling, which can be heard at the beginning of the track, and kept it on the final recording.

Michael was particularly excited about another title, 'Heaven Can Wait', which is about eluding death. "When I did that song with him," Riley recalls, "he held his heart and he said, 'Teddy, is this mine?' I said, 'It's yours if you want it, Michael.' He's like, 'I want it, let's go get it!' He was so excited. I have a couple of witnesses that were in the room when he said, 'I want that song. I need that song in my life'." Another song they worked on, '2000 Watts', was originally written by Riley and Tyrese Gibson for the singer's second studio album. But after hearing a demo of the hard hitting track Michael wanted it for his own album, and Tyrese was happy to pass it over. Michael and Riley also worked on a ballad, 'Don't Walk Away', and a screaming rock track, 'Shout'.

Michael finally appeared to be making some progress, but that didn't stop the album – now due in June 2001 – being delayed until the end of September. On a more positive note, it was announced that Michael would perform two concerts at New York's famous Madison Square Garden in September to celebrate his 30 years as a solo artist. It was revealed that Michael and his brothers would reunite on stage for the first time since 1984, and a duet with teen sensation Britney Spears was also in the works.

When Michael made a brief return to New York at the end of his two-week stay in Virginia he fired his management team, The Firm, run by Jeff Kwatinetz and Michael Green. Michael was furious with the pair, who had been taking care of affairs since early 2000 alongside John McClain, for not preparing a revolutionary marketing plan for his album.

Angry and intoxicated, Michael proceeded to fire them over the phone. "You're supposed to be working for me, fighting for what I want and what's best for this album," Michael yelled. "You haven't shown me a marketing plan. I've been asking for a plan for six months and I haven't seen a thing. You're purposely trying to sabotage this album. Fuck you, you're fired. If you don't believe in me, there are other people who do." Howard Kaufman and Trudy Green, of HK Management, were later brought in to replace The Firm.

After a brief stay in New York, Michael moved the final few weeks of production to the warmer climes of Miami. Michael may have regained focus in Virginia, but he was put off by the huge media attention his presence had caused in the state. It was hoped another change of scenery would inspire him on the final stretch. His mood no doubt improved as soon as he checked into his suite at the Sheraton Bal Harbour hotel north of Miami Beach, which had spectacular ocean views. Recording resumed at Miami's Hit Factory/Criteria studio, which Bruce Swedien described as a 'fantastic facility' with cutting edge, state-of-the-art equipment.

Michael and Swedien were joined in Florida by Riley, Rodney Jerkins and Brad Buxer, who all shared three rooms at the studio. Engineer Stuart Brawley was also invited back, among others. Michael and Riley continued working on the songs they'd recorded previously and Jerkins brought two new songs to the table, 'Unbreakable' and 'Threatened'.

'Unbreakable', like 'Speechless' and 'The Lost Children', quickly became one of Michael's favourite songs. He explained that the lyrics for 'Unbreakable' were written to portray him as 'invincible'. "I'm one of the few people, probably in show business, that have been through the ins and outs of so many different things," Michael said. "I'm just saying [in the song] I will continue to move forward no matter what." The song features a posthumous rap verse by Notorious B.I.G., which was originally recorded in 1996 for Shaquille O'Neal's song 'You Can't Stop the Reign'. It was Michael's idea to insert a rap, and Jerkins thought of the perfect part.

One of the most intense editing jobs Stuart Brawley was tasked with was to assemble a rap by Rod Serling from *The Twilight Zone* for the horror themed 'Threatened'. "Rodney had written a rap for 'Threatened' and wanted me to listen to all of the *Twilight Zone* episodes and find the required words to build into a rap," Brawley said. "It was a monumental task to not only find the words and phrases, but to have them flow rhythmically."

Brad Buxer described the Miami sessions as 'glorious'. "Those sessions were some of the best times I've ever had with Michael and Bruce, some of the best times of my life," he said.

THE FINAL DAYS

In June 2001, after close to four years of anticipation, delays and infighting, Michael finally decided to stop recording new music and wrap up production. The move to Florida clearly had the desired effect, but there were still a few twists and turns to come.

After mixing was completed, engineer Stuart Brawley began working with Brandy Norwood, who was also recording in Miami, on her album *Full Moon*. Brawley was hired to produce a song for the project, 'Come a Little Closer'. "At this point we had finished Michael's mixes, or so we thought, and I had moved on to other work," Brawley said. "I got a call from Tommy Mottola telling me to get back in the studio to mix a song for Michael. I remember telling him I was now on another project and that it would have to wait until I was available. Tommy's response was, 'I don't think you realise the seriousness of the situation.' It was a good reminder that there is a pecking order in the music industry. I immediately got a studio booked and made the changes to the mix for Michael."

On June 12, Sony held a special conference at the Hit Factory in New York to present Michael's new music to the label's executives from around the world. Sony helped Michael to choose the songs that would make the album, but Frank Cascio said Tommy Mottola didn't want 'The Lost Children' to feature, because he felt associating Michael with children would only serve to 'stir up' unpleasant memories of the 1993 allegations. But Michael demanded its inclusion, and got his way. 'Unbreakable', 'Heartbreaker', 'Invincible', 'Break of Dawn', 'Heaven Can Wait', 'You Rock My World', 'Butterflies', 'Speechless', '2000 Watts', 'Shout', 'Privacy', 'Don't Walk Away', 'Cry', 'Whatever Happens' and 'Threatened' also made the cut.

'Speechless' and 'The Lost Children' are the only songs Michael wrote himself. It was unfortunate, because with the exception of 'Rock With You', 'Human Nature', 'Man in the Mirror' and 'You Are Not Alone', arguably all of Michael's best songs across his career were written by the man himself.

Shortly after the Sony conference the album title was revealed to be *Invincible*, the name of one of the Rodney Jerkins tracks. Michael described it as a 'proper name', but as an album title it would take on a different meaning from the song, which is about a woman being 'invincible' as one pleads for her love. Explaining why he chose the title, Michael said, "I'm so proud and honoured that I've been chosen from the heavens, or whatever it is, to be 'Invincible', and to just continue to grow and to serve the people with wonderful entertainment."

Invincible became the longest album of Michael's career in terms of both running time and the number of tracks. Jerkins said the length was Michael's idea. "He didn't make that transition of doing shorter albums, it was literally nine songs on *Thriller*," the producer said. "We actually had that conversation where I was like, 'You should make it 10 songs and that's it.' You never know, maybe he felt like that would be his last album."

Songs that failed to make the final cut include the Jerkins tracks 'We've Had Enough', 'Can't Get Your Weight Off Of Me', 'Escape', 'Kick It' and 'It's Not Worth It'. Contrary to reports, Jerkins said he did not produce collaborations between Michael and Will Smith or Puff Daddy. Of the material left off the tracklist, Jerkins said, "I really want people to hear some of the stuff we did together which never made the cut. There's a whole lot of stuff, just as good, maybe better. People have gotta hear it." Jerkins said Michael loved 'Escape' in particular. "It was one of those songs where he specifically said to me, 'It has to see the light of day one day'," Jerkins said.

Other outtakes include the R. Kelly track 'One More Chance'; the Dr. Freeze tracks 'Blue Gangsta' and 'A Place with No Name'; 'I Have This Dream', written by Michael with Carole Bayer Sager and David Foster; 'Fall Again', written by Walter Afanasieff and Robin Thicke, and '(I Can't Make It) Another Day', a collaboration with Lenny Kravitz. Some of the Michael and Brad Buxer collaborations, including the funky 'Hollywood Tonight' and the ballads 'Beautiful Girl' and 'The Way You Love Me', were also left out.

Hip-hop superstar Dr. Dre was approached by Michael's management about a collaboration, but turned down the opportunity as he preferred working with new artists. "I can develop them from the ground up," Dre explained. "There's no standard that I have to live up to or anything like that. All I have to do is go in the studio and they're basically going to bust their ass to come in there and do their thing the way it's supposed to be done."

Michael's management was also offered several tracks composed by The Neptunes duo of Pharrell Williams and Chad Hugo, which were tailored specifically for Michael. These included 'Señorita', 'Like I Love You' and 'Rock Your Body', all eventually recorded by Justin Timberlake for his album *Justified*. According to Williams, Michael's management didn't feel they were adequate. Over a decade later, Williams said he was upset that the songs he wrote for Michael never 'made it' to him. "I did eight songs for him that never made it to him that ended up on Justin's record," Williams said. "Later he sang me all those songs and told me they should have been his, and I told him they were for him."

Meanwhile, Michael continued to tinker with the mixes. "I flew back to Los Angeles in June, and immediately received a call from Michael, who at this point was calling me directly, asking me once again to book a studio to make some changes to 'You Rock My World'," Stuart Brawley recalls. "Michael was a perfectionist. We ended up back at Record Plant and Bruce [Swedien] was also in Los Angeles to help get the mixes sounding the way Michael wanted."

It was during these last minute sessions when Brawley recorded a whistle solo for 'Whatever Happens'. Carlos Santana had already whistled at the beginning of the song while playing his guitar part, but Michael wanted more whistling throughout. "Michael asked if anyone in the room could whistle, and I immediately said yes," Brawley said. "It's something that to this day I enjoy putting in a song I'm producing. So I ended up going out to the microphone and whistling where Michael wanted it. I didn't think I'd ever end up with a whistling credit, let alone on a Michael Jackson song, but there you go." Brawley described his time working on *Invincible* as 'invaluable'. "It was an amazing year. I got to know Michael a bit as the months passed, and we even spent some time together at the piano. He loved to listen to others create music, and I often took a break by playing piano."

By July the mixes were finally completed, and the album was mastered shortly after at Bernie Grundman's facility in Hollywood.

MORE MONEY, MORE PROBLEMS

The cost of recording *Invincible* was estimated to be in the region of $30 million, making it the most expensive album ever made. That figure includes five-star accommodation and first-class travel for the recording team, over three years' worth of studio time and the hiring of several top producers. It was almost unheard of for producers such as Babyface, Puff Daddy and Wyclef Jean to be brought in, only for their work to be left on the shelf.

The escalating costs came as no surprise to engineer Brad Gilderman, who saw first-hand the money that was flying around during production. "Apart from the obvious things, it was also little things like all the food they constantly had available at the studios, totalling hundreds of dollars' worth a day," Gilderman said. "And if someone needed to be flown in, they flew first class." Gilderman said the huge costs weren't solely Michael's fault. "A lot of people took advantage of Michael financially, they were ripping him off," he said. "They knew they could sit in a studio and that Michael and Sony would still pay for things, and Sony could have kept on top of spending more."

Tommy Mottola said it didn't matter to Michael how much he spent to create his art, and blamed his 'handlers' for the spiralling production bill. "He thought he would make it [the money] back as soon as the album was released and became a megahit," Mottola said. "All of his handlers – and I mean all of them, every single one, allowed this to happen, no one said no."

Jim Morey, who managed Michael alongside Sandy Gallin between 1990 and 1997, said if Michael felt it was right for the art, then money was no object. "Michael is very bright, and Michael pretty much knew – even when he was advised something was too expensive – if he felt it was right for the art, he had the means to pay for it," Morey said. "He wasn't oblivious to what budgets were."

Berry Gordy believes the 'money is no object' attitude may have been another trait Michael picked up from him as a child. "He became more of a perfectionist than I was," Gordy said. "I would spend whatever money it took, and he knew that. I said money is less important than the quality of the work. So when he started doing his [own projects], he took that to major extremes." The costs of making *Invincible* are unlikely to ever be matched.

Even by Michael's impeccably high standards, four years was a long time to record an album. But music was no longer his sole priority, as he was also raising two young children. "I didn't have children before other albums, so I caught a lot of colds – I was sick a lot," he said. "So we had to stop and start again and stop and start."

Michael's lifestyle also contributed to the continuous delays – gone were the days of recording in one location such as Westlake. Around a dozen studios in four different corners of America were used. Production was constantly switched between Los Angeles and New York, due to legal wrangles or label executives insisting that he record on the East Coast under their supervision. Towards the end, Michael was also recording in Virginia and Florida.

Engineer CJ deVillar said moving studios and cities was impractical. "It means copies of songs are constantly floating between different people, different sessions and different studios," he said. "For *Invincible*, so many songs had a long evolution because of the different studios and schedules. There may have been a beatbox recorded on one reel, an orchestra on another, and vocals on another. And then everything had to be compiled later." One example of this was 'Break of Dawn'. The song was passed around between different studios, producers and engineers. Although Dr. Freeze wrote and produced the song, Rodney Jerkins and Teddy Riley also contributed to it at separate stages.

Michael also had a tendency to go abroad; over the course of the four years he made several trips to South Africa and nearly a dozen to Europe. Some were due to obligations such as press conferences, awards shows and concerts, but many were also vacations. Towards the later part of 2000 and early 2001 he was also entangled in the 'Heal the Kids' foundation with Rabbi Shmuley Boteach.

Close friend and assistant Frank Cascio said Michael's reliance on prescription drugs, such as Propofol and Demerol, also played a part. "It was apparent that he wasn't as clearheaded as he had been in the past, especially when one considered the impact the medicine was having on him," Cascio said. Eventually Michael sought help; between November 2002 and July 2003, he was treated for a Demerol dependency by Miami-based doctor Alimorad Farshchian.

From an artistic viewpoint, Michael's perfectionism was, as ever, also a major factor. Brad Gilderman described him as 'a soul that was never pleased'. "His thing was always more, more, more," the engineer said. "It needed someone to say, 'Michael, the song's great, it's done!' You never knew where a song was going to go. Things could change at the last minute.

Michael may suddenly think, 'This part needs a key change'!" Michael was also very slow to record material – it was simply his style. "The thing with Michael is he would record for an hour, and then maybe chat for an hour, then read a magazine for an hour," Gilderman said. "He would take his time. Sometimes six or seven hours would pass, and maybe only one verse would get done."

Michael admitted his perfectionism often got the better of him. "Of all my albums I would say this one was the toughest [to make], cause I was hardest on myself," he admitted. "It did take a while because I'm never happy with the songs. I'll write a bunch of songs, throw them out, write some more. People say, 'Are you crazy? That's got to go on the album.' But I'll say, 'Is it better than this other one?' You only get 75 minutes on a CD, and we push it to the limit. It is tough because you're competing against yourself. *Invincible* is just as good or better than *Thriller*, in my true, humble opinion. It has more to offer. Music is what lives and lasts."

Engineer Michael Durham Prince said Michael treated his songs like his 'kids'. "He was always a perfectionist and those songs were like his kids, he always felt they could be better and didn't really want to turn them in until they were perfect," Prince said.

Michael was also trying to juggle recording an album of new music with making inroads in the film industry. The contract he signed with Sony in 1991 included the chance to star in a full-length feature film. Those plans were left in tatters after the 1993 allegations, but Michael wouldn't give up on his dream.

Although Michael had thrown himself into the recording of *Invincible*, in late 1999 it emerged he had plans to play hard-drinking nineteenth century writer Edgar Allan Poe in a big-budget independent thriller, *The Nightmare of Edgar Allan Poe*. Poe died in 1849 at the age of 40 after a life of misery and madness, and an obsessive fascination with the supernatural. He was best known for his poems, short tales and literary criticism.

For one reason or another, the plan fell through, as did Michael's audacious attempt to purchase Marvel Entertainment, known for its Marvel Comics subsidiary, a publisher of comic books. The company had only been saved from bankruptcy in June 1998, and Michael sensed an opportunity to use Marvel's catalogue of characters, such as Spider-Man, to make superhero movies.

In 1999 Michael met with the former president and chairman of Marvel Comics, Stan Lee, and told him of his plan. Lee, who co-created Spider-Man, the Hulk, Iron Man, Thor, the X-Men and other fictional characters, had no stake in the company and was also interested in buying it. Michael asked Lee if he would help him run Marvel if his bid was successful, and Lee agreed. At the time, plans were in place for a Spider-Man movie, a role Michael was keen on playing. "He felt that [acquiring Marvel] would be the only way that he could play Spider-Man," Lee said. "I felt he wanted to be Spider-Man. That was the character that interested him. I think he'd have been very good."

One of Michael's many different business advisors at the time, Dieter Wiesner, said the acquisition of Marvel was Michael's big plan for the second part of his life. "Michael knew the stock markets and knew the shares in Marvel were at a low price," the German merchandising executive said. "So we worked all the details out, the banks put money on the table, and Marvel wanted $1.4 billion. Marvel was the plan for the second part of Michael's life. He had the Beatles catalogue on one side, and if he bought the Marvel catalogue, he had the second part."

Wiesner said the plan fell through when Sony refused to allow Michael to use his share of the Sony/ATV catalogue as collateral, although Michael's attorneys say complications arose due to Marvel's bankruptcy proceedings. In 2009, Marvel was bought by Disney for $4 billion, while the Marvel-character film franchises such as *Spider-Man*, *X-Men*, *Iron Man* and *The Avengers* have made billions of dollars in revenue. "Michael was right, he knew what was coming," Wiesner said.

In June 2001, Michael hired film producer Marc Schaffel to act as an advisor and to work with him on numerous projects. The two first met in 2000 at the home of their dermatologist, Arnold Klein, and developed a 'business relationship'. Together they formed Neverland Valley Entertainment, a company designed to fulfil Michael's film and video dreams. Michael liked Schaffel's ideas and was intent on making money that 'did not involve being onstage or in a studio'.

Schaffel claims that in 2000, Michael even stopped recording *Invincible* to work in secret at a small Los Angeles studio on a soundtrack for a planned remake of *Willy Wonka and the Chocolate Factory*, in an attempt to secure the lead role. "He thought it was the perfect role for him, and he planned to use the soundtrack, basically, to bribe his way into getting the part," Schaffel said. Schaffel said he attended several meetings with Warner Bros., the film distributors, but they were only interested in the soundtrack and not in Michael playing the lead role, which eventually went to Johnny Depp. According to director George Lucas, Michael also wanted the role of fictional character Jar Jar Binks in the 1999 blockbuster *Star Wars Episode I: The Phantom Menace*. But at the turn of the new millennium, Michael's movie plans still hadn't come to fruition.

Over the course of the *Invincible* sessions, Michael also became deeply frustrated with his record label. Ultimately, this conflict would contribute to the disappointing commercial performance of the album itself.

CHAPTER 16: *INVINCIBLE* BECOMES INVISIBLE

MID 2001 – MID 2002

After *Invincible* was completed, Michael began negotiating with Sony about what the first single from the album should be. He desperately wanted it to be 'Unbreakable', but Sony insisted on 'You Rock My World', which Michael wanted as the second single. Sony won out, but then wrangled with Michael over a budget for the video and the choice of director. Sony originally hired one of its own directors, Hype Williams, but Michael was unhappy with Williams's ideas and hired Paul Hunter instead.

After numerous delays Michael was said to be 'done' with the whole thing, and showed up late to the set. His mood was worsened by disagreements with his management and the director over the appearance of his face. Filming finally began in mid-August 2001, but ran $2–3 million over the original $2 million budget. There were expensive cameo appearances by high-profile actors Michael Madsen, Bill Drago and long-time friend Marlon Brando, and Michael was also said to have wanted Robert De Niro and Benicio Del Toro. *Rush Hour* star Chris Tucker, whom Michael first met in May, also made an appearance in both the video and on the recorded album track itself. The delay of the video production meant the album release date was also postponed, for the final time, to October 30.

In late August 'You Rock My World' was released as the first single from *Invincible* in the United States, but not commercially, with reports claiming Sony believed such a release could harm sales of the album. *Billboard* chart expert Fred Bronson said he was staggered by the decision, as a number one single would have served as a great promotional tool. The single reached number ten on the *Billboard* 100 on radio airplay alone. "Certainly, if a commercial single had been available, it would have peaked higher – perhaps even at number one," Bronson said at the time. "I thought it was a huge mistake not to release a single, given that there was no way for anyone to purchase the song in any configuration during the single's height of airplay popularity."

The single received a lukewarm response in the United States; it was considered to be a good track but lacking innovation or a sense of explosion, considering Michael had been absent from the charts for four years. Michael's choice of 'Unbreakable' would likely have had a much bigger impact as the lead single. More serious disagreements between Michael and Sony were yet to come.

After the filming of the 'You Rock My World' video, Michael's attention turned to his 30th Anniversary concerts, which were due to take place on September 7 and 10 at New York's Madison Square Garden arena. Tickets for the shows were the highest in show business history – the best seats cost $5,000, which included a dinner with Michael and a signed poster. Despite the prices, both concerts sold out within five hours and Michael reportedly earned $7.5 million for his appearances. CBS television network paid a huge figure to edit footage from both shows into a two-hour TV special that would air in November. Michael's continuing prescription drug problems saw the first concert delayed by an hour, after he overslept in his hotel room having received pain medication on the day.

The show included a seven-minute humanitarian speech by Marlon Brando, for which he was paid a staggering $1 million. Later, Elizabeth Taylor introduced The Jacksons' first performance together as a group since 1984, as they treated the crowd to a medley of classic hits. Justin Timberlake's band N'Sync joined them for a performance of 'Dancing Machine'. Despite the flawless performance, the brothers hadn't spent much time rehearsing. "Once we get on the stage it's a lot of magic and it all comes back to us," Jackie Jackson said. "We just feed off one another."

After the medley, Michael and Britney Spears sang 'The Way You Make Me Feel' together, before Michael finished off the show with 'Black or White',

'Beat It' and 'Billie Jean'. On the second night Michael also performed his new single, 'You Rock My World', with Usher and Chris Tucker. The next morning, tragedy struck America when the Twin Towers at the World Trade Center were attacked. Michael was still in Manhattan and quickly fled to the Cascio family home in New Jersey.

Only days later he announced his plans to record a charity single called 'What More Can I Give', in aid of survivors and the families of the victims of the terrorist atrocity. Michael originally began writing the song, then titled 'Heal L.A.', with Brad Buxer after the Los Angeles riots of 1992. From that point onwards the song evolved, and in 1999 it became 'What More Can I Give'. There were plans to release it in aid of the refugees of the Kosovo War, which ended that year, but they never materialised.

After Michael hired film producer Marc Schaffel in the summer of 2001, the two considered producing a charity record to try to duplicate the success of 'We Are the World'. The beneficiaries would be survivors and families linked to the next major humanitarian disaster, which came much sooner than expected with the New York attacks, after which Michael re-wrote the song. "I believe in my heart that the music community will come together as one and rally to the aid of thousands of innocent victims," Michael said. "There is a tremendous need for relief dollars right now and through this effort each one of us can play an immediate role in helping comfort so many people."

By September 20, artists such as Beyoncé, Usher, Celine Dion, Justin Timberlake, Mariah Carey and Shakira had all agreed to lend their voices, and Schaffel flew around the country in a jet chartered by Michael to record the vocals. A Spanish version, titled 'Todo Para Ti', was also recorded. According to Schaffel, the two songs cost $3 million to put together.

Michael signed away the rights to 'What More Can I Give' to Schaffel in a written contract some time before the terrorist strikes, without consulting his management or lawyers. Schaffel, who was appointed as the project's executive producer, said Michael was so excited about the project that he didn't have to beg him to come to the studio. "He really, really, really wanted to make it happen," Schaffel said. "He was like a different person when he was like that. He was convinced, and so was I, and so was everyone else, that we had two number one hits here, the English version and the Spanish version, which is actually the better of the two." Michael's label, Sony, agreed to manufacture and distribute the singles.

Michael later organised a benefit concert in aid of the victims of 9/11, which took place on October 21 at RFK Stadium in Washington D.C. The concert featured the likes of Beyoncé, Mariah Carey, James Brown, Rod Stewart, Usher, Pink, Puff Daddy and Aerosmith, among others, who joined Michael for a performance of 'What More Can I Give' at the end of the show.

THE HIATUS IS OVER

In mid-September, the recording of *Invincible* took a late, unexpected twist. At the very last minute, Michael decided to alter the tracklist by recording a new song, 'You Are My World', which John McClain had written together with Carole Bayer Sager and Babyface. Once the ballad was played for Michael, he fell in love with it and wanted it to be included on the album. Sager admitted her surprise. "I was shocked when I heard he was using it, I thought by then the album was shrink wrapped and ready to go," she said. But Michael only had a few days to record the song – it had to be mastered by the end of the week in order to be included on *Invincible*.

Engineer Jon Gass recalls the last minute rush. "On the Monday afternoon I got a call from the Babyface camp, asking if I could mix the song," he said. "We had such a tight deadline, because we had to go to mastering at 8am on the Thursday morning. So I went to Babyface's personal studio in Los Angeles, Brandon's Way, but there was nothing I could do. They were still cutting everything, including the musical track and the vocals. The next day I started getting some bits and pieces, drums, bass, acoustic guitar; basic stuff that Babyface had been playing. On the Wednesday the strings, arranged by Bill Meyers, were recorded at Capitol Studios. Later that night, at around 1am, I finally got Michael's vocals."

Although Gass was in the same building as Michael, he rarely saw him as he was recording in another area of the studio. "He liked his privacy when he was recording," Gass said. "With the album going to mastering only a few hours later, I only had seven hours to mix the song, do or die. It is tough when you get the vocals that late and have so little time. It was a long night!" At 7am the next morning, the mix was complete.

"At 8.30am I got a personal call from Michael, he thanked me for staying up all night and doing the mix, and he was very grateful," Gass recalls. "He is the only artist I ever got a call from like that. He was happy with the mix, and said it was brilliant. He really loved that song and was so happy it could get done and go on the album."

Michael changed the lyrics from 'You Are My World' to 'You Are My Life', and received a writing credit in the process. The song wound up replacing the Teddy Riley track 'Shout' on the final tracklist.

In early October the lead single, 'You Rock My World', was released commercially in the United Kingdom, peaking in the number two position. On October 30, 2001, four-and-a-half years after the release of *Blood on the Dance Floor* and six years after the release of *HIStory*, *Invincible* finally hit the shelves. Somewhat unfairly, many critics called it Michael's first album of all new material in ten years; overlooking the fact that 1995's *HIStory* had 15 new songs, making it as much of a studio album than anything he ever released. But after essentially six years away from the studio, the hype surrounding the album was enormous. It was viewed as Michael's big comeback, although he didn't see it that way. "I only do an album every four years, it's just that I've been on hiatus, writing," he explained.

Publicly, Tommy Mottola claimed *Invincible* contained some of Michael's best ever work. "Music lovers will be surprised and delighted by the power, depth and range of *Invincible*," the Sony Music chief gushed. But privately, he held a different view. "Everyone in the company thought that it was good, but by no means Michael's best work," Mottola later said. "After years of recording, we were not about to ask him to go back and cut some new tracks. For all we knew, that might take another two or three years."

The illustration on the album cover is simply a close up of Michael's face, inspired by an image taken in 1990 by fine art photographer Albert Watson of a child painted gold with curly locks. In 1999 Michael hired Watson for an album cover photo shoot, for which he was also painted gold by his hair/make-up artist Karen Faye. But Sony altered the final result. "The *Invincible* cover was retouched into something that was nowhere near the original photo shot by Albert Watson," Faye said. "I had painted Michael gold and he was wearing a hairpiece that was completely gold. I was very disappointed at what Sony did to the photo. The original photo was quite amazing."

The shoot was divided into two days; one for the front cover portraits and another for dance shots which were used inside the album booklet. Watson said he found Michael charming, cooperative, professional and a pleasure to deal with. When he arrived at Watson's New York studio, Michael spent a few minutes stretching before dancing in front of the mirrors to 'Billie Jean', which was played over the studio stereo system. "Because of the set-up and the preparation, it was hard not to get some magical shots in almost every frame during the roughly 30 minutes he danced in front of the camera," Watson recalls. "This was Michael Jackson dancing, after all. How could you go wrong?" The image, chosen over those taken by French photographer Arno Bani during a photo shoot in Paris, was available in five different colours – silver, red, orange, blue and green. "We just wanted the fans to have some fun with the pictures and with the colours and just to try something a little different," Michael explained.

To coincide with the release of *Invincible*, Sony issued special edition versions of *Off the Wall*, *Thriller*, *Bad* and *Dangerous*, complete with previously unreleased home demo recordings and outtakes, and special interviews with Quincy Jones and Rod Temperton. All four albums were completely remastered at a cost of several million; some tracks were said to have been remastered 20 or more times before Michael picked one he liked.

THE BATTLE

During the recording of *Invincible*, Michael had seen Sony's marketing plan and was exasperated by what he saw. It was part of the reason he lost motivation in his work. "To me it was an album that was going to do the big numbers," Teddy Riley said. "But when Michael saw the marketing plans he told me, 'I'll be surprised if this album does two million'."

Michael needed the album to be a success, not only to further enhance his legacy but also to bail him out of his financial troubles, as Frank Cascio put it. By 2001, Michael was $231 million in debt after borrowing from the Bank of America several times in the nineties, using his 50 per cent share in the Sony/ATV catalogue and catalogue of own songs, Mijac, as collateral. Michael also owed Sony for personal advances, recording costs, the imminent bill for album promotion and the millions the company paid to remaster his old albums.

Michael was particularly angry at Sony's budget cap for the videos, which were always so important to him due to his love for film. Michael had become frustrated with Sony's approach to the making of his videos as early as the *HIStory* campaign. It was then when Michael began to lose a degree of creative control over his work. "I'm submitting interesting projects at times," he said in 1998, "but I don't always get to do the things I want. Some people [at Sony] push me to do things fast, they don't care about the result, so they don't care that the videos will look like everyone else's, they don't want to be creative. They are limited…I always wanted to do videos that were innovative, and I want to continue like that. But some people only want that I put myself in front of the camera, and when the lights go on they hope something magic will happen…just like that, without thinking. Well, it doesn't work that way."

Sony chose to release 'Cry' as the album's second single (outside the United States) instead of Michael's preferred choice, 'Unbreakable'. When he saw the $1 million budget allocated for the video, it angered him so much that he refused to appear in it. In November 2001, Sony was forced to go ahead and shoot without Michael's participation. That same month, 'Butterflies' was released in the United States on radio airplay only and peaked at 14 on the *Billboard* 100. A commercial single was planned, but for whatever reason, was shelved. Like 'Cry', Michael was unhappy with Sony's pitch for the 'Butterflies' video and refused to participate in a project he did not believe in. A video was never filmed. 'Cry' was released commercially in Europe and Australia in December, but performed poorly on the charts. The weak video will have done little to promote it.

Michael was also annoyed Sony couldn't come up with an innovative marketing plan that didn't involve touring. Sony wanted Michael to tour to promote the album – touring is usually the most effective method. Michael agreed to begin a concert tour of America and Europe in the spring of 2002, but changed his mind after the 9/11 terrorist attacks. The tour was cancelled at Michael's request, which angered Tommy Mottola, even though other artists were also cancelling their tours due to the tragedy.

Though it cost him an estimated $100 million, the decision was made easier for Michael because he was tired of touring – he had done so all his life. "I love to entertain, but I don't like the system of touring," he admitted after the *HIStory* Tour. "You're jet-lagged. You're sleepy on stage. I don't know where I am half the time. I may not tour again. Ever." Michael would often lose ten pounds during his gruelling two-hour shows. "Then you get to your hotel and your adrenaline is at its zenith and you can't fall asleep," he said. "And you've got a show the next day. It's tough."

Instead of touring, Michael wanted to use both versions of 'What More Can I Give', which were ready by November, as a promotional tool for *Invincible*. But even though Sony had originally agreed to manufacture and distribute the singles it was now refusing to release them, further angering Michael.

According to documents, Sony actually refused to release the songs at the behest of Michael's own people. Baffled that he had signed away the valuable rights to 'What More Can I Give' to Marc Schaffel, his advisors launched an investigation into the unknown producer's background. In November 2001 they discovered that Schaffel was a producer and director of gay pornographic videos, triggering a damage-control effort. The advisors did not want Michael linked to Schaffel in any capacity, especially after the child molestation allegations of 1993.

Seemingly without Michael's knowledge, those advisors then asked Sony to terminate the 'What More Can I Give' project, or at least delay it until Michael recovered his rights. The label obliged by refusing legal permission for its stars to appear on the records. As Michael was contracted to Sony, he wasn't even able to get a third-party record company to release the singles.

Schaffel – who was dismissed by Michael's team following the discovery about his background but held onto the rights to 'What More Can I Give' – refutes that Sony refused to release the singles at the behest of Michael's own people. Instead, he claims the label was concerned the singles would compete with *Invincible.*

Despite all the disagreements behind the scenes, *Invincible* sold an estimated three million copies worldwide within five days of its release, and *Billboard* reported that this soon increased to 5.4 million. But sales suddenly stalled; within a month of its release the album tumbled out of the top ten in the United States. In the United Kingdom it was out of the top ten after three weeks, and after five it was out of the top 40 altogether. "Sales had completely stalled, we were all disappointed," Tommy Mottola said. "Michael's perception was that it was not acceptable and that we had failed him. It was certainly nowhere near the sales we needed to recoup the expenses." But promotion was set to continue into 2002 with the release of more singles, a Grammy performance and public appearances.

THE WAR

Michael believed the licences to his own recordings (masters) would revert back to him in 2000. If he held the distribution rights to his recordings, he would be able to release his own greatest hits albums or sell the rights to another label without having to split the profits with Sony. When Michael's team checked through the contract that was signed with Sony in 1991, they found that due to various clauses, the rights would not revert back to him until 2009/2010. Michael claimed he was unaware of these contract clauses, and was infuriated.

In early 2002, when John Branca began to renegotiate the contract with Sony, Michael demanded that his masters be returned to him in 2004 instead of 2009/2010, and that the label throw $8 million behind a video for 'Unbreakable'.

Unsatisfied with Sony's concept for the video, Michael came up with his own elaborate treatment. "Michael envisioned creating a dance for 'Unbreakable' that people would remember forever," friend Frank Cascio said. "He would be on the roof of a very tall building that was under construction, held over the edge by some thugs, and then they would let him go. He would go hurtling to the ground, seemingly dead, but slowly, his body parts would come together and he would turn into fire – dancing on fire from scaffold to scaffold as his body parts reassembled themselves."

Sony refused both requests, deeming Michael's vision for 'Unbreakable' too costly. Reports also suggest Sony thought the video was too violent, and the idea was shelved. Michael decided enough was enough, and told Sony he would not be signing another contract. He no longer wanted to work for a label he felt had betrayed him by not informing him of the master recordings clause, not supporting his video concepts or releasing 'What More Can I Give'.

It was agreed he could leave Sony, but only after fulfilling the remaining obligations on his contract, which were two more albums. Michael could walk away after releasing a greatest hits package and box set; the two albums would also have to include a handful of new songs between them. Although Michael was able to leave Sony and look for a new record deal elsewhere, the task would be made harder as he would not have his masters in hand – any prospective future record company would want the rights to Michael's previous hits.

In March 2002, Michael decided to fund the 'Unbreakable' video himself with Brett Ratner – whom he met in January – directing. But Sony told Michael not to bother with the video and cancelled all promotion for *Invincible,* including the prospective single releases of 'Butterflies' (commercially in the United States), 'Unbreakable', 'Threatened' and the radio airplay release of 'Heaven Can Wait'. An appearance at the 44th Annual Grammy Awards in February 2002 was also cancelled. At the end of March, only five months after its release, Sony deleted *Invincible* from its 'international priority' list of projects. The album became Michael's first as an adult where one of its singles failed to reach number one in either the United States or United Kingdom.

Michael had great visions for the album, especially for the videos accompanying each single. He was particularly excited about his concepts for

'Unbreakable' and 'Threatened'. "There's like an encyclopaedia of just great short-films to make from the album," he said in October 2001. "It's very exciting. I can't wait to do 'Threatened', I can't wait to get my hands on that one." Michael said he was coming up with new dances while listening to the music from the album. "They'll [the fans] be seeing all kinds of innovative things and movements that have never been seen before," he said. "We'll go places where we've never gone in dance before. All the hip-hop things that are happening now are beginning to look like aerobics, it's kinda getting annoying."

In April, the news that Sony had stopped promoting *Invincible* became public, and fan clubs began protesting against the label. The saga reached a low point in the summer, when Michael spoke out against Tommy Mottola publicly. Mottola said he was still on good terms with Michael 12 months earlier, when he was invited to the studio in Miami. "Michael was so welcoming that day, and he treated me and Thalia [his wife] as special guests," the Sony boss recalls.

In June Michael attended a fan demonstration at the Sony Music offices in London, riding on the top deck of an open topped bus which had been organised for him by a group of fans. Later he attended a fan-club event with Uri Geller at the Equinox nightclub, where he spoke for the first time of his problems with Sony and Mottola. Michael attended another fan demonstration at the Sony Music offices in Manhattan on July 6, again arriving on the top of a double-decker bus. Later that day, he went to Al Sharpton's National Action Network rally in Harlem to speak out against the music industry's treatment of artists, calling Mottola 'a mean, racist and very devilish man'.

At the time, executives from other labels said they believed Michael was piggybacking on the Sharpton artist rights movement to pressure and embarrass Mottola and Sony into allowing him to leave with his catalogue of master recordings early and look for a new deal elsewhere, without repaying the *Invincible* debts.

Mottola himself didn't comment on the fiasco until many years later. "We were all in shock when eight months after *Invincible* was released, the poor sales flipped Michael into becoming a different person," he said. "Something snapped and he decided to lash out at me publicly. Michael was trying to turn this into an escape hatch. He was singling me out in order to get a release from Sony. Did he really think he would embarrass Sony enough to walk away from approximately $50 million in debts or from our joint venture in the Beatles catalogue?"

The whole saga asks the questions:

WHY WAS THE INITIAL PROMOTION WEAK?

Mottola said Sony's executives 'put the full force of the company' in motion to promote the album with a huge $26 million campaign. But it's hard to believe how that amount was spent when only two videos were filmed. Sony spent an estimated $30 million on promoting *HIStory*, but that figure includes a teaser video, seven music videos and nine 32-foot statues of Michael.

Whether that figure is correct or inflated to make it look like Sony pulled out all the stops, the label did back Michael in terms of the funding of the videos that were filmed. At least $5 million was spent on 'You Rock My World' and 'Cry', three or four times what most companies budgeted for two videos at the time. But Sony was simply not willing to spend $8 million on a video for 'Unbreakable', because the label saw Michael's more elaborate videos as vanity projects rather than an effective method to sell more albums.

In 2002, Laura Holson of the *New York Times* said record companies were cutting costs due to faltering record sales, mainly thanks to illegal online file sharing services such as Napster, and were therefore unwilling to give large promotional budgets to artists who did not deliver profits. Michael usually delivered a supreme level of profit, but not this time with the huge amount of money that was spent making the album.

Sony still planned to promote *Invincible* by releasing at least four more singles and videos, but just not to the level Michael expected, as the executives saw it as uneconomical. No other artists at the time were given more than $2.5

million to make a video. Tommy Mottola felt he may have been the only person in the world who was able to say no to Michael. "When you are used to hearing 'Yes, Michael, yes, Michael, yes, Michael, yes', from everybody who is around you, it must be unbearable to hear, 'No, Michael, we cannot and will not put millions more into the promotion of this album'," Mottola said. Yet it seems baffling that Sony decided not to release 'You Rock My World' or 'Butterflies' commercially in the United States.

In the end, Sony blamed the so-called dismal sales on Michael's failure to tour and also complained that he failed to commit to a series of promotional appearances on both sides of the Atlantic. In February, Michael backed out of a commitment by his managers to appear on a 10-day promotional sweep of Europe. Marc Schaffel said many events were scheduled, but Michael was suddenly no longer interested in them. "That pissed off Tommy, who thought it was all because of 'What More Can I Give'," Schaffel said. "And a lot of it was. Michael wanted them to use 'What More Can I Give' to promote *Invincible*." Michael was apparently unaware that his own advisors stopped the project going ahead due to Schaffel's involvement.

Michael was so adamant Sony had cheated him that he contacted his friend Carole Bayer Sager to see if her husband, Bob Daly, who ran both Warner Music and the Warner Bros. studio, could investigate whether Sony was acting inappropriately. Daly reviewed the album's financing, but couldn't see any wrongdoing on the record label's part. "When I told him that, he sort of disappeared on me," Daly said. "Some people don't like hearing what they don't want to hear."

WHY WAS PROMOTION SUDDENLY CANCELLED?

Ever since 2002 there has been intense speculation as to why Sony suddenly cancelled promotion in March of that year. Perhaps the most popular theory is that Sony's Japanese executives wanted to acquire Michael's 50% share in the Sony/ATV recording catalogue, also known as the Beatles catalogue, and therefore deliberately tried to sabotage sales of the album by not promoting it sufficiently. Michael and Sony, of course, were joint owners of the catalogue after the 1995 merger.

As mentioned previously, Michael was reliant on *Invincible* selling well due to his huge bank loans and debt with Sony. If Michael struggled financially, it may have been in his interest to sell his 50% share in the catalogue, and Sony had first refusal. Michael himself believed it was a big conspiracy, although some said this allegation was part of his plan to heap further embarrassment on Sony. Mottola denied the theory. "It's total bullshit," he said. "Why would anyone sabotage anything when you're there to make money? That's the same thing as people saying our government was part of the 9/11 conspiracy. I mean, come on."

In reality, the decision likely had nothing to do with Sony wanting to push Michael into a corner. Michael had certain expectations; he felt Sony's marketing plan lacked innovation and that the budget wasn't sufficient, and he was also annoyed when the label refused to release 'What More Can I Give'. Sony, on the other hand, was irate that Michael wasn't cooperating with its campaign by refusing to tour, make promotional appearances or accept budgets and video pitches at a time when record companies were cutting costs due to faltering sales. "Ultimately, Michael's and Tommy Mottola's egos got in the way of promoting a great album," Frank Cascio said.

When Michael decided he would not be signing another contract with Sony, the label no longer needed him – he wasn't a company priority because he was leaving after *Invincible* anyway. Why spend millions promoting an artist that had no future with the label?

Many, including Michael's brother Jermaine, therefore feel Sony deliberately stopped promoting the album so he would find it harder to find a new deal elsewhere. If *Invincible* sold poorly, other labels may have felt Michael had lost his ability to sell records. "There is a saying in the music industry, 'Why fatten the frog for the snake?', usually heard when a recording artist's contract is about to expire, or he/she wants to leave," Jermaine said. "No label throws its promotional weight behind a want-away artist to big them up in the marketplace." It was a way of punishing Michael for his disloyalty.

Today, *Invincible* has sold at least 13 million copies worldwide, still putting it in the top 20 best-selling albums of the decade (2000s). Engineer Stuart Brawley believes *Invincible* – and Michael's others albums before it – were always compared unfairly with *Thriller*. "In my opinion *Invincible* was as good, if not better, than the other albums in his genre at that time," Brawley said. "You're lucky to get something like *Thriller* once; even Michael Jackson was going to struggle to make a *Thriller* part two." Regardless of the disappointing sales, Michael remained confident *Invincible* would still be appreciated in the decades to come. "Art – good art – never dies," he said.

CHAPTER 17: THE MOVIE DREAM

2002 – MID 2005

Although *Invincible* failed to perform as well as Michael had hoped, he was still looking to the future. Having delivered his final studio album for Sony, a new chapter in his career was set to begin. "I want to take several years off just doing film," he revealed in 2002. "I'd like to get six great movies behind me, and then I'll do a little bit of touring, then I'll do more filming."

As for music, it appeared he was true to his word when he said *Invincible* would be his last proper album. Dieter Wiesner, a German merchandising executive who officially became Michael's manager in early 2003, replacing John McClain and HK Management, said Michael had 'another career plan' after delivering *Invincible*. "Michael told me, 'I'm done with music, I did everything I could do, I did *Thriller*, and I don't want to be on stage touring at 50. Now is my time to do movies'. He never actually stopped making music, he still worked on ideas, but it was not his first focus anymore. He still wanted to do concerts, but only at big places like the pyramids in Egypt. I told him, 'But Michael, the people still want to see you.' But he wanted to do 10 or 15 concerts over two or three years, and not a full tour. Michael's dream was to be a director and an actor." Wiesner said Michael had no immediate plans to move to another label after his Sony contract ended, he simply wanted to move into film.

Michael began this process immediately after *Invincible* was completed, filming a small cameo scene in October 2001 for the Will Smith movie

Men in Black II. Four months later Michael and yet another new business partner, Kenyan-born producer and director Raju Patel, announced a $20 million investment deal with Canadian-based film company MDP Worldwide Entertainment. At the time MDP chief Mark Damon said Michael would be directly involved in choosing scripts, with the possibility of directing and also acting, if the right part came along 'for the Michael Jackson persona'. The deal was set to include Michael's own film division, Neverland Pictures. There were plans for Michael to play a werewolf in the first movie made under the banner, the gothic thriller *Wolfed*, but the entire MDP project collapsed due to Michael's financial troubles.

Michael also had another audacious plan up his sleeve. In the spring of 2002, he became aware of producer and media publicist Stuart Backerman's former role as the producer of *Peter Pan* on Broadway. Michael was interested in the possibility of playing the role of Peter Pan in a Broadway revival, and asked Backerman to set in motion the show's opening.

Meanwhile, in April 2002 Michael gave the last complete stage performance of his life – when discounting the few lines he sang of 'We Are the World' at the 2006 World Music Awards – at the famous Apollo Theater in Harlem. He performed a medley of hits from *Dangerous* at a concert to raise funds for the Democrat Party's 'Every Vote Counts' campaign, and was introduced to the stage by the former President of the United States, his good friend Bill Clinton. It is perhaps fitting that Michael's final performance came at the Apollo, due to its significance in launching The Jackson 5 in 1967.

In the summer of 2002, Michael made the fateful decision to invite British journalist Martin Bashir to Neverland to film a documentary. Hoping that it would allow the public to see who he really was, Michael put his full trust in Bashir, and over the next seven months, invited him into his world.

Bashir interviewed Michael at Neverland and in Las Vegas, where Michael conducted his infamous multi-million dollar shopping spree in an antiques shop at the Venetian Hotel. In November Bashir also travelled to Berlin, where Michael was presented with a Pop Artist of the Millennium Award. It was during this trip when Michael dangled his third child – nine-month old Prince Michael II (nicknamed Blanket) – from the balcony of Berlin's Hotel Adlon, leading to widespread criticism in the media. The incident put an end to Michael's hopes of playing Peter Pan in the Broadway musical, as he and Stuart Backerman decided the timing would be inappropriate. But the pair got along so well that Michael asked Backerman to become his spokesperson.

The highly anticipated Bashir documentary was aired in the United Kingdom and United States in February 2003, but was edited to portray Michael in a bad light. While narrating, Bashir said he felt uneasy about what he viewed as Michael's apparent obsession with children, and also questioned his conduct as a father. Michael was devastated and believed Bashir had betrayed him.

"I feel more betrayed than perhaps ever before, that someone who had got to know my children, my staff and me, whom I let into my heart and told the truth, could then sacrifice the trust I placed in him and produce this terrible and unfair programme," Michael said in a statement. "Everyone who knows me will know the truth, which is that my children come first in my life and that I would never harm any child."

In the following weeks, Michael and his team released a rebuttal to Bashir's documentary, as well as the light-hearted *Michael Jackson's Private Home Movies*. The aim of both programmes was to contradict how the documentary had portrayed Michael.

The documentary was a blow for Michael, but he had no intention of dropping his future plans. His newly appointed team – consisting mainly of manager Dieter Wiesner and publicist Stuart Backerman – began creating a vision for his future, called the MJ Universe project. After years of living like a recluse, Michael was about to be 'rebranded' with the aim of making him more accessible.

But it wasn't all about public relations; MJ Universe was also designed to help Michael make that transition from albums and touring to the fulfilment of his film and business dreams. "He was approaching fifty at that time, he told me a number of times that he didn't want to be an organ grinder's monkey doing 'Billie Jean' into his fifties," Backerman said. "He never really had his heart in performing again. He felt like that he was a father now; he had a responsibility to be with his family and that was a priority. For emotional and family reasons, he was willing to change in his mid-forties from a performer to a business man. That's what he really wanted."

But Michael didn't totally abandon his natural calling, and continued to create music in his spare time. In December 2002 he recorded a song in Miami with his friend Barry Gibb, of the Bee Gees, called 'All in Your Name'. Gibb explained that the collaboration came about simply because the two were close friends. "We gravitated towards the same kind of music and we loved collaborating and he was the easiest person to write with," Gibb said. "The more we got to know each other the more those ideas entwined and it all came to this song. 'All in Your Name' is in fact the message that Michael wanted to send out to all of his fans all over the world, that he did it all for them and for the pure love of music. This experience I will treasure forever."

Michael also continued to create music with his long-time collaborator Brad Buxer. In early 2003, while staying in adjoining hotel rooms in Las Vegas, the two came up with 'I Am a Loser'. Buxer was going through a breakup at the time, and Michael overheard him saying "I'm a loser" in a neighbouring hotel room. After hearing of Buxer's predicament he suggested they write a song about it, and together with engineer Michael Durham Prince they recorded a demo with scratch vocals using a portable recording studio in the hotel.

After the Bashir affair had seemingly blown over, Michael had plans to purchase a 51% stake in a Canadian animation features studio, CinéGroupe, as an alternative to the Marvel deal which had collapsed two years earlier. It was all part of the MJ Universe project. In anticipation of the takeover, the company invited Michael to Montreal in September 2003 to contribute ideas to *Pinocchio 3000*, a computer-animated film the studio was working on. "We spent some time in Canada and the contracts were signed," Dieter Wiesner said. "Michael was excited, this was his dream, and he was in a really good mood about everything."

MICHAEL'S DREAMS ARE QUASHED AGAIN

In November 2003 Michael spent time in Las Vegas to film a video for a new single, 'One More Chance', which he agreed to include on a new greatest hits album, *Number Ones*. Michael still owed Sony a greatest hits album and a box set, and *Number Ones*, which was scheduled to be released worldwide on November 17 and in the United States a day later, would fulfil half of that obligation. 'One More Chance' was originally written for Michael by R. Kelly as a possible track for *Invincible*, and was mostly completed during those sessions.

Michael began filming the video for 'One More Chance' at CMX Productions studio in Las Vegas with director Nick Brandt on November 17. Sony financed the video, and Brandt was its choice of director. The concept for the video was not Michael's idea, and the budget was modest. "Michael was not too happy about it," Dieter Wiesner recalls. "It was a relaxed situation but it was not what Michael really wanted to do. He looked still for the biggest thing and this was not something he would pick. It was not one of his high-class things he did before. When we arrived there, the set was already done. He was saying, 'This is like Smooth Criminal'. But he did his job. I think when he started to do something, he did it right. He was not so happy but he had to deliver something and that's what he did." Filming was due to resume the next evening, but Michael would never get the chance to complete the video.

On the morning of Tuesday, November 18, 70 members of the Santa Barbara County Sheriff raided Michael's Neverland Ranch for nearly 15 hours, shooting video and combing the grounds for evidence. The reason – a thirteen-year-old boy from an impoverished part of East Los Angeles had accused him of sexual abuse. Gavin Arvizo, a cancer survivor, had first been invited to spend time at Neverland with his family in 2000. Michael took pride in his philanthropy and humanitarianism, and Gavin became the latest sick child to benefit from his generosity; the family enjoyed vacations and received gifts in an all-expenses-paid lifestyle. Hoping that people would finally understand his relationship with children, Michael invited Gavin to appear in the Bashir documentary. But his appearance in the film had the opposite effect, and started a catalogue of events leading to the allegation.

After Michael admitted to Bashir that Gavin stayed in his bed while he slept on the floor, the journalist asked Michael how he would respond to criticism of such behaviour. "I feel sorry for them because that's judging someone who wants to really help people," Michael said. "Why can't you share your bed? The most loving thing to do is to share your bed with someone. You say, 'You can have my bed if you want, sleep in it. I'll sleep on the floor. It's yours'. Always give the best to the company, you know. Like to him [Gavin]. Because he was going to sleep on the floor and I said 'No, you sleep in the bed and I'll sleep on the floor'."

But a handful of psychologists and school officials didn't quite see it that way, and complained to California authorities. On February 14, 2003, only days after the documentary aired in the States, the Los Angeles Department of Children and Family Services and the Los Angeles Police Department launched a joint investigation. They interviewed the entire Arvizo family, including Gavin, his sister Davellin, brother Star, and mother Janet. All of them clarified that there was nothing inappropriate about the friendship and the case was closed, with the charges marked as 'unfounded'. The family also praised Michael in a rebuttal video to Bashir's documentary, for which Michael was paid millions of dollars by television networks. But then, Janet Arvizo changed her mind.

She sought the advice of Larry Feldman, one of the attorneys who represented the Chandler family in the first molestation case against Michael ten years earlier. Feldman suggested her sons see a counsellor and contacted psychologist Stan Katz, who interviewed Gavin and his younger brother Star in his Beverly Hills office. After Gavin alleged that Michael had molested him (he would later claim the abuse began after the documentary aired, when the whole world was already watching and complaints had been filed), Katz reported the case to the authorities.

The Santa Barbara County district attorney, Tom Sneddon, led the effort to prosecute Michael. Sneddon was considered by many to be motivated by a personal vendetta, having been defeated in the Chandler case. "If he thinks someone's guilty and slipped away, he doesn't forget that," said retired Superior Court Judge James Slater, who presided over the 1993 case. Those suspicions were furthered when Sneddon was criticised for his joking demeanour and making inappropriate comments at a press conference announcing Michael's arrest warrant.

Sneddon had also seemingly failed to investigate the Arvizo family background before deciding to proceed. Janet Arvizo had previously alleged sexual molestation, committed welfare fraud, sued retailer J. C. Penney after a shoplifting incident and solicited donations from celebrities for Gavin's medical expenses, even though they were covered by insurance. It would also later emerge that Gavin and his siblings had taken acting lessons ahead of the lawsuit against J. C. Penney.

Oddly the Neverland raid was carried out on the same day that Michael's new greatest hits album, *Number Ones*, was released in the United States, an act Michael felt was deliberate. Two days after the raid, Michael arrived at Santa Barbara Airport by private jet from Las Vegas and surrendered himself to police. He was driven to the Santa Barbara County sheriff's office and escorted inside, his wrists handcuffed behind his back. After posting a $3 million bail, posing for a mug shot and being advised of the charges against him, Michael walked free and returned to Las Vegas.

He was shell shocked. Just as he was about to complete possibly his last music video for Sony and finally make that transition into the movie industry, it was snatched away from him once again. Michael's plans for CinéGroupe were in tatters. "After the news became public, CinéGroupe stopped the deal and he lost everything," Dieter Wiesner said. "It shocked him, and killed him almost. It stopped all of his plans with the movies and the animated videos. I believe a part of him died that day."

Grand plans for the MJ Universe project were also ruined. After the completion of the 'One More Chance' video, Michael and his entourage planned to take a three-month trip which Stuart Backerman described as a 'triumphant publicity tour' around Europe, Africa and South America. "We were going to do all kinds of autograph sessions, record signings and fan events and we were going to do something at Harrods in London too," Backerman said.

Michael was going to present an award to Muhammad Ali at the Bambi Awards in Germany in late November, before taking a vacation at Elizabeth Taylor's chalet in Switzerland. After an event with Nelson Mandela in Africa the next stop would have been Brazil, where Michael was given permission to perform a midnight rendition of his new song, 'One More Chance', in Rio de Janeiro's famous Maracanã Stadium. It was also reported that Brazilian officials wanted him to perform in front of two million people on the iconic Copacabana Beach.

Although the allegations made headlines around the world, 'One More Chance' still managed to chart at number five in the United Kingdom after its release on November 20. The *Number Ones* album was a massive success, and like *Invincible* it became one of the top 20 biggest-selling albums of the decade, with around 13 million copies sold.

In December 2003 nine charges – later increased to fourteen – were brought against Michael, which included child molestation. Michael's brother Jermaine, who converted to Islam in 1989, brought in the Nation of Islam to provide security for Michael, who was feeling vulnerable. A religious movement founded in Detroit by Wallace D. Fard Muhammad in 1930, the Nation of Islam's stated goals are to improve the spiritual, mental, social, and economic condition of African-Americans in the United States and all of humanity. The organisation cut off all contact with many figures in Michael's life, including his manager Dieter Wiesner, publicist Stuart Backerman and business associate Marc Schaffel. Schaffel resurfaced in Michael's life in the summer of 2002, having initially been fired in late 2001 due to his background in the gay porn industry.

Before Christmas, Michael decided to move his family out of Neverland and into a $60,000-a-month rented mansion north of Beverly Hills. He felt the raid had tarnished his dream home forever, and vowed to never live there again. "It's a house now," he explained, "It's not a home anymore."

VICTORY

In April 2004, Santa Barbara County district attorney Tom Sneddon obtained an indictment before a grand jury, which decided there was enough evidence for a trial. In reaction to this crushing blow, Michael ousted the Nation of Islam from his life and hired a new defence attorney, Tom Mesereau, who entered a Not Guilty plea to all charges on his behalf. In the absence of a manager, younger brother Randy became his advisor for the foreseeable future.

The remainder of 2004 was a relatively quiet time for Michael, as he prepared for the start of his trial with his defence team. In November Sony released the box set that Michael owed them, titled *The Ultimate Collection*. The set features a handful of demos and completed songs which failed to make previous albums, but none were released as singles. It was the final album Michael owed his record company.

The trial began in February 2005 in the Santa Barbara County community of Santa Maria, a 45-minute drive from Neverland, where Michael had now returned (he slept in the guest quarters). The exhausting trial would last nearly four months. Michael's close friend and hair/make-up artist, Karen Faye, recalls the time she spent in his company during that period. "He was being really brave," Faye said. "I would go to Neverland Ranch at 3am every morning to get him ready by 7am. We had to be out the door by 6–7am to get to the trial. If we didn't show up on time they'd throw him in jail. We got him dressed every day. We made sure he looked really good. I washed his hair. Every day, we would hug, be arm in arm together and cry. I'd blow dry his hair. We'd listen to classical music. We'd watch Three Stooges videos."

Faye said everybody – including witnesses and accusers – was allowed to enter the courtroom via a back entrance, whereas Michael was paraded in through the front before the eyes of the glaring media. "They made it a parade, every single day," she said. "They had a red carpet, making him go into that courthouse every day. They made him, every single day, walk the red carpet. Just to put him on display, and give the media bites."

Although Faye saw signs that Michael was once again taking prescription drugs for his physical and psychological pain, she did not want to confront him at a time of enormous stress. "The time I spent with him was a time of peace, not confrontation," she explained. "It was my duty as a friend to make that time and space as peaceful and calm as I could before he had to go to where he had to go. And no matter what [drugs] he was doing, I could never blame him for that. Because of the pain. Physical, psychological, emotional pain."

On June 13, 2005, twelve jurors returned a unanimous Not Guilty verdict on all fourteen charges against Michael. The jury simply did not believe the claims of the Arvizo family, which the defence team successfully depicted as exhibiting a long history of attempting to extort celebrities and abusing the legal and governmental systems. "We expected some better evidence, something more convincing – but it just wasn't there," one juror said.

Defence attorney Tom Mesereau believes the prosecution case against Michael was malicious. "I think that he was treated in a way that no one else would've been similarly treated," he said. "It was because he was a mega-celebrity. Why 70 sheriffs searching Neverland Ranch, based upon what this accuser and his family said, before they'd even investigated the background of the accuser and his family?"

Mesereau also described the county of Santa Barbara's decision to spend millions of dollars on the case as 'absurd'. "They wouldn't do it in a murder case," he said, "They wouldn't do it in a serial killer case, but they did it because Michael Jackson is a superstar and they wanted to take a superstar down."

Mesereau said the media were sticking knives in Michael's open wounds both during and after the trial. For months, Michael watched as his carefully guarded life was laid open in the courtroom. "He was so hurt by what had been said and written about him," the attorney said. "He knew that many people – most of the people in the media – didn't believe him. I really think that by the time the trial was over Michael wasn't sure he wanted to live anymore."

During the trial, political commentator Matt Drudge accused the media of largely ignoring testimony and evidence that was in favour of Michael. "Out here Michael Jackson is being literally crucified," Drudge said. "I think if you did a pulse poll, of people listening to these local talk shows, they would say 95% that Michael Jackson did all this, because it's based on the coverage." British music journalist Charles Thomson later wrote a piece for *The Huffington Post* titled 'One of the Most Shameful Episodes In Journalistic History'. Thomson said the trial that was relayed to the public by reporters 'didn't even resemble the trial that was going on inside the courtroom'.

Michael may have been acquitted, but the damage was done. Could he possibly recover from such an ordeal? Rebuilding his career would certainly take time. For now, the love of his three children seemed to be enough.

CHAPTER 18: THE RECOVERY

MID 2005 – MID 2008

After the trial, Tom Mesereau gave Michael one final bit of legal advice: leave Santa Barbara County and never return. Mesereau felt the district attorney Tom Sneddon and the sheriff's department were obsessed with bringing Michael down; all it would take to open the door to another criminal charge is a child wandering onto the ranch. "I felt he could never live in peace if he stayed at Neverland," Mesereau admitted.

Michael heeded the advice and left America only six days after the verdict, arriving in Paris on a private jet with his children and a nanny in tow. But Michael's final destination would surprise many in the showbiz world. After a ten-day stay in the French capital, the Jacksons arrived in the desert kingdom of Bahrain, a tiny island nation tucked away just off the east coast of Saudi Arabia. Their host was the King of Bahrain's second son, Sheikh Abdullah bin Hamad bin Isa Al Khalifa. Michael first spoke to Abdullah over the phone during the trial after being connected by his brother Jermaine, who had several contacts in the Middle East.

Located over 8,000 miles from Hollywood, Bahrain was a remote place where the western media weren't going to hound Michael. Life on the island gave him everything he needed after the trauma of his trial – privacy, rest and, most importantly, the opportunity of recovery. By the end of the trial, Michael was so thin that his cheekbones were visible through his skin. The day after the verdict, Mesereau said Michael was going to have to go through a period of physical recovery. "He's exhausted," the attorney said. "He was not sleeping. He was not eating. It was a very, very traumatic experience for him and it's going to take a while for him to recover."

During the trial Abdullah agreed to pay Michael's utility fees for Neverland, and even footed his $2.2 million legal bill at the end of it. When the Jackson clan arrived in Bahrain, the sheikh put them up in a luxury palace and paid for transport, security, guests and even vacations to Europe. Over the course of nearly a year, he shelled out more than $7 million on Michael. But it wasn't merely a gift; in return for this huge advance Michael had to re-launch his career in the kingdom. A lover of music, Abdullah was keen to expand his new record label, Two Seas Records, and had cash to burn. "I saw the payment as an investment in Michael's potential," the sheikh said. "He said he would pay me back…through our work together."

Abdullah brought in British record producer Guy Holmes, the man behind the 2005 United Kingdom chart hit 'Crazy Frog', to run Two Seas Records and coordinate projects with Michael. "After Michael arrived in Bahrain I spent a bunch of time talking to him about what he wanted to do and how he wanted to get his career back on line," Holmes recalls. "The one thing we definitely weren't going to do was live shows. We felt he wasn't well enough, just looking at him and observing him." Together, they decided Michael would release at least two albums, write an autobiography and work on a Cirque du Soleil production based on his music, as well as a documentary series on his life. Abdullah then secured the agreement through a binding contract.

Several producers, including John Legend and Michael's former collaborators Bill Bottrell and John Barnes, flew to Bahrain to work on songs for the first album in a studio Abdullah built especially for the project. "Michael would come in and work in the studio for a couple of days and then have some time off, because he was also recuperating," Holmes said. "But he was serious about it, he made a list of all the microphones he used on his previous recordings and we went out and bought them all. A whole bunch of people would fly in and out to work with Michael, it was about getting the songs and the demos right first, before we would bring someone contemporary in to produce the whole thing at the end and bring it all together."

Holmes, who also acted briefly as Michael's manager, said he had a $24 million offer on the table from a major publisher for the autobiography, and he was also in discussions with Guy Laliberté of Cirque du Soleil about opening a stage show in Macau. If successful, the show would have been rolled out to other parts of the world. Holmes was also negotiating a deal with London-based television production company Mark Stewart Productions for an official Michael Jackson documentary series.

But by the spring of 2006, Michael had made little progress on these projects. To protect his investment Abdullah turned off the money taps, at least until Michael proved he was ready to get down to business. Michael, who believed Abdullah was going to build his family a house in the kingdom, was outraged. He responded in cold fashion; in late May, he told Abdullah he was travelling to London to give a deposition in a case filed against him by former advisor Marc Schaffel, before heading to Japan to accept an award. He would return soon, he told Abdullah, but it was the final time the sheikh ever saw Michael, who turned his back on Bahrain without completing the projects or repaying any of the $7 million he owed in expenses.

Michael's primary purpose for visiting Japan was to discuss the development of feature films, animation and video games with business figures and potential investors. The trip began with an appearance at the Japanese MTV Video Music Awards, where Michael was honoured with a Legend Award, and the next day he visited an orphanage in Tokyo. Over the following days Michael met with Japan-based concert promoter Broderick Morris and entertainment manager Qadree El-Amin, among others.

Morris and El-Amin claim Raymone Bain, Michael's Washington-based publicist who was originally hired as a spokesperson in 2003, enlisted their help to find willing investors and business partners to work on projects with her client. Back in Bahrain, Abdullah and Guy Holmes knew something was afoot. "We were really upset when Michael left," Holmes said. "We heard rumours that something was going on, but Michael promised us there wasn't. There were other people floating around, and he wouldn't have walked out on us if his bed wasn't feathered elsewhere."

After abandoning his stay in Bahrain, Michael decided to overhaul his business and management affairs. He fired his Bahraini lawyers and Los Angeles accountant, and placed Raymone Bain at the top of his organisation. Although Bain did not have an established history of managing musicians, she was now in a position of trust. Bain not only became Michael's new manager, but she was also appointed as president/chief operating officer of a new company formed to handle his personal and business affairs, The Michael Jackson Company (MJJ Productions came under this company and would still be used for music production). She would also receive 10% of any business she brought in.

Michael's entertainment attorney, John Branca, felt he was now listening to people who did not have his best interests at heart, and chose to resign after over 25 years of working together on and off. "He was surrounded," Branca explained. "He did not ask me to stay. I resigned amicably." Bain hired a new entertainment lawyer, Peter Lopez, and a business attorney, New York-based Londell McMillan.

Michael had also recently restructured his finances, with the help of lawyers Abdullah paid for. By 2004, Michael's debt – nearly all of which came from bloated Bank of America loans – stood at $275 million. In early 2005, after Michael was late with part of a $3 million quarterly interest payment, the bank chose to sell the loans to Fortress, a New York-based investment firm which specialises in distressed debt. But when the Fortress-owned loan came due in December 2005, Michael lacked sufficient funds to repay.

By early 2006, the amount owed had ballooned to $300 million, due to interest. Sony proposed that it would help Michael arrange new financing at a lower interest rate. Besides aiding a partner, the company was concerned Michael's half of Sony/ATV could end up in bankruptcy court – or in the hands of an outsider like Fortress. In exchange, Sony received a freer hand to make investment decisions without Michael's approval, and an option to buy half of his 50% stake for around $250 million.

Sony found a lender, Citigroup, but Fortress agreed to match the offer and refinanced the $300 million debt, which was collateralised by Michael's

50% share in the Sony/ATV catalogue. Fortress also provided a separate loan of $23 million, leveraged by the Neverland Ranch, increasing the total debt to $325 million. The refinancing wouldn't provide Michael with much spare cash though. As part of the package, he was forced to spend around $15 million buying back a 5% interest in the Sony/ATV catalogue he had given to his attorney, John Branca, in 1993 as a condition of his return.

THE EMERALD ISLE

In early June, when Michael left Japan after a week-long stay, he decided against returning to the United States and relocated to Ireland, via Paris. Bain said Michael wanted to base himself in Europe because of upcoming new music projects. The Middle East wasn't the ideal location to mount a comeback; geographically, it is a difficult place for producers to fly in and out of, and is very much disconnected from the western entertainment world. Broderick Morris and Qadree El-Amin claim they continued to work with Bain and Michael on various projects after the Japan visit, but none of the ideas that were discussed would come to fruition.

Michael and his children arrived in the Irish city of Cork on June 23 after taking a regular Aer Lingus flight from Paris, and headed straight to the medieval Blackwater Castle in the small village of Castletownroche. Castle owner Patrick Nordstrom said Michael chose Ireland over Paris as his next residence because he found it impossible to get away from the media attention during his week-long stay in the French capital. "They were virtually prisoners in their hotel room," Nordstrom explained. "He simply wanted to relax in peace with his children, like any father in his circumstances would want to. His management made enquiries about places in Europe where he could stay and be guaranteed some tranquillity."

After a two-week stay at Blackwater, the Jacksons moved briefly to Ballinacurra House in Kinsale, south of Cork, before a longer stay at the €30,000 a week Luggala Lodge estate in County Wicklow, near Dublin. But Tiger Woods had made a reservation to stay at the property while participating in the 2006 Ryder Cup competition, so once the golf superstar showed up, Michael moved on again.

This time he settled at Grouse Lodge, a Georgian estate located in the Irish Midlands about an hour west of Dublin. It was in the lodge's state-of-the-art recording studio where Michael was able to experiment with music again. Producers who flew over from America included Rodney Jerkins, Theron Feemster (aka Neff-U) and will.i.am, who admitted that working with Michael in an Irish cottage felt like a 'dream'.

The Black Eyed Peas singer even refused to take payment for his work. "A week before the trip, he [Michael] was like, 'My manager is gonna call you to make sure all the travel stuff [is taken care of]. Do you fly commercial or private?' I was like, 'Don't worry about my flights; I'll pay for my flights... So many people have taken advantage of you in the past...it will be my honour to take myself there and let's just make music. You don't pay for my flight, I won't charge you my fees and if we make good music then the song will make money.' He's had a history of people just taking advantage of his success and camping out in the studio and charging him outrageous rates."

Before will.i.am touched down in Dublin the pair sketched out around eight song ideas over the phone. During the producer's week-long stay at Grouse Lodge they worked on three songs, with a track called 'I'm Dreamin'' being the most complete. Michael promised will.i.am they would spend a whole month together in the New Year to complete the material.

In November 2006 Michael flew across to London, where he attended the World Music Awards to collect an award for selling over 100 million albums in his career. During the ceremony Michael joined a children's choir on stage to sing a few lines of 'We Are the World', much to the disappointment of the fans in attendance, who were expecting him to sing 'Thriller'. Michael told the media afterwards that there had been a 'misunderstanding'. It was the final time he stood on a stage in public.

After the awards, Michael finally felt ready to return home; he was never one for cold weather, and winter had arrived in Ireland. His luck was also running out in terms of privacy. After an interview in the Grouse Lodge studio with Access Hollywood's Billy Bush gave away his exact location, the paparazzi began flocking to the estate in droves. But the real reason Michael decided to come home was because he had entered talks with gambling dealmaker Jack Wishna over a return to the stage. Wishna, credited as the man behind the deal that brought the Trump Hotel to Las Vegas, tried to convince Michael to take up a residency show at a Sin City hotel. A staple of the Las Vegas Strip for decades, a residency means fans have to come from around the world to see the artist in one venue, rather than the artist going to the fans. Michael was receptive to the idea, so Wishna arranged for a private jet to collect him from Dublin and bring him to Nevada.

HOMECOMING

Michael and his children touched down at Las Vegas' McCarran International Airport on a frosty night in late December 2006. The Jacksons were met on the tarmac by their new security guard, Bill Whitfield, who took them to a seven-bedroom mansion on South Monte Cristo Way in the west of the city, leased on a six-month contract for a reported $1 million.

The residency plans aside, it was also more convenient for Michael to be closer to the producers he was creating his new music with. A portable recording studio was set up at the property, where Michael worked for a few months with long-time collaborator Brad Buxer and engineer Michael Durham Prince. He also continued to work with will.i.am and reached out to R&B star Ne-Yo, who submitted some songs. Michael had plans to eventually release his new music independently, without a record label. He planned to release it in a different way, putting out new singles every six weeks or so before compiling them all on an album later on. But he was in no great rush. "For the most part, he was just writing and creating music because he loved doing it," bodyguard Bill Whitfield observed.

As well as Jack Wishna, Michael also held talks with British megastar producer-manager Simon Fuller about performing shows in Las Vegas, while concert promoters around the world were clamouring for his signature. In April 2007, Michael and his entertainment attorney Peter Lopez met with Randy Phillips, the CEO of live entertainment promoters Anschutz Entertainment Group (AEG) Live, in the private wine cellar of a luxury condo in Turnberry Towers that AEG had rented for the occasion.

Together they discussed the possibility of Michael taking up another residency, this time at the 20,000 capacity O2 Arena in London, an arena which AEG operates. AEG was chasing the world's top entertainers to do residency shows at the arena, which had only recently opened. "Michael was at the top of the list," Phillips said. "It's a short list." In the meeting Michael reiterated his desire to make movies, and discussed the idea of playing King Tutankhamun in a television mini-series based on the story of the pharaoh. Phillips explained that AEG had the necessary connections after bringing a King Tutankhamun exhibition to the United States in 2005. The idea was presented to filmmakers at Walden Media, which is owned by AEG, but they did not feel the project was viable.

Michael also related his wish to release new music, and Phillips joked that he knew the right man who could help. "He did his whole story about what he wanted to do," Phillips recalls. "And I said, 'I have the perfect idea, the perfect guy to do this for you.' And he said, 'Who is that?' And I said, 'Tommy Mottola.' He was stunned that I said that and he took a pencil and threw it at me and actually hit me. His aim was good." Michael and the former Sony Music chief obviously hadn't made up since that feud in 2002.

But by the summer of 2007, it became clear that Michael wasn't ready to return to work in any capacity. Ultimately, Phillips was told by Michael's representatives that he simply wasn't capable of going back on stage at that time. The Las Vegas residency plans, which would have required Michael to perform only three shows a month, were also shelved because he was too 'debilitated' and 'incoherent', according to Jack Wishna. "As he stayed in Las Vegas, he started to get debilitated from a mental and physical standpoint," Wishna explained. "The family started to bother him again...His father Joe. I said, 'Michael, I think we should shelve it. I think we should put it on the shelf, come back to it when you are' – these are the words that I used – 'mentally, physically, and vocally capable of being a part of this project'." Raymone Bain also turned down an invitation for Michael to perform at the BET Awards, which were being staged at the Shrine Auditorium in Los Angeles on June 27. According to Bain, her client was in no fit state to perform or even make a public appearance.

In late June, with the lease on the Las Vegas property about to run out and plans for a residency show in the city abandoned, Michael went on a 'summer vacation' to Virginia. He stayed at a stately house at Goodstone Inn, a manor in the heart of Virginia's horse country which had plenty of acres for his children to enjoy. Michael was said to be interested in buying a vacation property on the East Coast, and it was also reported that Bain wanted him to be far away from his family members, who were bothering him in Vegas. Others believed that Bain, who was based in Washington D.C., wanted to bring Michael closer to the capital so she could exert more control over him.

Without a residence to call home, in August Michael and his children showed up on the doorstep of the Cascio family home in Franklin Lakes, New Jersey, to seek sanctuary. The Cascio family had been very close friends of Michael's since 1984. The stay was also convenient for his itinerary, as Bain organised two magazine shoots and interviews with Italian *Vogue* and *Ebony*, to take place in New York during September. Michael, whose liquidated cash was running out, ended up staying with the Cascios for three months, living a normal family life and staying in a modest room in the basement of the home. He was also biding his time, as another deal to refinance his $300 million loan with Fortress, which was due to be repaid in full in December 2007, was in the pipeline. The deal would free up money to settle lawsuits and pay other monies, and also provide cash so he could rent another property.

During his stay on the East Coast, Michael met with rapper Kanye West to discuss the remix of 'Billie Jean' for a surprise upcoming anniversary release of *Thriller*, titled *Thriller 25*. Sony announced the release of the album in November, exactly 25 years after the original record was released. Modern music stars West, will.i.am and Akon remixed some of the original *Thriller* hits for inclusion on the reissue, and Michael also decided to add a bonus track, 'For All Time', originally written by 'Human Nature' writer Steve Porcaro and his writing partner Michael Sherwood for *Dangerous*. Michael and Porcaro were supposed to meet at a studio to complete ad-libs and background harmonies, but Michael never showed.

In November 2007, Michael returned to the West Coast after accepting an invitation from Jesse Jackson to attend the civil rights activist's birthday gala in Los

Angeles. But Michael could barely afford the trip, so he and his entourage were flown to California at the expense of billionaire business magnate Ron Burkle, a friend of both Jacksons. Burkle's generosity didn't stop there, as he allowed Michael and his children to stay at his Greenacres estate in Beverly Hills for an entire month. After spending Thanksgiving in Los Angeles, Michael decided to return to Las Vegas, where a room was booked for him at the Green Valley Ranch resort. But after only two weeks, the Jacksons were asked to leave the hotel when Michael's credit card was declined. It was a desperate situation, but his entertainment attorney Peter Lopez came to the rescue. Lopez knew the owner of another Vegas hotel, the Palms Casino Resort just off the Strip, where the Jacksons were put up in a luxury suite free of charge.

FINANCIAL CHAOS

Fortunately for Michael, a deal on the latest refinance package was about to be completed by his advisors, following months of negotiations. British bank Barclays refinanced the $300 million Fortress debt (collateralised once more against Sony/ATV); another bank, HSBC, lent $30 million against Michael's own catalogue, Mijac, and a hedge fund loaned another $40 million, also against Mijac.

Although it was a financial lifeline for Michael, he wouldn't see much of the money. Most of the spare cash went on settling several lawsuits, debt payments, lawyer fees, back taxes and paying employees who had gone without wages over the preceding few months.

The $370 million package took Michael's total long term debt to $400 million (he also borrowed $23 million against Neverland in 2006, a debt still held by Fortress). With a further $100 million owed to other creditors, the total figure came close to half a billion dollars.

Although Michael was heavily in debt he was still asset rich, with his portfolio including his 50% stake in the huge Sony/ATV catalogue, which had an estimated value of up to $500 million. The ever-increasing value of the catalogue allowed Michael to borrow hundreds of millions of dollars and live beyond his means for years, and may therefore be the wisest investment ever made by a celebrity.

His own Mijac music catalogue was estimated to be worth $50–100 million, and he also owned the Neverland and Hayvenhurst properties, as well as millions of dollars' worth of antiques and art. Going by their estimated value, if Michael liquidated all of his assets there was the potential of being hundreds of millions in the black instead of the red. But he refused to surrender them while there were still alternatives, no matter how expensive they were.

After earning over a billion dollars throughout his career, the question arises, how did Michael end up in so much debt? Until the early nineties – he had as much as $30 million of debt by 1993 – Michael paid relatively close attention to his accounting and kept an eye on the cash that flowed through his business and creative ventures. Michael disbanded his original business team, which comprised manager Frank DiLeo, attorney John Branca and accountant Marshall Gelfrand, over the course of 1989 and 1990. Although Branca would return in 1993, it later became difficult to keep track of who was advising Michael in management, accounting and business, especially after Michael fired DiLeo's replacements, Sandy Gallin and Jim Morey, in 1997.

Michael's defence attorney from the 2005 trial, Tom Mesereau, said he listened to advice from people he shouldn't have trusted. "Because he generated so much wealth and so much profit, he became a repeated target of unsavoury characters, many of them mediocre, who tried to get near him, promise him the moon and then profit themselves by being around him," Mesereau said. Many advisors squandered tens of millions of dollars on deals that never happened, mainly theme park, casino and film projects.

From 1997 onwards Michael continually chopped and changed his management, and went on to affiliate himself with 'business' associates including Saudi Prince Al-Waleed bin Talal, Don Barden and South Korean businessman Myung-Ho Lee. They were followed by Marc Schaffel and Dieter Wiesner, Florida real estate mogul Al Malnik (a former lawyer for the late mafia mobster Meyer Lansky), veteran music publisher Charles Koppelman and even the Nation of Islam.

Michael's choice of advisors continued to raise eyebrows after he was acquitted of molestation in the summer of 2005. After a spell in Bahrain and a falling out with his host Sheikh Abdullah, Raymone Bain took centre stage, leading to Branca's resignation. Bain supervised the management and payment of Michael's day to day, weekly and monthly bills and also oversaw his living requirements, including insurances, personal requirements and expenses, travel, security and staff. In a nutshell, she had total control; Michael didn't even know where his own money was, or how much he had. But by late 2007 Michael had stopped trusting Bain, and transferred financial control over to his business attorney, Londell McMillan. In late December, with the loan refinancing complete, he officially dismissed Bain from his life, paying her $488,000 to walk away.

LAS VEGAS PART II

In January 2008 Michael was still living in a suite high atop the Palms hotel, which was the perfect location for him to continue creating music. The hotel boasts Las Vegas's first state-of-the-art studio, built in 2005 by owner George Maloof with the intent of bringing the city in line with the other big music cities in the United States. Maloof allowed Michael to use the $1,850 a day facility free of charge, in addition to the $40,000 a night suite he was occupying.

Michael worked in the $6 million studio with Akon, who had helped to put together the *Thriller 25* album, and Moroccan-Swedish producer RedOne, real name Nadir Khayat. RedOne was working on Akon's own album at the time and also co-produced Lady Gaga's hit album *The Fame*. One of the first songs Michael and Akon worked on together was called 'Hold My Hand', written by Akon together with Claude Kelly and Giorgio Tuinfort. Kelly said Michael loved the song because of its message. "The song is really, really emotional," the songwriter said. "It's about unity and has a message of friendship and togetherness that definitely struck a chord with Michael." But Michael wasn't content with the other material he worked on with Akon. "He was never satisfied," Akon admitted. "We might have passed up ideas that I know for a fact were smashes. He'd be like, 'Nah, nah – we got to come up with something better.' He always believed we could do better."

Thriller 25 was released in February 2008 and became a huge success commercially, especially for a commemorative re-release. If it had been eligible to enter the *Billboard* 200 chart, it would have reached number two, and in the United Kingdom it reached number three. The album sold an incredible three million copies within three months of its release, which eventually increased to ten million. Michael was delighted with this response from the public, and it inspired him to continue making new music. His gradual return to the limelight was set to continue when his representatives began talks over a performance at the 50th Annual Grammy Awards in Los Angeles on February 10, but the idea never came to fruition.

Thanks to the recent loan deal, Michael and his children were finally able to leave the Palms hotel at the end of February after a near three-month stay. They moved to a Mediterranean style mansion five miles up the road from the hotel at 2710 Palomino Lane, leased for six months for a modest $49,000.

Michael resumed work at the property with Brad Buxer and engineer Michael Durham Prince, again using a portable recording studio. Buxer was commuting to Las Vegas from Nashville during breaks from his job as a commercial airline pilot. Over the course of two spells in 2007 and 2008, Michael and Buxer collaborated on many songs together. But Buxer said Michael never actually mentioned the idea of releasing an album during this time. "He loved writing and working on songs but he didn't want to tour anymore," Buxer said. "All he wanted to do was film, so there wasn't much talk about the future regarding music." Together they simply created music, and continued to tinker with 'Adore You', 'Hollywood Tonight' and 'Shut Up and Dance', all of which came from the *Invincible* sessions, as well as 'From The Bottom of My Heart', a song the pair created in 2005 with the intention of benefiting the victims of Hurricane Katrina.

Later in the year Buxer had to leave the project, much to Michael's disappointment, as he couldn't afford to quit his flying job. Producer Neff-U – who worked briefly with Michael in Ireland in 2006 – took over, and the pair worked on titles including 'The Dark Lady', 'D.I.E.', 'Lady of Summer', 'H2O' and 'Silent Spring'. During this period Michael also received a visit from Dr. Freeze, the producer who contributed 'Break of Dawn' to *Invincible.* Freeze offered Michael a handful of songs and the pair brainstormed ideas, but nothing was recorded.

By early 2008, despite the recent restructuring of his financial empire, Michael had reached the peak of his cash flow crisis. He defaulted on repayments for his Neverland Ranch loan – a debt still held by Fortress and unaffected by the refinancing – and was told to pay off the entire $24.5 million balance by March 19 to prevent a foreclosure, which would have had disastrous financial consequences. Lenders were now refusing to loan Michael more money, but he was about to be tapped out for the final time.

Michael's brother Jermaine had just met a Lebanese-American businessman by the name of Dr Tohme Tohme (Tohme for short), who lived in Los Angeles. As Tohme was in real estate, Jermaine thought he may be able to help. His instincts were correct; Tohme was able to connect Michael to an associate, Tom Barrack, who made billions buying and selling distressed properties through his investment firm Colony Capital.

Barrack met with Michael at the Palomino residence and told him he was interested in a deal, but only if he agreed to return to work to increase his income. By 2008 Michael was earning $26 million a year, most of which came from his music catalogues, but his outgoings amounted to $42 million, with $25–30 million of that going on debt interest alone. Michael had been spending an average of $15–20 million more a year than he was earning for the past decade, a lifestyle sustained through borrowing, which was no longer an option. Either Michael had to sell his assets, or make some money.

"Where you are is an insolvable puzzle unless you're willing to go back to work," Barrack told Michael. "If you're willing to do that, then we can help, but if you're not willing to do that, it's just presiding over a funeral." But Michael was reluctant to tour again; all he wanted to do was make movies. "He really had a hard time with that [the idea of touring], and he struggled for about three days," Barrack recalls. "Finally, he calls back and says, 'You're right, I'll do it'."

CHAPTER 19: THE FINAL CURTAIN CALL

MID 2008 – JUNE 2009

After Michael agreed to return to the stage, Tom Barrack wrote a cheque and saved Neverland from being auctioned to the highest bidder on the steps of the Santa Barbara County courthouse. Under the terms of the agreement, if the property were to be sold, Colony would recoup its investment in the note plus accrued interest, its management and upkeep expenses, and around 12% of everything above that as a success fee. Michael would keep the rest. Barrack estimated that if marketed properly, the ranch could be worth as much as $60–70 million.

In early June 2008 Michael dined with Barrack at the Las Vegas Hilton, and the two discussed the options for a comeback. Barrack initially entertained the idea of having Michael do a residency at the Hilton, which Colony owned. As well as other concert promoters, Barrack reached out to his friend Phil Anschutz, who owns AEG Live, and informed him Michael was ready to return to the stage. AEG had of course already been in discussions with Michael a year earlier, but to no avail. Anschutz put Barrack in touch with AEG Live CEO Randy Phillips, who was introduced to Michael's latest primary advisor, the mysterious financier Dr Tohme.

Tohme claimed to have strong connections to wealthy figures in the Arab world, as well as being a medical doctor and a special envoy to the African country of Senegal. Tohme conceded that he is not a licensed physician, although he does possess a passport signed by the former president of Senegal, describing him the country's 'Ambassador at Large'. According to

Tohme, Michael was so happy with his role in helping to save Neverland that he signed over two separate powers of attorney, giving him control over both his financial and his business affairs. He also became Michael's new manager, despite his lack of experience in the entertainment industry. It was another example of Michael giving total control to a person he barely knew.

Tohme and Phillips met in mid-June at a bar in the Hotel Bel-Air, which Tohme treated as his office. They discussed loose terms which included a multi-year touring plan, starting with a residency at the O2 Arena in London, as discussed in 2007. Phillips noted that it takes a 'very special artist' to be able to do a major residency show. He recommended London because it was the hottest concert market in the world, bigger than New York and Toronto combined, and Michael's popularity was also less diminished in the United Kingdom. Phillips told Tohme he would do 'anything' to have Michael sign with AEG.

Following further conversations between Michael's representatives and AEG, Michael travelled to Los Angeles and met directly with Phillips at the Hotel Bel-Air in September 2008. To Phillips, it was apparent that Michael was now ready to get back on stage. For the first time, Michael spoke primarily about performing live rather than his film and music plans. "It was really then, looking him straight in the eye, that I actually realised this was not a wild goose chase," Phillips recalls.

Later that September, Michael and his representatives had a formal meeting with AEG executives at the MGM Grand in Las Vegas, where AEG chief Phil Anschutz has a villa. Phillips recalls Michael being 'laser focused' during the meeting. It was agreed in principle that Michael would perform a series of concerts at the O2 Arena in 2009, and his plans to release new music around the shows were also discussed. Michael also talked once more about his ambitions to write, produce, direct and star in films, and Anschutz, who has two film production companies, said he would help.

Meanwhile, on August 29, 2008, Michael turned fifty. To commemorate the landmark, Sony (which still held the licences to Michael's recordings) released a greatest hits album by the name of *King of Pop*. The album tracklist differs in each country it was released, because fans were given the opportunity to vote which songs should be included on each country's version.

While negotiations with AEG continued, Michael and the children moved to Los Angeles in late October, where they checked into a huge first floor suite at the Hotel Bel-Air. Michael returned to California at the behest of Tohme, who felt he should be closer to the centre of the concert industry. All musical equipment was brought over from Las Vegas, and Michael continued to work on music in the hotel with engineer Michael Durham Prince. Here, vocals were recorded for the pre-existing tracks 'I Am a Loser', which became 'I Was the Loser', and 'Best of Joy'. They were the final vocals Michael recorded in his lifetime. "Although we continued to work on music for a few more months, that was the last time that he truly sang," Prince said.

On Halloween Michael met again with Randy Phillips in his suite, and revealed the real motives behind his decision to tour again. In an emotional meeting, Michael told Phillips his children were now at an age where they could appreciate his talents, and he was still young enough to perform. Michael also admitted that he wanted his family to stop living like 'vagabonds'. He was tired of living in other people's houses since leaving Neverland in 2005, and finally wanted to settle down and find a permanent home for himself and his children. "We both broke down," Phillips recalls. "He got emotional. He teared up about his family and having a good life with them and a place to live and a residence they could call their own. I felt incredibly bad that this incredible star was at the point where he just couldn't buy a house with all this money he made. It just didn't make sense."

Michael had already identified his dream home, a palatial mansion at 99 Spanish Gate Drive in west Las Vegas. The 92-room walled compound, owned by the Sultan of Brunei's brother, is spread over 16 acres and was valued at around $60 million. In addition to the nine-bedroom main house, there are several guest villas and a sports house which contains an Olympic-sized swimming pool and squash courts. Bodyguard Bill Whitfield said

Michael would visit the property at least once a week while he lived in Las Vegas. "He wanted a property so huge that he could go outside and feel like he was free," Whitfield said. "He could go and climb a tree, do whatever. He said he was going to buy it and call it Wonderland."

But before Michael could sign with AEG, there was the small matter of securing a release from a contract with a Bahraini prince. Michael's representatives learned that he signed away the rights to his live performances when he entered into a contract agreement with Sheikh Abdullah while living in Bahrain in 2006. To complete the AEG deal Michael had to be released from the contract, which meant settling a lawsuit the sheikh had filed through a London High Court 18 months earlier. Abdullah claimed Michael owed him at least $7 million after he funded his living costs as an advance for restarting his career in the kingdom. But after spending nearly a year in Bahrain, Michael disappeared to Europe without repaying a penny or completing any projects. The case was settled out of court in late November; Michael agreed to pay the sheikh $3 million, and a release was granted.

100 North Carolwood Drive

With a settlement reached and negotiations with AEG progressing, Michael moved out of the Hotel Bel-Air to a huge seven-bedroom château on North Carolwood Drive in the plush Holmby Hills area of Los Angeles. The neighbourhood borders Beverly Hills and Bel Air, forming part of Los Angeles' illustrious 'platinum triangle'. Elvis Presley's old house, which he owned between 1970 and 1975, is situated about 200 feet away across the road at 144 Monovale Drive, and Walt Disney, Frank Sinatra, Barbra Streisand, Clark Gable and Gregory Peck all used to live about half a mile up the road. The Carolwood property, valued at $38 million in 2008, was owned by Ed Hardy clothing line executive Hubert Guez, and had previously been rented by James Bond star Sir Sean Connery. AEG was footing the $100,000 a month rent cost as part of any prospective contract with Michael, and signed a 12-month lease with Guez. Remarkably, the rent was cheaper than living at the Hotel Bel-Air full-time.

Michael finally signed a contract with AEG in the living room of the Carolwood home on January 28, 2009. The agreement outlined that Michael would perform a minimum of 18 shows, and a maximum of 31, starting in July and finishing in September at the O2 Arena in London. The number 31 was very significant – Michael wanted to do ten more shows than Prince had done in 2007, which would also break the record for number of shows performed at the O2 in the process. The meeting ended with a champagne toast and all parties high-fiving.

Phase one would see the announcement of an initial ten shows, which would most likely increase to anything between 18 and 31 shows, depending on public demand. If the demand for tickets was greater than 31 shows, the agreement could be amended for further shows to be added beyond the initial maximum of 31, based on Michael's approval.

Michael received a number of advances, including an initial $5 million artist advance, $3 million of which went straight to Sheikh Abdullah as a part of the court settlement. AEG also paid $1.2 million to lease the Carolwood mansion for a year, and agreed to advance $15 million for the down payment on Michael's dream Las Vegas home on Spanish Gate Drive.

For security, AEG had Michael sign a promissory note, with collateral being everything he owned. If Michael were to renege on the concert agreement in any way, AEG would take control of Michael's company and use the income from his assets, such as his music catalogues and royalties, to recoup its money. It couldn't, however, take an actual interest in any of those assets.

Although Michael would receive 90% of the tour profits (AEG 10%) once all the advances were deducted, he had to pay for 95% of the production costs. The production advance Michael would receive from AEG was capped at $7.5 million, but could be increased.

In handwritten notes later found in his Carolwood home, Michael revealed he would not have signed a deal with AEG unless it put up money for the development of films. After finishing the touring plan, Michael intended to retire from live performances permanently in order to finally pursue his movie dream. He felt if he didn't crack the film industry, he would have failed to achieve true immortality. 'If I don't concentrate [on] film, no immortalisation,' one note read. Michael also revealed that he wanted to be the 'first multibillionaire entertainer actor and director', and to be 'better than [Gene] Kelly and [Fred] Astaire' and 'the greatest ever, in the likes of [Charlie] Chaplin, Michelangelo and [Walt] Disney'.

As part of the contract, AEG contemplated entering into a separate agreement to develop three films. If a third party was interested in developing films with Michael, AEG would advance $1 million towards the development of a script. Michael's first ideas were to make two full-length 3D feature films based around his 'Thriller' and 'Smooth Criminal' videos; the latter would have been based around the 1960 movie *The Rise and Fall of Legs Diamond*. Michael felt the storylines of both videos had enough potential for the big screen, and wanted writers to work with him on these ideas during his time in London.

In his notes, Michael revealed that he wanted to make 'a movie a year for [the] next five years'. He loved movie classics from the forties, fifties and sixties and wrote a list of films he wanted to develop, including 'Jack the Giant Killer', 'The 7th Voyage of Sinbad', 'Aladdin', 'Ali Baba and the Forty Thieves', '20,000 Leagues under the Sea' and 'Mysterious Island'.

He was also desperate to play King Tutankhamun in a 'King Tut' movie or mini-series, a desire he had had for many years. 'AEG demand development of these movies', he wrote.

On February 21, after months of speculation, London's *Daily Mail* became the first media outlet to confirm Michael's return to the stage. "Michael Jackson is to launch a spectacular 30-date comeback at London's O2 arena this summer," it said. "The 50-year-old star has been in secret talks with organisers for months in a desperate bid to revive his career after recent personal problems."

'THE MIRACLE OF MARCH 5th'

With the contract signed, Michael began putting his tour team together. Towards the end of February he asked old friend Kenny Ortega, the director of his two previous world tours, to come on board as show director. "He was very excited," Ortega recalls, "and he used the expression 'this is it' a number of times during the phone conversation. I remember saying to him, 'You should just call it 'This Is It' you've said it so many times!' He was just very excited, [he said] 'this is it, this is the time, there is great reason to do this now and I want you to be a part of this with me'." Ortega was involved in other projects at the time, but after clearing his diary he accepted the offer on a $1 million salary.

It was decided the tour would indeed be called 'This Is It'; Michael chose the title because of its double meaning. "This is the last time I'm going to do this, and when I'm on stage, this is the place in the world to be," he explained to Randy Phillips.

A press conference to officially announce the shows to the world was scheduled for March 5 at the O2 Arena in London. But Michael was reluctant to attend. "He doesn't want to do these kind of things, but it was important to show Michael Jackson to the world if he wanted to do a Michael Jackson show," AEG executive Paul Gongaware said. To make matters worse, Randy Phillips was unable to reach Michael in the week before the conference. The only way Phillips was able to contact him directly was through Dr Tohme, but Michael wasn't taking his manager's calls.

Michael was angry with Tohme because of the way he handled an auction of over 2,000 of his personal possessions, which was scheduled to start on April 21. The items, most of which were stored at Neverland, were estimated to raise at least $12 million at a time when Michael needed it. Michael claimed he agreed to the auction on the basis that he would be able to view photographs of the items before deciding which ones to sell. But he soon learned that many 'priceless and irreplaceable' items of 'extraordinary sentimental value' were included in the auction, before he had a chance to review them. The auctioneer, Julien's Auctions, claimed the contract entitled it to auction anything it wanted. Michael blamed Tohme for the saga, as it was he who signed the deal on his behalf in August 2008. According to Tohme's attorney Dennis Hawk, Michael agreed for 'everything' to be auctioned when the agreement was made, but only changed his mind months later when he realised he would no longer need the cash due to the AEG deal. Yet Michael was also furious with Tohme for his general PR handling of the affair.

In the end Michael put his differences with Tohme to one side and agreed to attend the conference. On March 3 he flew into Luton Airport near London aboard a private jet with his three children, a bodyguard and a hair/make-up artist in tow. A limo then whisked them away to one of Michael's favourite London hotels, the lavish Lanesborough. Two days later Michael was due at the O2 Arena for his press call, but nerves began to creep in in the hours beforehand. When Randy Phillips arrived at the Lanesborough that afternoon he headed straight to Tohme's suite, where he waited alone. Eventually, Tohme returned from Michael's room. "We have a little issue, Michael got drunk," Tohme told Phillips, who began to panic as they were now running late.

Phillips decided to try and get into Michael's suite himself, but first he had to talk his way past Michael's bodyguard, Alberto Alvarez. "Alberto, you've got to let me in," Phillips told him. "This is a crisis situation." "He could see by my face it was not a time to stop me." Michael was still in his pants and robe, and an empty bottle of liquor lay on the floor next to the couch. "To me, he looked hungover," Phillips recalls. "I said, 'Michael are you OK?' He said to me that he was really concerned that there wouldn't be anyone there and maybe this would be a bust." Phillips informed Michael that he was quite wrong – there were thousands of fans and news organisations awaiting his arrival. The 2005 trial and accompanying media coverage had clearly damaged his confidence. "He was so nervous and really concerned as to how people would react to him after so many years," Phillips said.

Michael then went to the bathroom and changed into black boots, black trousers and a white V-neck t-shirt. Out of a choice of three different coloured shirts – black, red and blue – Phillips chose black because the background at the O2 Arena was red. But then Michael had trouble attaching the sequined armband to his black jacket. "He wouldn't leave unless he had the armband on," Phillips said. "That was more than I could take. I raised my voice and said, 'Guys, that's enough'!"

Soon after, Phillips sent an e-mail to his boss, AEG president Tim Leiweke:

> I screamed at him so loud the walls are shaking. Tohme and I have dressed him and they are finishing his hair. Then we are rushing to the O2. This is the scariest thing I have ever seen. He's an emotionally paralyzed mess, filled with self-loathing and doubt now that it is show time. He is scared to death. Right now I just want to get through this press conference.

Phillips admitted he might have overreacted. "I was so nervous," he said. "I created so much tension in the room, you could cut the tension with a knife." Once the party climbed into the SUV and bus transporting them to the O2 Arena, the mood lightened. Phillips said he went into 'jester mode', and Michael was also laughing and joking. As news helicopters circled above, the anticipation began to build.

Michael finally made it to the O2, albeit 90 minutes late. Phillips, who now calls the event 'The Miracle of March 5th', said the delay actually created more anticipation, as people doubted whether it would even happen. To the delight of over 3,000 hysterical fans and 350 reporters, Michael took to the microphone to announce he would be performing in London for the final time. "I just want to say that these will be my final show performances in London," he said. "This will be it, and when I say this is it, it means

This Is It." Michael then broke off, touching his chest – clearly elated at the huge reception he was receiving. "They [the fans] were telling him that they still loved him and I think that was really really important to him," Phillips said. "It underscored the point that he is just a human being."

"I'll be performing the songs my fans wanna hear," Michael continued. "This is the final curtain call. I'll see you in July. I love you. I really do, you have to know that I love you so much. Really, from the bottom of my heart. This is it, and see you in July."

JACKSON MANIA

Although Michael was contracted to perform between 18 and 31 shows – if the demand was great enough – only ten were initially announced. Phillips explained that in the concert business, promoters roll into the other shows and never put them all on sale at the same time. AEG executives were confident there would be enough interest for 20 to 25 shows; they were clearly not prepared for what was about to unfold.

The morning after the press conference, fans were invited to pre-register for tickets on a newly created website called michaeljacksonlive.com, to gauge the demand. But the site struggled to cope as 1.6 million people registered – enough to fill the O2 Arena more than 100 times – so AEG quickly added 20 more shows, for a total of 30. Only fans who registered were able to buy tickets – priced between £50 and £75 – when the pre-sale began. They sold out within minutes, causing ticket site Ticketmaster to crash due to the high traffic.

Phillips estimated Michael could have sold out as many as 150 shows, as people would want to see him more than once. So he called Michael and asked him if he would play more than 30 shows. Michael agreed, but only for a total of 50; he didn't want to spend an entire year in London. He also gave Phillips two conditions – first, he wanted the Guinness Book of World Records to attend the final show, as he knew 50 shows in one venue and one city was a feat no other artist or band was ever likely to beat. He also wanted AEG to rent him a country estate outside London so he and his children weren't trapped in a hotel suite for months on end. Michael chose the 28-bedroom Grade II listed Foxbury Manor, located about 19 miles away from the O2 Arena near Chislehurst in Kent.

Reports claimed Michael didn't actually agree to do 50 shows, and that Tohme went ahead and approved the extra dates behind his back. "I'm really angry with them [AEG] booking me up to do 50 shows," British tabloid *The Sun* quoted Michael later telling fans. "I only wanted to do 10, and take the tour around the world to other cities, not 50 in one place. I went to bed knowing I sold 10 dates, and woke up to the news I was booked to do 50." Yet a source close to the negotiations denied Michael was angry. "We couldn't have gone ahead with adding more shows, for a total of 50, without his direct approval," the source said. "And he wasn't pissed; there was no happier human being in the world, because to him, it showed the people still loved him."

Either way, all 750,000 tickets for the 50 shows were snapped up within hours, making This Is It the fastest selling concert series in history. Randy Phillips described it as a 'cultural phenomenon'. "Not only are these concerts unparalleled, these records will never be broken," he said. The phenomenal public response was mirrored by the media, which gave Michael favourable coverage for the first time in many years. On March 13, the *London Evening Standard* wrote, 'Jackson-mania is gripping London, and the world, transforming the figure of fun, never to be let near children, to the biggest draw on the planet once again'.

Michael would now be staying in London until the end of February 2010. But it was only the first phase; he still had the rest of the world hungry and waiting. There were plans to take This Is It around the globe as part of a three-year, 186-show international touring plan, with stops in Norway, Sweden, Germany, France, Switzerland, Italy, South Africa, Dubai, Japan, South Korea, Taiwan, India, Australia, New Zealand and South America. Finally, Michael would make a triumphant return to Canada and the United States.

AEG estimated Michael could walk away with over $30 million from the 50 London shows alone once all advances, expenses and production costs had been deducted. If he completed the full international tour he could net more than $130 million. This figure did not include income from potential commercial sponsorship deals, which would have been Michael's first since the 1993 allegations. There were plans to make a live 3D concert movie from the London shows, and AEG was also in talks to open a Michael Jackson merchandising store at the O2 Arena and to rent an empty store on Oxford Street, Europe's busiest shopping street, offering nothing but MJ merchandise. Michael seemed determined to be more careful with his money, vowing to sign all cheques over $5,000 himself and hire an accountant that he trusted.

Back in Los Angeles, Michael and Kenny Ortega began to assemble the This Is It team. Ortega set out to hire people he admired in lighting, production design, choreography and music. Travis Payne was hired as lead choreographer, Michael Bearden as musical director and Michael Cotten as the production and stage designer. Payne and Cotten had already worked with Michael on previous tours but it was the first time for Bearden, who took the position usually occupied by Greg Phillinganes or Brad Buxer. Other 'Team MJ' veterans brought back into the fold included costume designers Michael Bush and Dennis Tompkins, Michael's long-time friend and hair/make-up artist Karen Faye and former assistant Miko Brando.

Rehearsals began in late March 2009 at Center Staging in Burbank, a small venue where the initial production, music and staging ideas were laid out. Here, Michael was building the show conceptually with Ortega and Michael Cotten. They would spend several hours having creative conversations, going through Michael's vast archive of photos, videos and records. At one of the first meetings Michael revealed his grand plans for the concerts. "I want to push it to its limit, all the way," he said.

Each afternoon Michael was also rehearsing with Travis Payne in the basement studio of the Carolwood mansion. The choreography was based mostly on the previous tours, although Michael and Payne worked together to make it more dynamic and age appropriate. "When you're 30 [years old] you can do more than when you're 50," Payne explained. Michael's goal was to sing all of his vocals live in London, even the ones accompanying the big dance numbers, something he hadn't achieved since the first leg of the Bad Tour 22 years previously. Three or four times a week, Michael also worked out at home with actor and body-builder Lou Ferrigno, who played the Hulk in *The Incredible Hulk* TV series. Michael wanted to stay away from the weights and work mostly on flexibility and endurance.

In mid-April, 500 dancers from all over the world were flown to California for auditions at the Nokia Theater in Downtown Los Angeles. Michael was present on the final day of the three day process, when twelve dancers were selected to perform at both national and international venues on a two-year contract.

After the initial conceptual building of the show Michael didn't need to attend rehearsals as often, as the dancers were still getting up to speed. But he still visited Center Staging to attend production meetings and sing and rehearse with the band.

A MULTI-MILLION DOLLAR BATTLE

There was plenty of upheaval in Michael's camp in March and April 2009, as several figures tried to manoeuvre themselves into key positions ahead of a comeback tour potentially worth hundreds of millions of dollars. Michael was also sued by numerous individuals who claimed they were owed money. "You have the same thousand parasites that start to float back in and take advantage of the situation and that has happened a little at the edges," Tom Barrack noted at the time.

After returning from London in March, Michael cut off all contact with Tohme, the main reason being his role in the Neverland auction affair. Although the auction was later cancelled, it cost Michael money because he had to settle with the auctioneer. He was also influenced by his personal assistant and gatekeeper, Michael Amir Williams, who didn't trust Tohme and saw him as nothing more than a conman. His desire to be rid of Tohme would later be revealed in his personal diary, in which he wrote, 'Tohme away from my $ now, no contact', and 'no Tohme near me, no Tohme on plane or in my house'.

As early as September 2008, Michael told a spiritual advisor that he wasn't comfortable with the 'divide' Tohme had created between him and his own people, just as Raymone Bain had done. "This guy [Tohme], he just has ways about him," Michael said in a recorded phone conversation. "There's a divide between me and my representatives and I don't talk to my lawyer, my accountant. I talk to him and he talks to them. I don't like it. I wanna get somebody in there with him that I know and can trust. I don't know what's in my accounts." Tohme's dismissal wasn't made official until mid-April.

At the same time Tohme was on his way out, Michael made the surprise decision to bring Frank DiLeo back into his camp. DiLeo, whom Michael had dismissed 20 years earlier, was appointed as a 'representative' and 'tour manager'. In the weeks preceding the appointment, DiLeo had garnered Michael's attention because he promised him an associate of his had a special multi-million dollar fund for the pair to produce films. DiLeo also had support from Michael Amir Williams, who was desperate to see Tohme fired.

DiLeo admitted he was in discussions with Michael about movie projects shortly before he was hired, but denied it was simply a scheme to worm his way back into the fold. "We didn't really discuss what he was doing with AEG, we talked about movies," he said. "I never said to him, 'Do you need my help, can I be involved [with the tour]'." DiLeo said Michael later called him out of the blue to ask if he would manage him again. He accepted the offer, before asking Michael why he wanted him back. DiLeo claims Michael told him, "Well you know I'm doing these concerts, I need help. You know how to do this, you know what I want". DiLeo began working for Michael in April, but the appointment wasn't formalised until May.

There were whispers that DiLeo was hired by Randy Phillips against Michael's wishes; DiLeo allegedly convinced Phillips he could keep Michael focused on rehearsals and preparations for London, which was vital for AEG. Karen Faye, who claims Michael fired DiLeo in 1989 because he was stealing from him, also says Phillips brought him back. "Michael told me he would never hire him again," she said. Yet a source who dealt directly with Michael during this time said it was Michael's own decision to hire DiLeo. "It was Michael who brought Frank back in, after the falling out with Tohme he needed someone who knew the business to run his affairs and handle the music side of things," the source said. With DiLeo back in the fold, Michael now had many familiar people around him, people who were working with him at the height of his fame – on a creative level, the likes of Kenny Ortega, Travis Payne and Michael Bush, and on a personal level, DiLeo, Miko Brando and Karen Faye.

In an odd twist of events Michael brought Tohme back in later on, mainly to work on business affairs such as the purchase of the Las Vegas home at 99 Spanish Gate. DiLeo would continue to deal with the entertainment side of things, which Michael felt Tohme wasn't qualified to do. Michael's long-time attorney, John Branca, was also brought back to help with the negotiation of several deals. Michael's previous entertainment attorney, Peter Lopez, was fired by Tohme earlier in the year.

Amidst the managerial merry-go-round, Michael's cash strapped father also began meddling in his son's affairs. Joseph had been trying to organise a family reunion concert behind Michael's back since November, teaming up with ex-convict and 'family friend' Leonard Rowe, who promoted shows for the Jacksons in the late seventies, to make it happen.

At the behest of his mother, who was behind the reunion concert idea, Michael agreed to meet 'Joe and Rowe' on April 14. Michael made it clear that he couldn't perform with his family due to his deal with AEG, but the pair still tried to convince him they were the right men to manage his business affairs for the upcoming tour. Joseph wanted to wrestle control away from AEG. "I'm the only one who can do them [the shows] right," he reportedly told gossip columnist Roger Friedman on the phone a few weeks earlier. Joe and Rowe brought along a pre-prepared letter they wanted Michael to sign, which would appoint Rowe as his representative in all entertainment matters. Under pressure from his father, who was standing over him, Michael signed the letter. But first he changed the wording, giving Rowe permission only to 'oversee' the tour finances.

Four weeks later Michael was persuaded by his mother to take another meeting with Joe and Rowe, who were still trying to sign him up for a family reunion show. Michael explained to them, for the final time, that he was locked in a contract with AEG. In the days after the meeting Michael sent a letter to Rowe, which read, 'this is to inform you that you do not represent me and I do not wish to have any oral or written communication with you regarding the handling of my business and/or personal matters'. DiLeo said Michael 'forgot' all about Rowe's supposed role as a financial overseer, and planned to dismiss him much earlier. The entire situation was deeply confusing; even Randy Phillips admitted he found it difficult to keep track of who was in and who was out. "You needed a scorecard," he said.

In early May, AEG gave in to Michael's demands for a personal physician to accompany him for both the rehearsal period in Los Angeles and the shows in London. Initially, AEG tried to convince Michael that he did not need a costly full-time doctor simply to 'make protein shakes'. "I didn't want to spend $150,000 a month on a doctor, since we were playing in London, which has phenomenal medical resources," Phillips admitted. "He admonished me that he needed a doctor 24/7, the same way Barack Obama did, because his body is what fuels this whole business. Michael prevailed on that." The chosen physician, Grenadian-born cardiologist Conrad Murray, was hired at a rate of $150,000 a month. Michael first met Murray in December 2006, when he treated one of his children shortly after their arrival in Las Vegas.

NEW MUSIC

Michael continued to work on music with producer Neff-U and engineer Michael Durham Prince during the first few months of living at Carolwood, but by the time rehearsals began he no longer had the time. They kept a portable studio set up in the pool house of the property in case an idea came. "Michael always had a microphone in the house, he wasn't sitting in front of it, but it was there if he thought of a melody," Prince, who was also part of the tour team as an audio supervisor, said. Michael planned to continue recording music while he was in London – Prince said that by June 2009, recording equipment was being measured in preparation for transportation across the Atlantic.

Michael had a note pinned up in the Carolwood château with the titles of several songs he had been working on over the past few years, some of which he planned to finish. The list included the Akon duet 'Hold My Hand'; Akon revealed Michael wanted it to be the first single from his next album before it was leaked on the internet in the summer of 2008. But the song's appearance on the list may have meant Michael still had plans for it.

'I Was the Loser' and 'Best of Joy', the last songs Michael ever recorded, and the Neff-U tracks 'The Dark Lady', 'D.I.E.', 'Lady of Summer', 'H2O' and 'Silent Spring', were also on the list. 'The Way You Love Me', 'Hollywood Tonight', 'Shut Up and Dance', 'Beautiful Girl' and 'Adore You', songs Michael began recording with Brad Buxer and Prince during the *Invincible* sessions, also featured, as well as 'From The Bottom of My Heart', a song Michael and Buxer created in 2005 with the intention of helping the victims of the Hurricane Katrina disaster.

Older songs include the 2002-penned collaboration with Bee Gees singer Barry Gibb, 'All In Your Name', and 'You Were There', written in 1989 by Buz Kohan and performed by Michael for the only time at the Sammy Davis Jr. 60th Anniversary Special that year. Michael also wrote that he wanted to 'finish' 'Cheater', from the *Bad* sessions, and 'Scared of the Moon', a song recorded in 1984, also with Kohan.

Michael was still considering releasing singles one after another while on tour, before putting them all on a full album later on. "He would have released a single maybe every eight to twelve weeks while he was on tour, for a total of eight or ten, and then put them out as a full album at the end," Prince explained. "The tour got the world's attention, it was a great idea."

Michael also had a major surprise up his sleeve – as well as a pop record he planned to work on an album of classical music. At the end of April, composer David Michael Frank was invited to Carolwood, as Michael was looking for someone to arrange some music for orchestra. Frank, who first met Michael while he was working on the 1989 Sammy Davis Jr. special, said: "He told me, 'I have three projects going on simultaneously.' One was the tour, one was to be an album of pop songs. Then he said, 'The other one is that I want to record an album of classical music' – what he called classical music."

Frank described it as closer to film score music, but was impressed with Michael's knowledge of the genre. Michael once revealed that classical music was his 'first love'. "He said he listened to classical music all the time; it was his absolute favourite," Frank said. "I realised that almost all the classical pieces he mentioned are childlike, very simple and pretty, like Prokofiev's *Peter and the Wolf* and Tchaikovsky's *Nutcracker Suite*."

After Frank arrived at Carolwood the two went into Michael's pool house, where the studio was set up. "We headed out there, but Michael stopped when he saw the dog [Kenya, the children's pet] was outside, soaking wet from being in the pool," Frank recalls. "He didn't want us to get splattered. It was kind of funny. Michael got another assistant to hold the dog while we went to his pool house."

While Frank sat at the piano Michael played him two incomplete demos he had written, humming the missing parts. He was anxious to get the pieces orchestrated and record them with a large orchestra. "I asked if he could have someone call me to discuss the budget and he said he would take care of it," Frank said. Frank suggested they record the music in London, an idea which Michael liked.

In the meantime, Frank laid the music out on his computer and started on the orchestrations, and later he received a call from Michael's camp asking for a budget. "The pieces sound like pretty film score music, with very traditional harmony, and definitely very strong melodies," Frank said. Of course, the project would never come to fruition.

"THE TIME HAS COME, THIS IS IT"

On May 20, 2009, AEG announced it had to push back the beginning of This Is It by five days, meaning three shows had to be moved from July 2009 to March 2010. Director Kenny Ortega explained he needed an extra week to get the show ready because it had 'got so big', and they also required more rehearsal time in London. But the media chose to ignore the explanations and instead speculated that the delay was due to Michael's health.

The British tabloids were the main culprits when it came to outlandish Michael Jackson stories that circulated in the build-up to the shows. One story claimed Michael was secretly fighting skin cancer. Others detailed Michael's demands for elephants, monkeys and parrots to accompany him on stage in London, and that he planned to sing a duet with his twelve-year-old son Prince. The most outrageous one of all claimed it was a body double who had showed up to the press conference at the O2 Arena on March 5. Readers were also reminded that Michael had been using a wheelchair to go shopping as recently as the previous summer. The tabloid circus fuelled scepticism over whether Michael would turn up on the opening night, let alone perform 50 shows.

By June, the show had really begun to take shape. Although overall production costs were supposed to be capped at $7.5 million, the final costs ran closer to $25 million. This Is It was described as the most technologically advanced and most expensive arena show ever mounted. The $5 million 'Dome Project', consisting of a series of 2D and 3D films, was a major factor in the budget increase. The films were to be projected onto a huge LED screen behind the stage at different moments during the London shows, creating the first 3D concert experience in history.

Michael told Ortega the show's opening had to be something no artist had ever done before. The concept they chose was an LED video experience; Michael would float onto the stage in a body suit made of screens flashing with historical television images, before emerging and starting the show with 'Wanna Be Startin' Somethin''. For his grand stage exit, Michael came up with 'MJ Air'. The plan was to depart through a hole in the screen, to give the impression that he had boarded a jet and flown away.

'Smooth Criminal' was set to start with a short 2D film, which was made to look like Michael was appearing with Humphrey Bogart and Rita Hayworth in a stylish old film noir. Michael filmed his scenes against a green screen at Culver Studios in early June, which were then digitally inserted into sequences from several classic black-and-white Hollywood movies, including *Gilda*, *Dead Reckoning*, *In a Lonely Place* and *The Big Sleep*. The film was interactive; at one point Michael would have jumped out of the film before emerging on the stage. Ortega said it was one of the projects Michael was most excited about. "I said [to Michael], 'What if all the badass gangsters from all the old Hollywood movies were chasing you,' and Michael loved that," Ortega recalls.

The spectacular 'Thriller' performance was also interactive, and would have started with a 3D film including the recreation of the famous zombie scene from the 1983 video. The film was designed to act as a backdrop while Michael danced on stage. Towards the end Michael would emerge from underneath a black widow spider prop which had transferred from the screen, before performing the 'Thriller' dance with the zombies. Michael wanted ghost puppets to drop from the ceiling and fly over the audience and through the walkways, which he called the '4D' experience.

But 'Earth Song' was the video that was most important to Michael. The money and performing for his children weren't his only motivations for doing the tour; he also felt he had an important message to give. "He felt now more than ever that his music applied to our world situation," Ortega explained. "He wanted to use the stage as a platform to remind people the importance of us doing whatever we can to take care of this planet and each other."

His performance of 'Earth Song' would serve that purpose. "The planet is sick, like a fever," Michael said in 2009. "If we don't fix it now, it's at the point of no return. This is our last chance to fix this problem that we have, where it's like a runway train. And the time has come, This Is It." At the beginning of 'Earth Song', Michael wanted to show a video featuring a little girl playing with nature in a rainforest, complete with stunning colour and imagery. Towards the end, when Michael begins his raging ad-libs atop a cherry picker, the girl wakes up in a destructed wasteland on the screen behind. Finally, she meets a heavy digger which transfers onto the stage and stops in front of Michael.

Some of the numbers, including 'Human Nature', 'Billie Jean' and 'Man in the Mirror', were totally free of special effects so the audience could be alone with Michael, his voice, his dancing and the music.

This Is It had become a huge multi-million dollar production, which required Michael's full focus and attention.

"TIME TO GET REAL"

In the first week of June 2009, Michael spent most mornings on set at Culver Studios to film pieces for the Dome Project. At the same time, rehearsals moved from Center Staging to one of Los Angeles' major sports and concert arenas, the Forum in Inglewood. Preparations had advanced to the point where it was time to put the show on its feet and begin the staging phase at a larger venue. Michael was now expected to step it up and show more regularly for rehearsal, but he failed to attend as often as the production team would have liked. When he did show, rehearsals would usually begin in the late afternoon after his home session with Travis Payne, lasting up to seven hours.

Michael missed several rehearsals in the first two weeks of June, much to the frustration of Kenny Ortega and the production team. After Michael struggled at rehearsal on Friday, June 12 and skipped the Saturday session on the orders of his doctor, an increasingly concerned Ortega sent the following e-mail to AEG executive Paul Gongaware:

> MJ did not have a good Friday and he didn't show on Saturday. He has been habitually late (the norm). I realise he's up against a lot. I have a ton of love and sympathy for what he's been through. We must do all that we can as a team to stay on top of his needs everyday. He required more attention and management. As I mentioned I truly believe he needs nourishment guidance and physical therapy (massage) for his fatigued muscles and injuries. He is not in great physical shape. I believe he's hurting. He has been slow at grabbing hold of the work. We have twenty days we can't let him slip. I'm doing all I can every day to build up his confidence and to create a schedule that will help to ready him and to arrive us at our goals. Every time he is late or cancels it chisels

> away that possibility. There can be no more calls to Travis asking him to come to the house. MJ needs to be told that it's time to get real. He must take care of himself so that he can meet the schedule or there are going to be consequences. We need a healthy, rested and ready MJ at the Forum and Staples for all the remaining rehearsals as well as the few we have at the O2 in July.

Ortega explained in the message that he wanted Michael to be more in attendance with all the cast at the Forum, rather than just rehearsing at home with Travis Payne.

By the third week of June, Michael was absent from the Forum almost on a daily basis. On June 16, a meeting was held at the Carolwood mansion so Ortega, Gongaware and Randy Phillips could discuss with Michael his lack of focus and poor attendance at rehearsals. Michael, wearing a surgical mask, looked 'scared' before the meeting, his chef Kai Chase recalls. Chase said she heard a 'very, very expensive' vase smash at the beginning of the summit, and rushed into the room to clean up the pieces. "I was able to hear some of the conversation that was going on," she said. "It seemed they were very firm with him." It was reiterated to Michael that he needed to start showing up, partly for the sake of the dancers and the band. Michael was not only the performer but also the co-director of the show, so Ortega required his presence. Chase said an 'upset' Dr Murray, who also sat in on the meeting, later stormed out of the room. "I can't take this shit," she heard him say. In the days that followed, Chase noticed Michael was 'concerned, frightened and scared', and seemed to have 'the weight of the world on his shoulders'.

Gongaware, who had previously acted as a tour manager on both the Dangerous and *HIStory* tours, says he was never alarmed by Michael's absences. "Michael didn't like to rehearse, it didn't surprise me," he said. Michael barely rehearsed for the *HIStory* Tour but still nailed it, Gongaware noted. "I knew that when the house lights went up, he was going to be there," he added. "When it was game time, he would show up."

What caused the most alarm was Michael's sudden weight loss – he weighed 136 pounds – and strange behaviour. By June, those who were around him on a daily basis, including Kai Chase, Karen Faye and Travis Payne, among others, noticed his physical appearance had suddenly changed. "He looked great in April, he didn't look good in June," Chase recalls. "It was an obvious difference and concerned me greatly. He appeared very weak, he looked much thinner…undernourished…he didn't look as well as I had seen him." Faye became alarmed and sent two e-mails to Frank DiLeo, asking him to intervene. "I have seen with my own eyes, him deteriorate physically in a month," she told DiLeo. "Michael is painfully thin…his bones are protruding. I am [the] one person that has physical contact with him every day." Faye said several fans also e-mailed her with their concerns. Payne recalls questioning Michael about his sudden weight loss, but was told not to worry. "He said, 'I'm getting down to my fighting weight,' which I took to mean that he was preparing for the performances," Payne said.

Faye says Michael also began behaving oddly, often repeating himself and saying the same things over and over again. "This was not the man I knew," she admitted. "He was acting like a person I didn't recognise."

Michael's drug use became another concern; at some rehearsals, Payne recalls Michael appearing 'a little loopy', and 'under the influence of something', mostly when he would arrive straight from the Beverly Hills clinic of his long-time dermatologist, Dr Arnold Klein. Between April and June Michael made 18 visits to see Dr Klein, who was injecting his face with Botox and facial filler to prepare him for his return to the stage; he routinely had such treatments ahead of a major concert series.

Dr Klein admitted he would 'occasionally' give Michael the opioid painkiller Demerol, which he had been addicted to in the past, to sedate him during a procedure. An examination of Michael's medical records showed he was receiving as much as 375 milligrams of Demerol in a 90 minute period, more than seven times the recommended dose. Dr Robert Waldman, a specialist in medical addiction, said this amount would leave Michael sleepy and lethargic, and possibly difficult to arouse and unresponsive.

Dr Waldman testified that the treatment had 'probably' caused Michael to become addicted to Demerol once more. He consulted with dermatologists, who told him shots of Botox and Restylane (facial filler) were not painful enough to warrant the use of Demerol, although Michael was known to have a very low pain tolerance.

One thing Michael managed to hide from just about everyone, apart from Dr Murray, was his nightly struggle with insomnia. Michael had trouble sleeping during tour phases in the past, and this was no different. Dr Charles Czeisler, a Harvard Medical School sleep expert, believes Michael's tour insomnia may have been partly psychological. "He may have slept a little bit more than he thought, but from his point of view, he couldn't sleep well when he was tour," Dr Czeisler said. "And then this produced anxiety related to his sleep and in association with being on tour that made him very concerned about that impact." Dr Waldman said the insomnia may have been worsened by withdrawal symptoms from the Demerol, as he wasn't receiving it every day.

THE LOST BOY

On Friday, June 19, Michael showed up for what was scheduled to be the last rehearsal at the Forum. But he was in no fit state to even step onto the stage. Kenny Ortega said the Michael he saw that night frightened him. "I thought there was something emotionally going on, deeply emotional, something physical going on," he admitted. "He was cold. I observed Michael like I had never seen him before. It troubled me deeply; he appeared lost, cold, afraid. I felt Michael was in trouble and needed help."

Ortega, who couldn't understand why Michael was in such a condition when he had a personal physician, called Dr Murray to make him aware of the issue. Ortega and Karen Faye then tried to warm Michael, who was shaking and could barely hold a knife and fork, and gave him some food. "We talked, Karen put a heater by his feet," Ortega recalls. "I sat down on the floor and took off his shoes and I was rubbing his feet...and he told me it felt really great." Ortega couldn't believe it when Michael told him he'd never had his feet massaged before.

Michael asked to sit out the rehearsal and watch while Travis Payne took his place, before Ortega suggested that he return home early. After Michael left the building, Ortega and associate producer Alif Sankey became emotional. "We were both crying," Sankey recalls. "We were crying because he was not speaking normally to Kenny." Show production manager John Hougdahl then fired off an e-mail to Randy Phillips:

> I'm not being a drama queen here. Kenny asked me to notify you both MJ was sent home without stepping foot on stage. He was a basket case and Kenny was concerned he would embarrass himself on stage, or worse yet, be hurt. The company is rehearsing right now, but the DOUBT is pervasive. Time to circle the wagons.

Later that night Ortega also sent an e-mail to Phillips, expressing his deep concerns about Michael's recent physical and mental deterioration:

> My concern is now we've brought the doctor into the fold and have played the tough love, now or never card is that the artist may be unable to rise to the occasion due to real emotional stuff. He appeared quite weak and fatigued this evening. He had a terrible case of the chills, was trembling, rambling, and obsessing. Everything in me says he should be psychologically evaluated. If we have any chance at all to get him back in the light, it's going to take a strong therapist to help him through this as well as immediate physical nurturing. I was told by our choreographer that during the artists' costume fitting with his designer tonight they noticed he's lost more weight. Tonight I was feeding him, wrapping him in blankets to warm his chills, massaging his feet to calm him and calling his doctor. Finally, it's important for everyone to know, I believe that he really wants this. It would shatter him, break his heart if we pulled the plug. He's terribly frightened it's all going to go away. He asked me repeatedly tonight if I was going to leave him. He was practically begging for my confidence. It broke my heart. He was like a lost boy. There still may be a chance he can rise to the occasion if we get him the help he needs.

Ortega said he sent the e-mail because he wanted to be taken seriously. He admitted he did not think the show could go on at this stage. "I was torn, my instinct was to stop the show, but I didn't want to break Michael's heart," he said.

Phillips then replied, asking Ortega to remain calm:

> Kenny, it's critical that neither you, me nor anyone else around this show become amateur psychiatrist or physicians. It is critical we surround Michael with love and support and listen to how he wants to get ready for July 13th. You cannot imagine the harm and ramifications of stopping this show now. It would far outweigh "calling this game in the 7th inning". I'm not just talking about AEG's interests here, but the myriad of stuff/lawsuits swirling around MJ that I crisis manage every day and also his well-being. Please stay steady. Enough alarms have sounded. It is time to put out the fire, not burn the building down. Sorry for all the analogies.

John Hougdahl later sent another revealing e-mail to Phillips:

> I have watched him deteriorate in front of my eyes over the last 8 weeks. He was able to do multiple 360 spins back in April. He'd fall on his ass if he tried it now.

Only later would it become clear exactly why Michael had deteriorated at such an alarming rate, both physically and mentally.

Following the incident another summit was called, which took place the next afternoon at Carolwood. Ortega and Phillips began sharing their concerns with Michael and Dr Murray, but the doctor became angry with Ortega, telling him had no right to send Michael home. "[Murray said] Michael was physically and emotionally capable of handling all of his responsibilities for the show," Ortega recalls. "I was shocked because Michael didn't appear to me to be physically or emotionally stable at that moment." Murray then told Ortega to stick to his job and leave Michael's health matters to him.

Michael reassured both Ortega and Phillips that he was physically and mentally fit to continue, and that he would improve from this point onwards. "Michael told me that he was ready to take the reins," Ortega said, "that I should not be afraid, [and] that he was perfectly capable of handling the responsibilities. He wanted to do it [the tour], [he] wanted me to stay at his side, [and he] told me to believe in him. I told him I loved him, [that] I was concerned for his health and safety, and I said, 'That's the only reason why I brought these things up, because I care about you and I don't want any ill harm to fall upon you,' and he said, 'I'm fine Kenny I promise you,' and he gave me a hug."

It was also related to Michael once again that he needed to attend rehearsals at such an important stage of the production. Michael responded by explaining that he hadn't been as engaged as Ortega would have liked as he had been working with Travis Payne at home, and that he knew his routines. "I mean Michael was very clear that he was ready," Phillips said. "What he said to Kenny, is, 'You build the house, and I'll put on the door and paint it'." Michael said he understood his presence was needed for such a complex production, and promised Ortega he would now come to rehearsals. The director then told Michael to take the next two days off and spend some time with his children.

"I CAN TAKE IT FROM HERE"

On Tuesday, June 23 rehearsals moved from the Forum to the Staples Center in Downtown Los Angeles, which was a closer example of the O2 Arena in London. Eight rehearsals were scheduled to take place at Staples; the crew would then fly to London on July 5, allowing for five days of rehearsal at the O2 Arena before the opening show on July 13.

The Staples Center

When Michael showed up at the Staples Center that Tuesday night, he kept his promise – he was invigorated. Kenny Ortega could scarcely believe what was unfolding on the stage in front of him. "He entered into rehearsal full of energy, full of desire to work; full of enthusiasm, and it was a different Michael," Ortega recalls. The director even began wondering if he had seen a problem that didn't exist. "I doubted myself," he admitted. "I remember going, 'Did I see something that couldn't have been there?' Because Michael just didn't seem like the Michael that I had seen on the 19th. He was raring to go, fired up, in charge."

On Wednesday, Michael arrived at Staples at 6.30pm for a meeting with Randy Phillips, AEG president Tim Leiweke and television producer Ken Ehrlich. They discussed plans for a Halloween television special to be broadcast on CBS on October 31, 2009, which Ehrlich would produce; Michael wanted to combine his 1996 film *Ghosts* with segments of one of his live stage performances of 'Thriller' in London. He then spent the next hour reviewing the 3D segments for This Is It, before stepping onto the stage at around 9.30pm for rehearsal. Over the course of three hours Michael performed around a dozen songs, showing similar levels of energy and focus to the previous evening. The very last song he sang that night was 'Earth Song'. Michael then sat down with Kenny Ortega as they watched Travis Payne go through the 'Heal the World' rehearsal, so he could observe the lighting, staging and scenic elements of the song.

At the end of the session, Michael had a communal hug with Ortega and Payne before returning to his dressing room. Ortega was 'elated' with Michael's sudden transformation. "He knew we were over the hump," Phillips said. As they were walking out of the arena at 12.30am, Phillips said it felt 'like a million dollars' when Michael told him, "Now I know I can do this," and "Thank you for getting me this far, I can take it from here."

On Thursday Michael was due to begin rehearsing 'the illusion', which would transition 'Dirty Diana' into 'Beat It'. During 'Dirty Diana', Michael was to perform on a bed surrounded by flames while being pursued by a pole-dancing female aerialist, who would eventually catch him and tie him to one of the bedposts. A series of silk flames would then obscure him, before falling and revealing the pole-dancing female. Michael would then start 'Beat It' by floating over the audience on a cherry picker.

As Michael left the Staples Center, Ortega told him he would have everything prepared for him the next evening. "He felt like we were accomplishing the dream he saw before him in those rehearsals," an emotional Ortega recalls. "He asked me to thank everybody, to tell them that he loved them – the dancers, the singers, the band, the crew. I told him that I would have everything prepared for him the next day so that he could step right into the illusion rehearsal, and I told him that I loved him and he told me that he loved me more, and I gave him a big hug and he left the building."

THURSDAY, JUNE 25, 2009

The drive from the Staples Center to Carolwood Drive took about 30 minutes that night. As usual dozens of fans were camped outside the front gates to greet Michael when he returned. As his SUV approached the property at around 1am, Michael was in good spirits as he wound down his window and chatted briefly with fans before the vehicle proceeded through the gates.

But after stepping through the front door and retiring to his bedroom, his mood changed. As always after a hectic rehearsal, he struggled to wind down and relax. At 1.30am, after Michael took a shower, Dr Murray tried putting him to sleep with a tablet of diazepam, also known as Valium, a benzodiazepine drug with sedative properties. When this failed Murray gave Michael two stronger benzodiazepines, lorazepam and midazolam. Michael fell asleep, albeit briefly; after ten minutes he was wide awake again, according to Murray.

By 4.30am, Michael began to get desperate. "I got to sleep," he told Murray. "I have these rehearsals to perform. I must be ready for the show in England. Tomorrow I will have to cancel my performance. I cannot function if I don't get the sleep." Murray tried more lorazepam and midazolam, but by 10.40am, Michael was still not asleep. It was then when he told Murray, 'I'd like to have some milk. I know that this is all that really works for me.' What Michael was referring to was Propofol, an intravenously administered anaesthetic usually used only in a hospital setting. Murray reminded Michael that he had to be awake by noon to get ready for his next rehearsal at the Staples Center. "Just make me sleep, doesn't matter what time I get up," Michael responded.

Murray admitted he had been giving Michael Propofol every night for eight weeks to deal with his insomnia. Michael was familiar with the drug; he had used it for the same purpose during the summer of 1997 while touring Europe, and during the recording of *Invincible.* Because he was receiving the drug from a doctor, Michael believed it was safe. Over 48 hours earlier Murray began his attempt to wean Michael off Propofol, giving him less of that and more of the lorazepam and midazolam. On the Tuesday night, Michael slept reasonably well using only the benzodiazepines. This may explain why he was so invigorated at rehearsal.

Despite successfully getting Michael to sleep without Propofol the previous night, Murray gave in to the demands. "I decided to go ahead and give him some of the milk so he could get a couple hours sleep so that he could produce [rehearse], because I cared about him," Murray explained. The doctor administered 25mg of Propofol, slowly infused through an IV saline drip in Michael's leg. By 11am, as the drug surged through his bloodstream, Michael finally drifted off into a false sleep.

Phone records show that after administering the Propofol, Murray was busy talking to several people, including a girlfriend, between 11.18am and 12.05pm. When he returned to the bedroom he found Michael wasn't breathing, and his pulse was barely detectable. It's quite possible that Michael stopped breathing at least 45 minutes earlier. Murray started to perform CPR and mouth-to-mouth resuscitation on the bed, later claiming he couldn't move Michael off the bed on his own, but there was no response. Murray said he didn't call 911 immediately because the landline in the house wasn't working, even though he had access to a cell phone. Murray did manage to reach Michael Amir Williams, who was still at home in Downtown Los Angeles, using his cell. But instead of asking him to call 911, he told Williams to call Michael's security detail, located in a trailer outside the property.

At 12.17pm, security guard Alberto Alvarez took a call from Williams and sprinted up to the bedroom. But before asking him to call 911, Murray told Alvarez to place vials from the bedside cabinet in a bag and remove an IV drip from its stand, plus what appeared to be a bottle of Propofol. Finally, at 12.21pm, Alvarez called 911:

Alvarez: Sir, we have a gentleman here that needs help and he's not breathing. He's not breathing and we're trying to pump him but he's not…

911 operator: Okay, how old is he?

Alvarez: He's 50 years old sir.

911 operator: Okay. He's not conscious, he's not breathing?

Alvarez: Yes, he's not breathing sir.

911 operator: And he's not conscious either?

Alvarez: No, he's not conscious sir.

911 operator: All right, is he on the floor? Where is he at right now?

Alvarez: He's on the bed sir. He's on the bed.

911 operator: Okay, let's get him down to the floor. I'm going to have you do CPR right now okay. We're already on our way there. I'm doing as much as I can to help you over the phone. Did anybody see him?

Alvarez: Yes, we have a personal doctor here with him, sir.

911 operator: Oh, you have a doctor there?

Alvarez: Yes, but he's not responding to anything. He's not responding to CPR or anything.

911 operator: Oh okay. We're on our way there. If your guy is doing CPR and you're instructed by a doctor he has a higher authority than me.

Alvarez: Thank you sir. He's pumping his chest but he's not responding to anything.

911 operator: Okay, okay, we're on our way. We're less than a mile away, we'll be there shortly.

Murray was only just moving Michael onto the floor with the help of Alvarez when paramedics arrived at the château at 12.26pm. They treated Michael at the scene for nearly 40 minutes, giving him heart-starting drugs. Paramedic Richard Senneff began to think Michael had been dead for a while. At 12.57pm he spoke to a doctor at UCLA Medical Center, who gave him permission to pronounce Michael dead.

But Murray claimed he could feel a pulse, and demanded that he be taken to the nearby Ronald Reagan UCLA Medical Center in Westwood. Michael was loaded into an ambulance and transferred to hospital, but it was too late. Dr Michelle Cooper, who attended to Michael at UCLA, said he was 'clinically dead' on arrival at 1.13pm. After further resuscitation attempts, Michael was officially pronounced dead at 2.26pm.

Over at the Staples Center, Kenny Ortega was busy preparing the illusion rehearsal. His phone rang, it was Paul Gongaware. "Our boy is gone," Gongaware told him. Ortega didn't believe it was really Gongaware on the phone, and asked him to tell him something only the two would know to prove it was really him. "You have to sit down and get a hold of yourself," Gongaware told him. "Listen to me, Michael's gone." Ortega then collapsed in his seat and began crying, before gathering the rest of the team in a circle to tell them of Michael's passing.

THE AFTERMATH

American celebrity news website TMZ first broke the news of Michael's death at 2.44pm Pacific Time (10.44pm London time), only 18 minutes after doctors officially pronounced him deceased.

Family members rushed to the UCLA Medical Center to join Michael's three children, Frank DiLeo and Randy Phillips, who were already there, among others. By 4pm, thousands of people had gathered outside. Michael's passing instantly triggered a global outpouring of grief.

As the news spread, it caused unprecedented website issues from user overload. Both TMZ and the *Los Angeles Times* – the first news organisation to confirm the death at 3.15pm – suffered outages. Search engine Google initially believed that the input from millions of people searching for 'Michael Jackson' meant that it was under attack, and Twitter, Wikipedia and AOL Instant Messenger also reported crashes.

Vigils took place all over the world, and tributes poured in from the likes of Barack Obama, the President of the United States, and Nelson Mandela. Friend Liza Minnelli, clearly sensing that Michael's death would not be without its controversies, said, "When the autopsy comes, all hell's going to break loose, so thank God we're celebrating him now."

The day after Michael's death, a three-hour autopsy was performed on behalf of the Los Angeles County Coroner by the chief medical examiner.

A public memorial service was held on July 7 at the Staples Center in Los Angeles, attracting a global audience of up to one billion people. Michael's five brothers, sitting in the front row, each wore a white sequined glove in tribute, and Mariah Carey, Stevie Wonder, Lionel Richie, Usher and brother Jermaine performed, among others, while Berry Gordy, Brooke Shields, and Smokey Robinson gave eulogies. The Reverend Al Sharpton received a standing ovation when he told Michael's children, "Wasn't nothing strange about your daddy. It was strange what your daddy had to deal with."

Additionally, an emotional Marlon Jackson said, "We will never understand what he endured...being judged, ridiculed. How much pain can one take? Maybe, now, Michael, they will leave you alone."

The memorial is perhaps best remembered for the moment when Michael's eleven-year-old daughter, Paris, spoke publicly for the first time. Her voice cracking with emotion, Paris told the crowd, "Ever since I was born, daddy has been the best father you could ever imagine. And I just wanted to say I love him, so much."

Michael's will, signed in 2002, named his mother Katherine as the legal guardian of his three children, and his long-time on-off attorney John Branca and family friend and former manager John McClain as co-executors. The will divided Michael's estate into 40% for his mother, 40% for his children, and 20% for unspecified charities.

On August 28, the Los Angeles County Coroner made an official statement, classifying Michael's death as a homicide, after the drugs in his system were considered to have been intravenously injected by another. The county coroner stated that Michael died from acute Propofol intoxication with the effects of benzodiazepine drugs a contributor. As well as Propofol, the three benzodiazepines Dr Murray administered – diazepam, lorazepam and midazolam – were also found in Michael's blood.

When the combination of Propofol and benzodiazepines reached the lungs through the blood stream, they will have slowed the rate that the lungs inflate and deflate, decreasing their ability to pump oxygen around the body. The oxygen in the blood will have reached such a low level that it caused the heart to stop pumping.

Sleep expert Dr Charles Czeisler believes Michael may be the only human to have gone without REM (rapid eye movement) sleep for a period of 60 nights. Dr Czeisler said the coma induced by Propofol leaves a patient with the same refreshed feeling of a good sleep, but without the benefits that genuine REM sleep delivers in repairing brain cells and the body.

This means Michael is likely to have suffered from sleep deprivation for a period of eight weeks. Dr Czeisler said that symptoms of chronic sleep deprivation include a loss of weight and wasting, low body temperature, confusion, difficulty with balance and memory, paranoia and anxiety. These were the exact symptoms that those around Michael were concerned about in the last eight weeks of his life.

"The symptoms that Mr Jackson was exhibiting were consistent with what someone might expect to see of someone suffering from total sleep deprivation over a chronic period," Dr Czeisler said. "I believe that the constellation of symptoms was more probably than not induced by total sleep deprivation over the preceding chronic period."

Michael's service and burial took place at Forest Lawn Cemetery in Glendale, Greater Los Angeles, on September 3, ten weeks to the day after his death. Other famous figures buried in the cemetery include Hollywood legends Jean Harlow, Humphrey Bogart and Clark Gable, Michael's heroes Walt Disney and Sammy Davis Jr. and his dear friend Elizabeth Taylor.

In February 2010, Dr Conrad Murray was charged with involuntary manslaughter by prosecutors in Los Angeles. Murray pleaded not guilty and was released on bail. Eleven months later, the judge from Murray's preliminary hearing determined that the doctor should stand trial. In November 2012, Murray was found guilty of involuntary manslaughter for administering Michael too much dosage of Propofol, and served two years of a four-year sentence.

During the trial, Dr Steven Shafer, an anaesthesiologist who helped develop national guidelines for Propofol, testified about his review of the case and found that Murray committed 17 'egregious' violations of the standard of care, which he defined as acts that posed a foreseeable danger to Michael's life. These acts included a lack of monitoring equipment for his heart, breathing and blood pressure, and the failure to call 911 immediately.

In October 2013, Michael's family lost a negligence case against concert promoters AEG Live over his death. The family contended that AEG was liable for Michael's death by hiring and retaining Murray as his personal physician. Although a jury decided that AEG did hire Murray, they found that he was not unfit or incompetent for the job – and so AEG had not been negligent in hiring him. "It's easy to make us look like the corporate villains who took advantage of Michael Jackson," AEG Live CEO Randy Phillips said. "It's quite the opposite – we were the people who empowered Michael Jackson and gave him his dream back."

That dream would never be fulfilled, and neither would his desire to crack the movie industry. After achieving everything in music, movie success was the one type of success which Michael truly longed for, but one that would evade him forever.

It might be of small comfort to fans that Michael died just as he was about to show the world what it had been missing during those isolated years he spent in Bahrain, Ireland and Las Vegas. At the time of his death he was back in the public eye and treated like the King of Pop once more; he was no longer the fallen, reclusive figure that travelled the globe in the aftermath of the 2005 trial.

His passing made millions around the world put aside the eccentricities, the trials and the tribulations, and appreciate the man as an artist. But it can also be said those elements enhanced the notion that Michael Jackson was bigger than life, possibly the most famous person to ever walk the planet.

"Music has been my outlet, my gift to all of the lovers in this world.
Through it – my music, I know I will live forever."
Michael Jackson

AFTERWORD

In death, Michael has been enormously successful; according to *Billboard*, he sold an estimated 35 million albums worldwide in the 12 months following his passing. It is estimated he has earned more than $700 million posthumously, partly due to the release of two albums including previously unreleased material, *Michael* (2010) and *Xscape* (2014).

I made the decision not to cover these posthumous album releases in the book. During my five years of writing and researching, I discovered how much of a perfectionist Michael Jackson really was. He never felt any of his albums were truly ready for release, but at least he gave his blessing to the music he eventually allowed the world to hear.

The first compilation, *Michael*, features ten tracks that were re-produced by others posthumously. The eight songs on *Xscape* were also re-produced, but Michael's original, unfinished versions were included on a second disc. It is difficult to say with certainty what Michael would have wanted to happen to his unreleased music in death, but anything that was left behind in the vaults either wasn't considered good enough, or was incomplete and still needed work. In 1998, he admitted he was unhappy that others had remixed his songs from *HIStory* for inclusion on the *Blood on the Dance Floor* album. "I don't like it that they come in and change my songs completely," he said.

Fans were particularly upset with the *Michael* album. The authenticity of vocals on three of the tracks, 'Breaking News', 'Keep Your Head Up', and 'Monster', has been an ongoing controversy among fans and family members.

At the time, both Quincy Jones and will.i.am spoke out about the release and were of the opinion that none of Michael's unreleased work should see the light of day. "No way should it be coming out," Quincy said. "It should have all stayed in the vault. It's all to make money. He wouldn't have wanted it to come out this way. They must just be trying to make as much money as they can. I don't know why else they are doing it."

Will.i.am reiterated the point that Michael is a perfectionist. "I don't think that should ever come out. That's bad. He was a perfectionist and he wouldn't have wanted it that way. How you gonna release Michael Jackson when Michael Jackson ain't here to bless it?"

It's difficult for me to disagree.

APPENDIX

SOLO STUDIO ALBUMS RELEASED

ALBUM	LABEL	RELEASED	MICHAEL'S AGE
Got to Be There	Motown	January 1972	13
Ben	Motown	August 1972	13
Music & Me	Motown	April 1973	14
Forever, Michael	Motown	January 1975	16
Off the Wall	Epic	August 1979	20
Thriller	Epic	November 1982	24
Bad	Epic	August 1987	29
Dangerous	Epic	November 1991	33
HIStory	Epic	June 1995	36
Invincible	Epic	October 2001	43

OTHER NOTABLE SOLO ALBUMS

ALBUM	FORMAT	LABEL	RELEASED
Blood on the Dance Floor	Remix album	Epic	May 1997
Number Ones	Greatest hits album	Epic	November 2003
The Ultimate Collection	Greatest hits box set	Epic	November 2004
The Essential Michael Jackson	Greatest hits album	Epic	July 2005
Thriller 25	Anniversary reissue	Epic	February 2008
King of Pop	Greatest hits album	Epic	August 2008

SOLO WORLD TOURS AND CONCERTS

TOUR	DATES
Bad Tour	Sep 1987 – Jan 1989
Dangerous Tour	June 1992 – Nov 1993
HIStory Tour	Sep 1996 – Oct 1997
MJ & Friends	Two concerts in June 1999
Michael Jackson: 30th Anniversary Special	Two concerts in September 2001

NUMBER ONE HITS IN THE UNITED STATES (BOTH WITH THE JACKSON 5 AND SOLO)

SONG	YEAR WHEN AT NUMBER ONE
I Want You Back (The Jackson 5)	1970
ABC (The Jackson 5)	1970
The Love You Save (The Jackson 5)	1970
I'll Be There (The Jackson 5)	1970
Santa Claus Is Comin' to Town (The Jackson 5)	1970
Ben	1972
Don't Stop 'Til You Get Enough	1979
Rock With You	1980
Billie Jean	1983
Beat It	1983
Say Say Say	1984
We Are the World (as featured artist and co-writer)	1985
I Just Can't Stop Loving You	1987
Bad	1987

The Way You Make Me Feel	1988
Man in the Mirror	1988
Dirty Diana	1988
Black or White	1991
You Are Not Alone	1995

NUMBER ONE HITS IN THE UNITED KINGDOM (BOTH WITH THE JACKSON 5 AND SOLO)

SONG	YEAR WHEN AT NUMBER ONE
Show You the Way to Go (The Jacksons)	1976
One Day in Your Life	1981
Billie Jean	1983
We Are the World (as featured artist and co-writer)	1985
I Just Can't Stop Loving You	1987
Black or White	1991
You Are Not Alone	1995
Earth Song	1995
Blood on the Dance Floor	1997

ACKNOWLEDGMENTS

Writing this book has consumed my life for more than five years.

The loss of my mother only a year into the project was hard to take, but I know she would be proud that I persevered and completed it. I have dedicated this book to her memory.

There are many individuals to thank for helping to turn my vision into reality, but I am grateful in particular to the collaborators who gave up their precious time to share their experiences of working with Michael.

Firstly, this project would not have been possible without the kindness, generosity, memories and knowledge of Matt Forger. Matt, who I first met in Los Angeles in February 2012, has made an outstanding contribution to this book. He has answered hundreds of questions, read chapters and contributed the best foreword I could possibly wish for. You say it was an honour to work with Michael Jackson, but it must also have been an honour for Michael to work with you, because you're phenomenal.

Bruce Swedien is an immensely talented human being who connected me to several key individuals for this book. Bruce's memory may not be what it once was, but his intelligence and kindness remains. Thank you Bruce.

Russ Ragsdale, you had a big part to play, especially at the beginning of the project. I thank you for all of our conversations and e-friendship.

I am also indebted to Bill Bottrell, Brad Buxer, Steve Porcaro, Buz Kohan and Michael Durham Prince for answering endless questions in my relentless pursuit for new information and accuracy, and Sandy Gallin, Jimmy Jam, Michael Boddicker, Rob Hoffman, Dave Way, Bernie Grundman, CJ deVillar, Brad Gilderman and Thom Russo for the several hours you spent with me either in person or on the phone.

I also want to express my sincere appreciation to Tom Bahler, Glen Ballard, Jennifer Batten, Dan Beck, Stuart Brawley, Ndugu Chancler, Ed Cherney, Rob Disner, Shari Dub, Nathan East, Sam Emerson, Bert Fields, Jim Fitzpatrick, Mick Garris, Jon Gass, Geoff Grace, Gary Grant, Nelson Hayes, Guy Holmes, Jean-Marie Horvat, Kim Hutchcroft, Paul Jackson Jr., Rodney Jerkins, Craig Johnson, Bryan Loren, Brian Malouf, Jeff Margolis, Vince Paterson, Antony Payne, Greg Phillinganes, Randy Phillips, Glenn Phoenix, Tim Pierce, Bill Reichenbach, Seth Riggs, John Robinson, Mike Salisbury, Raff Sanchez, Andrew Scheps, Larry Stessel, Brad Sundberg, Bea Swedien, Dieter Wiesner, Larry Williams, Will Wilson, Bill Wolfer, Benjamin Wright and Dick Zimmerman.

All sixty-five of you have been remarkable. This book is also dedicated to you all.

Bruce Swedien, Matt Forger, Antony Payne, Brad Sundberg, Mike Salisbury and Jennifer Fasano Wolf also contributed their amazing photos to this book, and for that I cannot thank them enough. I chose the talented Sam Emerson's shot of Michael, taken during the filming of the 'Black or White' video, for the front cover. It's an incredible image and exactly what I envisaged.

Thank you to the team at Authoright, including Hayley, Gareth, James, Josh, Kate and Lucy.

Roslyn, you've put up with the stresses, the long hours and the sleepless nights. Thanks for being there for me. A special mention must also go to my father; without your support this book would quite simply not have been possible. I also express my gratitude to the other members of our small family; Gran, Jen, Matthew, Isaac, Ethan, James, Hebe, Max, Kevin and my grandparents in Deutschland. Plus, all my friends – you know who you are.

SOURCE NOTES

NOTE: I tried to interview absolutely everybody who has worked with Michael Jackson. I conducted sixty-five interviews.

Babyface, John Barnes, Tom Barrack, Michael Bearden, Nick Brandt, Paulinho Da Costa, Karen Faye, David Foster, Siedah Garrett, Paul Gongaware, Allen Grubman, Jerry Hey, Quincy Jones, Howard Kaufman, Jeff Kwatinetz, Jim Morey, Alif Sankey, and Rod Temperton told me either directly or through an agent/manager that they did not wish to be interviewed.

I did not receive a reply from direct messages or follow up telephone calls to Raymone Bain, Dr. Freeze, Miko Brando, Fred Jerkins III, Louis Johnson (who has sadly passed away), Charles Koppelman, Tommy Mottola, Kenny Ortega, Travis Payne, Teddy Riley, Cory Rooney, Dr Tohme or Walter Yetnikoff.

PROLOGUE

10. Loneliest man in the world: Michael Jackson, The Making of 'Stranger in Moscow', https://www.youtube.com/watch?v=ME5tH422ShA.
10. Sat on closet floor: Frank Cascio, *My Friend Michael* (New York: William Morrow/Harper-Collins, 2011), 60 (cited hereafter as Cascio).
10. "Outside my hotel"/"In the song": The Making of 'Stranger in Moscow'.
11. Triggered by pain/Worsened by stress: Michael Jackson, audio taped message, November 12, 1993.
12. "I've been through"/"I stop when": Michael Jackson, Online Audio Chat, October 26, 2001 (cited hereafter as Online Audio Chat).

CHAPTER 1: HUMBLE BEGINNINGS

13. BACKGROUND: Michael Jackson, *Moonwalk* (New York: Harmony Books, 1988), 29 (cited hereafter as *Moonwalk*); J. Randy Taraborrelli, *Michael Jackson: The Magic and the Madness* (Pan Books, 2004) (cited hereafter as *The Magic and the Madness*); Jermaine Jackson, *You Are Not Alone* (New York: Touchstone/Simon & Schuster, 2011), 42 (cited hereafter as *You Are Not Alone*).
14. Marlon joined same time/"He found octaves": *You Are Not Alone*, 42.
14. "When we sang": Michael Jackson: The Peter Pan of Pop, *Newsweek*, January 10, 1983 (cited hereafter as The Peter Pan of Pop).
15. Hear other children in street: Rabbi Shmuley Boteach, *The Michael Jackson Tapes* (New York, Vanguard, 2009), 73 (cited hereafter as Boteach).
15. Joseph used force/"We were nervous"/'Whatever's around': Michael Jackson, Interview with Martin Bashir, Living with Michael Jackson, February 6, 2003 (cited hereafter as Bashir).
15. MJ would get beaten more: *Moonwalk*, 29–31.
15. "Scared": Bashir.
15. Father verbally abused him: Boteach, 84.
15. Gordy knew at first audition: Berry Gordy, *To Be Loved* (Warner Books, 1994), 280.
17. "To come from": *Moonwalk*, 69.
17. "It didn't work": Sylvie Simmons, Michael Jackson: No Angel, But No Osmond Either, Creem, June 1983 (cited hereafter as Sylvie Simmons).
17. "Soul bubble-gum"/'Strange'/"See, my whole": The Peter Pan of Pop.
18. "In our early": John Pidgeon interview, January 1980, https://www.youtube.com/watch?v=N08cg2Ci20A (cited hereafter as John Pidgeon)

CHAPTER 2: THE ROAD TO *OFF THE WALL*

19. BACKGROUND: *Moonwalk*; *The Magic and the Madness*; *You Are Not Alone.*
19. Motown holding J5 back/Unhappy/Up to Michael: *Moonwalk*, 114–115.
19. "We want to try": Steve Rosen interview, 1980, https://www.youtube.com/watch?v=mu10Wu1nZJ4

20. "When you really": Bryan Monroe, Michael Jackson: In His Own Words, *Ebony*, December 2007 (cited hereafter as Bryan Monroe).
20. "Everybody has to start": Michael Jackson, TV Guide Interview, November 2001 (cited hereafter as TV Guide Interview, 2001).
20. CBS/MJ insurance policy: *Moonwalk*, 153–154.
21. "At Motown it's"/"That was the most": John Pidgeon.
21. "I had a meeting": Paul Grein, Michael Jackson: It's Tough Juggling Careers, *Billboard*, 1980 (cited hereafter as Michael Jackson: It's Tough Juggling Careers).
21. MJ unsure about life: *Moonwalk*, 134–135.
21. MJ/Quincy relationship: Ibid., 145.
23. "It's just exciting": Michael Jackson and Steve Rubell interview, 1977. https://www.youtube.com/watch?v=cQAFmYGjaU4
23. 'Renewed': Walter Yetnikoff, *Howling At The Moon: The True Story of the Mad Genius of the Music World*, Abacus, 102 (cited hereafter as Yetnikoff).

CHAPTER 3: LIVE IT *OFF THE WALL*

24. Walter Scharf: Stephen McMillian, Classic Soul Train Album Spotlight: Michael Jackson's Off the Wall, soultrain.com, June 4, 2012.
24. MJ surprised: *Moonwalk*, 146.
24. "I said, 'I'm ready": Bryan Monroe.
24. Too 'jazzy': Quincy Jones, *Q: The Autobiography of Quincy Jones* (New York: Doubleday, 2001), 231 (cited hereafter as *Q: The Autobiography of Quincy Jones*).
25. CBS preferred Gamble and Huff: Melinda Newman, Quincy Jones explains why Epic didn't want him to produce Michael Jackson's 'Thriller', hitfix.com, April 24, 2010.
25. "Epic felt": Ron Weisner, *Listen Out Loud* (Connecticut Lyons Press, 2014), 118 (cited hereafter as *Listen Out Loud*).
25. "White help": Katherine Jackson, *My Family, the Jacksons* (St. Martin's Press, 1990) (cited hereafter as *My Family, the Jacksons*).
25. "Eventually": *Listen Out Loud*, 120.
25. 'Appropriate'/'True start': Michael Jackson: The Ultimate Collection, Sony, 2004, compact disc. Liner notes, 22.
26. "Hard words": *Moonwalk*, 158.
26. "They understand": Sylvia Chase, 20/20, ABC, June 26, 1980, https://www.youtube.com/watch?v=MWxg9Gs90FM

26. "Someone with a good ear": Ibid., 155.
26. Appreciated show of trust: Ibid., 161.
26. Loved *Songs in the Key of Life*: Bryan Monroe.
26. Struggled writing lyrics/loved melodies: Craig Halstead and Chris Cadman, *Michael Jackson The Solo Years* (New Generation Publishing, 2003), 28 (cited hereafter as *The Solo Years*).
28. MJ shy: *Q: The Autobiography of Quincy Jones*, 232.
28. "Killer Q posse": Ibid., 232.
28. "We did": Gary Grant, personal author interview, March 2012 (cited hereafter as Gary Grant).
28. "Michael knew": Kim Hutchcroft, personal author interview, March 2012 (cited hereafter as Kim Hutchcroft).
28. "He went through": Michael Boddicker, personal author interview, March 2012 (cited hereafter as Michael Boddicker).
28. "He can come": *The Magic and the Madness*, 185.
28. MJ driving at the age of 19 not 21: Dad Says Michael's Big And Driving: A Rolls, *JET*, August 31, 1978, 60.
28. "He didn't like": Ed Cherney, personal author interview, February 2012 (cited hereafter as Ed Cherney).
28. "One memory": Jim Fitzpatrick, personal author interview, January 2015 (cited hereafter as Jim Fitzpatrick).
29. MJ and ballads: *Moonwalk*, 161.
29. "On my own album": Dennis Hunt, Michael Jackson: Hooked on the Spotlight, *Los Angeles Times*, December 17, 1979.
29. "Everybody seemed"/"After Quincy agreed"/MJ wanted 'She's Out of My Life' as first single/Not opening with ballad: Tom Bahler, personal author interview, May 2012 (cited hereafter as Tom Bahler).
30. "It's so pretty": John Abbey, The Jacksons: Ten Golden Years, *Blues & Soul*, February 1979.
30. "Michael was seated": Bruce Swedien, *In The Studio With Michael Jackson* (New York: Hal Leonard, 2009), 20–21 (cited hereafter as *In The Studio With Michael Jackson*).
30. "Quincy loved the way": Tom Bahler.
30. "The words suddenly": *Moonwalk*, 163.
31. "It really took": Tom Bahler.
31. "Michael was too embarrassed": *In The Studio With Michael Jackson*, 20.

32. "He had part"/"He was just like": Susaye Green, Fresh Touch Radio interview. http://www.blogtalkradio.com/wdkk-radio/2009/07/31/supremextremes-susaye-greene
32. "Stevie Wonder": Bryan Monroe.
32. "This is the vibe"/"If a certain author": Michael Boddicker.
33. More mature themes: *Q: The Autobiography of Quincy Jones*, 232.
33. Phillinganes/Thicker wall of sound: *Moonwalk*, 160.
33. 'Don't Stop' important for MJ: Ibid., 161.
33. Disco songs easiest for MJ: Ibid., 150.
33. "I just started singing"/"It turned out": Michael Jackson, The Dick Clark National Music Survey interview. http://mjjtime.blogspot.co.uk/2010/10/today-in-mjj-history_13.html
33. Katherine shocked/No reference to sex: *My Family, the Jacksons*.
34. "Michael wasn't even": Tom Bahler.
34. "I was like"/"Quincy called me": Benjamin Wright, personal author interview, March 2012 (cited hereafter as Benjamin Wright).
34. "That was on a Thursday": John Robinson, personal author interview, March 2012 (cited hereafter as John Robinson)."
34. 'Workin' Day and Night' autobiographical: Steve Demorest, Michael in Wonderland, *JET*, March 1, 1980.
35. "When we did": John Robinson.
35. "Going to Radio City": Tom Bahler.
36. "Smooth": Michael Boddicker.
36. "One of the best songwriters": *Q: The Autobiography of Quincy Jones*, 232.
36. "I simply loved": *In The Studio With Michael Jackson*, 4.
36. "In the end I wrote": Rod Temperton, Off the Wall (Special Edition). Sony, 2001, compact disc. Originally released in 1979 (cited hereafter as Rod Temperton Off the Wall).
37. "The first day we met": *In The Studio With Michael Jackson*, 4–5.
37. "Amazing": Rod Temperton Off the Wall.
37. MJ and Temperton similar: *Moonwalk*, 158.
37. "With all": Peter Feely, The Making of Michael Jackson, *Time Out Dubai*, December 2013.
38. MJ thrived with melody: Rod Temperton Off the Wall.
38. 'Rock with You' perfect for MJ: *Moonwalk*, 158.
38. Description of mixing: Chris Inglesi, The Basics of Mixing Your

Music, Music Industry Survival Guide, tunecore.com, http://www.tunecore.com/guides/basics_of_mixing.

38. "That opening": John Robinson.
38. "Own acoustic space": *In The Studio With Michael Jackson*, 9–10.
38. "The song was fabulous": Michael Boddicker.
39. "He was the epitome": Gary Grant.
39. "He knew exactly": Steve Porcaro, personal author interview, March 2012 (cited hereafter as Steve Porcaro).
39. "He comes in": Bryan Monroe.
39. Temperton surprise: Rod Temperton Off the Wall.
39. Artistic freedom/Could take chances: Quincy Jones, Off the Wall (Special Edition). Sony, 2001, compact disc. Originally released in 1979.
39. "Quincy got things": Michael Boddicker.
40. "Michael was so": John Robinson.
40. "He once held": Kim Hutchcroft.
40. "Quincy was criticised": Bruce Swedien, personal author interview, April 2012 (cited hereafter as Bruce Swedien).
40. "Gary Grant loved": Larry Williams, personal author interview, March 2012 (cited hereafter as Larry Williams).
40. "There was a lot": Gary Grant.
40. "When he was away": Ed Cherney.
41. "I told them": Mike Salisbury, personal author interview, May 2014.
44. "I just didn't like": *Moonwalk*, 152.
44. "In the meeting": Robert Hilburn, The Saga of Michael Jackson, *Billboard*, July 21, 1984.
45. CBS contract: *The Magic and the Madness*, 191–192.
45. "I was disappointed": *Moonwalk*, 176.
45. Disco backlash: Tony Sclafani, When 'Disco Sucks!' echoed around the world, today.com, July 7, 2010.
46. "In those days": Christopher R. Weingarten and David Browne, Michael Jackson's 20 Greatest Videos: The Stories Behind the Vision, rollingstone.com, June 24, 2014 (cited hereafter as Michael Jackson's 20 Greatest Videos).
46. One of the most difficult periods: *Moonwalk*, 164.
46. "Even at home": Robert Hilburn, Michael Jackson: the wounds, the broken heart, *Los Angeles Times*, June 27, 2009.

47. "This has been the": Paul Grein, Michael Jackson: It's Tough Juggling Careers.
47. Repay McCartney: *Moonwalk*, 188.
47. "One Christmas"/"We really had": Annie Leibovitz and Martin Harrison, Linda McCartney: *Life in Photographs* (Benedikt Taschen Verlag; Mul edition, 2011).
47. MJ/McCartney 1981 sessions background: Ray Coleman, *McCartney: Yesterday & Today* (Dove Books, 1995), 129–130 (cited hereafter as *McCartney: Yesterday & Today*).
48. MJ wanted two year gap: Michael Jackson: It's Tough Juggling Careers.
48. "It's an album": Michael Jackson, Jesse Jackson Interview, Keep Hope Alive radio show, March 27, 2005 (cited hereafter as Jesse Jackson Interview).
48. Biggest-selling of all time ambition: *Moonwalk*, 180.

CHAPTER 4: MAKING MUSIC HISTORY

49. "Always creating": Bruce Swedien, The making of Michael Jackson's Thriller, musicradar.com, October 1, 2009 (cited hereafter as The making of Michael Jackson's Thriller).
49. "I just let it go": Bashir.
49. "I started playing": Bill Wolfer, personal author interview, June 2015.
50. MJ knew he had a hit: *Moonwalk*, 192.
50. "I wrote this": HIStory: The Michael Jackson Interview, VH1, November 10, 1996, https://www.youtube.com/watch?v=IkGelnF-cuJI (cited hereafter as HIStory: The Michael Jackson Interview).
50. "We found people": Sylvie Simmons.
50. Awoke with melody: Robert Smith, AKA Robert Austin, Reynaud D. Jones, Clifford Rubin vs. Michael Jackson, Lionel Richie, Rod Temperton et al., United States Court of Appeals Ninth Circuit, 84 F.3d 1213, 1996 (cited hereafter as Robert Smith et al. vs. Michael Jackson et al.).
50. "Quincy called me": Fred Sanford vs. CBS, Inc. and Rose Records, Inc., United States District Court Northern District of Illinois, 83C3373, October 5, 1984 (cited hereafter as Fred Sanford vs. CBS, Inc. and Rose Records, Inc.).

50. "I called Michael 'Smelly'": *Q: The Autobiography of Quincy Jones*, 237.
51. "Shallow"/"There was even": The Peter Pan of Pop.
51. "I met Michael because": Matt Forger, personal author interview, February 2012 (cited hereafter as Matt Forger).
51. "Incredible"/"Michael and Paul": Steve Porcaro.
52. "Working with Paul": Fred Sanford vs. CBS, Inc. and Rose Records, Inc.
52. Unhappy with 'The Girl Is Mine': Michael Jackson, TV Guide Interview, December 1999 (cited hereafter as TV Guide Interview, 1999).
52. "Disco was just": Jesse Jackson Interview.
52. "Michael was certainly": Michael Boddicker.
53. "Quincy said to me": Jim Fitzpatrick.
53. MJ had higher hopes/"I admitted": *Moonwalk*, 180–181.
53. "You managed"/Demos/'Midnight Man': The Invisible Man: The Rod Temperton Story – Wise Buddah Creative for BBC Radio 2.
54. 'Just some'/"It was like electricity": Saeed Saeed, Michael Jackson's studio men lift the King of Pop's mask, The National, September 25, 2013.
54. 'Starlight' lyrics/"I thought kids": Robert Smith et al. vs. Michael Jackson et al.
54. "We bribed": *In The Studio With Michael Jackson*, 33.
54. "The idea"/"I frantically started": Rod Temperton, Thriller (Special Edition), Sony, 2001, compact disc, originally released in 1982 (cited hereafter as Rod Temperton Thriller).
55. "When the music track": *In The Studio With Michael Jackson*, 35–36.
55. 'The Lady in My Life' challenging: *Moonwalk*, 197.
55. "Smelly, I need": Steve Morse, "Right On Q: Love Songs", *The Boston Globe*, February 10, 1999.
55. "I like to just feel": Crystal Cartier vs. Michael Jackson, United States Court of Appeals Tenth Circuit, 59 F.3d 1046, 1995 (cited hereafter as Crystal Cartier vs. Michael Jackson).
56. "Find the right tunes": Michael Jackson, *Thriller 25: The Book, Celebrating the Biggest Selling Album of All Time*, (Orlando: ML Publishing, 2008), 14 (cited hereafter as *Thriller 25: The Book*).

56. "He would 'snapshot'": Matt Forger Speaks, mjdatabank.com, http://mjdatabank.com/memo/magazine/interviews/matt_forger/page02.htm (cited hereafter as Matt Forger Speaks).
56. Lingerie with 'Pretty Young Things': Jeff Lorez, James Ingram Interview, soulmusic.com, January 27, 2009.
56. "Quincy said he": Michael Boddicker.
56. "Song-writing": TV Guide Interview, 1999
56. Sonic personality: *In The Studio With Michael Jackson*, 37.
56. "The bottom line": The 500 Greatest Songs Since You Were Born, *Blender*, October 2005.
57. "Playing that": Ndugu Chancler, personal author interview, March 2012.
57. Never the same: Bruce Swedien.
57. "Michael was very specific": Nelson George, *Thriller: The Musical Life of Michael Jackson* (Da Capo Press, 2009), 127 (cited hereafter as *Thriller: The Musical Life of Michael Jackson*).
57. "During *Thriller*"/"Michael could also"/Voice info: Seth Riggs, personal author interview, April 2012.
58. "His timing": Gary Grant.
58. "A killer"/"This went on": The REAL Story on "Billie Jean", Gearslutz.com, https://www.gearslutz.com/board/bruce-swedien/84587-real-story-billie-jean.html
58. 'Not My Lover'/"Sitting here today": *Thriller 25: The Book*, 14.
58. "You could shave": Quincy Jones. Thriller (Special Edition). Sony, 2001, compact disc. Originally released in 1982 (cited hereafter as Quincy Jones Thriller).
58. 'Billie Jean' not strong enough: *The Magic and the Madness*, 224.
58. Flatly denied: *Q: The Autobiography of Quincy Jones*, 243.
58. Rolls Royce fire story: Nelson Hayes, personal author interview, January 2015 (cited hereafter as Nelson Hayes).
60. "That's how"/"The kid probably": *Moonwalk*, 192–193.
61. "This was quite"/"It was a nightmare": *Q: The Autobiography of Quincy Jones*, 234.
61. "He felt like this": Matt Forger.
61. "I felt like I was there": Gerri Hirshey, Michael Jackson: Life as a Man In the Magical Kingdom, *Rolling Stone*, February 17, 1983 (cited hereafter as Gerri Hirshey).

62. "Michael brought": Greg Phillinganes, personal author interview, April 2012 (cited hereafter as Greg Phillinganes).
62. "Michael draped Muscles": Shari Dub, personal author interview, January 2012.
62. "Girls came by": Larry Williams.
62. "A healthy young": *In The Studio With Michael Jackson*, 25.
62. "He was still very": Steve Porcaro.
62. "During a break": Gary Grant.
63. "We were at Westlake": Greg Phillinganes.
63. 'A little too poppy'/'Straightforward': Rod Temperton Thriller
63. Missing rock song: *Q: The Autobiography of Quincy Jones*, 237.
63. 'My Sharona'/'Human Nature' story: Steve Porcaro.
64. "All of a sudden": Quincy Jones Thriller.
65. "The deadline for": Matt Forger.
65. MJ held on to song/Shy/"He went crazy": *Moonwalk*, 185.
65. Lyrics not about encouraging violence: Ibid., 194–195.
65. Eddie Van Halen story: Matt Forger.
66. "I was a complete fool": Kevin Dodds, *Edward Van Halen: A Definitive Biography* (iUniverse, 2011), 92.
67. "He was this musical": Denise Quan, Eddie Van Halen deconstructs his collaboration on 'Beat It', CNN, November 30, 2012.
67. "Michael wanted a punchy": Matt Forger Speaks.
67. "Just as strong"/'The Toy': Fred Sanford vs. CBS, Inc. and Rose Records, Inc.
67. "I loved that one": Robert Smith et al. vs. Michael Jackson et al.
68. "Quincy wanted a certain": Greg Phillinganes.
68. "I guess I had": *Moonwalk*, 184.
68. "We went through": Ibid., 198.
69. "We listened": *In The Studio With Michael Jackson*, 30.
69. "Already I did not": Larkin Arnold, Pearl Jr Interview, michaeljacksoninsider.com, https://www.youtube.com/watch?v=FoK4hgeT5Bg
69. Mixed each song/'The Lady in My Life'/ 'Billie Jean' cut: *Q: The Autobiography of Quincy Jones*, 239.
69. "It felt so good": *Moonwalk*, 200.

CHAPTER 5: THE *THRILLER* PHENOMENON

70. 'Get it out of the way': *Moonwalk*, 188.
70. "Michael hid with me": *In The Studio With Michael Jackson*, 26.
71. "I was starting"/"That leather": Dick Zimmerman, personal author interview, May 2014.
71. "Michael said": Dick Zimmerman, THE CREATION OF THE "THRILLER" ALBUM COVER PORTRAIT, dickzimmerman.com.
71. MJ preferred *short-films:* Online Audio Chat.
71. "My brother Jackie": TV Guide Interview, 1999.
72. 'Stimulant': *Making Michael Jackson's Thriller*, directed by Jerry Kramer (Optimum Productions, 1983, VHS).
72. "Before *Thriller*"/"They came right": Joy Bennett, Michael Jackson: "The Thrill Is Back", *Ebony*, December 2007.
73. "I've never been": Yetnikoff, 155.
73. "Michael told me": Bill Wolfer, personal author interview, June 2015.
73. "He actually": *The Solo Years*, 55.
73. "Paul never had": *Moonwalk*, 188.
74. Anka songs recorded 1980 not 1983: Ira Jean Hadnot, Paul Anka: A new man for every decade, *The Milwaukee Sentinel*, May 22, 1981.
74. Anka collaboration background: Paul Anka, *My Way: An Autobiography* (St. Martin's Griffin, 2014), 234–235.
74. "He knew how"/'Steal'/"I'm trying": Ibid., 234–235.
75. 'Beat It' video stories: Antony Payne, personal author interview, June 2015 (cited hereafter as Antony Payne).
77. "While Mike": Nelson Hayes.
77. "There's so much": John Abbey.
78. 'Capture the moment'/"You capture it": *The Magic and the Madness*, 208.
78. "I remember driving": Gerri Hirshey.
78. "Michael made": Ambition to star as Peter Pan: Buz Kohan, personal author interview, May 2013 (cited hereafter as Buz Kohan).
78. "I worked": Michael & Son, *Life* magazine, December 1997.
78. "Michael had always": Anthony Breznican, Alternate-history Spielberg: Who ALMOST starred in his most famous movies?, *Entertainment Weekly*, January 18, 2015.

79. Ranch/'Say Say Say'/Publishing stories: Antony Payne.
81. "He'd berate me": Yetnikoff, 154.
81. "Who wants"/"It's simple": Nancy Griffin, The 'Thriller' Diaries, *Vanity Fair*, July 2010 (cited hereafter as The 'Thriller' Diaries).
81. Plenty of material for director: *Moonwalk*, 222.
81. MJ loved *An American Werewolf in London*: The 'Thriller' Diaries.
81. "It was a great opportunity": Mike Celizic, Director: Funds for 'Thriller' were tough to raise, today.com, June 29, 2008 (cited hereafter as Mike Celizic).
81. Red jacket: Lauren Goode, Deborah Landis, Designer of the Red Jacket Michael Jackson Wore in 'Thriller', *The Wall Street Journal*, June 30, 2009.
82. Cost $500,000/Exaggerated: Mike Celizic.
82. Funding the video: The 'Thriller' Diaries.
82. MJ stunned: *Moonwalk*, 224.
82. MJ felt he was the only person: *Moonwalk*, 181.
83. MJ burn details/Percocet: Dr Steven M. Hoefflin Discharge Summary, http://radaronline.com/wp-content/uploads/2013/10/jacksonmedicalrecords_redacted.pdf
83. "Michael had a huge": Katherine Jackson et al. vs. AEG Live, August 14, 2013.
83. Diagnosed with vitiligo in 1986: Michael Jackson Gives Revealing Record Breaking Interview To Oprah Winfrey, *JET*, March 1, 1993, 56.
84. DiLeo largely responsible for *Thriller* success: *Moonwalk*, 205.
84. Next album more successful: Yetnikoff, 156.
84. "They were great"/"It was a shame": Lesley-Anne Jones, *Mercury: An Intimate Biography of Freddie Mercury* (Simon & Schuster Export, 2012), 239.
85. MJ didn't want to tour: *Moonwalk*, 238.
85. Backwards step: *Listen Out Loud*, 155.
85. 'Coat-tailing'/"We never viewed"/'Stage addict': Ibid., 243–244.
85. MJ disappointed with staging: *Moonwalk*, 239, 242.
85. Jackie broken his leg: Margaret Maldanado Jackson and Richard Hack, *Jackson Family Values: Memories of Madness* (Newstar Pr, 1995), 29–30.

CHAPTER 7: THERE COMES A TIME

87. BACKGROUND: Stephen Holden, The Pop Life; Artists Join In Effort For Famine Relief, *The New York Times*, February 27, 1985; David Breskin, There Comes A Time…When We Heed A Certain Call, *Life* magazine, April 1985; Robert Smith et al. vs. Michael Jackson et al.; *The Magic and the Madness*, 341–344; *Q: The Autobiography of Quincy Jones*, 252–257.
87. "I was in my bedroom"/"We got together"/"I strongly": Robert Smith et al. vs. Michael Jackson et al.
88. "There's a bunch of": Gavin Edwards, Billboard Legend of Live Honoree Lionel Richie Remembers His Time With The Rolling Stones, Frank Sinatra and Michael Jackson (and His Snake), billboard.com, November 14, 2014.
88. "They were in shock"/"If we get it"/"The cassettes": David Breskin, There Comes A Time…When We Heed A Certain Call, *Life* magazine, April 1985.
89. MJ/Prince: We Are the World tune brings out the best of America's 46 stars, *JET*, February 18, 1985.
89. "I said to Quincy": Tom Bahler.
89. 'Like the Invasion': *Q: The Autobiography of Quincy Jones*, 252–257.
90. "He knew it"/"I went looking": James Desborough, Secrets behind the making of supergroup USA for Africa's charity hit We Are The World, mirror.co.uk, May 17, 2015.
90. "It has reached": Michael Jackson Simulchat, MTV, August 17, 1995 (cited hereafter as Simulchat).

CHAPTER 7: FOLLOWING *THRILLER*

92. "The Jacksons came"/"Michael was required"/"Michael would sit": Brian Malouf, personal author interview, June 2015.
93. "All kinds": Buz Kohan.
94. "I worked with": Matt Forger.
94. The Beatles catalogue background: Robert Hilburn, The Long and Winding Road, *Los Angeles Times*, September 22, 1985; Jack Doyle, Michael & McCartney, 1990s-2009, PopHistoryDig.com, July 7, 2009 (cited hereafter as Jack Doyle).
94. "Babies"/"Stonewalled"/"He will not deal": *McCartney: Yesterday & Today*, 137–138.

95. "I think it's dodgy": Jack Doyle.
95. "Michael saw": Gary Grant.
95: "When I was finished"/"It quickly": Christopher Currell, THE EVENT HORIZON – "SYNCLAVIER, MUSIC AND MICHAEL JACKSON", March 31, 2015, http://headphone.guru/the-event-horizon-synclavier-music-and-michael-jackson/#sthash.bBSO08fM.dpuf
96. "I was doing remixes": Post here if you worked on Michael Jackson's DANGEROUS album, Gearslutz.com, https://www.gearslutz.com/board/so-much-gear-so-little-time/403276-post-here-if-you-worked-michael-jacksons-dangerous-album.html (cited hereafter as Gearslutz thread).
96. Produce album without Quincy: Personal author interviews.
96. "Quincy signed": Matt Forger.
96. "Michael was beginning": Matt Forger.
96. "A teenager"/"Michael was growing": Gearslutz thread.
97. 'Stepping-stone': The 'Thriller' Diaries.
97. "I always do": *Moonwalk*, 265.
97. Socially conscious/Forger role: Matt Forger.
98. 'Sonically designing'/"He was happy": Bill Bottrell, personal author interview, November 2011 (cited hereafter as Bill Bottrell).
98. "I recall the": Gearslutz thread.
98. "I've lived with that": Michael Jackson, Interview with Barbara Walters, *20/20*. September 12, 1997.
98. "Sometimes the girls": Gerri Hirshey.
98. "There have been": Joseph Vogel, Abortion, Fame, and 'Bad': Listening to Michael Jackson's Unreleased Demos, *The Atlantic*, September 11, 2012.
99. "First, so that": *You Are Not Alone*, 265–266.
99. "He would never": Matt Forger.
99. "The thing I love": Joseph Vogel, Abortion, Fame, and 'Bad': Listening to Michael Jackson's Unreleased Demos, *The Atlantic*, September 11, 2012.
99. "Shuffling": *My Family, the Jacksons*.
99. "He'd sing his line": 50 Best Michael Jackson Songs: The stories behind the tracks that kept the planet dancing, *Rolling Stone*, June 23, 2014.

100. "It happens": Matt Forger.
100. 'Amazing fantasy': Quincy Jones. Bad (Special Edition). Sony, 2001, compact disc. Originally released in 1987 (cited hereafter as Quincy Jones Bad).
100. "I wrote that": Michael Jackson, Interview with *Ebony/JET*, September 1987.
100. "That's one of those": *Bad 25*, directed by Spike Lee (Optimum Productions, 2013, DVD) (cited hereafter as *Bad 25*).
100. No one in mind when writing: *Moonwalk*, 268.
100. 'Leave Me Alone' about relationship /"What I'm really": Ibid., 270.
100. "Stupid story": Michael Jackson, Interview with Oprah Winfrey, ABC, 10 February, 1993 (cited hereafter as Oprah).
100. Hated 'Wacko Jacko': Michael Jackson, Interview with Barbara Walters, *20/20*. September 12, 1997.
101. New tougher image: Quincy Jones Bad.
101. 'Goody-goody' image: *Moonwalk*, 277.
101. "You're cool": Michael Jackson, Interview with *Ebony/JET*, September 1987.
101. Prince didn't like song: Ronin Ro, *Prince: Inside the Music and the Masks* (St. Martins Press, 2011); *In The Studio With Michael Jackson*, 42.
101. 'Attitude'/'Feeling': Hugh Barnes, Whacko Jacko v Prince...battle of the mega pop stars, *The Glasgow Herald*, July 19, 1988.
101. "The line": Prince, Interview with Chris Rock, VH1 To One, February 1, 1997, https://www.youtube.com/watch?v=PcvhFjuqzx0
102. Westlake Studio D description: Quincy Troupe, The Pressure to Beat It, *Spin*, June 1987 (cited hereafter as Quincy Troupe).
102. "When we started": Bruce Swedien.
102. "There was the possibility": Matt Forger.
102. "This happened": Currell.
103. Yetnikoff furious: Quincy Troupe.
103. John Barnes departure: Matt Forger.
103. "Bruce Swedien and I": Craig Johnson, personal author interview, May 2012.
103 "He was looking": Currell.
104. "He had discussed": Currell.
104. "Something major": Personal author interview, confidential source.
104. "There was definite": Larry Williams.

105. "Michael and Quincy": Michael Boddicker.
105. "We fight": *Moonwalk*, 263.
105. Rap was 'dead': Katie Couric, Quincy Jones: 'I Miss My Little Brother', CBS News, July 8, 2009.
105. "On the song 'Speed Demon'": Larry Williams.
105. John Barnes departure: Matt Forger.
105. "We became friends": Bill Bottrell.
106. "It was wonderful"/"Michael asked me": Gearslutz thread.
107. "If I sat here": Bashir.
107. Never believed in writer's block: Online Audio Chat.
107. "He wasn't an artist": Joseph Vogel, *Man in the Music: The Creative Life and Work of Michael Jackson* (Sterling, 2011), 135.
107. "It's hard to take": Michael Speaks, *Ebony*, May 1992, 40.
107. "I could be walking": Robert Smith et al. vs. Michael Jackson et al.
107 "I never categorise": Adrian Grant, *Making HIStory* (Omnibus Press, 1998).
108. "He can convey it": Michael Goldberg, Michael Jackson's 'Dangerous' Mind: The Making of the King of Pop, *Rolling Stone*, January 9, 1992 (cited hereafter as Michael Jackson's 'Dangerous' Mind: The Making of the King of Pop).
108. "I first hear the music": Glenn Plaskin, Out Of The Mouth Of Michael, *Chicago Tribune*, August 16, 1992, http://articles.chicagotribune.com/1992-08-16/entertainment/9203140099_1_dreams-spirituality-daily-journal
108. "You have to be able": Bryan Monroe.
108. "Fashions change": Michael Jackson, At Large With Geraldo Rivera, February 2005.
108. "The one thing with": Teddy Riley, https://www.youtube.com/watch?v=siSSM9V8s3U
109. "It's very difficult": Robert Smith et al. vs. Michael Jackson et al.
109. "In my head, it's completed": Edna Gundersen, Michael in the Mirror, *USA Today*, December 14, 2001.
109. "He has an entire": Richard Buskin, Classic Tracks: Michael Jackson's 'Black or White', *Sound on Sound*, August 2004 (cited hereafter as Richard Buskin).
109. "The problem with Michael": Personal author interview, confidential source.

109. "Sometimes what musicians": Personal author interview, confidential source.
110. "These were situations": Matt Forger.
110. "Michael was better": Bill Bottrell.
110. "A good feel": Quincy Jones Bad.
111. "We have an"/"Four hours later": Paul Zollo, Siedah Garrett: Behind the Man In The Mirror: Working with Michael Jackson, https://bluerailroad.wordpress.com/siedah-garrett-behind-the-man-in-the-mirror-working-with-michael-jackson/ (cited hereafter as Paul Zollo).
111. "We were pleasantly": Glen Ballard, personal author interview, August 2014.
112. "I gotta be honest"/"Michael loved it": Quincy Jones Bad.
112. "I remember messengers": Currell.
112. 'Film noir' look/"I showed Michael"/"We had Michael": Michael Jackson's 20 Greatest Videos.
112. "We got to shoot": Vince Paterson, personal author interview, July 2014 (cited hereafter as Vince Paterson).
113. "You need a dramatic deadline": Michael Goldberg and David Handelman, Is Michael Jackson for Real?, *Rolling Stone*, September 24, 1987 (cited hereafter as Is Michael Jackson for Real?).
113. 'Man in the Mirror' background: Paul Zollo; *Bad 25*.
113. "That was such": Paul Zollo.
113. "It had everything": Michael Jackson Remembered: Glen Ballard on Making 'Man in the Mirror', *Rolling Stone*, July 9, 2009.
113. "I have lived": Glen Ballard, personal author interview, August 2014.
113. "If you want": *Moonwalk*, 267–268.
114. 'Didn't like'/"I didn't lose": Is Michael Jackson for Real?
114. MJ loved voice/Session: Paul Zollo; Charles A. Johnson, Garrett's Voice Turns Jackson's Head, Los Angeles Times, August 23, 1987.
114. "It came"/"It was exciting": Paul Zollo.
115. MJ and Wonder duet: *Moonwalk*, 268.
115. "We couldn't get": *Bad 25*.
115. "I was standing"/"Right in the middle": Gearslutz thread.
115. "Because of this": *Moonwalk*, 227.
116. "People who know": Quincy Troupe.

116. "He was very different": Steve Porcaro.
116. "I noticed": Kim Hutchcroft.
116. "Michael really liked": Steve Porcaro.
116. "For a while he drove": Tom LeBlanc, Integrator on Working for Michael Jackson, cepro.com, August 16, 2010.
116 'This Captain'/'A beautiful chic suit': Is Michael Jackson for Real?
116. "Westlake was always": Raff Sanchez, personal author interview, January 2012.
117. "The chimps": Tom LeBlanc, Integrator on Working for Michael Jackson, cepro.com, August 16, 2010.
117. 'Freaked'/"Small heart attack": Is Michael Jackson for Real?
117. "Michael was watching me": John Robinson.
117. "Michael was very loving": Greg Phillinganes.
117. "In the studio"/"My children would"/"At one stage"/"One day I looked": Larry Williams.
118. "It was my daughter's birthday": Kim Hutchcroft.
118. "In between takes": Gearslutz thread.
118. "Michael's cooks": Larry Williams.
119. 'The Slam-Dunk Sisters'/'Winner': *In The Studio With Michael Jackson*, 44.
119. "Of course": Russ Ragsdale, personal author interview, January 2012.
119. "When we shot": Vince Paterson.
120. "DiLeo helped me": Quincy Jones Bad.
120. "Too long": Greg Kot, Quincy Jones won't work with Jackson, *Chicago Tribune*, November 16, 1995.
120. "To Quincy, studio time": Michael Boddicker.
121. 'Make a difference': Yetnikoff, 220.
121. "Michael tried"/"'Bad' was the main"/"We created the": Larry Stessel, personal author interview, May 2014 (cited hereafter as Larry Stessel).
122. "I was set up": Sam Emerson, personal author interview, June 2014.
122. Terrified of confrontation with public: Quincy Troupe.
122. "It's very hard": *Moonwalk*, 265.
122. "I was replacing": Steve Porcaro.
122. "There was so much": Is Michael Jackson for Real?
122. "I've had musicians get angry": Online Audio Chat.

CHAPTER 8: THE *BAD* CAMPAIGN

123. 'One of the most': Quincy Troupe.
123. "Clearly, the jury": Paul Grein, Michael Jackson: Can Exiled King Reclaim His Throne?, *Los Angeles Times*, July 22, 1987.
123. "The critics get too": Bridget Byrne, Michael Jackson: An Eccentric Superstar Makes Marketing a Tricky Proposition, *Los Angeles Times*, October 11, 1987.
124. Equivalent to 'The Girl Is Mine': Quincy Jones Bad.
124. "She did not"/"Since the Synclavier": Currell.
125. "Michael was rehearsing": Larry Stessel.
125. First and final tour: Gill Pringle, Michael Jackson's flying circus, *Daily Mirror*, http://www.the-michael-jackson-archives.com/japan.html
125. Tokyo airport: Gill Pringle, The Greatest Show On Earth, *Daily Mirror*, http://www.the-michael-jackson-archives.com/japan.html; Bad Tour Programme (1988), Far East Report; Bad, Bubbles and Bananas, thisdayinmusic.com, http://www.thisdayinmusic.com/pages/bad_bubbles_and_bananas
126. "Bubbles was swinging"/"They thought the song": Currell.
126. "Unfamiliar": Martin Townsend, Bubbles the chimp reigns at Jacko's Japanese court, People, http://www.the-michael-jackson-archives.com/japan.html
126. "At one point": Jennifer Batten, personal author interview, April 2014.
126. "He didn't speak": Adrian Deevoy, Sheryl Crow interview, *Q Magazine*, October 1998.
126. "He invited me": Anderson Cooper 360 Degrees, CNN, June 25, 2009, http://edition.cnn.com/TRANSCRIPTS/0906/25/acd.01.html
128. "We put it all together": *In the Studio With Michael Jackson*, Facebook post, December 27, 2013, https://www.facebook.com/inthestudiowithmj/posts/237853733055195 (cited hereafter as Sundberg Facebook post).
128. Devastated and humiliated: Robert Hilburn, A Good–and 'Bad'—Night, *Los Angeles Times*, March 4, 1988.
128. "I didn't see him": Ian Winwood, Rise Before The Fall, *Rolling Stone Australia*, Issue 731, October 2012.

129. 'Smooth Criminal' remix story: Currell.
130. "You would never"/Greeted by employee/"This was a great way": Sundberg Facebook post.
131. "I can't go": Michael Jackson, Interview with Ed Bradley on *60 minutes*, December 2003 (cited hereafter as Ed Bradley).
132. "While Michael": Bill Bottrell.
132. "I wasn't completely satisfied": Crystal Cartier vs. Michael Jackson.
133. "It's time to pursue": Paul Grein, A New Stage for Michael Jackson, *Los Angeles Times*, January 27, 1989 (cited hereafter as A New Stage for Michael Jackson).
133. "I think he's going": Steve Dougherty and Todd Gold, All Bad Things Come to An End as a Tearful Michael Jackson Bids Bye-Bye to the Highway, *People*, February 13, 1989.
133. MJ disappointed with *Bad* sales/label ecstatic: The 'Thriller' Diaries.
133. 'The best'/"We made the best album": A New Stage for Michael Jackson.
133. Frank DiLeo's firing: Patrick Goldstein, Pop Star Jackson Fires His Manager, *Los Angeles Times*, February 15, 1989; Patrick Goldstein, Rock Managers: The Hiring and Firing, *Los Angeles Times*, February 19, 1989.
134. Fired for stealing: Karen Faye, Twitter, twitlonger.com, June 20, 2015, http://www.twitlonger.com/show/nk35pk
134. 'Talked into': Jack Silverman, Hit Man, *Nashville Scene*, November 22, 2007 (cited hereafter as Hit Man).
134. "I was talking to Walter": *Bad 25*.

CHAPTER 9: *DANGEROUS* DECISIONS

135. Quincy too much credit/MJ's entourage whispering: *Q: The Autobiography of Quincy Jones*, 243.
135. "People will think": Yetnikoff, 159.
135. "I remember when": Katie Couric, Quincy Jones: 'I Miss My Little Brother', CBS News, July 8, 2009.
135. Tough time over 'Smooth Criminal': *The Magic and the Madness*, 431.
136. "He has always": Brad Buxer interview, *Black & White Magazine*, November/December 2009.
136. Branca taking pressure off/*Decade*: *The Magic and the Madness*, 427–429.

137. Early sessions background: Matt Forger.
137. "His social commentary": Joseph Vogel, *Earth Song: Inside Michael Jackson's Magnum Opus* (BlakeVision Books, 2011), 15–16.
137. "Michael was getting me": Matt Forger.
137. Early Bottrell sessions: Richard Buskin.
138. "The first thing": Brad Buxer, personal author interview, July 2012 (cited hereafter as Brad Buxer).
138. "My favorite thing": Online Audio Chat.
138. The making of 'Black or White'/"Of course, it had to please": Richard Buskin.
139. "I originally started": Matt Forger.
139. "It just suddenly": Leo Hickman, Michael Jackson's biggest selling UK single wasn't Thriller or Billie Jean — but a song about the environment, theguardian.com, June 16, 2009.
139. Trilogy format: Bill Bottrell.
139. "I basically stole": Joel McIver, Guy Pratt interview, *Bass Player*, June 2006, 19.
139. "They came in": Joseph Vogel, *Earth Song: Inside Michael Jackson's Magnum Opus* (BlakeVision Books, 2011), 15-16.
139. "'Who Is It' was Michael's idea"/Hired a soprano: Bill Bottrell.
139. "Michael talked": Gearslutz thread.
140. "I knew it was coming": Bryan Monroe.
140. 'He wanted to be angry and cry': Alan Duke, Goodall: Chimps' plight inspired Jackson's 'Heal the World', CNN, October 24, 2009.
140. "With 'Heal the World'": Brad Buxer.
140. 'Children just'/"I just began": Matt Forger.
141. "The point is": Online Audio Chat.
141. "It really represented": Michael Boddicker.
141. MJ liked Loren's Shanice work: Bryan Loren, personal author interview, April 2014.
141. Indecisive about *Decade*: *The Magic and the Madness*, 429.
141. 'You Were There' story: Buz Kohan.
144. "I asked Michael": Stephen Holden, Quincy Jones's collage of African-descended pop styles, *New Straits Times*, December 10, 1989.
144. "I remember that day": Matt Forger.
144. "Michael didn't say": Rob Disner, My Brush With Badness, October 7, 2007, http://axecollectorblog.blogspot.co.uk/2007/10/

my-brush-with-badness.html (cited hereafter as Rob Disner, My Brush With Badness).

144. "I'm not sure yet": Adrian Grant, The Man In Black, *Off the Wall*, Issue 11, 9.
145. Unhappy with contract/Influenced by Geffen: Eric Pooley, Spinning Out: How Record Heavyweight Walter Yetnikoff Took the Big Fall, *New York*, November 5, 1990, 48 (cited hereafter as Spinning Out).
145. "John Branca called"/"Our conversation": Sandy Gallin, personal author interview, June 2015 (cited hereafter as Sandy Gallin).
146. 'Promise': Hit Man.
146. Geffen agenda: Spinning Out, 48; Fred Goodman, Who's the Biggest Hollywood? *Spy*, April, 1991, 42; Yetnikoff, 252.
146. "He was pissed at me"/Treated Grubman "like a schlemiel"/'Power tear': Yetnikoff, 252-253.
146. Turning MJ against Yetnikoff/Admired Geffen: Yetnikoff, 253; Spinning Out.
146. Geffen and contract/Branca: *The Magic and the Madness*, 431-432, 442.
146. "Rightly or wrongly"/Branca's representation of others: Patrick Goldstein, Is Rumpole on Michael Jackson's List?, *Los Angeles Times*, July 1, 1990.
147. Leaving CBS/Unable to: *The Magic and the Madness*, 432, 442.
147. MJ wouldn't deliver album/Secure better deal: Spinning Out.
147. Much to Yetnikoff's dismay: Yetnikoff, 253.
147. 'Outrageous': Ibid., 253.
147. Word got back to the Japan/MJ unhappy: Spinning Out, 48.
147. Transferred loyalty: Yetnikoff, 256.
147. Yetnikoff firing: Patrick Goldstein, CBS' Battle of the Bosses: Springsteen vs. Yetnikoff, *Los Angeles Times*, September 2, 1990; Spinning Out.
147. Yetnikoff says Geffen influenced MJ: Yetnikoff, 252-253.
147. Fields admitted: Bert Fields, personal author interview, June 2015 (cited hereafter as Bert Fields).
147. Ziffren severed ties: Patrick Goldstein, Is Rumpole on Michael Jackson's List?, *Los Angeles Times*, July 1, 1990.
148. "Michael changed"/"People want to": Spinning Out.
148. "Michael simply wasn't": Matt Forger.

148. Geffen influenced *Decade* decision: *The Magic and the Madness*, 429, 431.
148. "I was the influence": Richard Buskin.
148. 'A rock edge': Oprah.
148. 'Give In to Me' session: Bill Bottrell.
148. "He sent me": Michael Jackson's 'Dangerous' Mind: The Making of the King of Pop.
149. "We took that song"/"Tim laid down"/"All the time"/"He went": Richard Buskin.
149. "Firstly we did": Tim Pierce, personal author interview, March 2012.
150. "LTB stood for": Gearslutz thread.
150. "I was frustrated": Bill Bottrell.
151. "All the lights were off"/Michael still wasn't fully satisfied with it: Crystal Cartier vs. Michael Jackson.
151. 'Jam' making of: Bruce Swedien.
152. 'Gone Too Soon' making of: Buz Kohan.
153. 'Integral part'/"It seemed only fair": *HIStory: The Official Michael Jackson News Magazine*, Issue 3, 1996, 16.
154. Bryan Loren stories: Bryan Loren, "Michael and Me." Myspace.com.
154. More contemporary and modern/'Fire' and a 'driving snare': Crystal Cartier vs. Michael Jackson.
155. "Present something very street": Michael Jackson's 'Dangerous' Mind: The Making of the King of Pop.
155. MJ loved Riley's work with Guy: Bill Bottrell.
155. "I always tell her": Michael Jackson's Private Home Movies, Fox TV, April 24, 2003 (cited hereafter as Michael Jackson's Private Home Movies).
155. "We talked regularly before": "Michael Jackson: Recording Dangerous with Teddy Riley", musicradar.com, July 3, 2009 (cited hereafter as Michael Jackson: Recording Dangerous with Teddy Riley).
156. "Before we came out"/"We were working on": Dave Way, personal author interview, February 2012 (cited hereafter as Dave Way).
156. "His staff greeted"/"He said we'd go"/"He thought": *The Official Michael Jackson Opus*, edited by Jordan Sommers and Justyn Barnes (Guernsey: Opus Media Group, 2009) (cited hereafter as *The Official Michael Jackson Opus*).

157. "I had recently started"/The first session: Dave Way.
157. "He starts going": Michael Jackson's 'Dangerous' Mind: The Making of the King of Pop.
157. "Our first day": *The Official Michael Jackson Opus*.
158. MJ always wanted to create melody: *You Are Not Alone*, 290.
158. "I thought he was": *The Official Michael Jackson Opus*.
158. "I don't know how": Teddy Riley, https://www.youtube.com/watch?v=siSSM9V8s3U
158. "Michael was bemused": Dave Way.
158. "That's one thing": Teddy Riley, https://www.youtube.com/watch?v=siSSM9V8s3U
158. "It worked itself out": Dasun Allah, When Heaven Can Wait: Teddy Riley Remembers Michael Jackson, Hip Hop Wired, July 2009 (cited hereafter as Dasun Allah).
158. "Michael was happy"/Moved to Larrabee: Dave Way.
158. "There was a lot going"/Studio merry-go-round: Matt Forger.
160. "That was the last": Dave Way.
160. Sony contract background: Robert Hilburn and Chuck Philips, Keeping up with the Jacksons, *Los Angeles Times*, June 16, 1991; Jube Shiver Jr, Jackson Going for Big Royalty Increase, *Los Angeles Times*, November 15, 1990; Randall Rothenberg, Michael Jackson Gets Thriller of Deal To Stay With Sony, *The New York Times*, March 21, 1991; Alan Cintron and Chuck Philips, Michael Jackson Agrees to Huge Contract with Sony, *Los Angeles Times*, March 21, 1991; Spinning Out, 48.
160. "He will be developing new"/"My reading is that they were close": Randall Rothenberg, Michael Jackson Gets Thriller of Deal To Stay With Sony, *The New York Times*, March 21, 1991.
161. "Outrageous": Yetnikoff, 253.
161. 'Economic'/"If Michael continues": Michael Jackson's 'Dangerous' Mind: The Making of the King of Pop.
161. "I don't see the Sony deal": Robert Hilburn and Chuck Philips, Keeping up with the Jacksons, *Los Angeles Times*, June 16, 1991.
162. "By no means": Tommy Mottola, *Hitmaker: The Man and His Music* (Grand Central Publishing 2013), 231 (cited hereafter as *Hitmaker: The Man and His Music*).
162. MJ note/'MA & MJ duet': Michael Jackson, unpublished memo (circa early 1991).

162. "Teddy did some": Brad Buxer.
162. 'An experiment'/"He wanted to write a song"/Madonna was shocked/"I presented them to him": Madonna Interview, Jonathan Ross Presents: Erotica Madonna, October 1992, https://www.youtube.com/watch?v=4YB7yeb3x44
163. "They spent a little while": Rob Disner, More Musings on Michael, November 12, 2007, http://axecollectorblog.blogspot.co.uk/2007/11/more-musings-on-michael.html (cited hereafter as Rob Disner, More Musings on Michael).
163. "I have this whole vision"/'Up for it'/"I don't know": Don Shewey, Madonna: The Saint, The Slut, The Sensation, *The Advocate*, May 7, 1991, 42–51.
163. Liked spoken voice: Stéphanie interview on Radio Monaco, July 15, 2009, https://www.youtube.com/watch?v=UIWNAGi-1UI4&eurl=http%3A%2F%2Fprincely-family-of-monaco.blogspot.com%2F&feature=player_embedded
164. "She couldn't really sing"/"People were running around"/"Michael was goofy"/"Nancy and Michael": Thom Russo, personal author interview, February 2012 (cited hereafter as Thom Russo).
164. "He started sending"/'A special favour'/"Of course I agreed"/"Even though it was just"/"Michael left me this note": Rob Disner, My Brush With Badness.
165. "When I asked him what"/"He asked me to come"/"This was the pre-cell phone": Rob Disner, More Musings on Michael.
166. "I mean Teddy Riley": Thom Russo.
166. "One of the loves of my life": Boteach, 197.
166. Shields relationship: Alex Tirpack, Michael Jackson Remembered: Brooke Shields on Singer's "Pure Soul", *Rolling Stone*, July 13, 2009.
166. "I understand he's": Chuck Philips, Jermaine Jackson: 'Word to the Badd!!' a Call to Michael, *Los Angeles Times*, November 7, 1991.
167. "Teddy wasn't too happy": Dave Way.
167. "Lord I was shitting": Jean-Marie Horvat, personal author interview, November 2011.
167. 'Killer Teddy Riley dance grooves'/'Better than Knowledge': Michael Jackson, unpublished memo (circa early 1991).
167. "It came out perfectly": Michael Jackson: Recording Dangerous with Teddy Riley.

167. "I would walk": Sundberg Facebook post.
168. "We anticipated": Michael Jackson's 'Dangerous' Mind: The Making of the King of Pop.
168. "I thought he was"/"I could feel it": Michael Jackson: Recording Dangerous with Teddy Riley.
168. 'Simply overwhelming'/"His vocal performance": Jean-Marie Horvat interview, Le Numero Ultime, *Black & White Magazine*, November 7, 2009, 72–73 (cited hereafter as Le Numero Ultime).
169. 'Contemporary'/Wanted Riley to update sounds: Crystal Cartier vs. Michael Jackson.
169. "One day Bruce": Dave Way.
169. "Rene Moore and Bruce": Robert Doerschuk, Interview with Teddy Riley, *Keyboard*, February 1992.
169. Heavy D favourite rapper: Michael Jackson: Recording Dangerous with Teddy Riley
169. "I wasn't satisfied with it": Crystal Cartier vs. Michael Jackson.
169. "I was at the hotel": *Thriller: The Musical Life of Michael Jackson*, 196.
169. "No producer likes his track": Thom Russo.
169. "I never felt competition": Gearslutz thread.
169. "'Dangerous' had already been": Robert Doerschuk, Interview with Teddy Riley, *Keyboard*, February 1992.
170. 'Very professional'/"He'd come in with a groove": Michael Jackson's 'Dangerous' Mind: The Making of the King of Pop.
170. "He asked me to stay": *The Official Michael Jackson Opus*.
170. 'Aggressive, mechanical': Bernie Grundman, personal author interview, February 2012 (cited hereafter as Bernie Grundman).
170. "That was the sound": Michael Jackson: Recording Dangerous with Teddy Riley
170. "Michael looked up": Larry Stessel.
171. "That's when the intensity tripled": Brad Buxer.
171. "By the summer": Thom Russo.
171. "I would like to see children": Michael Speaks, *Ebony*, May 1992, 40.
171. "He was demanding": Michael Jackson: Recording Dangerous with Teddy Riley
171. "Michael was very slow": Thom Russo.
172. "Michael wouldn't do a vocal": Dave Way.

172. "Michael loved the work": Sandy Gallin.
172. "By then it was all go go go": Thom Russo.
172. "We'd drive to the studio": Michael Jackson's 'Dangerous' Mind: The Making of the King of Pop.
172. "One day there"/"We always had such fun with Michael": Bea Swedien, personal author interview, April 2014.
173. "Michael would come in": Thom Russo.
173. "He was a bad driver": Dave Way.
173. 'An awful driver'/"He hit everyone's car": Rob Disner, My Brush With Badness.
174. Landis reluctant/"Michael called": Rob Tannenbaum and Craig Marks, *I Want My MTV: The Uncensored Story of the Music Video Revolution* (Plume Books, 2012).
174. "The album had": Michael Jackson's 'Dangerous' Mind: The Making of the King of Pop.
174. 'Black or White' video background: Alan Citron and Daniel Cerone, There Are No Limits in Michael Jackson's World of Make-Believe, *Los Angeles Times*, November 14, 1991 (cited hereafter as There Are No Limits in Michael Jackson's World of Make-Believe); David Browne, Michael Jackson's Black or White Blues, *Entertainment Weekly*, November 29, 1991 (cited hereafter as Michael Jackson's Black or White Blues).
174. "We've pushed this": There Are No Limits in Michael Jackson's World of Make-Believe.
175. 'Keep the Faith' voice story: Michael Jackson's 'Dangerous' Mind: The Making of the King of Pop.
175. Voice cracked/Configurations: Brad Sundberg.
175. "He doesn't like": Michael Jackson's 'Dangerous' Mind: The Making of the King of Pop.
176. "Michael kept": Rob Disner, More Musings on Michael.
176. "He takes a song off": Bruce Swedien interview, *Black & White Magazine*, December, January and February issue 1994/1995 (cited hereafter as Bruce Swedien interview, *Black & White* magazine).
176. "One day he told": *The Official Michael Jackson Opus*.
176. "On every album": Michael Jackson: Recording Dangerous with Teddy Riley
177. "I was disappointed": Gearslutz thread.

177. "It was a song Michael was": Bill Bottrell.
177. "I couldn't believe": Dave Way.
177. "*Dangerous* was a rough period": Bryan Loren, Michael and Me. Myspace.com.
177. "Bryan Loren…you": Michael Jackson, *Dangerous* (Special Edition). Sony, 2001, compact disc. Originally released in 1991. Credits, 23.
177. 'For All Time' written for *Dangerous*/"Michael recorded it": Steve Porcaro.
177. "I wrote it originally": Robert Smith et al. vs. Michael Jackson et al.
178. "Michael said": Michael Jackson's 'Dangerous' Mind: The Making of the King of Pop.
178. MJ at Grundman's: There Are No Limits in Michael Jackson's World of Make-Believe.
178. "Nobody would be": Bernie Grundman.
178. "Everything was": Dan Beck, personal author interview, August 2014 (cited hereafter as Dan Beck).

CHAPTER 10: THE *DANGEROUS* CAMPAIGN

179. 'Black or White' video background: There Are No Limits in Michael Jackson's World of Make-Believe; Jackson Verdict: It's Nasty: *Sarasota Herald-Tribune*, November 16, 1991; Daniel Cerone, Michael's Video Takes Beating; 4 Minutes Cut, *Los Angeles Times*, November 16, 1991; Michael Jackson's Black or White Blues; Michael Jackson's 'Dangerous' Mind: The Making of the King of Pop.
180. "He wanted it to be": Michael Jackson's 'Dangerous' Mind: The Making of the King of Pop.
180. Own moniker/Bob Jones: Larry Stessel.
180. The *New York Post* and the *Chicago Sun-Times* use: Michael's doing just fine, *New York Post*, February 8, 1984; Adrienne Drell, Courtroom 'Thriller', *Chicago Sun-Times*, December 7, 1984.
180. Bob Jones wrote speech: Bob Jones, *Michael Jackson Man Behind The Mask* (Select Books Inc., 2009), 49.
180. "Ladies and Gentlemen": Elizabeth Taylor, award presentation speech, Soul Train Music Awards, 1989, https://www.youtube.com/watch?v=b1ZzxLsE7b8
180. "Michael loved": Sandy Gallin.

181. "Michael came into": Rob Tannenbaum and Craig Marks, *I Want My MTV: The Uncensored Story of the Music Video Revolution* (Plume Books, 2012).
181. "He commented on": Long Gone John, Overachiever Extraordinaire, *Juxtapoz* Magazine, Winter 1998.
182. Retiring from touring after Bad Tour: A New Stage for Michael Jackson.
182. "The only reason": Dennis Hunt, Jackson Plans World Tour to Fund Charity, *Los Angeles Times*, February 4, 1992.
182. "Prankster": Omoronke Idowu, Shani Saxon, Joseph V. Tirella, Josh Tyrangiel and Mimi Valdes, Action Jackson, *Vibe*, June/July 1995, 56 (cited hereafter as Action Jackson).
182. "We had a lot of fun": Naomi Campbell interview, Portrait, 1996, https://www.youtube.com/watch?v=dQ-NLEbRwBk
182. "They're arguably the best": Michael Jackson's 20 Greatest Videos.
183. "We had no time at all": Oprah.
184. 'Receptive'/"He was reclusive before": Dave Dimartino, Making sense of pop music, *Entertainment Weekly*, February 19, 1993.
184. "I knew that": Sandy Gallin.
185. Vitiligo/Denied bleaching skin: Oprah.
185. Skin whitening creams/Used for vitiligo: Thomas Watkins, Skin-whitening creams found in Jackson home, today.com, March 26, 2010.
185. "His became so severe": Arnold Klein, *Larry King Live*, CNN, July 8, 2009.
185. "The sudden coming-out": Daniel Cerone, Why Is This Man Talking?, *Los Angeles Times*, February 9, 1993.
185. 'Humanise'/"It made him": Sandy Gallin.
186. "In the past month I've": Michael Jackson, award acceptance speech, Grammy Awards, 1993, https://www.youtube.com/watch?v=XTXh0_OC98k
186. "We all breathed a big sigh": Dan Beck.

CHAPTER 11: TURMOIL

187. *Addams Family Values* film and song background: Monette Austin, Life Of Riley, *Daily Press*, May 2, 1993; Sound Bites, *SPIN*, August 1993, 30; Michael Fleming, Jackson off 'Addams' theme, *Variety*,

September 2, 1993; A.J. Jacobs, Action Jackson, *Entertainment Weekly*, November 18, 1994; Matt Forger; Mick Garris, personal author interview, January 2016 (cited hereafter as Mick Garris).

187. 'Monsterised': A.J. Jacobs, Action Jackson, *Entertainment Weekly*, November 18, 1994.

187. "Michael had become"/"The song was also titled": Mick Garris.

188. "I think people"/"Michael was a huge": Candace Williams, Michael Jackson Planned to Step into Jimmy Cagney's Shoes, Says 'Captain EO' Producer and Longtime Pal Rusty Lemorande, blog.blogtalkradio.com, June 29, 2009.

189. "That was the": Sandy Gallin.

189. 'Lonely, tortured musician': Andrew Lloyd Webber, Michael Jackson wanted to appear in Phantom of the Opera, telegraph.co.uk, June 27, 2009.

189. "The discussions": Dan Beck.

190. MJ pain summer 1993: Katherine Jackson et al. vs. AEG Live, May 9–10, 2013.

190. Surgery March 1993: Katherine Jackson et al. vs. AEG Live, August 13, 2013.

190. Hairpiece/Keloids: Katherine Jackson et al. vs. AEG Live, August 14, 2013.

190. Balloons/Pain six weeks/Wound/Hairpiece: Katherine Jackson et al. vs. AEG Live, May 9–10 and August 13, 2013.

190. "His schedule was so busy": Katherine Jackson et al. vs. AEG Live, May 9, 2013.

190. Percocet/Demerol: Katherine Jackson et al. vs. AEG Live, August 13, 2013.

191. Doctors took advantage/'Pissing contest'/Money. "Michael respected doctors"/Dilaudid/Condo/Concerned/Metzger/Programme/Progress: Katherine Jackson et al. vs. AEG Live, August 14, 2013.

191. Stress increased urge: Katherine Jackson et al. vs. AEG Live, July 8, 2013.

192. Rumours spread/Media could not confirm/Pellicano conference / Extortion: *The Magic and the Madness*, 500–502.

192. Jordan met MJ May 1992/Befriended/Jealous/Confronted ex-wife/ Dismissed worries/Hired attorney/Threatened to go public/Fields

hired Pellicano/Stepfather taped conversation/'Destroy'/"If I go through with this"/Played tape to Pellicano/"After listening to the tape"/$20 million demand/Still no accusation/Anaesthesiologist/ Sodium amytal/1952 study/Dental procedure/Rarely used for that purpose/Allegations made under influence of drug/Psychiatrist/ Allegation made in through three-hour session/Psychiatrist reported allegation/Informed police/Extortion charges filed late August: Mary A. Fischer, Was Michael Jackson Framed?, *GQ*, October 1994.

193. "Bert told me": Sandy Gallin.
193. $30 million of debt by 1993: Katherine Jackson et al. vs. AEG Live, August 12, 2013.
194. Morphine/Dehydration/Use of narcotics: Katherine Jackson et al. vs. AEG Live, July 8, 2013.
194. Dazed, stumbled: Katherine Jackson et al. vs. AEG Live, May 9, 2013.
194. $30 million civil lawsuit/Alleging/Dozen detectives/Collecting evidence/March 21, 1994/"They had a very weak case"/Mother switched sides/Fields hired Weitzman: Sonia Nazario, Jackson Sued by Boy Who Alleged Sexual Molestation, *Los Angeles Times*, September 15, 1993; Mary A. Fischer, Was Michael Jackson Framed?, *GQ*, October 1994.
194. 'In Our Darkest Hour': Michael Jackson, "Will You Be There", *Dangerous*, Sony, 1991.
195. "Michael had become"/"After Paramount"/"I was never paid": Mick Garris.
196. "I always had"/"I had a cassette"/"When I left the room": Brad Buxer.
197. "The lyrics": HIStory: The Michael Jackson Interview.
197. "It's because": Zack O'Malley Greenburg, *Michael Jackson, Inc.* (New York: Atria Books, 2014), 170–171 (cited hereafter as *Michael Jackson, Inc.*)
197. By Mexico narcotic use intensified: Katherine Jackson et al. vs. AEG Live, July 8, 2013.
198. 'A hot mess'/"He was depressed"/Unkempt/'A complete mess': Katherine Jackson et al. vs. AEG Live, August 14, 2013.
198. "You cannot go to Puerto Rico"/"Knew he had": Katherine Jackson et al. vs. AEG Live, August 14, 2013.
198. "The doctor said to me": Sandy Gallin.

198. Hotel state: *The Magic and the Madness*, 525.
199. "It was an entire organisation"/"Amazingly": Sally Brockway, My Diary: Psychotherapist Beechy Colclough, *Daily Mirror*, November 28, 1998.
199. Cancellation statement: Ernest Sander, Jackson Scraps Concert Tour, Cites Addiction, *Los Angeles Times*, November 14, 1993.
199. 'Was barely able': Bernard, Weinraub, Jackson Being Treated Abroad For Addiction, Lawyer Says, *The New York Times*, November 16, 1993.
199. "The press took": Mary A. Fischer, Was Michael Jackson Framed?, *GQ*, October 1994.
200. Puerto Rico/Arrested on United States soil: W. Speers, 2 Views On Why Michael Jackson's Still In Mexico, *The Philadelphia Inquirer*, November 12, 1993; Cascio, 68.
200. "Michael had to go on stage": Katherine Jackson et al. vs. AEG Live, May 9, 2013.
200. "All we're saying": Pepsi Drops Sponsorship of Jackson, *Los Angeles Times*, November 15, 1993.
200. "Initially the allegations": Dan Beck.
201. "It would be hard for anyone": *Hitmaker: The Man and His Music*, 232.
201. Three quarters of sales outside United States/Most international music star ever: Randall Sullivan, *Untouchable: The Strange Life and Tragic Death of Michael Jackson* (Grove Press, 2012), 115 (cited hereafter as Randall Sullivan).
201. Film ambitions destroyed by allegations: Sandy Gallin.
201. "The truth of the matter is": Candace Williams, Michael Jackson Planned to Step into Jimmy Cagney's Shoes, Says 'Captain EO' Producer and Longtime Pal Rusty Lemorande, blog.blogtalkradio.com, June 29, 2009.
201. "I don't think the studios": Sandy Gallin.
201. 'No role': Mike Thomas, Hey, what about that man in the glass booth?, *Chicago Sun-Times*, March 31, 2003.
201. Theme parks: Sandy Gallin.
202. 'Very strongly'/"I was convinced": Bert Fields.
202. Fields resigns/Cochran brought in/Pellicano leaves/Branca returns/Attorneys advise to settle/Concerns about justice/Extor-

tion accusations dropped: Mary A. Fischer, Was Michael Jackson Framed?, *GQ*, October 1994.

202. Cochran secured promise: William Plummer, Johnnie Cochran, *People*, June 13, 1994.

202. $2 million spent on investigation/200 witnesses questioned: *The Magic and the Madness*, 540–541

203. Settlement: Michael Jackson's $15 Million Payoff, The Smoking Gun, June 16, 2004, http://www.thesmokinggun.com/documents/celebrity/michael-jacksons-15-million-payoff

203. "I talked to my lawyers": Michael Jackson, Interview with Diane Sawyer, *Primetime Live*, June 14, 1995.

203. 'The worst decision': Randall Sullivan, 265.

203. Chandler not prevented from testifying: Michael Jackson's $15 Million Payoff, The Smoking Gun, June 16, 2004, 13–19: Confidentiality discussed. p. 16: Restrictions on sharing information apply to civil claims or actions only, except as may be required by law and the Chandlers may cooperate with subpoenas and investigations, http://www.thesmokinggun.com/documents/celebrity/michael-jacksons-15-million-payoff

203. "The criminal investigation": Jim Newton, Jackson Settles Abuse Suit but Insists He Is Innocent, *Los Angeles Times*, January 26, 1994.

203. Jordan Chandler refused to testify: Randall Sullivan, 265–266.

203. "Remember, this case": Mary A. Fischer, Was Michael Jackson Framed?, *GQ*, October 1994.

203. No witnesses could be found: Mary A. Fischer, Was Michael Jackson Framed?, *GQ*, October 1994.

203. No findings during search: *The Magic and the Madness*, 500–501.

204. Evan Chandler suicide: Bill Hutchinson, Evan Chandler, dad of boy who accused Michael Jackson of molestation, commits suicide in New Jersey, *New York Daily News*, November 17, 2009.

CHAPTER 12: MAKING *HISTORY*

205. "I was terrified": Robert E. Johnson, Michael Tells 'Where I Met Lisa Marie And How I Proposed', *Ebony*, October 1994, 124.

205. "We were reviewing tapes"/Team relocated/"Bruce and his wife Bea": Matt Forger.

205. 'The best in the world': Bruce Swedien interview, *Black & White*

Magazine.

206. "The idea was": Rob Hoffman, personal author interview, February 2012 (cited hereafter as Rob Hoffman).
206. "Maybe he was waiting": Matt Forger.
206. "Eddie was the engineer": Brad Buxer.
206. "Michael's apartment": Cascio, 82.
207. "There was a lot of political": Rob Hoffman.
207. "At this stage"/'Stranger in Moscow' first song/"When Michael finally"/Buxer co-writer/Wouldn't credit/"That song"/"Of course": Brad Buxer.
207. "Vocals were mostly": Rob Hoffman.
208. "One great thing": Geoff Grace, personal author interview, February 2012 (cited hereafter as Geoff Grace).
208. "Although the idea": Rob Hoffman.
208. MJ liked 'Owner of a Lonely Heart'/Rabin/"We had many": Gearslutz thread.
209. "That was one of": Gearslutz thread.
209. 'Innocent Man' lyrics: Michael Jackson, unpublished lyric sheet (circa 1994).
209. "They flew me": Larry Williams.
210. "Michael was a big fan"/'Little Susie': Rob Hoffman.
210. "Michael wanted some": Geoff Grace.
210. "We bought a bunch": Gearslutz thread.
210. "It's totally different": Rob Hoffman.
211. "They put a scarf on him": David Foster, *Hitman* (Pocket, 2008).
211. "What was fascinating": Rob Hoffman.
211. "They bounced ideas": Gearslutz thread.
211. "How could you not admire": Michael Jackson's Private Home Movies.
212. "Our personal history begins": *The Solo Years*, 135.
212. "If you really want": Ed Bradley.
212. "Michael did a bunch": Gearslutz thread.
212. "When we finished recording": *In The Studio With Michael Jackson*, 58.
213. "Michael has always": Richard Buskin.
213. "Foster became frustrated": Bill Bottrell.
213. "Michael went into the studio": Melinda Newman, New Jackson Set On Epic Aims To Make 'HIStory', *Billboard*, May 20, 1995, 13.
214. "We held a major meeting": Dan Beck.

214. "I had a meeting"/'Darker'/"Michael didn't speak out"/MJ loved Beck's idea: Dan Beck.
214. "HIStorical thinking": Michael Jackson, *HIS*tory: Past, Present and Future, Book I, Sony, 1995, compact disc. Liner notes, 8.
215. "This was how Michael": Dan Beck.
215. "When Michael left the studio": Rob Hoffman.
215. "She was very, very supportive": Robert E. Johnson, Michael Tells 'Where I Met Lisa Marie And How I Proposed', *Ebony*, October 1994, 124.
215. "They acted like two kids": Gearslutz thread.
216. "We actually"/"Janet called us"/"Michael didn't"/"Now the Hit Factory"/"Michael said"/Met in apartment/"So Michael said"/Anger/"-Michael came up"/Janet created title and bridge lyrics/"So we were sat there"/"I had never seen"/"It really showed": Jimmy Jam, personal author interview, May 2013 (cited hereafter as Jimmy Jam).
218. "The two of them singing": Gearslutz thread.
219. "Of course, this wasn't cheap"/"I think it was simply"/"He booked out": Bernie Grundman.
220. "So many new ideas": Matt Forger.
220. "In truth": *The Solo Years*, 132.
220. "That added to the price": Cascio, 88.
220. "His loyal followers": *Hitmaker: The Man and His Music*, 286.
220. "I came up for": Dasun Allah.
220. 'No Diggity': *Michael Jackson, Inc.*, 176.
220. 'Sounded too much': Gearslutz thread.
220. "My world crumbled": Katherine Jackson et al. vs. AEG Live, June 27, 2013.
221. "He gave it to us": *HIStory: The Official Michael Jackson News Magazine*, Issue 4, 1996, 22.
221. "My involvement"/"They were so nice": Steve Porcaro.
221. "He is indeed original": *In The Studio With Michael Jackson*, 55.
222. "He said, 'Chuck, I want"/"On and off": Ibid., 63.
222. "Michael wasn't even": Steve Porcaro.
222. "He got one of"/*Jurassic Park*/"The studio crew got free"/"We recorded a Christmas"/"Once, while we were"/"Bruce and I": Gearslutz thread.
223. "That pie that Michael": Brad Buxer.

223. 'Psyched'/"I feel I could": Kevin Chappell, R. Kelly: His Exciting Mansion And His Controversial Mix Of Shock And Salvation, *Ebony*, July 1996, 134.
224. Written after the losses: R. Kelly, *Soulacoaster* (Hay House UK, 2012), 198 (cited hereafter as R. Kelly, *Soulacoaster*).
224. "I think I am him": R. Kelly: The Man The Music The Mystery, *Vibe*, November 2000, 112.
224. 'Life'/'This song is for you': *The Solo Years*, 135.
224. 'A sense of climax': Adrian Grant, *Making HIStory* (Omnibus Press, 1998).
224. Co-writer's credit/"Naturally that got me"/Mistake: R. Kelly, *Soulacoaster*, 207.
224. "Wherever Michael": Ibid., 203.
224. "I knew he was a big kid": R. Kelly interview, Viva music channel, October 1999.
225. "When the manager appeared": R. Kelly, *Soulacoaster*, 206.
225. "He'd always stop": Ibid., 207.
225. "It was good": Jimmy Jam.
225. "He'd always go at peak": Robert Seidenberg, Jimmy Jam's work on "HIStory", *Entertainment Weekly*, 23 June, 1995 (cited hereafter as Robert Seidenberg).
225. "Them in the studio": Jon Bream, Jackson's New Jam, *Minneapolis Star-Tribune*, June 18, 1994.
226. "He's a perfectionist"/'Is It Scary'/"He asked us": Jimmy Jam.
226. "To my knowledge": Rob Hoffman.
226. "He really liked 'Is It Scary'": Brad Buxer.
226 "Winter had arrived": Matt Forger.
227. "In New York": Rob Hoffman.
228. "We were originally"/"The song was really simple": Jimmy Jam.
228. "We felt like the tabloids": Robert Seidenberg.
228. "I think he gave it": Jimmy Jam.
228. "Michael and Bruce": Gearslutz thread.
229. "I must say it's": Gearslutz thread.
229. "At that stage"/"He was a guy"/"The gift was": Jimmy Jam.
230. 'A knowingness'/"Even when my back": Adam White, Gordy Speaks, *Billboard*, November 5, 1994, 72.
230. "Berry insisted on perfection": *Moonwalk*, 77.

230. "Michael would work": Jimmy Jam.
230. "He's a kid at heart": Action Jackson.
230. "One night he told me": *HIStory: The Official Michael Jackson News Magazine*, Issue 2, 1995, 21.
230. "Once Michael said to me": Jimmy Jam.
231. "By 1995, he seemed even": Kim Hutchcroft.
231. 'Mad freedom'/"You're pressured by time": Action Jackson.
231. Notorious B.I.G. story: Gearslutz thread.
233. MJ's favourite Beatles song/"I just went in": Adrian Grant, *Making HIStory* (Omnibus Press, 1998).
233. Bottrell shocked/"Crude"/"I never intended": Gearslutz thread.
233. 'Very autobiographical'/"They come from": *The Solo Years*, 132.
233. 'Musical book'/"If you want to": Simulchat.
234. "Everything on": Robert Seidenberg.
234. "He sang what": Michael Jackson's Scream: HIStory in the Making, An MTV News Special, 1995.
234. 'Most persona'/'Most beautiful'/"He went above": Bruce Swedien interview, *Black & White Magazine.*
234. "I just kind of write"/Favourite songs/Emotions, message: Adrian Grant, *Making HIStory* (Omnibus Press, 1998).
234. "We wanted to pare it down"/"You shouldn't rush": Jimmy Jam.
235. "For the whole weekend": Rob Hoffman.
235. "I told him the story"/"This was a common": Gearslutz thread.
236. Mastering story/"This was no small": Gearslutz thread.
236. "It seemed like Michael": Bernie Grundman.
237. "No applause": *In The Studio With Michael Jackson*, 67–68.
237. Neverland party on Sunday, April 2: Andrew Scheps, personal author interview, March 2012.
237. "Janet called": Jimmy Jam.
238. "When Michael": Geoff Grace.
238. "It was the tail end": Gary Grant.

CHAPTER 13: THE *HISTORY* CHALLENGE

239. Super Bowl/Royal wedding: Jerry Crowe, Psssst–Heard About Michael's New Album?, *Los Angeles Times*, May 4, 1997.
239. 'Everything': *Hitmaker: The Man and His Music*, 287.
239. "At our end"/"By the mid-1990s": Dan Beck.

240. "Michael and Janet were"/"Firstly, Michael was very much": Jimmy Jam.
241. "Jew me, sue me": Michael Jackson, 'They Don't Care About Us', *HIStory: Past, Present and Future, Book I*, Sony, 1995.
241. "The most ridiculously": Steve Hochman, Jewish Leaders Call Jackson Lyrics Anti-Semitic, *Los Angeles Times*, June 16, 1995; Jerry Crowe, Jackson Promises Disclaimer in Future 'HIStory' Albums, *Los Angeles Times*, June 17, 1995.
241. 'Angry and outraged': Bernard Weinraub, In New Lyrics, Jackson Uses Slurs, *The New York Times*, June 15, 1995.
241. "My intention was for": Chris Riemenschneider, Jackson Will Re-Record 'Care' Lyrics, *Los Angeles Times*, June 23, 1995.
241. 'The TV event'/ 60 million: Marc Gunther, What Abc Gave To Get The Michael Jackson Interview, *The Philadelphia Inquirer*, June 29, 1995.
241. "It was me": Sandy Gallin.
243. "The original idea": Dan Beck.
244. $115 million to merge: Katherine Jackson et al. vs. AEG Live, August 12, 2013.
244. "This acquisition had nothing"/Third largest publisher: Michael Jackson And Sony Enter Joint Publishing Venture Valued At $600 Million, *JET*, November 27, 1995, 36.
244. Merger not sale/Needed cash: Pop star says he's not pressed for cash, *Herald-Journal*, November 10, 1995.
245. "We have been working": Michael Jackson And Sony Enter Joint Publishing Venture Valued At $600 Million, *JET*, November 27, 1995, 36.
245. 'A great deal'/"He basically": *Hitmaker: The Man and His Music*, 288.
245. "They thought"/Planned to perform *HIS*tory material: Jeff Margolis, personal author interview, January 2015 (cited hereafter as Jeff Margolis).
246. "From the very beginning": *HIStory: The Official Michael Jackson News Magazine*, Issue 4, 1996, 13-14.
246. Collapsed while rehearsing 'Black or White': David Stout, Michael Jackson Collapses At Rehearsal, *The New York Times*, December 7, 1995.
246. Face-first/"It was very frightening": Jeff Margolis.

246. Publicity stunt/Staged/"A little scheme": Rebecca Ascher-Walsh, Michael Jackson: The Thrill Is Gone, *Entertainment Weekly*, December 22, 1995; Robin Eisner, Jackson in intensive care, HBO concert postponed, Associated Press, December 8, 1995.
246. Ortega/Unhappy/'Anxious'/"I think that there were new choreographers": Katherine Jackson et al. vs. AEG Live, July 8, 2013.
246. "I worked so much to prepare": Michael Jackson interview, *Black & White* magazine, 1998, http://en.michaeljackson.ru/black-white-magazine/ (cited hereafter as Michael Jackson *Black & White* interview).
246. "He didn't think it": Sandy Gallin.
247. 'Definitely': Jeff Margolis.
247. 'Critical'/"He was dehydrated": Andrew Dys, Rock Hill doctor helped save Michael Jackson's life after 1995 rehearsal collapse, *The Herald*, July 8, 2009.
247. Show was ready/"It would have really": Jeff Margolis.
247. 'Wonderful'/"I adore this version": Michael Jackson *Black & White* interview.
248. "She begged and begged": Katherine Jackson et al. vs. AEG Live, May 9, 2013.
248. 'One of the world's': Patrice Apodaca, The Ride of Their Lives: Theme Park Design Team Seeks to Expand Its Empire, *Los Angeles Times*, November 28, 1996.
248. "Through Kingdom Entertainment": Michael Jackson, press conference, March 19, 1996, https://www.youtube.com/watch?v=Y4Q-GfKdJLY
249. "I wish": Mick Garris.
250. "There's some pathos": *Michael Jackson: The Making Of Ghosts*, VH1, 1997.
250. "Michael just always envisioned": Brad Buxer.
250. "I worked on *Ghosts*": Gearslutz thread.
250. "The song 'Ghosts'": Brad Buxer.
251. "It wasn't connected": Dan Beck.
252. 'A gift'/"Michael was divorced": Andy Geller, Two oldest kids not fathered by Michael Jackson: Ex-wife, *The New York Post*, June 29, 2009.
252 "I've being doing": Susan Essoyan, A Big Aloha for Michael, *Los Angeles Times*, January 6, 1997.

CHAPTER 14: *BLOOD ON THE DANCE FLOOR*

254. *HIStory Book II*/"It would have included": Rob Hoffman.
254. "The *HIStory Book II* concept": Brad Buxer.
254. Original idea four new songs/Nine remixes: Jerry Crowe, Pop/rock, *Los Angeles Times*, April 3, 1997; Melinda Newman, The Beat, *Billboard*, April 12, 1997, 12.
254. "The practical thing"/"It was then": Matt Forger.
255. "I think the trip": Matt Forger.
256. "I played every": Brad Buxer.
256. 'Vacuum clean': *Michael Jackson: For The Record* (CreateSpace Independent Publishing Platform; 2nd edition, 2009), 40 (cited hereafter as *For The Record*).
256. "When I heard it finished": Joseph Vogel, Michael Jackson's 'Blood on the Dance Floor', 15 Years Later, theatlantic.com, March 21, 2012.
256. 'Incredible time'/"Mike gave me": Vince Paterson.
256. 'Elizabeth I Love You': Buz Kohan.
257. "I do remember Michael": Bill Bottrell.
257. 'One of the greatest songs': Brad Buxer.
257. "I remember giving Michael": Bryan Loren interview, *Black & White Magazine*, April 1998.
257. 'Seven Digits' and 'Superfly Sister' background: Bryan Loren interview, *Black & White Magazine*, April 1998; Bryan Loren, personal author interview, April 2014.
258. "It seemed with this album": Dave Way.
258. "I kicked around a bit": Bill Bottrell.
259. "One day, we had": Dave Way.
259. Winston thought film should contain more music: Michael Jackson *Black & White* interview.
259. "We needed more"/"No dance scenes"/"We made new": Brad Buxer.
260. "Stan thought": Michael Jackson *Black & White* interview.
261. 'Tabloid Junkie' remix removed: *For The Record*, 362.
261. "The least I can say": Michael Jackson *Black & White* interview.
261. 'Pssssst': Jerry Crowe, Pssssst–Heard About Michael's New Album?, *Los Angeles Times*, May 4, 1997.
261. 'Hardly a sound': Andrew Ross Sorkin, King of Pop Faces U.S. Market With Subdued Promotion Effort, *The New York Times*, June 23, 1997.

261. 'Is witnessing an erosion': J.D. Considine, Michael Jackson is witnessing an erosion of fan base in U.S., *The Daily Gazette*, June 19, 1997.
261. 'The thriller is gone': David Bauder, Michael Jackson's sales figures: no thrill, *The Associated Press*, June 21, 1997.
262. "The album was": Matt Forger.
262. 'Completely behind'/"Michael is certainly": Andrew Ross Sorkin, King of Pop Faces U.S. Market With Subdued Promotion Effort, *The New York Times*, June 23, 1997.
262. "I did talk to Michael": Will Wilson, personal author interview, December 2014.
263. "But they weren't": Sandy Gallin.
263. Concerns over substance abuse/Concerts in danger of being cancelled: Le Numero Ultime, 45–49.
263. MJ using Propofol during tour: Katherine Jackson et al. vs. AEG Live, August 14–15, 2013.
263. Insomnia/"Michael was so buzzed": Katherine Jackson et al. vs. AEG Live, May 9, 2013; Katherine Jackson et al. vs. AEG Live, August 14–15, 2013; Katherine Jackson et al. vs. AEG Live, September 6, 2013.
264. "I think they tried it"/Rowe tried to warn: Katherine Jackson et al. vs. AEG Live, August 14–15, 2013.
265. MJ frustration: Michael Jackson *Black & White* interview.

CHAPTER 15: THE FINAL ALBUM

267. 'Street' sound: Matt Forger; *The Solo Years*, 165.
267. 'Simply fantastic': *The Solo Years*, 165–166.
268. "He takes an insane": Puff Daddy, Interview on MTV's *Total Request Live*, http://web.archive.org/web/20010609093708/http://members.aol.com/fascribes/albumnews.html
268. "I did not believe"/"'Break of Dawn' is just"/Favourite song/"That was his baby"/"He found it"/"The process in the studio": Elliot Straite aka 'Dr. Freeze', Interview with Quagmire, "MEETING MICHAEL WAS LIKE MEETING CAPTAIN KIRK," MJFrance, translated here, January 2011.
269. "I think that's partly": CJ deVillar, personal author interview, February 2012

269. "Michael was very calm"/"I went to the studio"/"He would drive"/"Some sessions"/"He would sit there": CJ deVillar, personal author interview, February 2012
270. "A song to take us": Jackson On A 'Quest' For Millennial Anthem, USA Today, February/March 1999.
270. "Our song will be": Michael Jackson News June 1999, michael-jackson-trader.com, June 10, 1999, http://www.michael-jackson-trader.com/news/1999/June/index.html
270. "Everyone wants to work": Daniel Rubin, Master Of Beat At 21, Songwriter And Producer Rodney Jerkins Jr. Is An R&b Wunderkind Who Goes For Energy With Beat, *The Philadelphia Inquirer*, February 9, 1999.
271. "You're not seeing"/'Shock the world': Rodney Jerkins interview, *Extra*, aired July 6, 2009, https://www.youtube.com/watch?v=0p-P2XQ_aeoM
271. "He just sat down": Michael Jackson Taps Rodney Jerkins, David Foster To Produce Next Record, mtv.com, March 11, 1999.
271. "At Record One": Brad Gilderman, personal author interview, February 2012.
271. "Michael would call me": Rodney Jerkins Says Working With Michael Jackson Was The Best Experience Of His Life, BOSSIP, published August 30, 2013, https://www.youtube.com/watch?v=9KMmKRSG6uc
271. "The place was swept": LaShawn Daniels Talks Michael Jackson's Invincible Album & What He Learned From The King Of Pop, Kempire Radio, published on November 11, 2012, https://www.youtube.com/watch?v=bEiEaf6Oeho
271. "I was slated to do": BMI Panel RODNEY JERKINS (Part 2) Talks about Michael Jackson, BMI Panel, published on February 13, 2008, https://www.youtube.com/watch?v=qGLqhjnHHM0
271. 'She Was Lovin' Me'/Michael loved it: Damien Shields, EXCLUSIVE: Michael Jackson's "She Was Loving Me", damienshields.com. August 29, 2013.
272. "We spent almost a month"/David Blaine: Chris Yandek, Industry Bigs: Music & Michael, cyinterview.com, July 8, 2009.
272. "I have an album": Michael Jackson: My Pain, *Daily Mirror*, April 12, 1999.

272. 'Keep doing album': TV Guide Interview, 1999.
273. 'He was standing': Michael Jackson News January 2000, michael-jackson-trader.com, January 25, 2000, http://www.michael-jackson-trader.com/news/2000/January/index.html (cited hereafter as Michael Jackson News January 2000).
273. "It was me": LaShawn Daniels Talks Michael Jackson's Invincible Album & What He Learned From The King Of Pop, Kempire Radio, published on November 11, 2012.
273. "He was really on it"/"In the end"/"When we were in New York"/"He would dance": Brad Gilderman, personal author interview, February 2012.
275. "My father told me": Cascio, 126–127.
275. "I thought": Katherine Jackson et al. vs. AEG Live, May 9, 2013.
275. "Up on the fifth floor": Cascio, 139–140.
275. "I'll talk to them"/"I think I'm": Gerri Hirshey.
276. "Sometimes he would": Jermaine Hall, V EXCLUSIVE: Rodney Jerkins Talks MJ's Last Studio Album, Invincible, vibe.com, September 5, 2009.
276. "I picked him up": Michael Jackson News January 2000.
276. "He said, 'We got the president": Rodney Jerkins talks Michael Jackson thru Harlem without security on Thermal Soundwaves Radio, Thermal Soundwaves, published on February 8, 2010, https://www.youtube.com/watch?v=Lu2edKnFooY
277. Drug use in New York/Propofol and Demerol/"This was a measure": Cascio, 171–172.
277. 'Millennium bug': Michael Prince, personal author interview, April 2014 (cited hereafter as Michael Prince).
278. "You ain't seen nothing yet": Michael Jackson, award acceptance speech, World Music Awards, 2000, https://www.youtube.com/watch?v=2mtuqU6HwlQ
278. 'One of the biggest': Michael Jackson News January 2000, January 12, 2000.
278. "There are these two sweet": Online Audio Chat.
278. "I hate to say that": Karen R. Good, Black Skin, White Mask, *Vibe*, March 2002, 116.
278. "We put the entire": Brad Buxer.
279. "I remember thinking": Cascio, 152.

279. Facilities not up to standard: Brad Gilderman, personal author interview, February 2012.
279. "It set the mood": Exclusive Interview with Bruce Swedien, Monster Cable, November 3, 2001, https://groups.yahoo.com/neo/groups/doo-doonews/conversations/topics/698
280. "There was some truly": Brad Gilderman, personal author interview, February 2012.
280. "He kept 'Rock My World'"/"He was like": Jermaine Hall, V EXCLUSIVE: Rodney Jerkins Talks MJ's Last Studio Album, Invincible, vibe.com, September 5, 2009.
280. "Michael called me": Rodney Jerkins interview, CNN, published June 29, 2009, https://www.youtube.com/watch?v=UZeX4pJwy0o
280. "You can push him": Online Audio Chat.
281. "You may have to turn": Brian Hiatt, Michael Jackson Nearing Completion Of New LP, mtv.com, December 21, 2000.
281. "He called me": Dasun Allah.
281. 'The Lost Children' and 'Speechless' among MJ's favourites: Online Audio Chat.
281. Michael's anthem and contribution to children: Brad Buxer.
282. 'Walking on air': Michael Jackson Marches On, nme.com, November 23, 2000.
282. Sony told him to return to the studio/Insulted and humiliated/Stopped showing at studio: Le Numero Ultime, 53.
282. "Bruce had gone home": Stuart Brawley, personal author interview, April 2014 (cited hereafter as Stuart Brawley).
282. "So he hits play": Everything you wanted to know about Floetry, official Floetry website (website defunct, article can be seen at http://www.fantasymusicleague.com/code/artist.php?artist=Floetry)
283. "My heart is literally": Michael Jackson by Marsha Ambrosius, soulculture.com (link defunct, article can be seen at http://www.positivelymichael.com/forums/archive/index.php/t-12241.html).
283. "It was incredible": Billy Johnson Jr, Songwriter Gets The 'Butterflies', Yahoo Music, November 15, 2001.
283. "Michael was a practical joker": Marsha Ambrosius Remembers Michael Jackson, rap-up.com, February 4, 2011.
284. "We were going"/"Michael was like": Teddy Riley Runs Down His Entire Catalogue, vibe.com, March 14, 2012.

284: Michael didn't write 'Whatever Happens': WHATEVER HAPPENS: LA GÉNÈSE DE CETTE CHANSON..., October 13, 2009, http://mjfrance.com/actu/index.php?post/2009/10/13/Whatever-Happens%3A-La-g%C3%A9n%C3%A8se-de-cette-chanson.../1791
284. "He was the nicest man": Online Audio Chat.
284. Loved Santana's whistling: Teddy Riley Runs Down His Entire Catalogue, vibe.com, March 14, 2012.
284. "When I did that": Dasun Allah.
285. The Firm/Furious/Angry and intoxicated/"You're supposed to be working for me": Cascio, 194–195.
285. 'Fantastic facility': *In the Studio With Michael Jackson*, 117.
286. 'Unbreakable' one of MJ's favourites/"I'm one of the few people": Online Audio Chat.
286. "Rodney had written a rap": Stuart Brawley.
286. "Those sessions": Brad Buxer.
286. "At this point": Stuart Brawley.
287. Mottola didn't want 'The Lost Children' on album: Cascio, 202.
287. "Proper name"/"I'm so proud": Online Audio Chat.
287. "He didn't make": Jermaine Hall, V EXCLUSIVE: Rodney Jerkins Talks MJ's Last Studio Album, Invincible, vibe.com, September 5, 2009.
288. No Will Smith or Puff Daddy duets: Rodney Jerkins, personal author interview, January 2015.
288. "I really want": *For The Record*, 141.
288. "It was one of those songs": Mesfin Fekadu, Posthumous Michael Jackson album due out May 13, yahoo.com, May 2, 2014.
288. "I can develop them": Corey Moss, Dre Passes On Michael Jackson Project, mtv.com, January 10, 2001.
288. "I did eight songs": Kathy McCabe, The new King Of Pop Pharrell Williams talks about missing out on working with Michael Jackson, news.com, March 9, 2014.
288. "I flew back to Los Angeles"/"Michael asked if anyone/"It was an amazing year": Stuart Brawley.
289. "Apart from the obvious"/"A lot of people": Brad Gilderman, personal author interview, February 2012.
289. "He thought": *Hitmaker: The Man and His Music*, 348.
289. "Michael is very bright": Timothy L. O'Brien, What Happened to

the Fortune Michael Jackson Made?, *The New York Times*, May 14, 2006 (cited hereafter as Timothy L. O'Brien).

289. "He became more": Michael Jackson, Inc., 74.
289. "I didn't have children": Online Audio Chat.
290. "It means copies of songs": CJ deVillar, personal author interview, February 2012.
290. "It was apparent": Cascio, 190.
290. Farshchian treatment: Katherine Jackson et al. vs. AEG Live, July 24, 2013.
290. "His thing was always": Brad Gilderman, personal author interview, February 2012.
292. "Of all my albums": Online Audio Chat.
292. "It did take a while": Edna Gundersen, Michael in the Mirror, USA Today, December 14, 2001.
292. "He was always a perfectionist": Michael Prince.
293. "He felt that"/"I felt he wanted": Stan Lee On Marvel Movie History, His Favorite Cameos And Michael Jackson as Spider-Man, moviefone.com, April 30, 2012.
293. "Michael knew the stock"/Sony refused: Dieter Wiesner, personal author interview, May 2014 (cited hereafter as Dieter Wiesner).
293. Complications due to Marvel's bankruptcy: Michael Jackson, Inc., 170.
293. "Michael was right": Dieter Wiesner.
294. Business relationship: F. Marc Schaffel vs. Michael Jackson, Los Angeles Superior Court, SC083501, November 16, 2004.
294. 'Did not involve': Randall Sullivan, 16–17.
294. "He thought it was": Ibid., 233–234

CHAPTER 16: *INVINCIBLE* BECOMES INVISIBLE

295. MJ wanted 'Unbreakable' first single/Sony 'You Rock My World': Cascio, 202.
295. MJ 'done' with video/Late on set: Ibid., 613.
295. Disagreements over face: Cascio, 203–204.
296. "Certainly, if a commercial": *The Solo Years*, 195.
296. Drug problems saw the first concert delayed: Cascio, 218–219.
296. "Once we get on the stage": Shaheem Reid, Jackson 5 Barely Rehearsing, Slash Refusing To Be Van Halen For Jackson Shows, mtv.com, September 6, 2001.

297. Duplicate 'We Are the World'/Beneficiaries victims of next disaster: Randall Sullivan, 19.
297. "I believe in my heart": Joe D'Angelo, Jackson Taps Britney, More For Song To Help Terrorism Victims, mtv.com, September 17, 2001.
297. "He really, really": Randall Sullivan, 21.
298. "I was shocked": Roger Friedman, Jacko Album Only Finished Five Weeks Ago, foxnews.com, October 30, 2001.
298. Recording 'You Are My Life': Jon Gass, personal author interview, March 2012.
299. Changed lyrics received credit: *The Magic and the Madness*, 613–614.
299. "I only do an album": TV Guide Interview, 2001.
299. "Music lovers": Epic Records to Release Michael Jackson's First Studio Album in Six Years: Invincible, prnewswire.com, August 23, 2001.
299. "Everyone in the": *Hitmaker: The Man and His Music*, 349.
300. Inspired by Watson image/"The *Invincible* cover was retouched": Albert Watson Photo Inspired Michael Jackson's Invincible Cover, March 28, 2012, http://www.mj-777.com/?p=8707&cpage=1
300. "Because of the set-up": Albert Watson, September 19, 2012, http://study-peace.tumblr.com/post/61691108214/michaelon-thewall-albert-watson-photoshoots
300. "We just wanted": Online Audio Chat.
300. "To me it was an album": Teddy Riley Runs Down His Entire Catalogue, vibe.com, March 14, 2012.
301. Bail him out: Cascio, 225.
301. $231 million of debt by 2001: Katherine Jackson et al. vs. AEG Live, August 12, 2013.
301. Several Bank of America loans/Used Sony ATV catalogue and Mijac as collateral: Roger Friedman, Hard Numbers Show Jacko in Constant Financial Peril, foxnews.com, July 26, 2002; Steve Chawkins and E. Scott Reckard, Prosecutor Says Jackson Is on the Brink of Bankruptcy, *Los Angeles Times*, March 12, 2005; Bad Fortune, *The Guardian*, June 15, 2005.
301. Michael owed Sony millions: *Hitmaker: The Man and His Music*, 355; Roger Friedman, Jackson Will Lose Beatles Songs Soon, foxnews.com, October 26, 2001; Roger Friedman, Michael Jackson Divorcing Sony Music, foxnews.com, June 18, 2002.

301. "I'm submitted interesting": Michael Jackson *Black & White* interview.
301. Refused to appear in 'Cry' video: *The Magic and the Madness*, 614.
301. Sony forced to shoot without MJ: Chuck Philips, Power, Money Behind Jackson's Attack on Sony, Insiders Say, *Los Angeles Times*, July 9, 2002.
301. Unhappy with pitch for 'Butterflies' video/Refused to participate: Chuck Philips, Power, Money Behind Jackson's Attack on Sony, Insiders Say, *Los Angeles Times*, July 9, 2002; *The Magic and the Madness*, 614.
302. Annoyed Sony couldn't come up with plan that didn't involve touring: Cascio, 234-235.
302. MJ agreed to tour/Pulled out after 9/11: Chuck Philips, Power, Money Behind Jackson's Attack on Sony, Insiders Say, *Los Angeles Times*, July 9, 2002; *You Are Not Alone*, 366.
302. Mottola angry MJ didn't tour: *You Are Not Alone*, 366.
302. Not touring cost $100 million: The People of the State of California vs. Michael Joe Jackson, Supreme Court of the State of California, No. 1133603, April 8, 2005.
302. "I love to entertain": Michael & Son, *Life* magazine, December 1997.
302. "Then you get to your hotel": Edna Gundersen, Michael in the Mirror, *USA Today*, December 14, 2001.
302. MJ wanted to 'What More Can I Give' to promote *Invincible*: Randall Sullivan, 22.
302. Own people killed 'What More Can I Give'/Schaffel dismissed/ Sony refused permission: Chuck Philips, New Spin on Collapse of Jackson's Charity Project, *Los Angeles Times*, July 13, 2002.
303. Sony worried singles would compete with *Invincible*: Roger Friedman, Mottola Steps Up Spin War on Jacko, Implicates Producer, foxnews.com, July 15, 2002.
303. "Sales had completely"/"Michael's perception": *Hitmaker: The Man and His Music*, 353.
303. Masters revert back 2000/Advisors checked contract/Rights revert back in 2009–2010/MJ unaware: Chuck Philips, Power, Money Behind Jackson's Attack on Sony, Insiders Say, *Los Angeles Times*, July 9, 2002; *The Magic and the Madness*, 611–612; *You Are Not Alone*, 364.

303. Renegotiated contract early 2002/Demanded masters returned to him 2004/Sony back $8m 'Unbreakable' video: Laura M. Holson and Lynette Holloway, Sony and Its Star Go to War Over the Promotion of Album, *The New York Times*, July 10, 2002.
303. Not satisfied with David Meyers's concept: Lance Fiasco, Michael Jackson Picks A Second 'Unbreakable' Video Director, idobi.com, March 22, 2002.
303. "Michael envisioned creating": Cascio, 202.
304. 'Unbreakable' too costly/Violent: Chuck Philips, Power, Money Behind Jackson's Attack on Sony, Insiders Say, *Los Angeles Times*, July 9, 2002; Laura M. Holson and Lynette Holloway, Sony and Its Star Go to War Over the Promotion of Album, *The New York Times*, July 10, 2002.
304. Michael decided to leave Sony/No longer wanted to work for label/ Two more albums: *The Magic and the Madness*, 612; *Hitmaker: The Man and His Music*, 353–354.
304. New contract difficult without masters: Chuck Philips, Power, Money Behind Jackson's Attack on Sony, Insiders Say, *Los Angeles Times*, July 9, 2002.
304. Promotion and singles cancelled/Deleted from 'international priority' list: Paul Martin, It's War; World Exclusive: Michael Jackson Breaks His Silence In His Feud With Record Boss, *Daily Mirror*, May 15, 2002.
305. "There's like/"With the music": Online Audio Chat.
305. "Michael was so": *Hitmaker: The Man and His Music*, 348.
305. Demonstration/'A mean': Jennifer Vineyard, Michael Jackson Shocks Al Sharpton By Calling Tommy Mottola A Racist, mtv.com, July 8, 2001.
305. Piggybacking on artist rights movement: Chuck Philips, Power, Money Behind Jackson's Attack on Sony, Insiders Say, *Los Angeles Times*, July 9, 2002; *Hitmaker: The Man and His Music*, 348, 354–355.
305. Leave without repaying *Invincible* debts: Paul Martin, It's War; World Exclusive: Michael Jackson Breaks His Silence In His Feud With Record Boss, *Daily Mirror*, May 15, 2002; Laura Holson, Recording Industry Questions a Bitter Attack by a Pop Star, *The New York Times*, July 8, 2002.

305. "We were all in shock": *Hitmaker: The Man and His Music*, 348, 354–355.
306. Sony claims $26 million was spent: Chuck Philips, Power, Money Behind Jackson's Attack on Sony, Insiders Say, *Los Angeles Times*, July 9, 2002; *Hitmaker: The Man and His Music*, 355.
306. "Put the full force": *Hitmaker: The Man and His Music*, 355.
306. At least $5 million on videos/Three or four times normal budget: George Rush, Joanna Molloy, Lola Ogunnaike, Kasia Anderson, Jacko Bags A Hollywood Heavyweight, *New York Daily News*, August 30, 2001; Chuck Philips, Power, Money Behind Jackson's Attack on Sony, Insiders Say, *Los Angeles Times*, July 9, 2002; Nick Brandt interview, Le Numero Ultime, 65–67.
306. Record companies cutting costs: Laura Holson, Recording Industry Questions a Bitter Attack by a Pop Star, *The New York Times*, July 8, 2002.
307. "When you are": *Hitmaker: The Man and His Music*, 353.
307. Sony blamed dismal sales on failure to tour/Promo appearances: Randall Sullivan, 23.
307. "That pissed off Tommy": Randall Sullivan, 23.
307. MJ adamant Sony cheated him/"When I told him that": Richard Siklos, The fight over Michael's millions, *Fortune*, October 23, 2009 (cited hereafter as Richard Siklos).
308. Sony ATV theory/In his interest to sell 50% share in catalogue: Roger Friedman, Jacko Pawned $2 Million Watch to Raise Dough; Banker Claims: 'I've Kept Him Alive', foxnews.com, April 19, 2002; Maggie Farley and Chuck Philips, Jackson Takes Glove Off Against Sony, *Los Angeles Times*, June 6, 2002; Nekesa Mumbi Moody, Invisible 'Invincible', *The Spokesman-Review*, June 16, 2002; Laura Holson, Recording Industry Questions a Bitter Attack by a Pop Star, *The New York Times*, July 8, 2002.
308. Sony first refusal: Bad Fortune, *The Guardian*, June 15, 2002.
308. MJ believed it was a conspiracy: Jesse Jackson interview; Cascio, 195.
308. Plan to further embarrass Sony: Nekesa Mumbi Moody, Invisible 'Invincible', *The Spokesman-Review*, June 16, 2002.
308. "It's total bullshit": Michael Jackson, Inc., 189.
308. "Ultimately": Cascio, 235.
308. "There is a saying": *You Are Not Alone*, 365.

309. "In my opinion": Stuart Brawley, personal author interview, April 2014.
309. "Art – good art – never dies": Michael Jackson speech, June 15, 2002, https://www.youtube.com/watch?v=Mx0Un9K5dKQ

CHAPTER 17: THE MOVIE DREAM

310. "I want to take": Michael Jackson: Why I'm going to be a movie star, *Gold*, December 2002.
310. 'Another career plan'/"Michael told me"/No plans for another label: Dieter Wiesner.
311. MDP deal/'For the Michael Jackson'/Neverland Pictures: Carla Hay, *Billboard*, March 16, 2002, 99.
311. Neverland Pictures/*Wolfed*: Mike Goodridge, Michael Jackson to produce and star in werewolf movie, screendaily.com, May 19, 2002.
311. MDP deal collapse: Dieter Wiesner.
311. Backerman and *Peter Pan*: Valmai Owens, Interview With Stuart Backerman, Michael Jackson Tribute Portrait Online Magazine, April 1, 2011.
312. "I feel more betrayed": Michael Jackson's statement, CNN, February 6, 2003.
312. "Rebranded"/Wanted to reach out: Charles Thomson, How Michael Jackson's Movie Dream Turned Into A Nightmare, Sawf news, November 2010, http://www.charles-thomson.net/one_more_chance.html (cited hereafter as How Michael Jackson's Movie Dream Turned Into A Nightmare).
312. "He was approaching fifty": Valmai Owens, Interview With Stuart Backerman, Michael Jackson Tribute Portrait Online Magazine, April 1, 2011.
313. "We gravitated towards": Bee Gees' Barry Gibb reveals Michael Jackson collaboration, nme.com, May 25, 2011.
313. 'I Am a Loser': Damien Shields, EXCLUSIVE: The origins of Michael Jackson's "I Am A Loser" revealed!, damienshields.com. September 8, 2013.
313. "We spent some time": Dieter Wiesner.
314. "Michael was not too happy": How Michael Jackson's Movie Dream Turned Into A Nightmare.

314. The People of the State of California v. Michael Joseph Jackson background: Matthew Davis, Profile: The Arvizo family, BBC News, June 13, 2005; Aphrodite Jones, *Michael Jackson Conspiracy* (Aphroditejonesbooks, 2010).
315. "I feel sorry for them": Bashir.
315. "If he thinks": Wendy Thermos and Catherine Saillant, D.A. in Jackson Case Failed in 1993, but Has Reputation for Persistence, *Los Angeles Times*, November 20, 2003.
316: Jovial conference: Art Harris, Tom Sneddon: Jovial Press Conference Was 'Inappropriate', CNN, November 26, 2003.
316. Failed to investigate Arvizo family: Tom Mesereau, Larry King Live, CNN, June 14, 2005.
316. Neverland raid/*Number Ones*: Tracy Wilson, Steve Chawkins and Richard Winton, Warrant Out for Michael Jackson, *Los Angeles Times*, November 20, 2003.
316. Surrender/Handcuffed/Bail: John M. Broder, Michael Jackson Is Booked on Molesting Charges That He Calls Lies, *The New York Times*, November 21, 2003.
316. "After the news became": Dieter Wiesner.
316. MJ Universe project ruined/"Triumphant publicity tour"/"We were going"/"Michael was not too": How Michael Jackson's Movie Dream Turned Into A Nightmare.
317. Taylor/Maracanã/Copacabana: Randall Sullivan, 32.
317. Nation of Islam for security: *You Are Not Alone*, 384-385.
317. Nation of Islam history and goals: Mother Tynetta Muhammad, Nation of Islam in America: A Nation of Beauty & Peace, March 28, 1996, http://www.noi.org/noi-history/
317. "It's a house now": Ed Bradley.
318. Nation of Islam ousted/Mesereau hired/Randy: Roger Friedman, Jacko Fires the Nation of Islam, foxnews.com, April 27, 2004; *You Are Not Alone*, 385.
318. "He was being"/"They made it a parade"/"The time I spent": Katherine Jackson et al. vs. AEG Live, May 9–10, 2013.
319. Extorting celebrities/Abusing systems: Aphrodite Jones, *Michael Jackson Conspiracy* (Aphroditejonesbooks, 2010), 205–211, 275–288.
319. "We expected some": Michael Jackson cleared of abuse, BBC News, June 14, 2005.

319. "I think that"/'Absurd'/"They wouldn't do it": Tom Mesereau, *Larry King Live*, CNN, June 14, 2005.
319. "He was so hurt": Randall Sullivan, 370–371.
320. "Out here Michael Jackson": Matt Drudge interview with Roger Friedman, The Drudge Reports about the Michael Jackson trial (part 2), https://www.youtube.com/watch?t=305&v=AWOhMT-Pl9mM
320. 'Didn't even resemble': Charles Thomson, One of the Most Shameful Episodes In Journalistic History, *The Huffington Post*, June 13, 2010.

CHAPTER 18: THE RECOVERY

321. Mesereau advice/"I felt he could never": The Secret Life of Michael Jackson, *Dateline NBC*, aired February 5, 2010, https://www.youtube.com/watch?v=m11gOHxgTPM
321. Cheekbones visible through skin: Randall Sullivan, 7.
321. "He's exhausted": Tom Mesereau, *Larry King Live*, CNN, June 14, 2005.
322. "I saw the payment"/Owed $7 million: Bahrain prince sues Michael Jackson, china.org.cn, November 18, 2008.
322. "After Michael arrived"/Projects/"Michael would come"/Stopped money/House: Guy Holmes, personal author interview, May 2015; William Lee Adams, Michael Jackson Settles Out of Court with Sheik, *Time*, November 24, 2009.
323 Bain, Morris and El-Amin: William Dotinga, Men Claim Share of Michael Jackson's Estate, courthousenews.com, May 9, 2013.
323. "We were really upset": Guy Holmes, personal author interview, May 2015.
324. "He was surrounded": Jackson had long history with estate executor, *USA Today*, August 14, 2009.
324. $275 million debt in 2004: Katherine Jackson et al. vs. AEG Live, August 12, 2013.
324. Late with payment/Loan sold to Fortress early 2005: Edna Gundersen, Jackson's freedom isn't free, USA Today, June 13, 2005.
324. MJ lacked funds to repay Fortress/Owed $300 million by 2006: Charles Duhigg, Indebted Jackson to Sell Part of Music Catalog, *Los Angeles Times*, April 14, 2006 (cited hereafter as Charles Duhigg).
324. Sony new financing deal: Richard Siklos.

324. Fortress loan collateralised by Sony/ATV: Charles Duhigg; Katherine Jackson et al. vs. AEG Live, August 12, 2013.
325. $23 million Neverland loan: Roger Friedman, Michael Jackson: Deal to Save Him Won't Include Neverland, foxnews.com, November 6, 2007.
325. Total debt $325 million: Charles Duhigg; Katherine Jackson et al. vs. AEG Live, August 12, 2013.
325. $15 million to Branca/Condition of return: Charles Duhigg; Joseph Jackson's Objection to Appointment of John Branca and John McClain as Executors of the Estate of Michael Jackson, Los Angeles Superior Court, BP117321, November 9, 2009.
325. "They were virtually": Bill Browne, Jackson's Cork hideaway, *The Corkman*, July 2, 2009.
326. "Dream": Fred Topel, Will.i.am on music and acting, craveonline.co.uk, June 12, 2009.
326. "A week before": World Entertainment News Network (WENN), Michael Jackson – Will.i.am Worked With Michael Jackson For Free, contactmusic.com, January 5, 2012.
326. 'Misunderstanding': Michael Jackson returns to stage, news.bbc.co.uk, November 16, 2006.
327. "For the most part": Bill Whitfield, Javon Beard and Tanner Colby, *Remember the Time: Protecting Michael Jackson in His Final Days* (Scribe Publications, 2014), 116 (cited hereafter as *Remember the Time: Protecting Michael Jackson in His Final Days*).
328. "Michael was at the top": *Michael Jackson's This Is It*, directed by Kenny Ortega (Sony Pictures, 2009, DVD) (cited hereafter as *This Is It*).
328. King Tut/"He did his whole story"/MJ wasn't ready: Katherine Jackson et al. vs. AEG Live, May 31 and June 11, 2013.
328. "As he stayed in Las Vegas": Jackson Confidant Jack Wishna Opens Up About Michael & The Tour That Never Was, accesshollywood.com, January 8, 2010.
328. 'Debilitated' and 'incoherent': Alan Duke and Saeed Ahmed, Portrait of Jackson's pill consumption emerges, CNN, July 10, 2009.
328. 'Summer vacation'/Goodstone Inn/Property: *Remember the Time: Protecting Michael Jackson in His Final Days*, 160
329. Away from family/More control: Roger Friedman, Michael Jackson's Family Calls for Help, foxnews.com, June 29, 2007; Roger

Friedman, Michael Jackson Evidently Moving to Rental Home in Virginia, foxnews.com, July 3, 2007.

329. Fortress loan due December 2007: Richard Siklos.

330. Jesse Jackson gala/Barely afford trip/Expense of Burkle/Stayed at Burkle's home: Jacko, Kids Squat With Burkle, *New York Post*, November 20, 2007; *Remember the Time: Protecting Michael Jackson in His Final Days*, 227–228, 234.

330. Green Valley Ranch/Credit card declined/Lopez and Palms: *Remember the Time: Protecting Michael Jackson in His Final Days*, 235–238.

330. Refinance deal completed December 2007: Raymone Bain vs. Michael Jackson, District Court District of Columbia, 2009-0826, May 7, 2010.

330. Barclays refinanced $300 million Fortress debt/HSBC lent $30 million/Fund loaned $40 million: Richard Siklos.

330. Went on lawsuits/Debt/Fees/Back taxes/Paying employees: Richard Siklos.

330. Long term debt $400 million: Katherine Jackson et al. vs. AEG Live, August 12, 2013.

330. Neverland loan remained with Fortress: Roger Friedman, Michael Jackson's Neverland Foreclosed; Auction Date Set, foxnews.com, February 26, 2008.

330. $100 million owed to creditors: Katherine Jackson et al. vs. AEG Live, August 13, 2013.

330. Sony/ATV stake estimated value up to $500 million: Christopher Palmeri, Settling Michael Jackson's Estate May Be a Thriller, businessweek.com, June 25, 2009; Tim Arango and Ben Sisario, Jackson's Estate: Piles of Assets, Loads of Debt, *The New York Times*, June 26, 2009; Michael Jackson, Inc., 212.

331. Mijac estimated worth $50–100 million: Tim Arango and Ben Sisario, Jackson's Estate: Piles of Assets, Loads of Debt, *The New York Times*, June 26, 2009.

331. Earning over a billion dollars throughout career: Michael Jackson, Inc., 250.

331. Until early nineties MJ paid close attention to his accounting: Timothy L. O'Brien.

331. "Because he generated": *Michael Jackson: The Life of an Icon*, directed by Andrew Eastel (Universal Pictures UK, 2011, DVD).

331. Advisors spent million on deals: Gerald Posner, Missing Millions, thedailybeast.com, August 2, 2009.
331. Advisors: Jeff Leeds, Advice from a team in turmoil, *Los Angeles Times*, January 13, 2004; Gerald Posner, Missing Millions, thedailybeast.com, August 2, 2009.
331. Al Malnik former lawyer for Meyer Lansky: Timothy L. O'Brien.
332. Bain responsibilities: Raymone Bain vs. Michael Jackson, District Court District of Columbia, 2009-0826, May 7, 2010.
332. Didn't know where money was/How much he had: *Remember the Time: Protecting Michael Jackson in His Final Days*, 193.
332. Michael stopped trusting Bain: Ibid., 215.
332. McMillan took control: Gerald Posner, Missing Millions, thedailybeast.com, August 2, 2009; *Remember the Time: Protecting Michael Jackson in His Final Days*, 227.
332. Bain dismissed December 2007/$488,000 to walk away: Raymone Bain vs. Michael Jackson, District Court District of Columbia, 2009-0826, May 7, 2010.
332. "The song is really": Kimbel Bouwman, Interview with Claude Kelly, hitquarters.com, May 24, 2010.
332. "He was never satisfied": Jocelyn Vena, Michael Jackson Was 'Never Satisfied' With His Music, Akon Says, mtv.com, October 23, 2009.
333. MJ delighted with response: J. Randy Taraborrelli, As he turns 50, is this what Michael Jackson should really look like?, dailymail.co.uk, August 28, 2008.
333. "He loved writing": Brad Buxer.
334. Neverland loan: Roger Friedman, Michael Jackson: Deal to Save Him Won't Include Neverland, foxnews.com, November 06, 2007; Roger Friedman, Michael Jackson's Neverland Foreclosed; Auction Date Set, foxnews.com, February 26, 2008; Roger Friedman, Can Michael Jackson Find 11th-Hour Help?, foxnews.com, February 28, 2008.
334. $26 million/$42 million/$25–30 million debt interest/Overspending/Lenders refusing to loan more: Katherine Jackson et al. vs. AEG Live, August 12, 2013.
334. "Where you are"/"He really had": Benjamin Wallace, Monetizing the Celebrity Meltdown, *New York* magazine, November 28, 2010.

CHAPTER 19: THE FINAL CURTAIN CALL

335. Colony would recoup investment/Expenses/12% success fee/ Michael keep rest/Ranch worth $60–70 million: Richard Siklos.
335. Connections to Arab world/Medical doctor/Senegal/No licence: Roger Friedman, Jacko's Mystery Manager Revealed, foxnews.com, March 16, 2009; Kim Masters, Michael Jackson's Strange Final Days Revealed in Dueling Lawsuits, *The Hollywood Reporter*, July 19, 2012; Roger Friedman, Flashback 2009: Michael Jackson Manager Tohme Tohme Said Star Could Do "100 Shows", showbiz411.com, July 19, 2012.
335. 'Ambassador at Large': Randall Sullivan, 304.
336. Michael happy with Tohme: Ibid., 231.
336. Signed over powers/Tohme manager: John Branca and John McClain, Co-Executors of the Estate of Michael Jackson, Los Angeles Superior Court, BP117321, February 17, 2012.
336. 'Very special artist'/London bigger than New York, Toronto: The People of the State of California vs. Conrad Robert Murray, October 25, 2011; Katherine Jackson et al. vs. AEG Live, June 11, 2013.
336. 'Anything': Randall Sullivan, 238.
336. "It was really then": *This Is It.*
336. "Laser focused": Richard Siklos.
337. Move to LA at behest of Tohme: Randall Sullivan, 236.
337. "Although we continued": Michael Prince.
337. 'Vagabonds'/"We both broke down": Katherine Jackson et al. vs. AEG Live, June 12, 2013.
338. "He wanted a property": *Remember the Time: Protecting Michael Jackson in His Final Days*, 136.
338. Abdullah settlement: Roger Friedman, Michael Jackson Sued by Bahraini Prince, foxnews.com, August 14, 2007; Michael Jackson 'betrayed' Arab sheikh by walking out on pop deal, telegraph.co.uk, November 18, 2008; Richard Siklos.
338. $3 million paid to Sheikh/The contract and meeting/Advances/ Promissory note/Prince and 31 shows/Toast: "Agreement" between The Michael Jackson Company, LLC and AEG Live LLC, January 28, 2009 (Katherine Jackson et al. vs. AEG Live, Exhibit-677-150-to-677-177); Katherine Jackson et al. vs. AEG Live, June 12, 2013.

340. Wouldn't have signed AEG deal/Notes to self: Michael Jackson, Notes to self, published by *New York Post* in September 2013.
340. Retire to do movies/'Thriller 'and 'Smooth Criminal' movies: The People of the State of California vs. Conrad Robert Murray, September 27, 2011; Katherine Jackson et al. vs. AEG Live, July 10, 2013.
340. AEG film agreement: Katherine Jackson et al. vs. AEG Live, May 22, 2013.
341. "Michael Jackson is to launch": Simon Cable, Michael Jackson chooses London's O2 arena for the 'greatest comeback in history', dailymail.co.uk, February 21, 2009.
341. "He was very excited"/Cleared diary: The People of the State of California vs. Conrad Robert Murray, September 27, 2011.
341. "This is the last time": Katherine Jackson et al. vs. AEG Live, June 12, 2013.
341. "He doesn't want": Katherine Jackson et al. vs. AEG Live, May 31, 2013.
341. Phillips unable to reach Michael/Angry with Tohme: Katherine Jackson et al. vs. AEG Live, June 5, 2013.
342. Auction/'Priceless'/'Extraordinary': MJJ Productions, Inc. vs. Julien's Auction House, LLC and Darren Julien, Los Angeles Superior Court, BC408913, March 4, 2009.
342. Blamed Tohme/'Everything'/Changed mind/PR handling: Randall Sullivan, 302–303.
342. Lanesborough room incident: Katherine Jackson et al. vs. AEG Live, June 12, 2013.
343. "He was so nervous": *This Is It.*
343. "I screamed at him": Katherine Jackson et al. vs. AEG Live, June 5, 2013.
343. "I was so nervous"/O2 journey/'The Miracle of March 5th'/More anticipation/3,000 fans and 350 reporters: Katherine Jackson et al. vs. AEG Live, June 12, 2013.
343. "I just want to say"/"I'll be performing": Michael Jackson press conference at the O2, London 2009, published March 5, 2009, https://www.youtube.com/watch?v=c00CwFA5JNE
344. "They were telling him: *This Is It.*
345. "I'm really angry"/Tohme: Tim Nixon, Michael Jackson's 50 gig fury, *The Sun*, June 2, 2009; Randall Sullivan, 302.

344. "We couldn't have": Personal author interview, confidential source.
345. 'Cultural'/"Not only are": Jackson to play 50 gigs at the O2, news.bbc.co.uk, March 12, 2009;
345. 'Jackson-mania is gripping London': Amar Singh and Robert Mendick, Detoxing brand Jacko, standard.co.uk, March 13, 2009.
346. Vow to sign all cheques over $5,000: Michael Jackson, Notes to self, published by *New York Post* in September 2013.
346. "I want to push it": *This Is It.*
346. "When you're 30"/Goal to sing all vocals live: Katherine Jackson et al. vs. AEG Live, May 14, 2013.
347. "You have the same": Chris Lee and Harriet Ryan, Deep pockets behind Michael Jackson, *Los Angeles Times*, May 30, 2009.
347. Tohme out: Yazmeen, Interview with Patrick Allocco – President of AllGood Entertainment, muzikfactorytwo.blogspot.co.uk, May 24, 2011; John Branca and John McClain, Co-Executors of the Estate of Michael Jackson, Los Angeles Superior Court, BP117321, February 17, 2012; Randall Sullivan, 300–302.
347. 'Tohme away from'/'No Tohme near me': Michael Jackson, Notes to self, published by *New York Post* in September 2013.
348. "This guy, he just has ways": Michael to June Gatlin, NEW MJ's audio tape released — Mystery Man Behind Michael Jackson, published August 24, 2009, https://www.youtube.com/watch?v=x-UoA4k9XTnE
348. DiLeo and film fund: Personal author interview, confidential source.
348. DiLeo helped by Williams: *Remember the Time: Protecting Michael Jackson in His Final Days*, 285.
348. "We didn't really discuss": Frank DiLeo interview, PART 3 Raffles van Exel Frank DiLeo, November 4, 2009, https://www.youtube.com/watch?v=i1pg4TqJdtU
348. DiLeo in by April: Katherine Jackson et al. vs. AEG Live, June 3, 2013 (made official May 2: Letter appointing Frank DiLeo as 'tour manager', dated May 2, 2009).
348. Phillips hired DiLeo: Interview with Patrick Allocco – President of AllGood Entertainment, muzikfactorytwo.blogspot.co.uk, May 24, 2011.
348. Phillips hired DiLeo/"Michael told me": Karen Faye, Twitter, twitlonger.com, June 20, 2015, http://www.twitlonger.com/show/nk35pk

349. "It was Michael": Personal author interview, confidential source.
349. Tohme back: Katherine Jackson et al. vs. AEG Live, June 11, 2013.
349. Branca back/Lopez fired: Jackson had long history with estate executor, USA Today, August 14, 2009; Randall Sullivan, 291.
349. Joseph family concert/Leonard Rowe/"I'm the only": Letter appointing Leonard Rowe as 'a financial overseer', dated March 25, 2009 (signed April 14, 2009); Roger Friedman, Jacko Hit With Ridiculous Lawsuit, showbiz411.com, June 10, 2009; Interview with Joe Jackson and Leonard Rowe, *Larry King Live*, CNN, July 20, 2009; Roger Friedman, Joe Jackson's Partner: Jail Sentences and Lawsuits On Resume, showbiz411.com, July 22, 2009; Frank DiLeo interview, PART 2 Raffles van Exel Frank DiLeo, November 4, 2009, https://www.youtube.com/watch?v=1cNeJjA6LlM; Yazmeen, Did Michael Hire Leonard Rowe as His Manager?, muzikfactorytwo.blogspot.co.uk, February 22, 2011; Yazmeen, Interview with Patrick Allocco – President of AllGood Entertainment, muzikfactorytwo.blogspot.co.uk, May 24, 2011; *Untouchable: The Strange Life and Tragic Death of Michael Jackson* (Grove Press, 2012), 379.
349. Mid-May meeting/Rowe dismissal/'Forgot': Frank DiLeo, *Larry King Live*, CNN, August 4, 2009, Randall Sullivan, 379.
350. "You needed": Katherine Jackson et al. vs. AEG Live, June 5, 2013.
350. Murray hired early May/$150,000 a month: Katherine Jackson et al. vs. AEG Live, Exhibit-177-1, May 20, 2013.
350. 'Make protein shakes'/"I didn't want to spend": The new Michael Jackson movie: How Jackson fought for Dr. Conrad Murray, *Entertainment Weekly*, October 15, 2009; Michael Jackson: His Final Days, CNN, June 22, 2014, http://edition.cnn.com/TRANSCRIPTS/0907/03/sbt.01.html
350. "Michael always had"/Equipment transportation/"He would have released": Michael Prince.
351. "He told me"/"He said he listened"/"We headed out"/"I asked if"/"The pieces": Tim Smith, More details on instrumental album Michael Jackson started before his death, and his love of classical music, *The Baltimore Sun*, July 10, 2009.
352. 'First love': Simulchat.
352. 'Got so big'/Tabloids: Paul Harris, The square chin. The deep voice. But was it really Michael Jackson?, dailymail.co.uk, March 14,

2009; Jackson delays opening tour dates, news.bbc.co.uk, May 20, 2009; Alison Boshoff, Comeback king? Michael Jackson has managed TWO of 45 rehearsals for his £65m concerts, dailymail.co.uk, May 22, 2009; *This Is It*.

353. Production/Dome Project/"I said"/"He felt now"/"If we don't fix": Harriet Ryan and Chris Lee, Michael Jackson rehearses near Burbank airport, *Los Angeles Times*, May 12, 2009; David Germain and Ryan Nakashima, Michael Jackson Shot 3D Video Project Before Death, billboard.com, June 30, 2009; *This Is It*; People of the State of California vs. Conrad Robert Murray, September 27, 2011; Katherine Jackson et al. vs. AEG Live, Exhibit-641-20-to-641-28; Katherine Jackson et al. vs. AEG Live, May 8, 2013; Katherine Jackson et al. vs. AEG Live, May 20, 2013; Katherine Jackson et al. vs. AEG Live, July 9, 2013.

355. Missed rehearsals June 1–14: Katherine Jackson et al. vs. AEG Live, May 8, 2013; Katherine Jackson et al. vs. AEG Live, July 9–10, 2009.

355. "MJ did not have a good Friday": Katherine Jackson et al. vs. AEG Live, Exhibit-447-19-to-447-21, July 12, 2013.

356. June 16 meeting: Katherine Jackson et al. vs. AEG Live, Exhibit-274-AEGL-54639 and Exhibit-664-371-to-664-372; Katherine Jackson et al. vs. AEG Live, June 18, 2013; Katherine Jackson et al. vs. AEG Live, July 9–10, 2009.

356. "Michael didn't like to rehearse"/HIStory Tour/"I knew that": Katherine Jackson et al. vs. AEG Live, May 29–June 3, 2013.

357. "He looked great in April": Katherine Jackson et al. vs. AEG Live, June 18, 2013.

357. Karen Faye e-mails: Katherine Jackson et al. vs. AEG Live, Exhibit-330, May 9–10, 2013.

357. Repeating/"This was": Katherine Jackson et al. vs. AEG Live, May 9, 2013.

357. "He said, 'I'm getting down"/'A little loopy'/'Under the influence'/Klein: Katherine Jackson et al. vs. AEG Live, May 14, 2013.

357. Klein visits/Waldman: The People of the State of California vs. Conrad Robert Murray, October 27, 2011.

357. 'Occasionally': Arnold Klein, *Larry King Live*, CNN, July 8, 2009.

358. "He may have slept": Katherine Jackson et al. vs. AEG Live, June 20, 2013.

358. Insomnia/Demerol: The People of the State of California vs. Conrad Robert Murray, October 27, 2011.
358. June 19 incident/"I thought there"/"We talked"/Ortega couldn't believe it: The People of the State of California vs. Conrad Robert Murray, September 27, 2011; Katherine Jackson et al. vs. AEG Live, May 29, 2013; Katherine Jackson et al. vs. AEG Live, July 10, 2013.
359. "We were both crying": Katherine Jackson et al. vs. AEG Live, May 8, 2013.
359. "I'm not being a drama"/"My concern is now"/"Kenny, it's critical": Katherine Jackson et al. vs. AEG Live, Exhibit-307-AEGL-137453-137456.
359. "I was torn": Katherine Jackson et al. vs. AEG Live, July 11, 2013.
360. "I have watched him": Katherine Jackson et al. vs. AEG Live, June 6, 2013.
360. "Michael was physically"/Murray then told Ortega/"Michael told me": The People of the State of California vs. Conrad Robert Murray, September 27, 2011.
361. "I mean Michael": The People of the State of California vs. Conrad Robert Murray, October 25, 2011.
362. "He entered into rehearsal": The People of the State of California vs. Conrad Robert Murray, September 27, 2011.
362. "I doubted myself": Katherine Jackson et al. vs. AEG Live, August 8, 2013.
362. 'Elated'/"He knew"/Walked out of the arena/'Like a million dollars': Katherine Jackson et al. vs. AEG Live, June 13, 2013.
362. "Now I know I can do this"/"Thank you": Gil Kaufman, Promoter Describes Michael Jackson's Final Moments, mtv.com, July 1, 2009; Claire Hoffman, The Last Days of Michael Jackson, *Rolling Stone*, August 6, 2009.
363. Ortega would prepare/"He felt like/"He asked me": The People of the State of California vs. Conrad Robert Murray, September 27, 2011.
363. Murray treatment/"I got to sleep"/'I'd like to'/"Just make me"/"I decided": Los Angeles Police Department Internal Affairs Group Transcript of Recorded Interview with Dr Conrad Murray, June 27, 2009.
364. Safe from doctor: Katherine Jackson et al. vs. AEG Live, May 9, 2013.

364. Phone records: Guy Adams, Eighteen months on, the Jackson circus comes to town again, independent.co.uk, January 5, 2011.
364. Call to Williams: The People of the State of California vs. Conrad Robert Murray, September 28, 2011.
365. Alvarez/911 call: The People of the State of California vs. Conrad Robert Murray, September 29, 2011.
365. Paramedic treatment/'Clinically dead': The People of the State of California vs. Conrad Robert Murray, September 30, 2011.
366. "Our boy is gone"/Call: Katherine Jackson et al. vs. AEG Live, July 10, 2013.
367. "When the autopsy": Liza On Autopsy: All Hell Will Break Loose, cbsnews.com, June 26, 2009.
367. "Wasn't nothing"/"We will never"/"Ever since": Michael Jackson Memorial (Funeral) – Full Complete Version HD, published June 25, 2014, https://www.youtube.com/watch?v=eoDS7krlenw
368. Homicide/Autopsy: Bob Tourtellotte, Jackson death ruled homicide, focus on doctor, reuters.com, August 28, 2009; Certificate of Death, Jackson, Michael Joseph, County of Los Angeles Department of Health Services, September 1, 2009.
368. Means of death: Autopsy: Michael Jackson's Last Hours, Channel 5, January 7, 2014.
368. Czeisler testimony/"The symptoms": Katherine Jackson et al. vs. AEG Live, June 20, 2013.
369. Murray charged/Trial: Jack Leonard, Harriet Ryan and Victoria Kim, Jackson's physician charged with involuntary manslaughter, *Los Angeles Times*, February 9, 2010; Harriet Lee, Michael Jackson's doctor to stand trial in manslaughter, *Los Angeles Times*, January 12, 2011; Harriet Ryan and Victoria Kim, Conrad Murray convicted in Michael Jackson's death, *Los Angeles Times*, November 8, 2011.
369. Shafer/'Egregious' violations: The People of the State of California vs. Conrad Robert Murray, October 19, 2011.
369. AEG case: Alan Duke, AEG not liable in Michael Jackson's death, jury finds, cnn.com, October 3, 2013.
369. "It's easy": Richard Siklos.
370. "Music has": Quote Of The Day, michaeljackson.com, April 28, 2011.

AFTERWORD

371. *Michael*/Authenticity: Exclusive: Will.i.am Explains His 'Disgust' for New Michael Jackson Album, rollingstone.com, December 13, 2010; Authenticity of Michael Jackson songs challenged by fans, sunshinecoastdaily.com.au, November 12, 2013.
371. "No way": Quincy Jones: Lady Gaga is "Madonna, Jr.", usmagazine.com, November 22, 2010.
372. "I don't think": Will.i.am Doesn't Support New Michael Jackson Album, billboard.com, August 3, 2010.

ABOUT THE AUTHOR

Mike Smallcombe is a journalist who currently resides in England. Mike, who spent his youth living in Germany and Cornwall, graduated from the University of Exeter with a degree in English Language before relocating to London, where he completed his journalist training with the Press Association. Mike then returned to the South West, where he joined the staff at Devon and Cornwall Media. For more, follow Mike on Twitter (@mikesmallcombe1) and visit his website (www.makingmichael.co.uk).

Printed in August 2019
by Rotomail Italia S.p.A., Vignate (MI) - Italy